Interp Communication for Canadians

MW00721253

Interpersonal Communication for Canadians

An Interdisciplinary Approach

Jennifer MacLennan

OXFORD

UNIVERSITY PRESS

OXFORD

UNIVERSITY PRESS

70 Wynford Drive, Don Mills, Ontario M3C 1J9
www.oup.com/ca

Oxford University Press is a department of the University of Oxford.
It furthers the University's objective of excellence in research, scholarship,
and education by publishing worldwide in

Oxford   New York

Auckland   Cape Town   Dar es Salaam   Hong Kong   Karachi
Kuala Lumpur   Madrid   Melbourne   Mexico City   Nairobi
New Delhi   Shanghai   Taipei   Toronto

With offices in

Argentina   Austria   Brazil   Chile   Czech Republic   France   Greece
Guatemala   Hungary   Italy   Japan   Poland   Portugal   Singapore
South Korea   Switzerland   Thailand   Turkey   Ukraine   Vietnam

Oxford is a trade mark of Oxford University Press
in the UK and in certain other countries

Published in Canada
by Oxford University Press

Library and Archives Canada Cataloguing in Publication

MacLennan, Jennifer

Interpersonal communication for Canadians: an interdisciplinary approach/Jennifer MacLennan.

Includes index.

ISBN 978-0-19-542102-6

1. Interpersonal communication—Textbooks. I. Title.

BF637.C45M18 2007   153.6   C2007-903802-6

Cover Image: Ryan McVay/Getty Images
Cover Design: Sherill Chapman

This book is printed on permanent (acid-free) paper ∞.
Printed in the United States of America
2 3 - 16 15

Contents

Appendix C   Communication Case Studies

Preface

Anyone who teaches interpersonal communication in a Canadian college or university already enjoys a seemingly wide choice of introductory textbooks on the subject. Most cover the same ground using pretty much the same assumptions and the same approach. Why, then, add another book to the already bulging market?

It's a question I have frequently asked myself as I have worked to integrate materials from several quite different theoretical orientations. However, it is also one that contains its own answer: the embedded assumptions of most texts and the standard approach to teaching this material have troubled me for two decades, from the time I first taught interpersonal communication in a Canadian college in the early days of my career.

Even then I found something about the course material, and the orientation of the book, a poor fit for my students, but at the time it wasn't entirely clear to me what the trouble was. The source of my unease became clearer when I moved to the US to undertake a Ph.D. in rhetoric, a specialty that was not available in Canada at the time. Rhetoric, like interpersonal communication, is part of the discipline of speech communication,[1] and my graduate teaching assignment included the opportunity to teach interpersonal communication in its original disciplinary (and cultural) context. At the same time, I was carrying out research for my dissertation on the rhetoric of Canadian identity, and in the confluence of these two experiences I discovered part of the answer to the question that had lingered so long in the back of my mind: why had the interpersonal communication course seemed so ill-suited to my Canadian students?

As I have since argued in a slightly different context,[2] the problem seems to be that the entire discipline of speech communication is a fundamentally *American* phenomenon: its roots are American,[3] and so are most of its theoretical developments, its academic departments, its scholarly organizations, and its textbooks. These books, with their roots in an exclusively American tradition, naturally take for granted a range of American cultural values and attitudes, which in turn are conflated with, and taught as part of, the discipline's assumptions and theories. Thus, the study of communication as represented in these American texts not only 'naturalizes' a disciplinary model, but also implicitly encodes a set of identifiable cultural values and assumptions.

Like many Canadian educators, I believe that our students deserve better than to have their own cultural context obliterated, particularly in culturally sensitive fields such as communication. Yet few American communication texts recognize any context other than an American one; I have found only one book apart from 'Canadianized' versions in which Canada gets any sort of mention at all,[4] and that only when the authors assert that the two cultures are 'increasingly connected'. Even when the writers acknowledge various 'co-cultures' within so-called 'mainstream North America', Canada receives no mention at all.[5] And despite plenty of research to indicate significant patterns of divergence in cultural and social values between the two nations,[6] Canada is asserted to be, just like the US, a 'highly individualistic' culture.[7]

This situation is so typical that a Canadian instructor who hopes to find an interpersonal communication book in which American cultural assumptions are *not* naturalized is pretty well out of luck. Except for one or two Canadianizations, the field is dominated exclusively by American texts written by American academics for audiences of American students. Even 'Canadianized' texts can—and frequently still do—manifest the same American values, since these values are embedded in the theoretical foundations of the discipline.

But it's not just the pervasive American slant of the books that has troubled me; the *approach* of the books seems unnecessarily narrow as well. As a rhetorician, I know that the study of human interaction has a much longer and richer history than is typically acknowledged by standard texts on interpersonal communication, which tend to have an exclusively social scientific orientation. What this means is that although many of the topics and processes studied in such books are highly rhetorical (negotiation, leadership, motivation, language, and identity formation, to name a few), valuable insights into human motivation derived from centuries of rhetorical study are altogether neglected. This has always seemed to me a shame, not only because the broader discipline of speech communication has been enriched by contributions from both humanities and social scientific traditions, but also because rhetorical study, with its emphasis on the nature of motivation, offers such abundant possibilities for enhancing our understanding of interpersonal dynamics. That all human interaction is embedded in persuasion is well understood, yet books that come out of this quantitative, social science tradition typically ignore what rhetoric—traditionally the study of persuasion—has to teach us about the subject.[8] As well, though most interpersonal texts include a chapter on verbal communication, the significant rhetorical dimensions of linguistic behaviour are disregarded.[9] And though many of the books treat topics such as 'communication climate', the groundbreaking work of rhetoricians on the role of situation in shaping communication is ignored, presumably *because* it comes from the field of rhetoric.[10] Finally, insights into human motivation derived from the work of the great rhetorician Kenneth Burke remain unmentioned, despite the fact that they have been widely embraced by sociologists and others in quantitative fields.[11]

I recognize that there are those for whom 'interpersonal communication' remains exclusively a label for one of the formal divisions of speech communication: for them, it names a purely social scientific subdiscipline distinct from the other subfields of instructional, small-group, and organizational communication, philosophy of communication, and—most especially—rhetoric. However, while such turf divisions may be useful for some purposes, preserving them isn't my primary concern, in part because such labels are arbitrary, and in part because they have so little meaning for those outside the discipline, for whom my book is intended.

My audience is made up of future practitioners in a variety of professional fields who are currently studying in Canadian colleges or universities, and for their instructors, the majority of whom have come to the task from academic specialties other than communication. I understand their situation: I came late to the formal study of communication myself, since it wasn't an available major in Canada during my undergraduate days, and over the course of my career I have taught beside people from a wide variety of other disciplines—literature, classics, philosophy, history, and religious studies, to name a few—who had to master this material for their own classes without themselves ever having formally studied it. Those from a humanities background will instantly recognize the usefulness and value of an approach that includes insights from humanistic study of communication as well as those from social scientific approaches to the subject.

An exploration of human motivation is necessarily—as Kenneth Burke so firmly established—a rhetorical undertaking,[12] and it has been my goal to add these important insights to the foundational concepts covered in all introductory textbooks on interpersonal communication. In writing this book, I have sought to provide a comprehensive theoretical foundation for understanding how, and why, human beings communicate on an interpersonal level, and in so doing to enhance the coverage and understanding of such topics as identity formation, leadership, language, motivation, negotiation, and the dynamics of interpersonal influence. This is not to say, however, that my book is *exclusively* rhetorical or that it is always self-consciously Canadian in focus; I have simply chosen to recognize the ubiquitous presence of 'rhetorical motive . . . where it is not usually recognized, or thought to belong',[13] and to eliminate embedded American values and assumptions. I believe the result is a richer book; I trust that my Canadian audience will think so too.

Acknowledgements

As always when a book is finished, there are many people to thank for their contributions both direct and indirect, and especially for their moral support. I am therefore immensely grateful to many friends and colleagues who have helped me to keep my perspective through the onerous process of creating a book that straddles—as this one does—two quite different academic specialties, and through the upheaval of office renovations, curricular development, and computer disasters.

I begin by thanking Burton Urquhart of the Graham Centre at the University of Saskatchewan for his indispensable help with this and a second manuscript I was preparing at the same time. His good humour, his reliable record-keeping, and his research assistance—not to mention his cat-sitting—have all been an immense help to me over the past several months. I would like also to acknowledge Jeanie Wills, Deb Rolfes, and Rebekah Bennetch, also of the Graham Centre, who, along with Burton, thoughtfully read the first draft of the manuscript and gave me their helpful comments. All four of these remarkable people are colleagues in the fullest sense of the word, and I am thrilled that they have chosen to direct their considerable talents to the success of the Graham Centre.

I owe a debt of gratitude also to the former Dean of Engineering, Claude Lague, who has been a consistent support to me in so many ways, and especially in our quest to establish the Centre for the Study of Communication; I know that it would not have come about without his commitment. I would also like to acknowledge Lynn Danbrook, College of Engineering Development Officer, whose hard work brought the dream closer to reality. I am grateful, too, to D.K. Seaman, who has always fully supported my efforts to develop innovative programming for engineering students and professionals, and who gave us his blessing as we sought to extend the responsibilities and the scope of the Chair he established. It goes without saying, of course, that I am deeply indebted to Ron and Jane Graham for their faith in the approach I wished to take in the new Centre for the Study of Communication, and I promise to do everything in my power to make them proud of what their most generous gift has allowed us to do.

My friends and mentors David Male, Emeritus Professor of Mechanical Engineering, John Thompson, President Emeritus of St Thomas More College, and Richard Burton, Professor of Mechanical Engineering, have also provided me with inspiration and support, for which I am enormously grateful. This has been a gruelling year in many ways, but it has been brightened immeasurably by their thoughtfulness and constancy. I am humbled by their continued commitment to what I am doing here, and I can't help but wonder at my remarkable good fortune at being blessed with their friendship.

I have been glad of the patient understanding I've received from the editorial staff at Oxford University Press, in particular Roberta Osborne, Dina Theleritis, and Eric

Sinkins, all of whom have been models of collegiality and professionalism, who have respected my efforts and understood the enormous and competing demands on my time over the past year. My e-mail conversations with Cliff Newman continue to be a source of genuine pleasure, and I look forward to his never really retiring. My professional association with David Stover is now 20 years old (happy anniversary, David!), which I am sure surprises him as much as it does me. I hope it delights him in equal measure, as it does me.

Without the support of David Cowan, my most treasured friend, my closest confidant, and the funniest, kindest, wittiest, and most patient and unflappable man in the world, the demands of this past year would have been impossible to meet. I would be utterly lost without him.

Finally, I am deeply grateful to the remarkable Malcolm Reeves, Assistant Dean in the College of Engineering, for his incredible patience and steadfastness, his hard work and dedication, and especially his gift for strategy. In his every action he is a model of outstanding communication, both interpersonally and rhetorically. It is just one small indication of how dearly we in the Graham Centre love him that I dedicate this book to him.

Introduction

Throughout the time that I have been engaged in writing this book, I have also been involved in what will undoubtedly turn out to be one of the most exhilarating, demanding, rewarding, and exhausting experiences of my life: the establishment of the Ron and Jane Graham Centre for the Study of Communication. It is no accident that this book and the Graham Centre have emerged simultaneously; both are parts of the same scholarly and pedagogical vision aimed at creating a Canadian home, and a Canadian tradition, for the study of communication.

Until relatively recently, it wasn't possible to study human communication (as distinct from mass communication or journalism) in any meaningful way at a Canadian university. This is still true, especially at the graduate level, though there has been some scattered growth in undergraduate offerings in the past 10 years or so.

The problem is not simply that there has been a dearth of opportunities for study, though that's serious enough. Just as problematic is the lack of a Canadian scholarly tradition. As I suggested in the Preface, human communication as an academic specialty is fundamentally American in its assumptions and outlook, and this fact pervades most of its theoretical developments, particularly in the social sciences. It creates a certain disciplinary blindness, particularly as regards Canadian practices, which are typically perceived by Americans as identical to their own. While American theorists clearly understand cultural difference to be a factor when they deal with visibly 'foreign' cultures such as China, Russia, or Pakistan, they tend to overlook cultural factors when they are dealing with Canada. As I saw repeatedly when I was studying in the US, American communication theorists and scholars have little interest in the nuances of Canadian cultural practices and values, even where such differences have been validated by scholars in other fields,[1] and even when they point to important insights into human communication. A claim based on 'difference' may thus be rejected on the grounds that it 'isn't theoretically sound'—when in fact it simply challenges the received view of Canadian culture as nothing more than an extension of, or reaction to, American culture. It seems clear that if we are to 'grow' a tradition of communication study in Canada, we need our own contributions to the scholarly tradition, and our own course texts.

The almost total absence of a humanistic approach to the study of communication is a related, and just as serious, problem in the Canadian academy. As a rhetorician whose primary interest lies in the articulation of Canadian identity, I have keenly felt this lack. Relatively few Canadian academics specialize in rhetoric as a communication discipline, and relatively little rhetorical analysis—as distinct from political, journalistic, or literary analysis—is carried out on Canadian speech and performance. Those who do carry out such research find few publication outlets for their work, and thus have little chance of contributing to a truly Canadian tradition of scholarship and pedagogy.

An obvious place where Canadian scholars could make a contribution to the study of communication is in the study of identity formation, a subject that has already received the attention of several of our most prominent writers and scholars—including Pierre Berton,[2] Margaret Atwood,[3] Northrop Frye,[4] and George Grant,[5] to name only a few. But although the question of Canadian identity has 'obsessed the media and the politicians and a great many ordinary, thinking Canadian people',[6] it has received little sustained scholarly analysis. Because rhetoric is quintessentially the study of identification at both personal and social levels, it offers an ideal methodology for a genuinely Canadian tradition of scholarship. And because cultural expressions—from advertisements[7] to political autobiographies,[8] from parliamentary speeches[9] to television programs[10]—are rhetorical texts, they merit insightful analysis that can help us to understand not only our own cultural preoccupations, but the nature of identity in general. Such analysis would have the added bonus of providing a corrective to the American perspective that so dominates communication study, while at the same time producing more reliable—because less culturally skewed—understanding of human motivation and interaction.

This book is interdisciplinary because it recognizes, as most on the subject do not, the inescapable rhetoricity of all human communication. It therefore incorporates a rhetorical and humanistic perspective not normally encountered in a textbook on interpersonal communication, a subject that is usually treated from a purely social scientific—and emphatically American—perspective. The inclusion of insights gained from thousands of years of rhetorical study demonstrates how such an approach can enrich the study of human identification on an interpersonal as well as social, political, and cultural level. As this book demonstrates, because interpersonal communication is so inescapably about personal identity and the formation of community, it is also inescapably rhetorical. A comprehensive study of interpersonal communication should not overlook this important feature of human interaction.

Chapter 1

Foundations of Communication

Learning Objectives

- To understand what is meant by interpersonal communication.
- To understand the functions of interpersonal communication.
- To understand the interrelatedness of perception and communication.

We spend our lives immersed in messages, and yet, for most of us, the ways we create meaning remain largely unexamined. Communication, after all, is a natural process that happens whether or not we spend much time thinking about how exactly it works. And most of the time, it works well enough for us to meet our needs. As a rule, only when we run into some kind of conflict do we pay conscious attention to our patterns of interacting with others, and then—well, conflict is inevitable, isn't it? We pause briefly to reflect, chalk it up to experience, and continue pretty much as before.

Most of us have developed our communication habits more or less by accident, copying them from our families, our friends, and our social or cultural surroundings. We may be aware that our strategies are sometimes less than perfect, but our communication style is so much a part of us that it is very difficult to modify it, even if we could discover how to do so without feeling that we are trying to change our entire personalities. Besides, the habits of a lifetime are difficult to change. 'That's just the way I am', we rationalize, 'and people will have to accept that.'

But we really do need to understand our communication better, if only because we do so much of it: studies have suggested that as much as 75 per cent of the average person's day is spent communicating in some way. This percentage, as high as it is, is even higher if you're in college or university. While you are a student, it is estimated that just about all your waking time is spent communicating: roughly 69 per cent on speaking and listening, 17 per cent on reading, and 14 per cent on writing.[1] As one expert has put it, 'we listen a book a day, we speak a book a week, read the equivalent of a book a month, and write the equivalent of a book a year.'[2]

You'd think with all this practice we'd be pretty good at communicating, and that we'd pretty much be able to avoid misunderstandings and conflict. Even a brief reflection on your own lived experience will convince you that this isn't so: think of the challenges of communicating with parents, siblings, roommates, friends, and partners; if you expand your consideration to include classmates, neighbours, professors, and service providers, to name only a few, you can rapidly see how much of your communication time actually is spent managing relationships with others. This function of communication—the care and maintenance of relationships—is known as **interpersonal communication**, and this book is about how we can improve our skill and make our interactions more effective and satisfying.

In the field of communication studies, interpersonal interaction is usually distinguished from other categories or classifications of communication study, such as group communication and leadership, rhetoric and persuasion, public speaking, organizational communication, mass communication, and intercultural communication; each category is treated as a separate, independent subject. In this book, however, we will approach the subject of interpersonal relations a little differently, drawing insights from other branches of communication study in order to enlarge our understanding of how people establish and maintain relationships, form identities, and become members of communities. This approach makes two important assump-

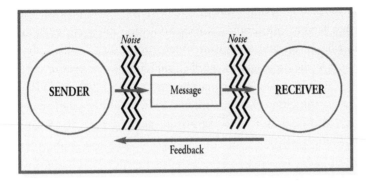

Fig 1.1
The Shannon-Weaver Model of Communication

tions. First, there is a sense in which *all* communication is interpersonal, since every interaction contributes to the establishment of social connection and human intimacy. Second, our interpersonal relationships are affected and shaped by political, rhetorical, cultural, and organizational contexts and pressures, and understanding these will make us more adept interpersonal communicators.

What Is Communication?

If pressed for a definition of **communication**, we might come up with something similar to this: 'the transmission of information by speaking, writing, or other means'.[3] As soon as we start thinking about interpersonal communication, however, we see how unsatisfactory this definition is, since it treats communication merely as a vehicle for transferring information from one person to another. This conception of communication, known as the 'bullet' or radio transmission model, has its basis in information theory. This model is frequently presented in textbooks that emphasize an exclusively social scientific approach to the study of communication, and can be illustrated by a diagram known as the **Shannon-Weaver model**[4] (Figure 1.1).

According to this model, a 'sender' transmits a message to a 'receiver' through a 'channel'. Notice that the message, or the sender's meaning, is treated as a separate entity, independent of the sender and the receiver. The sender 'encodes' this meaning into a form (for example, an off-the-cuff remark, a thoughtful conversation, a letter, a video diary) appropriate to the chosen 'channel' (for instance, a telephone call, a face-to-face interaction, an e-mail message, a television broadcast). As it travels through the channel, the message may encounter 'noise' or interference, which may make it difficult for the receiver to interpret what has been said or written or taped. The model includes the possibility of feedback from the receiver to the sender, which allows the sender to receive confirmation and inquiries from the receiver.

While it may be easy to visualize and understand, this model of communication is ultimately inadequate, since it implies that communication is little more than an exchange of information. By emphasizing the centrality of the message over the inter-action between the people involved, the Shannon-Weaver model provides an incomplete understanding of what's actually going on when people communicate, whether they do so personally or socially.

In practice, communication is less like a process of information exchange than it is like a process of negotiation, which almost always involves the interplay of feelings, assumptions, values, ethics, public status, self-definition, and social needs. Because the Shannon-Weaver model tends to obscure the human dimensions of interaction, reducing people to 'senders' and 'receivers' of information, it can't satisfactorily account for the complex nature of interpersonal communication.

Throughout this book, we will assume that communicating effectively means not only making a message clear, but also creating an appropriate and effective relationship with the person or persons you are addressing, and establishing or maintaining a sense of social belonging and personal credibility.

The Roots of Communication Study

People have been thinking about these questions for a long time, perhaps longer than they've been studying nearly anything else. For example, the oldest book in existence (dating to 2675 BCE) is a collection of tips on effective communication.[5] Probably the most influential book on communication in history, however, is a practical advice book written by Aristotle nearly 2,500 years ago (c. 330 BCE). Although Aristotle's main focus was public communication rather than face-to-face interactions, his insights are still useful to those who would like to communicate more effectively, thoughtfully, and ethically in all situations.

Although Aristotle's book focuses on public communication rather than on inter-personal interaction,[6] it nevertheless provides valuable insights into human motivation and behaviour. Aristotle's primary interest was understanding how we influence each other through our communication, and how we can manage our own influential messages more effectively. While not all scholars recognize the role of influence in interpersonal communication, many others recognize the role that persuasion plays in all our interaction.[7] For instance, influence expert Robert Cialdini's work explores the relationship between psychology and persuasion;[8] the linguist Deborah Tannen examines the language of interpersonal and conversational dynamics in order to shed light on such issues as 'who gets heard, who gets credit, and who gets ahead'[9]—issues that are inescapably both rhetorical and interpersonal. And in some colleges and universities, it is possible to take courses in the rhetoric of interpersonal communication,[10] which explore—as this book does—the role of persuasive forces in

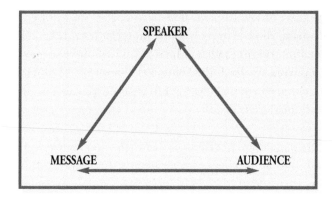

Fig 1.2
The Rhetorical Triangle

the shaping of the self, the extent to which interpersonal communication is rhetorical, and the ethical dimensions of interpersonal-rhetorical interaction.

From the perspective of interpersonal communication, the most important part of Aristotle's theory is a model of communication that has come to be known as the **rhetorical triangle**, illustrated in Figure 1.2. What makes this model especially useful is its emphasis on the interactional nature of communication. Like many contemporary theorists, Aristotle understood that communication is a dynamic process of observation, judgement, and adaptation, that it is an interaction rather than a simple transaction or exchange of static information.

The arrows in the model indicate the vectors of influence or connection—the relationships—that exist between each pair of elements: the speaker builds a relationship with the listeners (speaker–audience vector), demonstrates a connection and investment in the message (speaker–message vector), and makes clear the relevance of the message to the listeners (audience–message vector).

The rhetorical triangle model of communication differs from the Shannon-Weaver model in that it recognizes that human communication is about more than information; it's a complex and unpredictable process that also involves elements of relation-building—the establishment of credibility and trust, for instance, and an ability to recognize and respond to the needs and expectations of those with whom we are communicating. While the message is important, it is far from the only factor in an interaction.

One of the most important features of Aristotle's approach is his emphasis on the important role that the speaker's own character plays in communication. He called this quality of self-projection **ethos**, a word that in Greek combined the ideas of ethics and habit.[11] Just as contemporary scholars recognize the role of communication in establishing our sense of identity, both public and private, and our sense of belonging or community,[12] Aristotle understood that people establish or confirm their public selves through the content, tone, and style of the things they say, and he argued that any person who wishes to be heard, accepted, and heeded by others must demonstrate three important qualities. These are (1) good will, by which he meant genuine respect and concern for others' interests and views; (2) good judgement of the situation and issues, which includes a sensible and reasonable point of view based on a full understanding of the issues; and (3) good character—that is, integrity and credibility.

For Aristotle, these qualities of character that make up someone's ethos are central because they create the foundation of trust on which all effective communication depends. He knew that believability depends as much on our confidence in a speaker's character as on the quality of the message content. People who have forged a bond of trust with us are seen as more believable, while we are inclined to doubt or even reject messages from someone we do not trust, no matter how accurate their information may be.[13] Consider, for example, how many times you have found yourself resisting messages from someone you did not find credible or trustworthy, even if the person's information was factually correct.

The rhetorical model of communication in Figure 1.2 also shows the importance of the relationship a speaker forms with others, since it can also influence how the message is heard and whether it is accepted. A successful communicator must demonstrate both understanding of and consideration for others by recognizing and affirming the things that the listeners value, need, hope for, fear, or care about. He or she must also exhibit respect and concern for the audience. Aristotle called this aspect of communication **pathos**, so named for its recognition of the feelings of others. Pathos and ethos together form the relational foundation of an interaction, and Aristotle argued that these are very important if you are going to be listened to or understood.

In the remainder of this chapter, and indeed in the remainder of this book, we will explore the ways in which this dynamic understanding of communication can provide a foundation for understanding interpersonal interaction.

The Functions of Communication

The ability to communicate effectively can have a dramatic impact on a person's quality of life, far more than most people realize. Research shows a strong correlation between communicative ability and happiness,[14] life satisfaction,[15] professional success,[16] and even good health.[17] The absence of meaningful interaction not only compromises our quality of life, but can make us vulnerable to a variety of health problems, including various kinds of cancer, epilepsy, inflammatory bowel disease, heart disease, and arthritis.[18] Thus, effective interpersonal communication is important to our well-being.

We communicate for many reasons, but most messages fulfill one or more of the following three functions: **expressive messages**, **pragmatic messages**, and **symbolic messages**. Expressive communication typically is not directed to a specific listener; instead, such messages give voice to, and thus help us come to terms with, our own emotional experiences. The capacity to cope with emotional ups and downs is important to our psychological well-being, and thus indirectly to our interpersonal effectiveness, but expressive communication is not so much about building relations with others as it is about getting things off our chest. Because it is 'only imperfectly aware of an audience',[19] expressive communication is not as important to our study of interpersonal communication as the other two functions.

The second function of communication is to perform practical tasks. Pragmatic messages focus mainly on task or content and are primarily intended to get things done. They are meant to appeal to a listener or listeners, mainly because the co-operation of others is necessary to accomplishing our ends. Pragmatic messages may have an instrumental purpose, aimed at fulfilling our basic physical needs (for example, we communicate in order to obtain food and shelter, such as when we shop for groceries or rent an apartment). Pragmatic messages also assist us in establishing task-based co-operation with others and in enlisting aid in practical circumstances. For example, if you are lost and need directions, you may communicate with a stranger who can tell you the way, or if you want to paint your apartment, you might communicate with a friend to obtain her assistance.

Finally, pragmatic messages can have a decision-making function, providing us with the background we need to draw well-founded conclusions as a basis for action. For instance, when faced with an unfamiliar situation we may seek the advice of someone more knowledgeable, as when you ask your parents for assistance with filling out your first income tax form, or approach your communication professor for advice on writing a letter of application.

Because they require us to engage with others, pragmatic messages are relevant to our understanding of interpersonal dynamics. However, it is the third category, symbolic messages, that is of greatest interest, since its motives are rooted deeply in our nature as social beings. On this level of function our communication enables us to fulfill our emotional, psychological, and social needs.

The separation between pragmatic and symbolic communication is not absolute, of course, since some apparently pragmatic messages can have a deeper symbolic or psychological purpose, and any single message can fulfill several functions for the individual. The theorist Kenneth Burke explains the difference between a symbolic act and a practical act as follows:

> if a man climbs a mountain, not through any interest in mountain climbing, but purely because he wants to get somewhere, and the easiest way to get there is by crossing the mountain, we need not look for symbolism. But if we begin

to discuss *why* he wanted to get there, we do get into matters of symbolism. For his conception of purpose involves a texture of human relationships; his purposes are 'social'; as such, they are not something-in-and-by-itself, but a function of many relationships; which is to say that they are symbolical.[20]

In other words, people sometimes do things for reasons that have nothing to do with practical tasks. They are motivated by other, more profoundly personal or psychological reasons that have to do with their identity and symbolic satisfaction.

The 'person-building' function of communication that takes place on the symbolic level is essential to our psychological and emotional health. As social beings, humans derive satisfaction just from interacting with others. We use communication to make this connection, to establish emotional ties with others, and to participate in our families and communities. Beyond these important social functions, communication also allows us to build relationships on a number of levels of intimacy, and through these relationships to establish our sense of self and the sense of others as selves too. Finally, it is through the symbolic function of our communication that we are able to develop an ethical orientation, an important function of communication that we will discuss more fully in Chapter 11.

While the three functions of communication are theoretically distinct, in practice our messages may significantly overlap the categories. A communication that is apparently purely expressive may have a pragmatic purpose, while a pragmatic message can carry symbolic meaning. For example, when Gwen woke up late for class last week, she exclaimed, 'Oh no! My alarm didn't go off! I'm going to miss my exam!' While such a statement arguably is purely expressive, it also may be intended to serve a pragmatic purpose. Although Gwen has not specifically requested a ride to school, her message may nevertheless elicit the offer of a ride from her roommate. The relationship is one of long-standing, and in such a context, the request doesn't have to be made explicitly in order to function as a pragmatic message. It's also possible that this same message can function symbolically, since it affirms the closeness of their friendship, which involves mutual concern and support for each other. Gwen has not had to explicitly ask for help, but her friend hears her expression of concern and offers the needed assistance anyway. To understand the symbolic import of the interaction, imagine what would have happened to the relationship if Christa, hearing her roommate's cry, had not offered the needed ride.

Kenneth Burke teaches that, beyond the fulfillment of our most basic physical needs, the fundamental motive of all human communication is the creation of **identification**, a sense of connectedness and intimacy, with others. All communication is in this sense symbolic, and at the same time persuasive.[21] Social scientific research supports Burke's insights. The absence of meaningful relationships—interpersonally effective relationships—not only compromises our joy in life but can actually shorten its duration.

THE FUNCTIONS OF COMMUNICATION

- Expressive messages (focus mainly on self-expression)
  - Express and cope with emotional experience
- Pragmatic messages (focus mainly on task and content)
  - Instrumental: fulfill basic needs
  - Co-operative: obtain assistance with practical tasks
  - Decision-making: make more informed decisions
- Symbolic messages (focus mainly on relation-building and identification)
  - Obtain social affirmation and psychological fulfillment
  - Form relationships with others
  - Participate in family, community, and society
  - Establish and maintain a sense of self
  - Build trust
  - Establish an ethical foundation for action

Perception and Communication

Perception—how we see or hear what goes on around us—has a profound influence on the way we understand the world, and thus on the way we communicate. Indeed, the word 'perception' can be used not only to mean the ability to see or hear, but also to refer to qualities of insight and interpretation.

Perception begins with the raw cues that come to us through the senses, such as light waves, sound waves, or molecules in the air that carry odours, but it doesn't end with the reception of these molecules or energy waves by our sense organs. Instead, the process we know of as perception takes place in three stages: selection, classification, and interpretation.

If you've ever listened to eyewitness accounts of an event, you know that reports of the same event by different observers may be incompatible. Part of the reason for this is the selective nature of our perceptions. The flow of information from the world around us is constant, and we can't possibly pay attention to all of it. As a result, much of it escapes our conscious notice as we attend to the easiest, most available, or most familiar details.

Selection is the process whereby we choose which of the many sensations that surround us will register on our minds. First, of course, we select based on our own physiological limitations: not all the sounds that occur around us fall within the normal range of human hearing, for example, nor are all light waves visible to the human eye. But even beyond these obvious limitations, each of us has different sensory acuity, and we will tend to notice different stimuli within the range of our own abilities.

In an environment of competing sensations, we tend to notice things that stand out from their surroundings: a loud noise in the midst of the din of conversation; sudden movement; a flash of light in a dark room; a stillness in the midst of a hubbub of activity; and so on. We are also attracted to rhythm and repetition; for example, even a low sound can become intolerable when it is repeated—a dripping tap or a ticking clock can keep us awake, though the sound may not be especially loud. On the other hand, we tend not to notice persistent sounds or sights to which we have become accustomed; these simply fade into the background. For example, if your apartment overlooks a busy intersection, you will soon stop noticing traffic noise. Even sirens, if they occur with frequency, will pass almost unnoticed.

We also select what to attend to on the basis of our own orientation and concerns. What you notice is partly a function of what you're interested in, your goals, your expectations, your experience, or your needs. If you buy a new car, for example, you will suddenly notice all the similar models that pass you on the road, when you never noticed them before. If you're late for an appointment, you'll probably notice every clock that you pass or every red light that impedes your progress. If you suspect that your parents don't like your new friend, you will notice every disapproving look that passes between them when she comes to your house for supper. Your own physical sensitivities also influence the things you notice; think of how different the world feels when you have a headache from how it feels when you are well.

Selection is only the first stage in the perceptual process; **classification**, or organization, is the second. When faced with a new sensation, we automatically slot it into

an appropriate category of experience, since sense experience means little to us until we have classified or organized it within a familiar frame of reference. Only then can we understand what the sensation is. Inescapably, the categories into which we organize our perceptions tend to gloss over subtle differences in experiences; thus, all such classification involves some degree of simplification. The more complex an experience or the more ambiguous it is, the more subtleties are overlooked.

Human beings classify all their perceptions in this way, but it is the classification of interpersonal experience that is of greatest interest to us here. We tend to see people in terms of their similarity to or difference from ourselves, organizing them by sex, age, and ethnic origin, followed by style of dress, attractiveness, and general attitude or demeanour. Other significant aspects include occupation, social status, religion, the friends they associate with, the hobbies they pursue, where they live, and so forth. The categories we have available depend in part on our previous experience, as does the way we place people within these categories. For example, if I have never had a friend from a different background or age group than my own, I may be unlikely to view someone significantly older or of a different ethnicity or socio-economic background as a potential friend. In general, the more people appear to have in common with us, or the more they seem to be like others we are familiar with, the more comfortable we feel with them and the more favourably we tend to view them.

The final step in the perceptual process is interpretation, through which we give meaning to the information we have selected and classified. Interpretation involves making **inferences**, which are judgements about what we don't know based on what we do know. Inferences involve 'filling in the blanks' by attributing to others traits we associate with the ones we've observed. The whole process looks like this: some quality or action of another person catches our attention; in response, we make a **snap judgement** about her. This first impression may be accurate or inaccurate, but it can continue to colour our judgement of someone even after we have had a chance to get to know her better.

On the basis of this initial **attribution**, we interpret the person's general motivation as residing either in his character or in the situation he's in. For instance, we notice that Bill behaves generously to someone and because we approve of him, we regard this gesture as further evidence of what a nice guy he is. On the other hand, we have noticed that Larry serves himself first, so when he behaves generously we assume either that there must have been some outside pressure on him that forced him into doing something nice, or that he is hoping to gain some advantage through the gesture. We use this attribution of motive to further confirm our approval or disapproval, our like or dislike, and our categorization of the person as decent or a jerk.

The final stage of this attribution process is using our general impression of someone to predict a whole range of potential behaviour and actions. 'Don't invite Larry to your party', we tell a friend. 'He'll just find some way to turn the whole thing to his own advantage.' The attribution process tends to reproduce itself, since whenever the person acts, we are inclined to interpret the actions in ways that confirm our initial impression.

There is an important distinction to be made here between the kind of snap judgement we are discussing and a reasonable inference about another person's future behaviour. Obviously we can, and need to, make informed judgements about the behaviour we might expect to encounter from people we know. Since past behaviour is the best predictor we have of future actions, it is not unreasonable to expect that someone who has consistently behaved with personal integrity in the past can most likely be depended upon to behave with integrity in the future; similarly, someone who has made a habit of lying and deceiving others will likely continue to do so. We would make ourselves foolishly vulnerable to a range of interpersonal and other abuses if we were unable to make such judgements.

What is at issue is the *basis* upon which our inferences rest. If we are going on a single initial impression, or on one action that may have been misread or misinterpreted, or on similarly limited experience and observation, we need to bear in mind that such inferences, however reasonable they may appear to be, can be mistaken. Where we need to be especially cautious is in inferring an entire range of behaviour and future action based on such scant knowledge. This is a qualitatively different thing from making reasonable, informed judgements based on long-term patterns or adequate opportunity to observe someone's behaviour. Although even such well-founded inferences can be mistaken for a variety of reasons, they are usually more reliable than our quick inferences.

It may seem remarkable that we can be so quick to infer entire personalities based on only one or two character traits, but there are a few reasons for this. As communication theorist Erving Goffman points out, the capacity to 'profile' or interpret the conduct and character of others is a basic social process,[22] as well as an essential skill, particularly when we are dealing with those who will remain more or less strangers to us—classmates, customers of a business where we work, staff members of the college with whom we interact only occasionally. The process of attribution is not in itself 'wrong'. In fact, we need to be able to make such inferences in order to manage the large amounts of information that come our way in the course of a day. If we could not quickly make sufficiently accurate inferences to get us through our daily tasks, we would be paralyzed and vulnerable.

The problem is not with the process of attribution so much as it is with our tendency to forget that our snap judgements are provisional and based on only partial information. We rely on our ability to make accurate inferences because we need to be able to do so, and we forget that we sometimes have difficulty distinguishing between significant, representative behaviour and accidental misinterpretations. Where we run into trouble in the inferential process is in taking our initial inferences as the final word on someone and allowing that snap judgement to colour every subsequent encounter with the person. This persistence of the initial impression can show up in several ways.

First, we tend to treat our first impressions as representative of the person's whole attitude or manner of being. For instance, a classmate has always been confident and willing to speak in class, so you infer that he is intelligent; the clerk in the registrar's office greets you pleasantly and treats you with genuine friendliness, so you judge that she's very good at her job; your roommate's boyfriend is attentive and thoughtful whenever he visits, so you and your friend assume he is faithful.

In each of these examples, your initial impressions could be correct, but additional information could also show them to be mistaken: it could be that the classmate just likes to hear himself talk, whether or not he has anything valuable to say; that the clerk would rather pass the time of day than attend to her filing; and that the attentive boyfriend has actually been cheating on your friend. Refusing to supplement your initial judgements with further insights as they become available is a bigger problem than the original interpretation itself.

We make inferences about people's motivations for a variety of actions, and we may tend to be more generous in interpreting the actions of people we know well, especially if we are on a friendly basis with them, than we are towards strangers. Jeanie and Julian are colleagues and friends; when Julian passes her in the hall without saying hello, Jeanie assumes that he must be preoccupied and wonders whether there is something wrong. 'Poor Julian', she thinks to herself, 'he must have a lot on his mind.' On the other hand, the same behaviour from Peter, whom she sees in the hall several times a week and who has been introduced to her a couple of times at meetings, makes her dismiss him as socially dysfunctional.

Our inferences are shaped by past experience, as well as by our current needs and expectations. They can also be affected by our state of health or well-being; we can be influenced by fatigue or hunger or pain or infirmity. In such circumstances, we may be so preoccupied with our own discomfort that we lose track of what might be motivating others. Melinda, who is diabetic, has just ordered a meal at her favourite restaurant when she feels her blood sugar start to drop. When the server comes by to tell her there's been a mix-up and her order will be delayed, Melinda snaps at him as though he's deliberately tried to inconvenience her. When Frank has a migraine, it seems to him as though the idiots who live in the apartment below him deliberately choose that moment to turn up the music as loud as it will go.

Our judgement can also be coloured by age and level of experience, as well as by rigid adherence to social roles or occupational hierarchy. For example, Richard has just met an attractive young woman at a party. He is shocked to discover that she is a newly minted Ph.D. in mathematics and has just started teaching at the university. 'No way you're a math prof', he tells her. 'They're all a hundred years old and male.' Adrian is team leader in his part-time job at a local fast-food restaurant, where several of his classmates work. He's good at his job and proud of the fact that his group has been designated this month's 'A-team' because of his leadership. However, he joins a study group for one of his courses, and he is shocked when, in response to his suggestions, one of his team members from work responds edgily, 'We're not at work now, Adrian. This isn't your call.'

We rely on our ability to make accurate inferences, and we need to be able to do so. But as much as we rely on our perceptual acuity and our ability to make reliable inferences, we need to remember that we can make mistakes.

How Perceptions Can Be Wrong

It is true that our ability to communicate effectively sometimes depends on our being able to rapidly 'size up' what we see, make a quick judgement, and infer a lot of information based on that judgement. It is through this process that we are able to read a situation, deduce its constraints and expectations, and respond appropriately. We quite correctly prize this skill of quick apprehension and response as an ability to 'think on your feet'. In a job interview, in an oral presentation, or at social events, for example, the ability to react quickly and appropriately is a definite benefit.

However, interpersonal perceptions are not always reliable. They can be compromised in a number of ways. First, we tend to over-attribute based on qualities that are most visible: the way someone dresses, her age, even her 'race'. We react to this social information because it is most available, and sometimes—as with dress—it is used deliberately to create a certain kind of impression. Such features as age, ethnicity, or group affiliation are powerful triggers for the unspoken attributions of others, and, because they are so visible, they can easily become the foundations for stereotypes.

Because Canada, especially in its large urban centres, is both multi-ethnic and multicultural, we should be especially careful about how quickly and on what basis we classify and interpret cues from those whose cultural or ethnic backgrounds differ from our own. In college or university, we are likely to encounter—sometimes for the first time—people whose appearance, dress, or social conventions are unlike what we are used to. When we have no reliable experience to help us interpret such unfamiliar cues, we may tend to react defensively or negatively. Just as in any situation where we have to interpret the actions of someone who is unknown to us, we should bear in mind that our initial judgements and our interpretations will likely need refinement as we become more comfortable with the cultural and ethnic diversity of our new surroundings.

Many of us have been misjudged at one time or another based on the attributions made by other people, and we have all made snap judgements about others on such bases. We judge others by their clothes, by their manner of speaking, by their age, sex, or social memberships. While it is not wrong to make attributions, it is risky to assume that our first impressions are always correct or to hold onto our initial interpretations when additional information shows them to be flawed. Even otherwise thoughtful, enlightened, and intelligent people are capable, in some situations, of making unfounded judgements, but what shows them to be thoughtful, enlightened, and intelligent is their willingness to revisit those first impressions to accommodate a greater level of observation and understanding.

In addition to making judgements based on highly visible social information, we also tend to overgeneralize from scraps of information, treating them as if they are representative of the whole. We do this in part because consistency is a feature of social identity, and social identity in turn is believed to provide reliable indicators of personal identity. This makes sense, but in order to make reliable inferences, we need—as Goffman cautions—to be able to distinguish between an individual's 'more or less abiding characteristics, as opposed to the moods, feelings, or intents that he might have at a particular moment'.[23] If we mistake a passing mood for an abiding characteristic, we are likely to make a misattribution.

Interpretation can also be faulty because of the tenacity with which we hold onto our initial snap judgements and preconceptions. Thus, instead of using subsequent observations to refine and improve our initial impression, we often selectively distort them so as to confirm that first reading of the person's character. We also have a tendency to draw cause–effect relationships where they may not exist.

For example, Jenna recently left her job to return to university to obtain a Master of Professional Communication degree. She'd been thinking of going back to school for a while now, and is very interested in studying communication. Her boss, knowing of Jenna's interest in obtaining the master's degree, encouraged her to apply under a new company policy that offers financial support for those who wish to pursue further education. Her boss feels that Jenna's successful completion of her MPComm will enhance both her usefulness to the company and her future career prospects. Jenna knows it will be a lot of work to juggle school and a full-time job, but she has a plan and has discussed it with her boss and with an advisor at the university.

Imagine Jenna's surprise when a friend recently reported to her that she was the subject of gossip among their circle of acquaintances, who have attributed her choice to a variety of causes: one suggested that she must have been about to lose her job, since nobody would otherwise willingly take on the grind of more schooling; another claimed that she is just a ruthlessly ambitious careerist who will stop at nothing to get ahead; a third said she was obviously compensating for feelings of inadequacy; a fourth claimed that she was simply doing the degree because she wanted to go trolling for a husband.

When making our interpretations of other people's motivations, we are influenced by our own interests, fears, and experiences. We also tend to overlook the complex nature of motivations and reach for a simple, one-dimensional explanation that can be neatly stated and categorized: 'Bob's just worried and is taking out his frustration on Jane'; 'Jenna's just looking for a husband'; 'Lisa's just a fool when it comes to money.' We may forget to consider the power of a situation to shape and motivate behaviour. People have choice and will, it's true, but they are also subject to the powerful influences of a situation. For example, perhaps without the encouragement of her boss and without the company's new policy of providing financial support, Jenna's dream of returning to school would not have materialized. Jenna brought the motivation, but in a different situation she might have contented herself with taking some professional development seminars on communication instead of the degree she is now pursuing.

Finally, when we make inferences we are likely to validate negative information more than positive information. We also tend to be more favourable about our own motives than about those of others, and in judging the same behaviour in two different people we are more willing to give the benefit of the doubt to someone we like than to someone we don't like. In addition, we are likely to be more approving of behaviour or choices that we might undertake ourselves than of those that we would not be likely to consider. Notice, for example, that Jenna's acquaintances all made negative attributions about her motives for pursuing an action that none of them could imagine doing themselves.

Considering all the ways that it's possible to go wrong in making attributions of motive, why don't we stop doing it altogether? The answer is that we could not get along without the ability or skill to 'read' a situation and respond appropriately. We can never stop making such judgements, nor would we want to. What we can do, however, is learn how to make better assessments and keep ourselves from mistaking our interpretations for facts.

How To Improve Your Perceptual Skills

There is an old fable about a man who spent his days seeking the meaning of life. After many years of searching, he at last reached a mountaintop where there lived a wise guru who was reported to have the answer to the man's quest. When the man asked for this insight to be shared, the guru gave him this response: 'Pay attention, pay attention, pay attention.' Whatever its value as a recipe for a meaningful life, this is certainly good advice when it comes to increasing your interpersonal skill, and especially to improving your perceptual abilities.

Since perception is a three-step process, it makes sense that, to increase your skills, you need to alter your habits on all three levels. First, then, you need to practise your powers of observation so that you develop some greater awareness of the features of an interaction that may be influencing you. Pay attention to exactly how you form impressions of others. When you find yourself making an attribution—'He's nervous' or 'She's a snob'—try to pinpoint exactly what it is in the person's behaviour that has triggered this judgement. Force yourself to become more conscious of exactly why you are judging actions and people in the way you do—create a kind of 'quality control' for yourself by asking 'Why do I think this?' The more you remind yourself to qualify your judgements, the more careful and better an observer you will become. At first it will be cumbersome and time-consuming to query every judgement that you make about people, but with persistence you will find that your interpretations will automatically become more thoughtful and also more amenable to adjustment with additional information.

Second, you should keep reminding yourself that your attributions are just that—interpretations, not facts. As you observe others, ask yourself how you are categorizing them and why you've chosen to group them in that way. On what basis, for instance, have you decided that Lucie is an airhead? Why do you think Alvie is a genius? Is there any chance that further information would qualify that judgement? I once heard a female television performer tell an interviewer 'people think because I'm happy, I must be an idiot.' Do you make similar sorts of leaps in classifying people? What sorts of associations do you use to make your quick assessments? Try to identify, if you can, the qualities to which you attach the most meaning.

You can also check your perceptions and judgements against the perceptions of a friend or partner. Did you both 'read' the same event or person in a similar way? If so, does this validate your perception or simply confirm that you and your friend share similar values and expectations? If not, what does this tell you about the way you have judged the situation?

In addition to examining your own process for judging others, you should also

seek out and consider how others form their impressions. When you hear a friend make a pronouncement about someone else's character or motivations, ask him to tell you why he thinks as he does. Although some people may become defensive about this kind of probing of their judgement, others will willingly tell you how they've arrived at their conclusions. Compare their interpretations with your own, and evaluate how their assumptions differ from yours.

You can also learn more about the process others use for making their judgements by paying close attention to how they seem to be categorizing and interpreting your actions. One way to do this is through the process of **metacommunication**, which means communicating about the process of communication itself. This can be a rich source of insight, but you should be aware that it can be risky when feelings and judgements that are normally submerged are made explicit. If you have a close friend with whom you share confidences, you might try asking her or him to discuss your perceptions and evaluations of each other. But understand, if you decide to undertake this kind of metacommunication, that you must be prepared to handle some surprises; not everything that your friend thinks about you will be entirely flattering or easy to hear. Remember the interpretations Jenna's friends offered of her motives for returning to school?

Finally, keep an open mind. Try to remember that your attributions are only provisional, and don't take them for fact at least until you have sought out further information to help clarify and qualify your assessments. You can, if you pay attention to your perceptual processes, increase your awareness of your own typical inaccuracies and develop ways to compensate for them. When you encounter a new situation, try to make conscious your process of observation and judgement. Describe to yourself what you witnessed—not what you thought it meant, but what you actually saw. Delay attaching meaning to the things you observed for as long as possible. Then think of at least two different ways of 'reading' the event you witnessed and try to imagine the motivations and circumstances that might have led to what you saw. As you do this, think about how you might have behaved in the identical situation. Finally, if it's appropriate to do so, seek clarification of what you saw before coming to a final judgement.

If you practise this process regularly, you will find that in time you will significantly increase your ability to 'read' a situation with greater accuracy. By taking the time to consider the influences that may shape the actions of others, you will also increase your ability to empathize with them, which in turn will make your interpersonal communication more effective.

Summary

While is true that we obtain our factual knowledge of the world primarily through our communication with others, the purpose of interaction is not simply, or even mainly, to gather facts. Instead, it is through our communication that we find ourselves, forge friendships, and express our dreams. Our communication is what enables us to create the social and other relationships that help to form us, that provide our frame of reference, our understanding of right and wrong, our sense of where we belong in the world. Communication allows us to gain the trust of others and give them our trust in return. Communication enables the co-operation that defines any society.

Our communication is greatly influenced by the process of perception, through which we select, classify, and interpret the actions and motives of others. We are subject to error at all levels of this process—we may select the wrong details to pay attention to, we may organize what we see in a misleading way, or we may draw conclusions on partial or faulty information. To improve our interpersonal skills, we must start with our perceptual abilities and learn to qualify our judgements as more information becomes available.

In the rest of this book we will approach the study of interpersonal communication with two central assumptions. The first is that our quality of life depends in large part on the quality of our interactions with others. The second assumption, implicit in our discussion so far, is that humans are social beings, drawn towards relationships and identification with others rather than towards isolation and division. The study of interpersonal communication focuses on the building and maintenance of these relationships; it is, in effect, the opposite of impersonal messages, which tend to treat people as though they are objects rather than feeling, choosing, reflective beings who not only dwell in a physical environment but are immersed in messages that shape their understanding of themselves, others, and the world.

The study of interpersonal communication is not concerned with manipulating or triumphing over others; it is not about determining who is 'right' in an interaction or dispute; it is not about affirming your own point of view over that of another. Instead, interpersonal communication is concerned with getting along more effectively, with helping each of us to achieve more satisfying relationships, and with making all of our interactions more effective and fulfilling.

The key to effective interpersonal communication does not lie in the content of your messages; it doesn't lie even in the mastery of communication techniques and strategies; instead, it lies in the quality of the relation you establish, in your ability to understand another's perspective, to establish intimacy, to handle conflict, and to manage interpersonal risk. This book is intended to help you better understand your own communication and that of others, to improve your skills, and to manage your communication in a more effective and beneficial way.

Key Terms

attribution
classification
communication
ethos
expressive messages
identification
inferences
interpersonal communication
interpretation
metacommunication
pathos
perception
pragmatic messages
rhetorical triangle
selection
Shannon-Weaver model
snap judgement
symbolic messages

Suggested Readings

Barry Brummett, *Rhetoric in Popular Culture* (New York: St Martin's Press, 1994). Brummett's text explores the messages encoded in the symbols and artifacts of popular culture. This book is intended for senior undergraduates, but it is quite readable.

Dale Carnegie, *How to Win Friends and Influence People*, new edn (London: Vermilion, 2007). First published in 1936, this popular classic in the interpersonal self-help genre has sold millions of copies worldwide and has never been out of print. It provides practical advice on how to communicate more effectively by establishing a genuine connection with and understanding of others.

John Fiske, *Introduction to Communication Studies* (New York: Methuen, 1982). Fiske's book is a good general introduction to the study of communication, and provides an overview of foundational theory in the field.

Ann Gill, *Rhetoric and Human Understanding* (Prospect Heights, Ill.: Waveland, 1994). Gill's book provides an introduction to communication from a rhetorical perspective, beginning with symbolism and language, and including an overview of the Western intellectual tradition.

Todd Gitlin, ed., *Watching Television: A Pantheon Guide to Popular Culture* (New York: Pantheon, 1986). The essays in Gitlin's collection cover a range of popular culture, including news broadcasting, soap operas, children's television programming, and advertising.

Exercises and Assignments

1. Circulate within the class. Introduce yourself and talk for a few moments with five people you did not know before. List the names of the five people on a piece of paper. This exercise is more anxiety-producing for some than for others. Were you at all uncomfortable during any part of the exercise? Why might that be?

2. Choose a partner, someone you do not already know, and if possible, someone you did not meet in the first part of the exercise. Converse for four or five minutes, and prepare a brief (two-minute) introduction of your partner for presentation to the rest of the class. Like Exercise #1, this exercise is more anxiety-producing for some than for others. Were you at all uncomfortable during any part of the exercise? Was it more or less stressful than Exercise #1? Why do you think that might be?

3. Present the introduction you prepared in Exercise #2. Apart from the usual nervousness arising from speaking in public, did you feel any added social or interpersonal pressure during this exercise? Why might that have been? In this exercise, whom does the audience learn more about: you, or the person you are introducing? For whom is face primarily being established?

4. Over the next week, keep track of the number of times you hear the word 'rhetoric' used. Does it seem to you to occur more frequently than before you began this course? If so, why do you think that might be? How exactly does the word seem to be used by the speakers you've heard? Is it ever used in the context of interpersonal interaction? Be prepared to discuss your findings with the class, as directed by your instructor.

5. Prepare a short written self-introduction (100–250 words) that will help your instructor become acquainted with you. The specific content and the approach are up to you, but bear in mind that you are helping to set the tone for the relationship between yourself and the instructor over the course of the term. Hand

in the introduction as the first assignment for what will become your interpersonal communication portfolio. The portfolio, a collection of all your written work for the course, is intended to aid you in reflecting on your interpersonal communication skill development. To create the portfolio, keep all of your assignments and reflective writing over the term and organize them, along with a table of contents, into a small binder or Duo-Tang folder. At intervals during the term, and again at the end of the term, you will be asked to submit this portfolio of your work for comments and grading. You should insert a blank page or two at the front of the portfolio, just behind the table of contents, to accommodate your instructor's comments and responses. Your instructor may regularly assign brief reflective or analytical writing tasks specifically for inclusion in the portfolio.

6. Read each of the following case studies and follow the instructions below.

Case Study 1: Martine got married at 18, right out of high school, to the 'older man' of 25 she had been dating for three years. After her marriage, she went to Starlets Beauty College for a six-month course that earned her diploma in Hair Design. By the time she was 25, she had two daughters of her own; by 30 she was divorced and living in a small town where she runs a modest salon out of her home.

Case Study 2: Victor is an 18-year-old, second-year student who is taking pre-law. He's at the top of his class, and is regarded by his peers as well-read and articulate. He has a startlingly large vocabulary, and is knowledgeable about classical music, literature, international culture, and politics. Interestingly, Victor never went to high school; instead, he was home-schooled—entirely by himself; that is, without a tutor. When he's not reading or practising the oboe, Victor can be found wandering the back alleys of town in the early morning wearing rubber boots and carrying binoculars, looking for unusual birds.

Case Study 3: As the only child of a successful cardiologist, Lena had just about everything money can buy. For example, she was the only student in her high school class who had her own credit cards, her own late-model car, and her own exercise room complete with a hot tub and a big-screen TV. But Lena's dreams of becoming a doctor like her dad were dashed when she didn't get past the med school interview. After earning her undergrad degree in biology, Lena drifted from one thing to another, but nothing seemed to pan out. She tried her hand at being a radio announcer, but that fizzled when she got tired of working nights; her dad set her up with a small restaurant, but that went under. Then Lena thought she'd write a novel, but after seven years of frustration, she hasn't even finished a single chapter. She's not sure what she's going to do next. She's toying with the idea of getting her master's, but she's really not sure.

Case Study 4: Prof. Krabb recently joined the Faculty of Management after several years in the corporate world. In nearly every class meeting he draws explicitly on the professional experience that sets him apart from the other profs in the program, who have only ever taught in the university and therefore, he says, don't really know what managers need to learn. He makes it clear that much of what other profs are teaching—and he's not afraid to name names—is a waste of time. After all, he himself was a practising manager for years, making more money than any of his colleagues, and he got along just fine without knowing anything about subjects like interpersonal communication or negotiation, two of the courses in the program that he is particularly critical of. His philosophy of management, he says, is 'just do it', and if you're no good at it you should find a different line of work.

Choose any THREE of the following attributes that you think most accurately apply to the individuals in each of the case studies above. Then choose three that you believe to be the OPPOSITE of each of these individuals. There are no 'right' answers; simply choose those you believe are most apt. Be prepared to discuss your choices with the class, as your instructor directs.

able	bored	determined	gracious	open
accomplished	caring	dim-witted	happy	original
adventurous	childish	discreet	hare-brained	passionate
aggressive	commanding	dishonourable	helpless	perverse
agitated	compatible	domineering	honest	pleasant
ambitious	competent	dramatic	impatient	popular
amicable	concerned	dynamic	individual	possessive
anti-social	confident	effective	inferior	powerful
appealing	congenial	efficient	informal	professional
apprehensive	content	empathetic	inquisitive	reckless
approachable	conventional	energetic	insecure	reflective
arrogant	co-operative	entertaining	inspired	resistant
assertive	courageous	extroverted	intelligent	resourceful
attention-	creative	fearful	interesting	ruthless
seeking	credible	forceful	introverted	sad
attractive	creepy	formal	lazy	self-controlled
authentic	curious	friendly	likable	self-disciplined
authoritative	defensive	genuine	misguided	self-indulgent
bashful	deferent	good-willed	nurturing	self-reliant

self-respecting	strong	uncertain	unmotivated	well-adjusted
shallow	stupid	unconven-	uptight	wise
sincere	timid	tional	vulnerable	
skilful	trustworthy	unethical	warm	
sociable	unapologetic	unhappy	weak	

7. Reread the case studies above and answer the following questions, either as part of the class discussion or in writing, as directed by your instructor.

   a) Would you be interested in having a conversation or coffee meeting with any of the people described? Why or why not?

   b) At first glance, do you think it likely that you would become friends with any of these people? Why or why not?

   c) Did you react strongly to any of the individuals in the case studies? Why?

8. Following the class discussion, write an analysis (250–500 words) of the experience. What differences were there among the attributions made by your class? Were there any significant consistencies? Based on what we have learned about interpersonal communication, what conclusions can be drawn regarding these interpretations? Place your assessment into your Interpersonal Communication Portfolio along with your attributions, as directed by your instructor.

Chapter 2

Nine Axioms of Communication

Learning Objectives

- To understand the principles that govern all communication.
- To develop a theoretical foundation for understanding communication.
- To understand context and risk as fundamental to communication.
- To understand the pervasiveness and ambiguity inherent in communication.

Interpersonal communication, like all other forms of communication, is conditioned and influenced by a variety of factors that may not always be evident to those who are communicating. This chapter describes Nine Axioms that help to explain what happens when people interact.

An **axiom** is a principle or foundational truth that operates across cases. In other words, it's a proposition that holds no matter who the communicators are or what the circumstances are. The Axioms that follow are not 'tips' or methods for improving your communication, although understanding them will help you to communicate more thoughtfully and effectively. The Axioms are also not a matter of choice, nor do they describe elements that you could leave out of your communication if you wanted to. Instead, they are principles that operate in your communication whether you choose to acknowledge them or not.

These Axioms about the practice of communication are informed both by the tradition of rhetoric dating back to Aristotle and by more recent research confirming that communication is a dynamic process of interaction that involves judgement, choice, attitudes, feelings, status, and identity. Once we have established the Nine Axioms, we will explore these concepts in greater detail.

Some of these principles may surprise those who are used to thinking of communication as primarily information exchange, but they make sense once we recognize that communication is about more than just the content of a message. It is also about building relationships.

NINE AXIOMS OF COMMUNICATION

- Communication is an interaction between people.
- Communication involves an element of relation as well as content.
- Communication involves an element of interpersonal risk.
- Communication takes place within a context of 'persons, objects, events, and relations'.
- Communication is the principal way we establish identity, both individual and social.
- Communication is the main means through which we establish co-operation and influence.
- Effective communication is other-centred, not self-centred.
- Communication frequently is ambiguous: what is unsaid can be as important as what is said.
- Communication is pervasive: you cannot *not communicate*.

1. Communication Is Not Simply an Exchange of Ideas or Information, but an Interaction between People

This most fundamental of the Nine Axioms emphasizes the dynamic nature of communication discussed in Chapter 1—it's not simply something you do (an action), nor is it an exchange (a transaction). Instead, communication is a living process in which two or more people participate together (an interaction). This Axiom is also intended to remind us that all genuine communication—even when it occurs through e-mail or the Internet, and even when it is as impersonal as possible—nevertheless has a personal dimension and a personal impact. Finally, it emphasizes that messages are not simply static commodities in an exchange; their meanings are negotiated, understood, interpreted, and 'spun' in complex ways by the participants in an interaction.

It is true that, for the sake of consistency or efficiency or simplicity, some routine communicative tasks can be formalized, decontextualized, and depersonalized—the standardized forms we use for many purposes, from job applications to insurance claims to incident reports, are examples. The primary goal of these standardized devices is efficiency; they enable their users to process large amounts of information quickly and easily, and make categorization and filing easier.

If communication were simply about exchanging information, this bureaucratic approach would be appropriate for all our interactions. But communication, especially in our interpersonal relationships, is about much more than—and sometimes, about something completely other than—the exchange of information. Thus, although efficient management of information is sometimes important, it is not the top priority when it comes to interpersonal interaction. In fact, an emphasis on efficiency can even be detrimental to effective interpersonal relations.

If you have ever dealt with government agencies, insurance companies, or other bureaucratic organizations, you will almost certainly have received some kind of standardized message. In fact, chances are the last time you received correspondence from your college or university it was a form letter. What is your typical response to such a letter? Do you feel that you've been heard? That your specific concerns have been understood and addressed? That any real communication has occurred? In all likelihood the answer is no, since form letters treat you as 'typical' rather than individual, and the frustration you feel in such situations is a natural response to the absence of real human contact.

Imagine, instead, receiving a business letter genuinely addressed to you by someone in an organization who has taken the time to deal directly with your request or situation. Even if the message content is negative—a rejection letter for the job you applied for or a denial of your application for a loan, for example—the sense that you have been acknowledged and your feelings considered goes a long way to promoting good will, and can even take the sting out of a rejection.

But, you might protest, the government, the university, the insurance company are all bureaucracies, and processing information efficiently is what bureaucracies do. They *have* to reduce every individual case to the simplest common denominator, because to do otherwise would slow the process to unacceptable levels. We shouldn't take it personally. Or should we?

The problem with this view is that communication is *always* personal. We need to be wary of accepting bureaucratic practices without thinking much about them, because the values that underlie them have a way of creeping into our everyday interactions, even at the interpersonal level. Placing efficiency first means tacitly accepting the view that communication is about content only, and that 'fairness' involves treating individual cases as though they are identical. Fortunately, most of us don't behave like bureaucratic entities—or at least we don't intend to do so. But if we are not vigilant, our interactions with others can become tainted by the same kinds of assumptions about communication, about fairness, and about responsibility and ethical interaction.

There is a sense in which all communication is interpersonal communication, in that it involves the negotiation of our social and public selves and fulfills our desire for a sense of belonging. As we choose the manner of our communication, and as we interact with the various bureaucratic institutions that surround us, we need to remember that the more impersonal and conventionalized an encounter becomes, and the more it is reduced to a simple exchange of information, the less actual communication takes place.

Because of its role in creating connections between people, communication has been described as a process of 'building community by exchanging symbols'.[1] This definition rightly emphasizes the relationships that are formed when we communicate, rather than simply the information exchanged. Every time we communicate, whether in face-to-face exchanges, by telephone, through letters or reports, or via e-mail, we should ask ourselves what kind of community we are helping to build. Our second Axiom focuses on this process.

2. All Communication Involves an Element of Relation As Well As Content

Once we realize that communication is an interaction between *people* rather than simply an exchange of information, we can begin to understand the role of human relationships in all communication. This element of *relation* is frequently as important as—and often more important than—the content or information that the message contains. In fact, ignoring this quality of relation is, as we will see, one reason that messages can fail.

All communication establishes some kind of relationship, or **footing**, between the participants.[2] This is not to say that all such relationships are identical: they are not. The relationship we are building may be a supportive, intimate relationship; it may be a formal, professional relationship; it may be a cordial, collegial relationship. It may be characterized by admiration, liking, respect, and good feelings.

Unfortunately, however, the relation established by our communication isn't always positive and rewarding. Messages can also create unpleasantness between participants through a mismanagement or disregard of relation, and the footing we create may be characterized by condescension, dislike, hostility, defiance, and discomfort. A message may, for example, communicate an air of superiority or disdain; it may indicate a lack of consideration or a disregard for the feelings of another; it may even imply contempt for another's concerns, intelligence, or values. This negative relation may be unintentional, or it may be deliberately encoded in a message; it may even be the result of attempting to contain or eliminate personal engagement.

As we have already seen, organizations and bureaucratic structures are often justifiably criticized for depersonalizing their messages in the mistaken belief that doing so will make their communication more 'professional'. However, since depersonalizing means treating others as if they are objects rather than beings, things rather than people, there is nothing professional about it. In fact, we need to be very clear that such officiousness is not a sign of professionalism or sophistication in communicating; in fact, by refusing to really engage another person, such messages are actually the *opposite* of communication. Frequently, their purpose is to avoid communicating, while still appearing to participate in an interaction.

You will certainly have seen this kind of obfuscation in form letters. You may even have encountered bureaucratic representatives who assume this same style in their interactions with members of the public. If so, you'll be familiar with the drill: a refusal to really hear your concern, a tendency to cite policy instead of engaging your question, a superior or condescending manner, and a seeming inability to respond to you on a human level. Although this depersonalized style may be an attempt to contain or eliminate the personal, it is important to realize that these messages don't make relation disappear; instead, they created relation that is entirely negative. The reason that bureaucratic communication is problematic is that this same refusal to engage others in a meaningful way can also show up in the interpersonal style of some people.

Consider these examples: have you ever encountered someone who jokes around all the time, no matter what you're talking about, to the point that it seems you can never have a serious discussion about anything? Someone who holds himself aloof from an interaction, seemingly as a way of displaying superiority or uniqueness? Someone who fires off angry e-mails when something upsets him, saying things he would never think of saying if he were face-to-face with the other person? In all these cases, the individuals have in some way managed to depersonalize their interaction, whether by deflecting others, by outright refusal to engage, or by disregarding other people's feelings. Dealing officiously with the public is bad enough, but allowing such disregard or disdain to poison our more immediate interactions can be even more harmful, since it can distance us from others, compromise trust, and build defensiveness. E-mail is especially prone to failures of relation-building because of the built-in distancing and depersonalizing effects of the technology, and it needs to be handled with particular care.[3]

Although the strategies just described are ultimately counterproductive, it's likely that these individuals are attempting to minimize the interpersonal risk that all communication entails. This risk is the subject of our third Axiom.

3. All Communication Involves an Element of Interpersonal Risk

This Axiom recognizes a close relationship that exists between your communication and your sense of social and personal worth. As social beings, we all need the approval and affirmation that comes from interactions with others. We want to be taken seriously, we want acceptance and approval, we want to see our good opinions of ourselves reflected in the reactions of those around us.

Our sense of worthiness as individuals—as members of a family or community, as friends and colleagues, even as professionals—depends on the acceptance and affirmation of others, and that approval in turn depends on the quality of our communication. Those who already know us expect to see our character reinforced; new acquaintances need to see a demonstration of our credibility and worthiness. Both our self-worth and our sense of public affirmation—the positive social value that communication theorist Erving Goffman calls **face**[4]—depend on the continued good will of those with whom we interact.

As Goffman explains, whether we are aware of doing so or not, we tend to act and communicate so as to support and maintain that approval. As we will learn in greater detail in Chapter 3, each time we enter into a new interaction, we encounter what Goffman calls **face risk**—the risk of being judged and possibly rejected. Thus, each encounter with others carries the risk of 'losing face', an experience that can shame and discredit us.[5]

To see for yourself how pervasive face risk is, consider the following common communication activities:

- seeking a favour from a friend;
- phoning a stranger;

- inviting an acquaintance on a date;
- asking a professor to reconsider your grade;
- requesting a raise;
- applying for a loan;
- selling an item door-to-door;
- canvassing for a charity;
- running for office;
- attending a job interview;
- giving a speech.

Does the idea of carrying out one or more of these actions make you uncomfortable? If so, it's because in each case we confront the possibility of public disapproval, rejection, even ridicule. Should any of these occur, we will experience shame and a loss of face. The amount of risk each poses varies somewhat with each individual, but most of us will experience some level of 'face threat' from all of these activities.

As social beings, we wish to establish, and maintain, that important public character that Aristotle called ethos. We wish to communicate competence and integrity; we wish to be accepted and respected. Each interaction presents a danger that this public image may be compromised, and thus each contact involves risk.

4. All Communication Takes Place within a Context of 'Persons, Objects, Events, and Relations'[6]

This Axiom reminds us of the connection between communication and context. If we are to better understand the communication of others or become more effective and sensitive communicators ourselves, we need to remember that no message ever stands entirely on its own; *all* messages arise out of, and are given their meaning by, the particular situation in which they originate. The **context** for understanding a message may be familial or social; it may be political or historical; it may be public or private; it may be professional or personal; it may be conventional or original; it may be a combination of these and other factors. But make no mistake: messages *always* arise in some kind of context, and to consider a message in the absence of its context is to remove any real hope of understanding what took place.

Similarly, the context in which we are communicating shapes the kinds of things we say and do. We adapt and adjust our messages to the needs and expectations of the person with whom we are communicating, to the relational history we have with that person, to the place and time when we are communicating, to the rest of the people who may be present, and to a host of other constraints. The ability to accommodate your communication content, tone, and style to the situation in an appropriate way is a measure of your personal and professional judgement and competence, and those who are unable, or unwilling, to moderate their communication in this way are generally judged to be ineffective or incompetent as communicators, and perhaps socially inept or even dysfunctional.

Some time ago, I read a report about a judge who was asked to assess an interaction between a police officer and a witness, in order to determine whether the comments and reactions of the officer had been 'appropriate'. To make his determination, the judge requested a transcript from which the witness's words had been deleted, so that only the officer's remarks remained. The judge said that he did not wish his assessment to be 'tainted' by knowledge of how the witness had interacted with the officer.

The judge in this case was no doubt well-intentioned, but he was certainly not very well-informed about communication. Like many people, he appears to have believed that a message is a kind of self-contained commodity with an independent meaning that is stable no matter who is involved or what the context is. Unfortunately for the officer concerned, the judge could not have been more wrong. In fact, the whole notion of 'appropriateness' makes sense only if a context is provided, since appropriateness is a measure of fittedness between the message and its situation.

It would have been difficult enough to recreate the fullness of any interaction from a mere transcript, even if it had included all the words that were exchanged; to expect to render a meaningful or informed judgement on the basis of *half* a transcript

is absurd, and in this case even tragic, since the judge's decision would have serious consequences for the lives of those involved. The judge worried that knowledge of the context might taint his judgement, but he did not seem to recognize that ignorance of the context would cripple his judgement entirely.

If we wish to improve our own communication and our understanding of the communication of others, we need to recognize how much our professional, social, cultural, political, historical, and interpersonal circumstances contribute to the meaning and interpretation of our messages. We need to recognize, for example, that each message is inextricably part of the situation in which it arises and for which it is created, that it is the result of a whole range and collection of influences at play in a given context. We need, in short, to be smarter than the judge in the example.

5. Communication Is the Principal Way We Establish Identity, Both Individual and Social

Take a few minutes to think about how you would answer the following question: How do you know who you are?

It's hard to imagine an answer to this question that does not depend on communication. For example, you may define yourself in reference to others: your family, your ethnic group, your religious affiliation, your work. But these affiliations wouldn't even exist without communication.

Let's try again. You understand yourself based on your memories, on your reflections, on your thoughts. However, these, too, are dependent on communication. After all, thoughts and reflections, memories too, are different from the experiences they record, interpret, or reflect on, and without the ability to communicate you would be unable to formulate any thoughts or reflections in the first place.

Finally, you may decide to define yourself based on your likes or dislikes, your affiliations or dissociations, your preferences and tastes. But the very act of forming affiliations or dissociations is itself an act of communication, because they depend on observing, interpreting, and organizing sensations into a coherent framework of understanding. In any case, the very attempt at definition is in some ways a trap, because to define anything, least of all yourself, you need to be able to communicate, to think abstractly, to understand similarities and differences that can only be articulated through communication.

As we will see later in this book, the ability to communicate through symbols—and in particular language—is a distinctly human trait. Although recent studies suggest that animal communication may be more sophisticated than we have previously understood, the human ability to think abstractly and to communicate symbolically remains central to most of our understanding of culture, religion, philosophy, and psychology. In fact, definitions of what it means to be human almost always begin, as the great rhetorician Kenneth Burke's does, by acknowledging the centrality of symbol-using to the nature of a human being.[7]

Thus, no matter how we answer the question 'Who are you?', it seems certain that in many respects we are who, and how, we *say* we are. The link between communication and **identity** is inescapable: it is through our communication with others, both individually and collectively, that we create the social and other relationships that help to form us, that provide our frame of reference, our understanding of right and wrong, our sense of where we belong in the world. It is through our communication that we establish our presence in the world, and through our communication that we find ourselves, forge friendships, and express our dreams. Communication allows us to gain the trust of others and give them our trust in return. It is communication that enables the co-operation upon which any society depends.

In a very real sense, then, we are what we communicate.

6. Communication Is the Main Means Through Which We Establish Co-operation and Influence

Influence—the ability to gain co-operation and compliance from others—is a fundamental requirement for our survival, comfort, and success. For this reason, influence is central to effective interpersonal communication.

It's easy enough to see that our physical survival and comfort depend on co-operation. For example, few of us are sufficiently skilled to provide all the necessities of life for ourselves. The food we eat, the clothing we wear, the homes in which we live, the vehicles we drive, the roads we travel, and many other goods and services, large and small, are substantially provided for us by others. To have these needs fulfilled, we rely on a network of social co-operation that extends well beyond our own immediate circle of family and friends. It's not surprising that some theorists, such as linguist S.I. Hayakawa, identify co-operation—not competition, as many people think—as the fundamental principle of human social organization.[8]

In Canada and North America at least, our social structure is organized to provide most of us with access to the physical necessities of life, and it does so efficiently most of the time. But human beings need more than just food and shelter: we also need a sense of belonging, of social acceptance, of respect and regard. We need love and friendship, affirmation, and the comfort of understanding.[9] These, in turn, depend on our ability to communicate and to forge the co-operation and sense of community on which effective and satisfying relationships depend.

As we learned in Chapter 1, the theorist Kenneth Burke believed that, beyond the fulfillment of our most basic physical needs, the fundamental motive of all human communication is obtaining the sense of connectedness and intimacy with others that he called identification. For this reason, Burke argued, all communication is persuasive[10] because it seeks to influence the way in which we are perceived by others. Social scientific research has confirmed that the absence of meaningful interaction not only compromises our quality of life,[11] but can make us vulnerable to a variety of health problems, including various kinds of cancer, epilepsy, inflammatory bowel disease, heart disease, and arthritis.[12]

Human connectedness is not something we can achieve as readily as we can satisfy our physical and survival needs. For example, if we have the financial means, we can easily purchase food, clothing, and shelter without ourselves having to do the work necessary to create them. But no matter how wealthy we may be, we cannot rely on anyone else to establish rapport and identification on our behalf. To have happy, fulfilling, and healthy lives, we must be able to forge these connections for ourselves. Establishing bonds with others may not at first seem to be a matter of persuasion and influence, but as Burke has shown and as we will see later, it is the very essence of persuasion. If we cannot establish identification with others, we compromise our quality of life, our professional success, and even, potentially, our health.

7. Effective Communication Is Other-Centred, Not Self-Centred

As we have seen already, communication is not simply about the exchange of information. If it were, then you could improve your effectiveness merely by improving your own skills. However, no amount of technique will improve your ability to communicate effectively if your attention remains on yourself. In fact, because it can tempt you into thinking that effective communication is all about *you*, such an exclusively skills-based approach can actually make your communication *less* effective than it already is. It is important to be reflective about your own communication habits, but there is danger in focusing exclusively on your own abilities, since communicating effectively on an interpersonal level involves a genuine willingness to listen to and connect with others.

This Axiom is intended as a corrective to the dangers of self-absorption by reminding us that simply polishing our skills will not make us better communicators so long as we remain focused exclusively on our own preoccupations and desires. To be truly effective, and to satisfy our social and emotional needs, we must be able to focus on the concerns and interests of those with whom we interact.

This is not to say that communication can never serve a purely expressive function; clearly there are times when such a purpose is legitimate. For example, James McCroskey describes **expressive communication** as a self-centred or 'source-centred' form in which the main purpose is to express emotion rather than to engage the response of a listener.[13] This kind of communication expresses strong feelings—I cry out in pain when I've been stung by a bee, in delight when I've won a lottery, in frustration when I discover that I've left my wallet on the bus, in mourning at the loss of a loved one. The fact that I do so even when nobody is there to hear me suggests that none of these expressions is particularly intended for an audience. Instead, their purpose is to express, and help me to cope with, the feeling of the moment. Interestingly, various art forms from literature to painting have also been characterized as 'expressive'[14] for similar reasons—that is, they are intended to express some powerful experience of the human heart.

So what's wrong with communicating expressively? Obviously, nothing whatsoever. Expressive communication helps us to cope with overwhelming emotional experience; it also has produced great artistic achievement. Expressive communication is necessary to human experience, but most theorists distinguish it from the bulk of our day-to-day communication, which is intended to engage more directly and immediately with those around us. The problem arises from the fact that too many of us habitually approach *all* of our communication as if it were mainly about self-expression. We focus on what we want to say rather than on how our words and actions will affect those around us, concentrating on ourselves instead of considering them.

The fact is, however, that little of our normal interaction requires a purely expressive response. Instead, most of our day-to-day communication involves a relational interaction that establishes identity and community, engenders intimacy, maintains relationships, and exercises influence. Each of these goals requires the affirmation, like-mindedness, and co-operation of people whose preoccupations, attitudes, expectations, experiences, concerns, and dreams may differ widely. The effective communicator must be able to pay attention to the needs and concerns of others, to bring diverse and sometimes contradictory interests into harmony, to build—so far as it is possible—consensus and common ground. An effective communicator must also be able to recognize those points on which agreement is unlikely and to take steps to manage conflicts and preserve face.

Because it is essentially self-centred, expressive communication is useless for achieving these goals. Interpersonal communication that focuses on the speaker's views and needs at the expense of shared interests and goals will be unfulfilling and ineffective. If we are interested in engaging others, in obtaining social approval and affirmation, in achieving a sense of common purpose and community, we must learn to understand another's point of view rather than simply insisting on our own perspective.

8. Communication Is Frequently Ambiguous: What Is Unsaid Can Be As Important as What Is Said

Human beings are complex, and their motives, needs, and concerns are also complicated. Many of the reasons for which we communicate—to establish a sense of social worth, to create a sense of belonging, or to obtain an affirmation of identity—carry a great deal of face risk. In order to manage and reduce these risks, both to ourselves and to others, we have developed an extraordinary capacity for indirection through social codes of fare and politeness. In other words, much of the meaning of many of our interactions is carried in the unexpressed and often unacknowledged subtext of interaction: the message behind the message.

The relational dynamic that an interaction establishes is part of that unspoken subtext. As we will see in Chapter 6, it is communicated partly through non-verbal cues such as eye contact, facial expression, vocal tone, gestures, physical movement, stance and posture, manner of dress, personal hygiene, or overall attractiveness. Non-verbal expressions, commonly referred to as 'body language', can communicate trust, affection, happiness, pleasure, approval, and delight, or they can exhibit distrust, dislike, unhappiness, displeasure, disapproval, and disappointment. They can display assertiveness, confidence, self-possession, energy, enthusiasm, co-operativeness, reliability, and truthfulness— or their opposites. Such elements constitute the emotional quality of our messages, our level of engagement with the content, and our relationship to those with whom we are interacting.

But the 'message behind the message' in any interaction is not simply a matter of emotional patterning. It also results from unspoken assumptions about ourselves, about our audience, and about the content and context of our messages, assumptions that may never be stated outright, in part because we take them so much

Photo: Jeff Greenberg/World of Stock

for granted that we don't even recognize they are there. To us, they are simply common sense. Emphasis, elision, positioning, and word choice, in combination with habitual patterns of figurative language, can carry clues to the unspoken assumptions on which the communication is based. Finally, the positioning of the message with respect to the relational history between the individuals who are communicating can also carry implications that are not made explicit.

Non-verbal signals and implicit cues are present in every interaction, and they can strengthen the conviction and passion inherent in what you are communicating. However, in cases where they do not seem to coincide with explicit content, they can compromise or even discredit your communication, making you appear untrustworthy or manipulative. Although it is not possible to completely control your nonverbal or unspoken messages, you can learn to pay closer attention to the way you position your messages, both orally and in writing, through unconscious nonverbal cues and unstated assumptions. You can also become more adept at 'reading' the cues of others. We will cover these issues in more detail in Chapters 6 and 9.

9. You Cannot 'Not Communicate'

This final Axiom recognizes the pervasiveness of communication and of the human need to interpret symbolic meanings. Interestingly, even non-messages are typically read as having communicative meaning.

For example, imagine you have been on a blind date. You feel that the evening went well and you agree to go to a play together next week. Your date offers to pick up the tickets, and promises to call to confirm the arrangements. If a length of time passes without your hearing anything, you will undoubtedly interpret this lack of communication as itself a negative message. This simple example demonstrates that once a channel of exchange has been opened, anything that occurs—even if it is nothing at all—will be read as a message. As soon as we have entered into any form of interaction with others, we are engaged in a relationship in which non-communication becomes impossible.

Channels can be opened not only by choice, as in the blind date scenario, but also by coincidence—as long as you live, work, attend school, socialize, or shop where there are other human beings, you are immersed in a social environment filled with messages. Participating in this pervasive environment is inevitable, because each action of yours will be read by others for its communicative meaning. Even a refusal to participate in communication is a form of communication that others will interpret, just as we read meaning in the non-messages of others.

For example, suppose that you attend classes with a young woman who habitually arrives late to class. Every morning, about 10 minutes after class has begun, she sweeps into the room and announces, out loud for everyone to hear, something like:

'I'm sorry I'm late. My ride was delayed. The roads are just awful this morning.' Instead of a coat, the woman wears a cape. She crosses to the front of the room and selects a seat where the rest of the class have an unobstructed view of her whenever they look at the professor. Her remarks during discussion period seem almost intended to engage the professor in a private conversation and are rarely directed towards the rest of the class.

Your class is small enough that everyone in the group knows each other, at least by sight if not by name, and you have all noticed this young woman. As it happens, you pass her in the halls nearly every day as you come and go from other classes. Although you used to say hello, she has never acknowledged your greeting or greeted you in return. In fact, she always looks right through you as though you're not there, and you have pretty much given up acknowledging her, as well.

Have you found yourself attributing meaning to this young woman's unconventional attire and ostentatious actions? Perhaps you have judged her to be arrogant or vain, or perhaps you have pegged her as insecure and attention-seeking. You might have felt compassion for her, or perhaps irritation. You might even have begun to wonder whether she is suffering from some kind of self-esteem problem or even if she is socially dysfunctional. Your inferences may be accurate or inaccurate, but some form of inference will be inescapable, because the woman's resistance to normal social interaction itself constitutes a message, as she likely intended it to do.

Once a context for communication has been established, there is no possibility of non-communication. Although you are probably not as flamboyant as the woman in the example, every action you perform will send messages that will be understood—or in some cases misunderstood—by others.

Summary

The Nine Axioms of communication offer a way of conceptualizing how communication works. Although they are not themselves intended as a method of improving your communication practice, they do offer the possibility of deeper understanding, which can translate into improved skill. When we understand the role of interaction in fulfilling our need for comfort, connection, and solace, and when we recognize that all communication is in some degree about relation, we can begin to better understand how we might make ourselves better communicators and find greater life satisfaction through improved relationships.

The Axioms teach us that all communication is in some measure both interpersonal and rhetorical. It is interpersonal in that it contributes to our sense of well-being and to our capacity to form satisfying relationships that will improve our quality of life. It is interpersonal also in that it helps us to form our sense of personal identity. Communication is rhetorical in its role as an activity through which we establish community and influence. As Kenneth Burke has noted, wherever there is communication, there is some kind of invitation to a shared way of seeing the world, and thus to persuasion. Communication is a tool that we can use to help us to live satisfying lives. It is intimately connected to our survival, our health and well-being, and our happiness. Without it, life would be desolate and barely—if at all—worth living. The study of interpersonal communication is, in a sense, a study of relationships as much as a study of skill development.

Key Terms

axiom
context
expressive communication
face
face risk
footing
identity

Suggested Readings

Marcus L. Ambrester and Carolyn Gardner Buttram, *A Rhetoric of Interpersonal Communication* (Chicago: Waveland Press, 1977). Ambrester and Buttram's book explores the connection between interpersonal and rhetorical dynamics in communication, including identity creation and interpersonal influence.

Jennifer MacLennan, 'Understanding the Communicative Situation', in MacLennan, *Effective Communication for the Technical Professions* (Scarborough, Ont.: Prentice-Hall Canada, 2003), 1–13. This introductory chapter provides a different perspective on the Nine Axioms by considering them in a different context, that of professional communication.

Brigid McGrath Massie with John Waters, *What Do They Say When You Leave the Room?* (Salinas, Calif.: Eudemonia Publications, 1998). Massie's book is one of many popular self-help books on communication that purports to offer tips for better handling interpersonal relationships. Massie promises strategies to increase what she calls 'personal effectiveness', which involves, among other things, 'developing potent relationships'.

Deborah Tannen, *That's Not What I Meant! How Conversational Style Makes or Breaks Relationships* (New York: Ballantine, 1986). One of her many popular books on language and interactional style, Tannen's work concentrates on the relationship between interpersonal effectiveness and a speaker's rhetorical-linguistic style. Although Tannen is a linguist who has published many scholarly articles, her popularizations are geared for a lay audience and are very readable.

Burton Urquhart, 'Bridging Gaps, Engineering Audiences: Understanding the Communicative Situation', in Jennifer MacLennan, *Readings for Technical Writers* (Toronto: Oxford University Press, forthcoming). By examining a case study of an inventor presenting his idea before a group of investors, Urquhart's essay explores the audience-centredness of all communication.

Exercises and Assignments

1. As a class, prepare a list of at least 15 communication activities that involve some face risk, such as giving a speech, inviting someone on a date, or interviewing for a job. Have someone record the suggestions on the board. Once you have generated a reasonably long list, rank them from least risky to most risky. Was there any disagreement among class members about whether a given activity involves risk? Was there any dispute about the level of risk associated with the activities? Why do you think such disagreements might have arisen?

2. Your instructor will divide the class into pairs. Sit facing your partner, approximately two feet apart, for two minutes. During that time, do your best to avoid communicating anything to the other person. When the two minutes are up, discuss the experience as a class, considering the following questions:

   a. How uncomfortable was the exercise? Why? What risks might have been involved?

   b. How self-conscious did you feel? Why do you think these effects occurred?

   c. How did the exercise affect your non-verbal behaviour?

   d. Were you successful in avoiding any communication? Was your partner successful?

3. Fill out the following 'Perceptions and Initial Impressions Survey' form and submit it to your instructor. Do not put your name on the form and do not reveal your responses to anyone else in the class. Once everyone has completed and submitted the anonymous survey forms, your instructor will provide each class member with one or more forms to interpret. If the group is small, you may be given the entire batch to assess.

   On a separate page, write one word that best summarizes the impression you believe you make on others. Then write one word that best summarizes the way you think of yourself. Turn in the survey to your instructor, but retain the separate page to be used in following up the class discussion.

   As you read each of the forms you have been given, answer the following questions as honestly as you can. Don't try to guess whose form you're reading;

Perception and Initial Impressions Survey

Please type or print your responses. Do not put your name on the form or reveal your responses to anyone else in the group.

1. Two TV programs you regularly watch _____

2. A magazine or on-line blog you regularly read _____

3. An activity you enjoy in your leisure time _____

4. The most satisfying feature of your chosen major _____

5. The thing you hate most about your chosen major _____

6. The website you visit most often or have visited most recently _____

7. The last two books you read _____

8. Do you consider yourself a religious person? _____

9. The kind of music you most often listen to _____

10. A word that best describes your style of dress _____

11. Something that makes you laugh _____

12. Your favourite childhood memory _____

13. One thing you are proud of _____

14. Your favourite food _____

15. The food you dislike most _____

16. The most 'fun' thing you can think of _____

17. The most boring thing you can think of _____

18. The ugliest thing you can think of _____

19. A prized possession _____

20. The thing you admire most in others _____

21. The thing you dislike most in others _____

22. The world would be a lot better place if _____

_____

_____

_____

instead, focus on the person's answers and, as far as possible, base your assessment on those. Work as quickly and as thoughtfully as you can; you are aiming to record your first impressions. Depending on the makeup of your class, your instructor may direct you to add questions to this list or to disregard some of those shown.

a. List five words you would use to describe the person.

b. List three words that are opposite of the person.

c. Choose one word that best summarizes your overall impression.

d. List one word that reflects how you think the respondent would like to be seen (not necessarily the same as how you saw the person).

e. Would you be interested in conversing with this person? Briefly say why or why not.

Discuss your assessments with the rest of the class, as directed by your instructor. Place your completed form into your Interpersonal Communication Portfolio.

4. Once the 'Perceptions and Initial Impressions Survey' exercise is complete and each person's form has been interpreted by one or more classmates, consider the following questions. Your instructor may ask you to be prepared to discuss these with the class, or to write your responses for inclusion in your Interpersonal Communication Portfolio.

a. Did you have in mind a particular impression you wanted to create as you filled out the form? Were your answers deliberately crafted to fit the situation or simply the first thing that came to mind, without reference to the context?

b. Look again at the words you recorded on your separate piece of paper. Do you think you were successful in presenting yourself as you would like to be seen?

c. Did others' impressions of you, as reported in the discussion segment, align with the impression you wanted to create?

d. Is a survey like this an adequate way of establishing identity within a new group? Is it a more effective way or a less effective way than the kind of face-to-face interaction you would normally have in a class? If less so, what was missing? If more so, what does the form provide that is unavailable to you in ordinary class interaction?

e. Did you observe any significant misattributions or misinterpretations, either of your own intentions or of the intentions of anyone else? Why might these have occurred?

f. Did the exercise cause you to re-think any of the assessments you might already have made of other people in the group? How?

g. Did any aspect of this experience make you uncomfortable? Why do you think that might be?

5. Below you will find a table showing the actual answers to this survey given by five people in an Interpersonal Communication class like yours. Study the collected responses carefully to uncover any significant patterns in the answers, either in the attitudes of a single respondent, or in the group's overall orientation. Then answer the questions as fully as you can.

SUBJECT #1	SUBJECT #2	SUBJECT #3	SUBJECT #4	SUBJECT #5
1. Television programs you regularly watch				
Tag, Everwood	*Prison Break, The OC*	I don't watch TV	N/A	*22 Minutes, Trailer Park Boys*
2. A magazine or on-line blog you regularly read				
Interline (company newsletter)	Popular Mechanics	none	Western Standard	Harper's
3. An activity you enjoy in your leisure time				
playing pool	playing soccer	sports	martial arts	watching movies
4. The most satisfying feature of your chosen major				
learning problem-solving	learning about things that interest me	good job market	financial security (flexibility)	lets me create something new

SUBJECT #1	SUBJECT #2	SUBJECT #3	SUBJECT #4	SUBJECT #5
5. The thing you hate most about your chosen major				
struggling with problem-solving	seven classes, two terms straight	lack of room for elective options	statistics package (computer program)	at the moment, the writing
6. The website you visit most often, or most recently				
weather website	dell.ca	weather network	hotmail.com	university website
7. The last two books you read				
Into What Far Harbour	*The DaVinci Code, The Wealthy Barber*	*Harry Potter & The Goblet of Fire, Can You Keep a Secret*	*Phaedrus, The Art of War*	*Harry Potter & The Half Blood Prince, Human Amusements*
8. Do you consider yourself a religious person?				
sure	yes	yes	no	not in the way people usually mean
9. The kind of music you most often listen to				
rock	rock	hip hop	alternative rock	rock, jazz
10. A word that best describes your style of dress				
casual	casual	normal	cheap	casual dress
11. Something that makes you laugh				
small children	a funny movie	Dane Cook	when my girlfriend gets mad at me (but not really mad)	Ricky wiping out
12. Your favourite childhood memory				
helping my grandfather repair his swather	going to the pool	Disney World	shooting guns with my grandpa and father	the summer I met my friend Shaun

SUBJECT #1	SUBJECT #2	SUBJECT #3	SUBJECT #4	SUBJECT #5
13. One thing you are proud of				
my son	making it to where I have in life	winning a public-speaking contest	my family	my jeans
14. Your favourite food				
hamburgers	McDonald's	steak	pizza	teriyaki beef, no mushrooms!
15. The food you most dislike				
parsnips	sushi	anchovies	tuna	dill pickles
16. The most 'fun' thing you can think of				
spending time with friends	playing competitive soccer	backpacking in Europe	shooting	making things
17. The most boring thing you can think of				
company meetings	senior critical methods course	political lecture	studying	cocktail parties
18. The ugliest thing you can think of				
Alien (creature from the movie)	smoking cigarettes	hairy wart	Metaphorically speaking, lack of human rights in other countries	violence passed off as entertainment
19. A prized possession				
motorcycle (I sold it to afford university)	my jeep, soon to be traded for a better car	watch	N/A	my gadgets
20. The thing you admire most in others				
honesty	respect	patience	intelligence	courage
21. The thing you dislike most in others				
dishonesty	jealousy, back-stabbing	rude comments	ignorance	lying

SUBJECT #1	SUBJECT #2	SUBJECT #3	SUBJECT #4	SUBJECT #5
22. The world would be a lot better place if				
there were no wars	people would just slow down	racism didn't exist	everyone got along, but that's not going to happen, so what I would enjoy is for people to question what they learn and not just swallow up everything they hear or read. In questioning one gains a true understanding of the material, that means that one will be intelligent rather than ignorant.	people kept their word

Now answer the following questions:

a. Read all the responses for each item in turn. Circle any that seem out of place with the others. Did any particular pattern emerge?

b. Read each individual's responses. Do the answers as a whole point to any particular concerns, interests, attitudes, or assumptions?

c. Did any of the respondents stand out strongly from the rest? Why?

d. Are the members of this group more similar to each other or more different from each other? Explain.

e. Can you discern which of the answers were given by women and which were given by men? Justify your answer.

f. One of the respondents is the professor. Can you tell which one? What elements made you choose the one you did? Your instructor will be able to reveal the correct answer.

6. Your instructor will provide you with copies of four or five of the completed survey forms. Make a table of the responses similar to the one shown in #6. Compare the responses to each item, and then consider all of the answers of each respondent. What themes can you detect, either from the group as a whole or from an individual's answers?

7. As directed by your instructor, write an analysis (250–500 words) of the experience to be included in your Interpersonal Communication Portfolio along with your Initial Impressions Survey and your notes of the results of others' interpretations. The class will return to this exercise later in the course.

8. Keeping in mind Axiom #5—Communication is the principal way we establish identity, both individual and social—return to the self-introduction that you wrote during the first week of class. Given what we have learned so far about the link between your communication and your sense of self-presentation and face, what does your self-introduction reveal about you? Would you write the introduction any differently if you were to re-do it now? What has changed?

Photo: Keith Levit/World of Stock

Chapter 3

Self and Others

Learning Objectives

- To understand the relationship between communication and identity.
- To understand how the self-concept forms and how it functions.
- To understand the relationship between intimacy, disclosure, and interpersonal risk.
- To understand the nature and causes of defensiveness.

Our study of the Nine Axioms has suggested how important a role communication plays in establishing a sense of self, both individually and in relation to others or to the social structure. This chapter explores in greater detail the notion of 'self' and its relationship to communication, beginning with some definitions.

What Is the Self?

When we speak of the self, we are referring to those qualities that distinguish a person from everyone else while also providing a sense of social belonging and wholeness—what the psychologist Erik Erikson called 'ego identity'.[1] In other words, the idea of 'self' has both individual and public or social significance.

We are not born with a **sense of self**. Little babies do not recognize themselves as beings separate from their mothers; in fact, they can't even perceive where they end and the rest of the world begins. The ability to differentiate the 'me' from the mass of experience that is 'not me' develops, along with language, as a child grows.

Identity, or your sense of self, is inseparable from your communication. This close connection between how you communicate and who you are is a fundamental assumption of communication theory,[2] as well as of psychoanalytic theory.[3] The rhetoric scholar Thomas Benson, for example, describes communication as primarily 'a way of constituting the self'.[4] Our sense of self is formed by a process of identification—with other people, with institutions, with family or friends, with social or ethnic background, with political or religious entities, with groups or organizations. Identification, as you may recall from our discussion in Chapter 2, is the primary goal of all communication,[5] through which we establish our social connections and sense of community. From our affiliations we get our values, beliefs, attitudes, and ethical sense. We establish both a **social identity**, made up of features that we share in common with various others, and a **personal identity**, which is the unique combination of all our attributes. This personal identity is 'not found to hold, as a combination, for any other person in the world.'[6] Both of these contribute to **self-concept**—our own assessment of who we are.

Self-Concept and Identity Formation

Self-concept refers to the way you see yourself—it is your understanding of who you are, your own self-definition or self-image.[7] Your self-concept isn't a given, granted to you at birth; instead, it is accumulated through your interactions with the world. Self-concept is made up of your attitudes, your values, your beliefs; it includes your perception of your abilities and talents, your character traits, your level of attractiveness or likeability; it encompasses your relations with your family, your friends, and your community, as well as your relationship to the divine.

Self-concept isn't what you *are* like; instead, it's what you believe yourself to be like.[8] How accurate your perceptions are depends on a number of factors, and in particular on the quality of your self-reflection. Few of us see ourselves exactly as we 'really' are, or as others see us.

Thus, the first significant feature of the self-concept is that it is subjective, meaning that it is an interpretation rather than a factual representation; it is an expression of your own view of yourself. Your self-concept won't necessarily match up with reality, or with others' sense of you, and even if you have fairly accurate self-perception in some areas, you will still be blind in others.[9]

There are several reasons for this mismatch. First, though your self-concept includes information that you have internalized from others, you can't see yourself from the outside; you may have features that are evident to others but that you can't see for yourself.

Second, you have access to information about yourself that others don't: your doubts, your fears, your secret dreams. This information can also influence your self-assessment, so that your perceptions are different from those of your friends in part because you have information they don't have access to.

The self-concept may be inaccurate for a third reason as well. Most people have a tendency to emphasize their flaws in disproportion to their strengths; at times we take to heart the critical remarks of others more than their praise, and we can also be our own harshest critics, measuring ourselves against sometimes impossible standards. Thus the self-concept may be somewhat distorted, since it is affected by information that we don't have, or that we don't usually share, and since it is filtered through our tendency to self-deprecation.

The second major feature of the self-concept is its complexity; it includes more than one configuration of your sense of self.[10] For example, your concept of yourself as a student may be different from how you think of yourself as a friend; your view of yourself as a sibling differs from your sense of what kind of employee you are. You conduct yourself differently when you're playing competitive hockey than when you are leading a seminar in your communication class, and yet in each of these roles and circumstances you are 'really' you. Thus, we say that the self-concept is complex because it encompasses the entire range of your roles and experiences.

Related to its complex, multi-dimensional nature is the third important feature of the self-concept: its remarkable flexibility.[11] Far from being a rigid conception of the self that stays the same no matter what, it is elastic enough to allow for growth and change: for example, I may not be a very good public speaker and fear having to make a presentation, but I can alter both my level of skill and my confidence by taking a course in public speaking.

The self-concept is also flexible enough to allow me to establish an appropriate footing for different contexts. For instance, successfully completing my public-speaking course has made me a better and more confident public speaker, and compared to my friend Nancy, I have become expert enough to provide advice when she seeks it. But when I compare my abilities with those of my public-speaking instructor, I am no longer an expert; in that context, I understand that I am still very much a novice. Thus, my self-concept can adjust to accommodate changes in my circumstances or grow as a result of experience.

Finally, although it is *capable* of alteration and adaptation, the fourth important feature of the self-concept is that it doesn't automatically adjust to changes in our level of knowledge or experience. Once our assumptions about ourselves have become established and taken for granted, they can be remarkably persistent, and our view of ourselves often tends to lag behind the reality.[12] It is for this reason that a shy person who develops confidence may nevertheless continue to regard herself as shy long after she no longer experiences social discomfort; the young man who has outgrown childhood may still resist thinking of himself as an adult; the woman who has lost a significant amount of weight may still tend to view herself as 'too fat'; the office wunderkind may be shocked one day to discover that he is now one of the old guard. This is especially true in cases where such self-judgements are confirmed by the words and actions of others. In order to maintain a realistic and meaningful view of ourselves, we need to 'update' our self-concepts periodically as our circumstances and experiences change.

CHARACTERISTICS OF THE SELF-CONCEPT

- Subjective interpretation
- Complex and multi-dimensional
- Flexible enough to accommodate various situations
- Resistant to change

Where Does Your Sense of Self Come From?

Self-concept is moulded by a variety of influences, and carries connotations of the value we place on ourselves as human beings.[13] Your own perception and self-assessment play a part in how you identify yourself, particularly if you are reflective about your own behaviour. When you review how you did something or think over your part in an interaction, when you evaluate these things or justify them to yourself, when you worry whether what you did was right, you are contributing to the development and maintenance of your self-concept. Your habitual self-talk—the things you rehearse internally or sometimes even say aloud—is both a product of and a shaping force for your self-concept.

As powerful as your self-talk is, however, your own point of view is not the only source, or even the primary source, of the information and attitudes that make up your self-concept. To understand how a person's self-concept is formed, we have to trace back to the messages communicated by influential adults during the person's childhood. Your opinions about your identity begin with such social influences and continue to be affected by them throughout your life. The feedback you receive from others provides a way of interpreting and assessing your behaviour that can become habitual; for example, Aunt Maisie tells your mother, 'That child is so clumsy!' and 'She'll never amount to anything!' Such judgements can become internalized and help to form a frame for interpreting subsequent information. This can work in either of two ways: you may indeed turn out clumsy and unsuccessful, bearing out Aunt Maisie's prediction, or you may set out to prove her wrong, becoming both graceful and successful. However, in both cases the judgement of an influential other has helped to shape both beliefs and behaviour.[14]

Consider Nicki's reaction when her grandmother repeatedly described her as a klutz when Nicki was a child. As an adult, Nicki has become a champion figure skater known for her elegant style. In addition, her modesty has made her a favourite of interviewers. What they don't know, however, is that her gracefulness is a compensation; secretly, Nicki still believes she is awkward and ungainly, and she is terrified that the world will find her out. For Nicki, Grandmother's judgement remains more powerful than all the competitions she has won or the compliments she has received from her peers and the public, because Nicki still believes it to be the 'truth' about herself that she is simply concealing from others.

Influential feedback from others doesn't end with childhood, of course. Even when you are an adult, people continue to contribute to your self-concept with explicit messages:

> 'You've been a really good friend to me.'
> 'Here you are finally, late *again*.'
> 'You're such a talented musician.'
> 'How on earth do you always manage to spill something on your shirt?'
> 'I wish I could write as well as you do.'

Flattering or not, such messages can contribute to your self-assessment and thus to your conception of who you are.

The messages from others need not be so direct or explicit; indirect responses can also influence your self-perceptions. For instance, every time you raise your hand to speak in class, two or three of your classmates roll their eyes; as you successfully perform a difficult piece of music, you see your music teacher nodding and smiling in your direction; when you walk into a room, the conversation between two of your friends falls silent. How you interpret these events will in part be a result of your self-concept, but will also contribute to its development.

Even the messages contained in popular culture and advertising have the power to influence how we see ourselves: our judgement of our attractiveness, popularity, or relationship success can be shaped by television, magazines, and other forms of persuasive communication that surround us. Whether these messages are explicit or implied, there is no doubt that external influences contribute in powerful ways to the formation of our sense of self.[15]

In addition to our own self-appraisal and the input we receive from outside, our self-concept is formed in part by the roles we play in our lives, whether these are familial, social, or professional. For instance, within the family you may be the black sheep, the favourite, the quiet one, the brainy kid, a daddy's girl or mama's boy, the one that takes after Uncle Charlie, the responsible big sister or brother, the mischievous little brother or sister. You may be the independent first-born, an indulged only child, the stable middle child, or the spoiled baby of the family.[16] Socially, you might be a bit of a class clown, a princess, a loner, a brown-noser, a deep thinker, a nerd, a jock, a brainiac, a tomboy. Finally, your employment status—from unemployed to shopkeeper to Prime Minister—carries with it particular expectations of skill or status that help to shape your sense of self.[17]

Photo: Marcelo Pinheiro/World of Stock

WHERE THE SELF-CONCEPT COMES FROM

- Self-appraisal and self-talk
- Judgements of others
  and from cultural images
- Familial, social, and professional roles

Self-Concept and Communication

The way we view ourselves can influence the way we communicate interpersonally, because our attitudes and beliefs about ourselves shape the choices we make when we communicate. As we interact with others, we tend to act in ways that reinforce our view of ourselves and others, and of how we fit into the situation.[18] We also try to act in ways that will gain or maintain what Erving Goffman calls '**positive social value**'.[19] According to Goffman, our verbal and non-verbal actions, taken together, form a kind of pattern or '**line**', which is an outward expression of the self-concept and a means of negotiating and preserving face needs.

Self-concept shapes our communication behaviour in at least three distinct ways. First, it is a predictor of what we will do or how we will experience a given event, since we will tend to act in ways that confirm the view we already have of ourselves. For example, a person who views herself as shy and socially awkward expects to feel uncomfortable at social gatherings; she behaves in ways that make this true, and the next social encounter reaffirms the accuracy of her self-perception. Similarly, someone who perceives himself as outgoing and socially adept expects to enjoy social encounters, and usually does, confirming his view of himself. In this way the self-concept creates a pattern for future actions that we will tend to fulfill. This patterning is one form of **self-fulfilling prophecy**,[20] a kind of self-prediction that conditions us to expect a certain outcome, such as success or failure, based on whether we believe ourselves to be good or not so good at a particular task. Because our beliefs and expectations condition how we behave, we can actually bring about the very success or failure that we have come to anticipate.

HOW SELF-CONCEPT AFFECTS COMMUNICATION

- Predicts future actions
- Filters current interactions
- Shapes unspoken assumptions and body language

Second, in addition to creating a pattern for future interactions, a self-concept acts as a kind of filter for our current interactions. In particular, we tend to select from the conversations of others those words or actions that confirm our own judgements of ourselves. Messages that challenge our self-concept may be ignored, downplayed, or dismissed as exceptions, while those that confirm what we believe are more readily accepted.[21]

For example, Sam privately thinks he is not smart or good-looking enough, so he is inclined to discount feedback that suggests he is intelligent or handsome. Julia is convinced she is no good at mathematics, and despite doing well all term in her calculus class she sees her poor showing on the latest assignment as confirmation that she is unable to succeed at math. Although Ian has never sung anywhere but in the shower, he dreams of winning the next *Canadian Idol* competition. When his friends respond unenthusiastically to his karaoke debut, he angrily dismisses their comments as nothing more than jealousy. Since high school, Laura has nurtured her writing ability by keeping a journal and writing poetry; however, her university essays have earned only mediocre grades. Frustrated, she concludes that her professors must be too dim-witted to recognize real talent.

Finally, the self-concept conditions the unstated aspects of our communication— the tone and footing, and the ways in which we word our messages. Our language choices, as well as our non-verbal idiosyncrasies, reveal to those who know how to read them a whole range of information about our unspoken assumptions and attitudes, about how we see ourselves in relation to others, and about how we view our role in the situation. In this way, the unstated 'message behind the message' is shaped in part by self-concept. We implicitly understand this connection between self-concept and communication, and we show it when we react to another's inappropriate behaviour by asking 'Who do you think you are?' or 'Who do you think you're talking to?' Who we think we are and who we think we're talking to condition the choices we make when we set out to communicate with others.

Self and Others

Our every interaction contributes to the formation, maintenance, and negotiation of our self-concept. Although we tend to act in ways that confirm what we already believe about ourselves, and although in general we tend to filter out messages that don't accord with our self-perception, there is also a sense in which our conceptions of self are continually challenged and renegotiated through interaction.[22]

As social beings, we all need approval and affirmation. We want to be taken seriously; we want acceptance; we want to see our good opinions of ourselves reflected in the reactions of those around us. In order to achieve these emotional and psychological necessities, we adjust our behaviour, and with it, our self-concepts. Thus, our views of ourselves are gradually shaped by how satisfactory our encounters are and how effectively they allow us to fulfill our social needs. In Chapter 4 we will examine the importance of such needs in greater detail.

At the same time as we are negotiating our own sense of self, we are also contributing to shaping the self-perceptions of others. Thus, at any one time, in any given interaction, I am attempting to manage a combination of at least four perspectives about who I am and what line I can or should take in this interaction. First, there are my own assessment and perceptions of who *I* am. Second, there is my sense of who *you* are, and how I can accommodate your role and contribution to the situation. Third, there is my impression of how you perceive me or value me or consider me. Finally, there is my sense of how you view yourself.

At the same time, you are attempting a parallel task: managing your own sense of self, combined with your understanding and perception of me and my role, influenced in turn by what you believe I think of you, and finally shaped by your perception of how I see myself. All in all, the interaction involves a complex of at least eight possibly competing points of view, which may in turn influence self-concept for either of us. Table 3.1 summarizes this relationship more clearly.

Table 3.1 **The Negotiation of Selves**	
Factors influencing my communication with you	Factors influencing your communication with me
My self-perception	Your self-perception
My perception of you	Your perception of me
My perception of how you view me	Your perception of how I view you
My perception of how you view yourself	Your perception of how I view myself

If we add a third person, or more, to the mix, the model becomes even more complicated, as the additional people add their perspectives on each of us and on our combined attitudes. As well, we are also negotiating our understanding of the situation we are in and the purpose of our interaction.

As we interact, we influence not only elements of our own self-concepts, but also, to a greater or lesser degree, those of others. The more important those others are to us or the more powerful they are, the more influence they will have in shaping our definition of self. It is in this sense that communication theorists talk about 'negotiation of selves'.[23] Every interaction contributes to this negotiation and to this process of coming to terms with who we are.

Face, Self-Concept, and the Johari Window

As we have already learned, the self-concept strongly influences the way we communicate interpersonally, since our attitudes and beliefs about ourselves shape the choices we make when we communicate. These choices involve the tone of our interactions, the footing or relationships we establish with others, and the line we take in any interaction. Not surprisingly, then, there is an important connection between the self-concept and the 'face' we can claim in a given encounter.

Like self-concept, the face we present to others is not a complete picture of what we actually are like. In fact, it isn't even a complete picture of what we *believe* we are like. Face is only a partial representation of the self-concept, selected and shaped in part by the constraints of the situation and by the way we would like to be seen by others. If we are to communicate effectively, we need to be able to respond and adapt to the demands of the context in which we are communicating. Failure to do this is a mark of insensitivity, as well as of communicative weakness.

You should be careful not to mistake the partial and selective nature of face for a deliberate deception or misrepresentation. It is neither. Instead, it is measure of what used to be called **decorum**—the ability to conduct yourself appropriately in a given situation. This includes recognizing what is and is not an acceptable level of self-disclosure. After all, everyone's self-concept contains some information that the person considers private, and to present everything indiscriminately would mark a person as socially inappropriate, lacking in judgement, and perhaps even disturbed.

We choose to present what we deem to be appropriate to that situation and the people we are speaking to, and our ability to match our level of disclosure to the demands and constraints of the situation is one measure of our communicative and interpersonal skill. We may disclose different kinds and amounts of information, depending on the level of intimacy in the relationship. Factual data, such as last night's hockey scores or the formatting of a business report, are least risky and require the least intimacy, followed by opinion and thoughts, and finally, feelings and emotions.

Not everyone discloses at the same level or to the same extent. Some people are comfortable with a relatively large degree of self-revelation, whereas others are more private. However, everyone, no matter how 'open' they may be, has some self-knowledge that is not shared, since disclosing everything about yourself would in most cases be inappropriate, as well as leave you excessively vulnerable to risk or rejection.

To help us understand the ways in which levels of disclosure might affect our interpersonal relationships, we can turn to the **Johari window**, an interpersonal mapping device created by two communication theorists, Joseph Luft and Harry Ingham.[24] The Johari window is intended to help you to discover the intersections between your self-knowledge and the knowledge that others have of you, as shown in Figure 3.1.

The diagram shows a square split vertically and horizontally into four quadrants. The two quadrants to the left of the vertical central line represent the things I know about myself. The two quadrants to the right represent information about myself that I am unaware of. Splitting the square horizontally, the two quadrants above the horizontal dividing line represent the things that others know or have observed about me. Finally, the two quadrants below the horizontal line represent the things that others do not know.

Each pane of the 'window' thus formed represents an intersection of what I know about myself and what others know about me. Starting at the lower left and moving clockwise, we begin with the quadrant or pane labelled 'hidden', which represents private information that I know about myself but may for whatever reason prefer not to disclose to others. Above it, the upper left quadrant, or pane, is labelled 'open', since it shows the information about me that I willingly share or that is readily available, so it is known both to me and to others. The upper right quadrant or pane represents my 'blind' spots about myself—information that others can see, but to which I am oblivious. Finally, the bottom right quadrant is 'unknown' because it represents information about me that I have repressed or that is unavailable either to me or to others.

Photo: Bill Stevenson/World of Stock

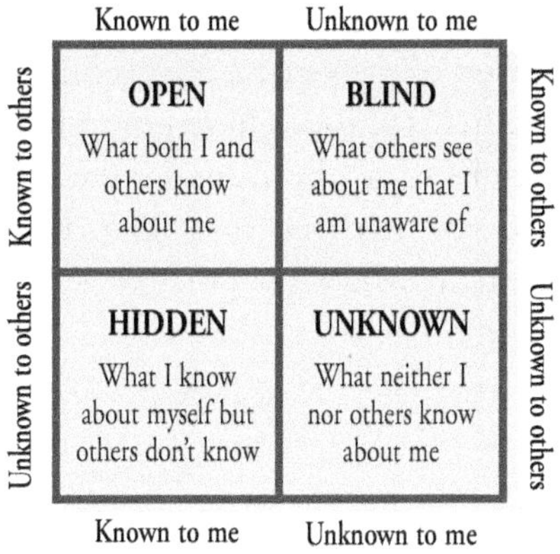

	Known to me	Unknown to me	
Known to others	**OPEN** What both I and others know about me	**BLIND** What others see about me that I am unaware of	**Known to others**
Unknown to others	**HIDDEN** What I know about myself but others don't know	**UNKNOWN** What neither I nor others know about me	**Unknown to others**
	Known to me	Unknown to me	

Fig 3.1
The Johari Window

The Johari window can be used in two ways. First, it can be used to map your general pattern of self-reflection and self-disclosure. Although of course everyone shares personal information at different levels in different kinds of relationships, each of us has a 'typical' comfort level with acquaintances and friends that the window can be used to display.

Since people are not equally self-aware, and since everyone discloses different amounts of information and at different rates, everyone's window will look different. The example in Figure 3.1 shows the quadrants to be of equal sizes, but in practice they may vary in configuration. For instance, the greater a person's self-awareness and self-reflection, the larger will be the left half of the window. If that person also discloses freely, the top half of the diagram will also be enlarged. This is the case for Kay, whose Johari window (Figure 3.2) shows a much larger 'open' quadrant, a much smaller 'unknown' quadrant, and compensatory changes in the 'blind' and 'hidden' quadrants. Kay is highly self-reflective, and she is comfortable with self-revelation.

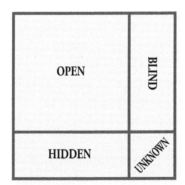

Figure 3.2
Kay: Johari Window Showing Higher
Levels of Self-Knowledge and Self-Disclosure

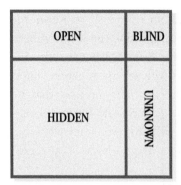

Figure 3.3
Jim: Johari Window Showing High
Self-Awareness but Less Inclination
to Disclose

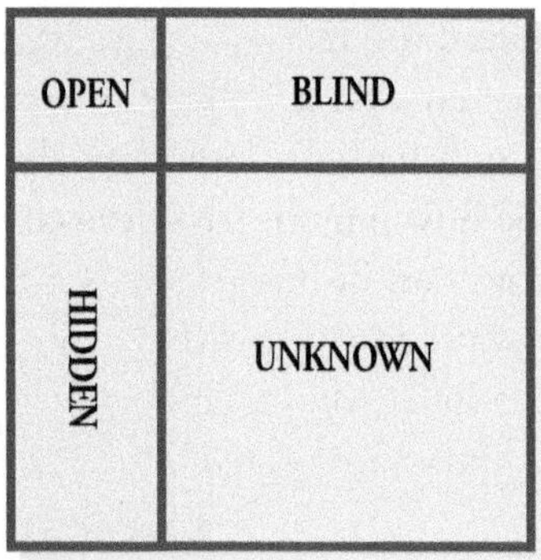

Figure 3.4
Kevin: Johari Window Showing Low
Self-Reflection and Low Disclosure

On the other hand, Jim (Figure 3.3) may be just as self-aware as Kay, but less forthcoming; his 'blind' and 'unknown' quadrants are reduced in size, but his 'hidden' segment has enlarged, reflecting the greater amount of insight that he generally keeps to himself. Though Jim is self-reflective, he is also a private person and more reserved than Kay.

Finally, Kevin, who finds self-reflection uncomfortable and who does not much like to talk about himself, might be expected to have a reduced 'open' quadrant, with a correspondingly larger 'unknown' one (Figure 3.4). Because Kevin doesn't like to reflect on his feelings or actions, his motives are largely obscure to him, and because he does not reveal much of himself, they aren't known to others either.

While the Johari window is useful for representing a person's 'typical' interaction style, it can also be used to map someone's pattern of disclosure in a particular relationship. For example, the map of Kay's relationship with her friend Theresa will show a greater openness than the map of her relationship with Wendy, whom she does not know so well and with whom she is not so comfortable.

The Johari window provides a graphic means of understanding the relationship between self-understanding and self-disclosure, and in particular how one affects or influences the other. In general, a greater degree of self-reflection means greater self-understanding, and usually a better quality of interpersonal communication. A generally high level of self-disclosure, while easing the challenge of social situations (Kay is comfortable talking to just about anyone), isn't required for every relationship in someone's life. As long as each person has one or two others with whom there is a meaningful level of self-disclosure, that person will have a healthy interpersonal life. For example, although Jim is generally reserved with his acquaintances, he has three or four close relationships in which he is able to freely share his deeper concerns, and thus he is able to feel emotionally supported.

However, self-reflection does have an impact on all our relationships. Kevin, for example, may find it difficult to establish close relationships, since he is uncomfortable not only with disclosure but also with self-reflection. Even if he has friends with whom he is willing to share his feelings, his discomfort with self-examination would likely compromise his interpersonal effectiveness, since he can't disclose what he doesn't understand himself. Kevin's Johari window suggests that he is likely something of a loner who doesn't easily get close to others and who resists understanding himself very well. If Kevin is lucky, he will meet one person with whom he can establish a bond of closeness and learn to become more comfortable with self-reflection; if not, it is likely that he will be lonely throughout his life.

Intimacy and Self-Disclosure

Intimacy is a state of close familiarity that exists between friends, members of a family, or partners. As we have already seen, intimacy is the goal of our interpersonal communication, and the fulfillment of our need for connectedness and identification. Intimacy is closely related to the trust that we establish with others, which in turn depends on self-disclosure.

Self-disclosure can be defined as divulging or revealing something about yourself that the other person would be unlikely to know or understand without your having made it available. Self-disclosure of some form is involved in all human relationships, with greater disclosure occurring where there is a greater level of trust and intimacy. Self-disclosure to an acquaintance may involve primarily factual information, such as biographical data and details: where you grew up or went to school, how many brothers and sisters you have, or what you do for a living. As you get to know the person better and your comfort level increases, you will likely share more personal thoughts and opinions. Once a relationship has become intimate, you can openly express your deeper feelings and concerns.

Self-disclosure is a prerequisite for intimacy.[25] As the level of disclosure increases, the level of relational closeness that is possible also increases, enabling us to fulfill our most pressing psychological and emotional need: the need for communion with others. However, in order to achieve this identification, we must place ourselves at risk. Interpersonal risk—the risk of being hurt or betrayed by someone else—increases with greater intimacy.[26] That is, the more knowledge the person has about you, the more profoundly you can be hurt. All rejection is hurtful, of course, but betrayal by an intimate in whom you have placed a greater degree of trust is much more painful. However, no one can live without love and intimacy, and the benefits of these things far outweigh the grief that we can sometimes encounter.[27]

Self-disclosure has a reciprocal quality;[28] my offering of personal information invites a similar level of disclosure from you. If for some reason you choose not to share with me at the same level of closeness, I may feel embarrassed and uncomfortable, and will likely withdraw somewhat. By the same token, while my disclosure invites a similar level of intimacy from you, I cannot make you disclose information you do not want to share.

Self-disclosure creates trust, but it also requires trust from both participants in the interaction. For this reason, it ought not to be forced or demanded. How much you disclose is up to you, and most of the people with whom you interact will recognize and respect that boundary. Anyone who tries to push you too quickly to an uncomfortable level of disclosure is likely not behaving in your best interest.

Finally, self-disclosure can contribute to the building of your self-concept in part through a process of **perception-checking**. Articulating your feelings and perceptions to others in a tactful way can help you correct misunderstandings before they become entrenched, and can help you understand yourself and others better by encouraging self-reflection and analysis. It can provide confirmation or correction of your perceptions, and can help you to sharpen your judgement both of yourself and others by providing a more realistic sense not only of how you interpret the actions and words of others but of how others perceive you.

CHARACTERISTICS OF SELF-DISCLOSURE

Self-disclosure:
- involves risk.
- is a prerequisite for intimacy.
- builds and requires trust.
- is voluntary.
- contributes to the formation of self-concept.

Disclosure, Face Risk, and Betrayal

Although in normal social interaction we cannot usually be forced to make ourselves vulnerable by revealing more than we are comfortable with, there are some situations in which we may find ourselves making disclosures that we would not ordinarily have chosen. Because these exceptions can possibly cause us harm, it is well to be aware of them. For example, it is known that many people will provide information they would not normally disclose if they are asked a direct question. This knowledge underlies the process of cross-examination in court, and is also sometimes exploited in professional contexts. For example, George recently started working for an insurance and financial planning company. In his training, he was taught to ask very direct questions about people's spending and saving habits when interviewing potential clients. George finds these questions intrusively personal and would not want to answer them himself, but on his first day of interviewing he was shocked to discover how much private information people will volunteer, even when they don't really want to do so, just because he has asked them directly.[29] For George, even *asking* these direct questions is uncomfortable and face-threatening, and he has found the whole process so uncomfortable that he has begun looking for a different kind of job.

Why do people reveal personal details just because someone asks them a question? The first reason is that a direct question, especially if it's unexpected, is psychologically compelling and imposes a kind of obligation on a respondent. The compulsion to answer is so strong that we may feel no choice but to disclose even when we would normally not have chosen to share this information. As well, most of us have learned that an out-and-out refusal to answer a question is an act of rudeness, even when the question itself is impertinent. To respond even with something like 'I'm sorry, but I don't think that's any of your business' represents too direct a face threat, and many of us cannot bring ourselves to say this. Sometimes, rather than refusing to respond, we will instead divulge information that we might not normally disclose. As we will learn in Chapter 9, once we have committed to answering the first in a series of questions, we generally find it harder to refuse to answer subsequent ones.

Shirley recently had an experience of this sort when she was being interviewed for a job that she really wanted. Interspersed with legitimate questions, the interviewer

asked several that were inappropriately personal and therefore technically illegal in a job interview. Before the interview, Shirley had imagined that if she were ever faced with such a situation, she would politely but firmly say 'I'm not sure what bearing this has on the job we're discussing', but when it happened to her, she found herself unprepared for such a dramatic and forceful gesture. Faced with the interviewer's direct questions in a context where answering questions was expected, she seemed unable to prevent herself from disclosing information about her domestic arrangements, her relationship with her fiancé, and her religious affiliation. Only when the situation became completely intolerable was she able finally to excuse herself from the interview.

Afterwards, Shirley was angry with herself for answering any of the inappropriate questions, especially since she ended up walking out on the interview anyway. Why had she done so? In part, she had responded to the first question because she did not want to jeopardize what she thought might be her dream job. She continued answering subsequent questions because her answer to the first one seemed to have committed her to a course of action that she felt she could not abandon. Somehow the direct questioning compelled her to provide answers even though she was uncomfortable doing so, and once she had begun to divulge personal information it was as though she had given the interviewer tacit permission to pursue the line of questioning further. Now that she's been burned once, Shirley says she will be more prepared the next time this happens, and she plans to deflect questions that make her uncomfortable rather than answering them.

Sadly, there are those who use disclosure in unprincipled ways. They may lead others into disclosures that make them vulnerable, or use what they know to betray others. For instance, consider what recently happened to Heather and Betty, who have been best friends since childhood. They recently met James and have started to become friends with him. One day James reports that Heather has divulged one of Betty's secrets. The story is not true, but in her anger at the supposed betrayal, Betty retaliates by telling James some private information about Heather. James repeats the information to several of their acquaintances, and now Heather and Betty are no longer on speaking terms.

Or consider the case of Les, who belongs to a small, close-knit social community. Les and Donna recently split up, and Les had a brief but intense affair with Alana. The liaison ran its course quickly, and now Les and Donna are back together. But Les is appalled to discover that what he considers his private business seems to be known by everyone in their social circle, and now they're all treating him like one of the untouchables.

Literature and film are filled with stories like these, and all of us at some time experience some form of betrayal by a friend or other intimate who violates our trust, leaving us deeply wounded. Why, then, do we continue to engage in such risky interactions? The answer is that we need intimacy and connectedness as a matter of survival, and that the rewards of close relationships always are greater than the risks that they entail. What we get from our interpersonal interactions is nothing less than ourselves—our understanding of who we are, our friendships and family connections, and our social and personal identity. Through our interactions with others, we enjoy company, we encounter kindness, we experience understanding, and we achieve fulfillment. That we also sometimes feel pain and hurt is part of the price we pay for the gift of intimacy and social approval.

Summary

Self-concept, or how we view ourselves, plays an important role in our communication. Our sense of self contains elements that distinguish each of us from everyone else, while at the same time providing a sense of social belonging and identification. Thus, we have both a personal and a social identity. The self-concept is flexible and adaptable, but it is also remarkably persistent and occasionally needs to be updated.

The way we see ourselves has a huge impact on how we communicate because it conditions our choices and forms a kind of pattern for our interactions with others. The self-concept complicates interactions for several reasons. First, it is through our social interactions that we maintain, and reinforce, a sense of who we are, and it is through these interactions that we obtain the social affirmation that we all need. Second, at the same time that we are managing our own identifications and negotiating the demands of a given communication situation, others are doing the same, making interpersonal communication potentially very complex.

Our self-concepts are tied up with our capacity for self-reflection and our willingness to disclose personal information. These features of our interpersonal behaviour are governed in part by our own level of comfort and in part by the situation: we disclose more, and more willingly, in the presence of friends than in the presence of strangers. Our level of disclosure is intimately tied to the notion of face, and we all take steps to protect ourselves from becoming too vulnerable to face attacks.

Our interpersonal communication is also influenced by motives we can't always see. Our actions, especially our socially significant or symbolic ones, may be embedded in motivations that are invisible to us or that are too deeply held to be revealed to anyone. We can gain access to some of these motivations by recognizing the extent to which we are governed by deeper motives and by practising habits of self-reflection. One way to examine the relationship between our self-awareness and our interpersonal communication is the Johari window, a device for modelling the interaction between self-reflection and self-disclosure.

Finally, greater disclosure carries with it an elevated level of face risk, and so can engender defensiveness. Rejection, ridicule, and betrayal can all cause us to lose face and to respond defensively. Defensiveness, in turn, can constitute a face attack on someone else, thereby causing the other to become defensive and effectively destroying the trust that is necessary to interpersonal communication.

Because it is so intimately tied to our sense of self, and because it carries the potential for enormous face loss, interpersonal communication can be very challenging at times. But because it is what enables us to find social affirmation and intimacy, to establish our sense of self as individuals and as social beings, and because it provides the fulfillment and security of emotional closeness, it is worth the potential risks. Our ability to forge satisfying interpersonal relationships ensures not only our emotional and psychological well-being, but better health, and even greater longevity. Improving our interpersonal skills is a way of committing to a better quality of life.

Key Terms

decorum
intimacy
Johari window
line
perception-checking
personal identity
positive social value
self-concept
self-disclosure
self-fulfilling prophecy
sense of self
social identity
trust

Suggested Readings

Stephen Duck and Julia T. Wood, eds, *Composing Relationships: Communication in Everyday Life* (Belmont, Calif.: Wadsworth, 2006). Duck and Wood provide a reasonably accessible treatment of social relationships and communication in the conduct of our everyday interactions.

Anthony Elliott, *Concepts of the Self* (Cambridge: Polity Press, 2001). Elliott explores numerous contemporary controversies over the notion of 'self' as it is defined by social scientific theory. Elliott moves easily between scholarly and popular works, and includes political, interpersonal, and sociological aspects of self-identification. The book is aimed at a lay reader who wishes to understand the relationship among self, society, and everyday life.

Erik H. Erikson, *Identity: Youth and Crisis* (New York: Norton, 1968). This classic text, written for the expert but readable by a determined lay person, explores the formation of identity among youth through a process of crisis and resolution.

Al Gini, *My Job: My Self* (New York: Routledge, 2000). Gini's book takes literally the maxim 'You are what you do', exploring the relationship between our work and our sense of self. The essence of his argument is that adults need to work as a way of defining themselves and their roles in the social order, and that they depend on their work as a means of establishing identity.

Erving Goffman, *The Presentation of Self in Everyday Life* (New York: Anchor Books, 1959). This classic and influential work studies the dynamics of face in social interaction. Goffman's prose is somewhat dense, but his exploration of how we construct and maintain a public self is insightful and provocative.

Amin Maalouf, *In the Name of Identity: Violence and the Need to Belong*, trans. Barbara Bray (New York: Penguin, 2000). In a departure from the usual study of identity formation, Maalouf studies the relationship between violence and the desire to belong. Maalouf suggests that social identifications that reduce identity to a single affiliation are productive of violence against those who are defined as 'the other'.

Hendrik M. Ruitenbeek, *The Individual and the Crowd: A Study of Identity in America* (New York: Mentor/New American Library, 1965). Ruitenbeek presents the notion of identity in a historical context, and explores the phenomenon of 'anomie', the sense of having lost one's identity. This brief book attempts to answer some of the crucial questions of human existence: Who am I? Where am I going? Where do I belong? The book is a scholarly rather than a popular treatment, and may present some challenges to a lay reader (Ruitenbeek is a sociologist and psychoanalyst), but the insights it offers are still pertinent 40 years after its original publication.

Exercises and Assignments

1. Read the form letter 'Mark C is Caught in the Middle' (Appendix B). Using what you have learned about the way our sense of self is shaped by the confirmation or disconfirmation we receive from others, consider how this spam ad exploits both interpersonal and cultural dynamics. What can we learn about the interpersonal quality of the communication that some corporations use with their clients? About the power of the self-concept and self-doubt in general? Can you provide any other examples of your own of similar tactics? Present your analysis in writing or as part of a class discussion, as directed by your instructor.

2. Read Rose De Shaw's 'Guilt, Despair, and the Red Pottery Pig' (Appendix B). What is the meaning of the pig to the members of the group? What are the author's feelings about being the recipient of the pig? On reading this article, one of my friends described it as 'the Pig of Shame'. Is he correct? If so, what is the role of shame in the shaping of self-concept? To what extent is the pig an expres-

sion of social control? Does it fit into our understanding of the functions of communication described in Chapter 2? Why or why not?

3. Draw a Johari window that represents as closely as possible your own average level of self-knowledge and self-disclosure. Include a brief explanation to aid in interpreting the window. Without discussing it with the class, clearly label it with the date and place it in your Interpersonal Communication Portfolio.

4. Following the guidelines in Appendix A, create your own Personal Icon. Be prepared to bring the Icon to class for analysis and discussion. Be sure to adhere to the guidelines provided, and preserve the anonymity of your creation until it is time for the 'reveal'.

5. Once the Personal Icons have been created and submitted, but before the class has had an opportunity to examine them carefully or interpret them, the class will be given the opportunity to discuss their initial impressions of the experience of creating such a self-representation. As you prepare to contribute to that discussion, consider the following:

   a. Do you have any observations about the experience of making your own Icon? Was it more difficult or easier than you expected?

   b. On first seeing the Icons, but before examining any of them carefully, what was your initial reaction? Did you find that seeing what others had produced gave you any second thoughts about your own icon? Why might this have been?

   c. Drawing on what you have so far learned about interpersonal communication, discuss the particular challenges associated with presenting yourself through this kind of exercise. As a way of establishing your place within the group, is it more effective than the usual classroom interaction, or less effective? Why?

6. When the class has finished the Personal Icon exercise, draw a second Johari window that represents what was communicated by your Icon. Once again, include a brief explanation. Either through class discussion or in written form, compare this Johari window with the one you drew for Assignment #1. Are there any differences? Are they significant? Why might that be? Has the Icon exercise caused you to rethink your initial estimate of your level of self-disclosure? What else was revealed to you in the course of the exercise?

7. When the class has finished viewing and discussing the icons, you will probably

have made some observations about the presentation and negotiation of self in communication. Write a short paper (approximately 600 words) in which you analyze the experience in light of concepts discussed in class. What have the preparation and discussion of the Personal Icons revealed about communication and presentation of self? Please choose only one of the two approaches outlined below:

a. You may have noticed from the class discussions that others frequently read the icons differently from what their creators intended. Such an experience should remind us how misleading first impressions can be and how dependent we are on context for making useful interpretations. Using a specific example of one of the class Icons, contrast your initial reaction to and interpretation of the Icon with the description and explanation given by the person who made it. Consider the following questions in your analysis. Would you have interpreted the Icon differently had you known beforehand who owned it? Why might this knowledge have made a difference to you? What elements of the icon led to your interpretation? What might you have brought to it yourself that influenced that interpretation? In your analysis, you should consider what we have learned about perception and communication, as well as about self-concept and negotiation of self.

b. You may equally have been the victim of misunderstanding in the interpretation of your Icon by your classmates. If this was so, what might have happened to cause such a misreading? Do you think your Icon would have been clearer to others if you had been able to explain it to the class? What elements of your Icon do you feel were particularly misinterpreted? Did the comments of others give you any insights into your own self-representation? If you found yourself wishing you could make changes to your Icon once you saw those of others and heard some of the comments, explain why you think this might have happened. What did you learn about your own views of private versus public self? About the amount and kind of risk you were willing to take in sharing your self-concept?

Photo: Dennis MacDonald/World of Stock

Chapter 4

Theoretical Dimensions of Interpersonal Communication

Learning Objectives

- To distinguish among different types or levels of interpersonal interaction.
- To develop some theoretical foundations for understanding interpersonal communication.
- To understand the life cycle of relationships.

The study of interpersonal communication is concerned with the care and maintenance of the relationships on which we depend; it is intended to help us to develop
the skills we need to understand those relationships and to manage them more effectively, to assist us in dealing with the inevitable conflicts we will face, and to give us
insight into how relationships develop, how they are sustained, and why they sometimes come to an end.

Interpersonal communication, like all other forms of communication, is conditioned and influenced by a variety of factors that may not always be evident to those
who are communicating. This chapter describes several theoretical models intended
to help explain the motivations that influence our interpersonal communication
behaviour. Although knowledge of theory by itself does not guarantee improvement
in our skills, it does provide a foundation upon which skill may be developed. We
will begin with a few definitions.

The Nature of Interpersonal Relationships

An **interpersonal relationship** has been defined as 'a series of interactions between
two individuals who are known to each other'.[1] However, although it seems intended to include all the possible interactions that may occur between individuals, this
definition appears to place greater emphasis on the events than on the people
involved in them, de-emphasizing the relational qualities we are most interested in
studying. Another way to think of interpersonal communication is as an emotional
association or involvement between two people that extends over several encounters.
Such associations can take many forms and occur on a variety of levels, from an
acquaintance through friendship to intimate relationships.

LEVELS OF INTERPERSONAL INVOLVEMENT

- Acquaintanceship
- Friendship
- Intimate relationships or close friendships

Acquaintances are people with whom our interactions, though pleasant, are constrained in both quality and quantity. Conversation in such relationships is usually
limited to exchanging factual information, which is easiest to share since it involves
the least interpersonal risk. **Acquaintanceships** are frequently tied to particular contexts, such as the classroom or workplace, community groups or organizations to
which we belong, or church, temple, mosque, or synagogue.

In such instances, our associations depend as much on setting as on mutual interest; for instance, as long as they are assigned to the same project at work, Dave may interact daily with Malcolm. However, when either of them moves to a different project or to a different department in the company, their interactions will be reduced, or may even cease unless they have also become friends. Tess might have coffee regularly with the group of people she takes classes with, but when classes end, she may find that there is little left to bring them together.

Acquaintanceships may also be a product of the social roles we fulfill, which may be quite clearly defined and relatively structured: relationships between students and professors, doctors and patients, or lawyers and clients are clearly of this sort; even the interaction we have with the clerk at the dry cleaner or the server at the local fast-food hangout qualifies as a role-based acquaintanceship. These are people we know, who perform the services on which we depend, and with whom we may exchange pleasantries when we meet, but with whom we do not share much beyond what is required by the nature of our professional interaction.

If, over time, we find that we have more in common with an acquaintance than simply our mutual context, the relationship may develop into a **friendship**. Friends, as opposed to acquaintances, are those with whom we choose to spend our discretionary time, and with whom we have voluntarily chosen to become more deeply involved.[2] As a friendship develops, we are more likely to go beyond exchanging factual information to sharing opinions and thoughts, followed, as the relationship deepens, by more personal feelings. Obviously, a friendship involves greater levels of self-revelation and deeper levels of trust than does an acquaintanceship, and thus poses both greater interpersonal risk and greater opportunities for emotional support and fulfillment.

Acquaintances become friends based on a variety of factors. We tend, at least initially, to become friends with those we find appealing or attractive. We are also more likely to be drawn to those who show an interest in us or concern for our feelings. It makes sense, too, that we tend to seek further association with those who display good social skills rather than with those who are surly or unpleasant. Similarity and shared interests may also play a role, though it can also be true that we become friends with someone who is different enough to complement our strengths. Not surprisingly, research confirms what most of us understand intuitively: people tend to seek out friendships that fulfill their social and psychological needs.[3]

Most of us instinctively know the difference between acquaintanceships and friendships, adapting or constraining our level of disclosure to suit the relational intimacy we have reached. Lasting friendships, though they may grow out of acquaintanceships, go beyond the original context, developing higher degrees of self-disclosure and commitment, as well as a sense that the relationship will endure even if circumstances change. Friends choose to spend time together and enjoy talking and sharing experiences with each other. Friendships also involve a greater degree of commitment than do acquaintanceships, and a greater degree of investment in each other's well-being. Friends willingly sacrifice time and energy to help a friend who is in need.

Some friendships develop into close or intimate relationships that are marked not only by frequent contact but by significant levels of disclosure. Close friends differ from 'ordinary' friends in the level of emotional investment each brings to the relationship and the level of intimacy they share. They wholeheartedly like each other and feel genuine warmth and affection for each other. Close friends actively seek each other's company and share their deepest concerns and feelings. For some, a **close friendship** may be more intimate in this sense than the relationship the person has with a partner or spouse. Most of us have only a few such relationships; while we may have many acquaintances and even perhaps many friends, there are few who are true intimates.

Social Scientific Theories of Interpersonal Relationships

Just as Kenneth Burke argued that the fundamental motive of all human communication is the creation of identification—a sense of connectedness and intimacy—with others,[4] social scientists have advanced theories to help explain interpersonal relationships. Many of these are, like Burke's theory, based on the idea that motivation arises from social, psychological, and symbolic needs.

SOCIAL SCIENTIFIC THEORIES OF INTERPERSONAL COMMUNICATION

- Hierarchy of needs (Abraham Maslow)
- Interpersonal needs theory (William Schutz)
- Four basic wants (Murray Banks)
- Social exchange theory (John Thibaut and Harold Kelley)

Probably the best-known 'needs' model of human motivation is Abraham Maslow's **hierarchy of needs theory** (Figure 4.1), first proposed in 1943.[5] Although it wasn't specifically intended to explain interpersonal relationships, Maslow's pyramid does demonstrate the central importance to human life of social connectedness and a sense of belonging, and thus provides a foundation for understanding interpersonal dynamics.

Maslow became interested in the study of motivation when he noticed that, even among animals, some needs take precedence over others: physical survival is more fundamental than socialization, for example. Maslow began to ponder the influence of needs on human motivation, particularly at the social and symbolic levels, but rather than basing his theories of human motive on the study of the psychologically disturbed, as Freud and others did, Maslow conducted a qualitative study of the lives and personalities of some of history's greatest thinkers and achievers, including writers, scientists, musicians, philosophers, and theologians.

Maslow's analysis led him to posit five fundamental categories of human need, arranged in a hierarchy from most basic (physiological needs and security needs), through social and psychological needs (belonging and self-esteem or ego needs), to the level of self-fulfillment that Maslow referred to as self-actualization. Maslow emphasized that needs are only needs as long as they remain unfulfilled; in the moment of fulfillment, the need disappears, only to reassert itself later for further replenishment or affirmation. For example, we are not hungry if we have just eaten or sleepy if we have just awakened from a full eight hours of sleep, but we will experience both needs again.

MASLOW'S HIERARCHY OF NEEDS

- Physiological or 'body' needs: water, food, sleep, warmth, physical activity, procreation
- Safety and security needs: protection from environmental hazards and dangers
- Social needs: love and belonging, a sense of identity, preservation of face, respect
- Self-esteem or ego needs: a feeling of accomplishment, healthy pride, appropriate social status
- Self-actualization: fulfillment of potential, personal growth

The most basic needs described by Maslow are physiological, or 'body' needs, for the bodily necessities without which we could not survive. These include such essentials as air to breathe, clean water to drink, food to eat, warmth, sleep, procreation, and physical activity. These needs form the base of Maslow's pyramid because our very existence depends on their being fulfilled. Until these needs are met, other needs do not even manifest themselves.

The second level in Maslow's hierarchy of needs is safety and security. If we are to live, we need protection from the dangers imposed by our environment, such as predators, extreme temperatures, or harsh weather conditions. Like those on the first level, these needs are essential to our continued existence, and so must be fulfilled before we turn our attention to satisfying our social and psychological requirements. Maslow called these first two levels **deficit needs**, since if they remain unanswered, we will not survive.

But Maslow's hierarchy demonstrates that human life depends on more than physical survival and safety. Once these are assured, we will begin to experience what he termed **growth needs**: those that arise from our social, psychological, and symbol-

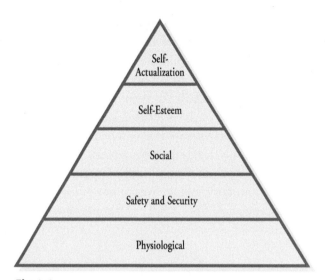

Fig 4.1
Maslow's Heirarchy of Needs

ic natures. Unlike the deficit needs, fulfillment of growth needs is not essential for our immediate physical survival. However, while the adverse effects are much less immediate than the lack of water, sleep, or food, a lack of fulfillment at the social and psychological level has a significant impact on the quality of life, and, over the long term, on our health and well-being.

These growth needs are featured in the three remaining levels of Maslow's pyramid: social needs, self-esteem or ego needs, and self-actualization needs. The social needs that make up the third level include the need for a sense of identity and community, and for a feeling of belonging; the need to feel respected and valued by others; the need to establish and preserve face for ourselves and others; and, most important, the need to love and be loved by someone else. Since they are fulfilled primarily through our interpersonal communication, we will return to these needs throughout much of this book.

The fourth level of Maslow's hierarchy is

what he described as self-esteem or ego needs. These include a feeling that we have achieved a satisfactory level of social status and can take healthy pride in our accomplishments. We need to feel that we are good at something, that we are worthy of regard, that we are able to make a worthwhile contribution. The self-esteem that Maslow describes comes from a sense of actual achievement, of having 'made the grade' in some significant way.

However, it does not mean necessarily being the top of the class, the captain of the team, the dean of the college, or the president of the corporation; instead, it refers to a sense that we have achieved a level of accomplishment and social status commensurate with our abilities, expectations, and interests, and that whatever distinction we have obtained is ideally the result of our own efforts. Like our social needs, these self-esteem needs are fulfilled largely through our interpersonal interactions, and so will be addressed further as we work through the remainder of this book.

The final level of Maslow's hierarchy is the need for **self-actualization**. At this level, we need to feel not only that we have achieved social status and ego satisfaction, but that we have fulfilled our deepest human potential. The need for self-actualization arises out of our symbolic nature; this level has a transcendent, spiritual quality marked by a search for a deeper sense of meaning and value, and a sense of going beyond mere self-gratification to identify with something greater or more profound than the self. For some, the search for self-actualization may involve a spiritual quest; for others, it may reside in acts of selflessness that serve others, in service to a community, in profound and concentrated intellectual work, or in acts of great physical courage and daring.

Self-actualization, like all of the states described by Maslow, is not a permanent condition. Instead, it comes to us in **peak experiences**—moments of insight and an intense feeling of well-being. Such moments are described as self-validating, self-justifying moments with their own intrinsic worth. Not everyone achieves self-actualization, but those who do may experience these 'peak moments' at any level of the pyramid. While the peak experience itself is short-lived, its effects may be longer lasting. For example, consider how the celebrated Canadian scholar Northrop Frye described a moment of insight that came to him when he was writing his famous study of the poet William Blake:

> [S]uddenly the universe just broke open, and I've never been, as they say, the same man since. . . . [it was] a feeling of an enormous number of things making sense that had been scattered and unrelated before, a vision of coherence. That's the only way I can describe it. Things began to form patterns and make sense. . . . I've had two or three nights where I have had sudden visions of that kind. They were I suppose ultimately visions of what I myself might be able to do.[6]

Frye, a scholar and university professor, found his 'peak experiences' in intellectual work, but such moments of profound insight can come from any form of intense human experience—physical, spiritual, psychological, or intellectual.

Like Abraham Maslow, William Schutz also saw human motivation as a product of fundamental needs. However, because Schutz's focus is specifically on explaining interpersonal interactions, his **interpersonal needs theory** begins with what Maslow termed 'growth' needs: the social and psychological necessities of human interaction, taking basic survival for granted.

Schutz argues that interpersonal relationships develop and are maintained primarily because each person meets the interpersonal needs of the other, and he identifies three fundamental needs that humans fulfill through their interpersonal interactions: affection, inclusion, and control.[7] Schutz's theory acknowledges the centrality of the human need to love and to be loved, or in Schutz's words, 'the need to establish and maintain a satisfactory relation with others with respect to love and affection'.[8] He notes that the need for affection works in two directions: people not only need to feel loved themselves, but they also need to express love for others.

Like the need for affection or love, the sense of inclusion also involves both a need for and a desire to provide others what Schutz calls 'a satisfactory relation with people with respect to interaction and association'.[9] Inclusion involves achieving a sense of belonging, or identification, for yourself and extending that same sense of belonging to others; it is devoted to building a sense of community and social connectedness. Schutz's theory thus confirms what we have already learned about the importance of identification to our sense of well-being and identity.

Finally, Schutz posits a third interpersonal need that shapes the kinds of relationships people seek out: 'the need to establish and maintain a satisfactory relation with people with respect to control and power'.[10] The need for control, like the need for affection or inclusion, expresses itself in more than one way: it can manifest as a need to be directed by others or as a desire to take control of your own situation and actions. In the extreme, the need for control may express itself in a desire to manage not just your own but also others' behaviour.

People differ in the level of need they feel in each of the three areas of affection, inclusion, and control. Consider Jenn, whose orientation towards control appears extremely high, especially to the members of the project team she worked with for a recent class assignment. Jenn was charged with gathering the group's submissions and assembling them into a final report for presentation to the professor; however, without telling her group mates what she was going to do, she completely rewrote their contributions to meet her own standards before handing in the final report.

While they're not complaining about the grade they received for their project, Benjamin and Daniela are still pretty ticked that Jenn made so many extensive editorial changes without consulting the rest of the team. Among other choice names for her, they now refer to her as the 'control freak'.

What Jenn did was clearly not appropriate, since the rest of the group had no idea their work would be edited, and she altered their contributions without their consent. But what, if anything, can be said in her defence? Is she, as her friends have concluded, really a control freak? While her actions certainly show a need to control the situation and the outcome, Jenn may not be quite as directive as it first appears. Jenn's need for control seems to focus on results more than on others' behaviour, since even her classmates acknowledge that she made no attempt to direct their work habits or tell them what to do. All of her efforts at control were centred on consequences.

If we know that this incident is typical of Jenn's behaviour, we might speculate that her particular pattern of needs ranks control ahead of affection, since she willingly risked alienating her peers by changing their work without their permission. As well, events like this one suggest that her need for control may also be greater than her need for inclusion, since acting unilaterally in this way would clearly set her apart from the group. We should expect that, in professional situations at least, Jenn's need for control will normally take precedence over her need for inclusion or affection, but that this need will express itself in a results orientation and not in micromanaging of others' actions.

Schutz suggests that an individual's particular pattern of needs for inclusion, affection, and control is formed in childhood and remains fairly stable throughout life. For this reason, he argues that it is a useful predictor of how someone will behave in future situations. In this respect, Schutz joins Kenneth Burke, who observed in a person's behavioural patterns 'the sustaining of an attitude . . . a character repeating his identity'.[11]

In Jenn's case, we should expect her to behave in ways that provide the level of control of situations and outcomes that she needs in order to feel comfortable. This doesn't excuse her for changing the group's report, but it does give some insight into what makes her tick.

 ## COMPONENTS OF INTERPERSONAL NEEDS THEORY

- Affection
- Inclusion
- Control

A final model of interpersonal motive based on human needs is the **basic wants model** offered by Murray Banks, a psychiatrist whose lively and entertaining presentation style made him popular as a speaker and media celebrity in the 1950s and 1960s, much as Dr Phil McGraw is today. Although Banks's model is a popularization, it demonstrates, like the previous 'needs' theories, the centrality of interpersonal communication to a full and satisfying life.

In one of his popular speeches,[12] Banks outlined what he called the 'four basic wants' that drive human interaction: I want to live, I want someone to love me, I want a feeling of importance, I want a little variety. According to Banks, emotionally healthy people possess a strong survival instinct, followed by just as powerful a desire to be loved and to love in return. We also desire a feeling of personal worth akin to the self-esteem needs identified by Maslow. Finally, Banks observed that human beings need to feel challenged, to have a sense of accomplishment and growth. Banks saw these things as prompted by what he termed 'variety'. As you can immediately see, Banks's model parallels both Maslow's hierarchy and Schutz's interpersonal needs theory, emphasizing the centrality of social connectedness to psychological well-being and a healthy and fulfilling life.

Although the understanding of human needs as a source of motivation is widespread among theorists, it is not universal. A well-known theory that has offered direct explanation for interpersonal relationships is **social exchange theory**, which departs from the 'needs' paradigm by treating relationships as a kind of economic transaction of rewards and costs.

According to this theory, advanced by John Thibaut and Harold Kelley,[13] people seek relationships that will offer the greatest benefit for the least effort or investment of time and energy. Social exchange theory assumes that people more or less deliberately weigh the costs and benefits of a given relationship and decide to continue or abandon it according to what shows on a kind of internalized balance sheet. It is this ratio of rewards and costs that determines whether someone will enter into a relationship or even an individual interaction.

Social exchange theory, not surprisingly, has come under criticism[14] for its reduction of human interaction to a kind of economic behaviour. The economic metaphor is problematic because it not only assumes that we operate instinctively according to a cost–reward ratio, but also that we can accurately anticipate the payoffs of a variety of interactions. It assumes, too, that we are able to compute a rational analysis of our choices based on available data and then act accordingly—much like a computer would do.[15]

Unfortunately, as we learned in the previous chapter, people rarely behave according to rational models, and their motives are often a mystery even to themselves. While the social exchange model may tempt us to think of human beings as computer-style data-processing machines,[16] our communicative behaviour is actually much more complex than this. As we have learned, our emotions, our psychological make-up, our interests, and even our values all play a part, so that we do not respond in equal measure to each bit of information, or even to the same information received at different times in different contexts.

Despite the drawbacks of seeing interpersonal interactions as mere cost–benefit transactions, however, an analysis of the kind described by Thibaut and Kelley can be helpful in situations where we face a dilemma and must choose between two attractive alternatives. For instance, Nani, who works as a communication officer at a medium-sized company in Halifax, was recently offered a slightly more senior position at a bigger firm in Kitchener. Though the salaries were comparable, the

Kitchener job was slightly higher profile and offered some perks that her current company couldn't match: flex-time, an on-site fitness facility, education leave, and a stock-option plan. As well, the move would have brought Nani closer to her family, who live in Kenora.

Nani was very tempted by the new position, but staying in Halifax also offered some definite benefits: for example, the company's plans for expansion, if realized according to the fiscal plan, would offer her the opportunity to enhance her skills and her role in the organization. Leaving Halifax would cause her to lose what she had already paid into the pension plan, and the new salary, though comparable to her current earnings, was slightly less than what she anticipated her salary would be after this year's cost-of-living increase. Her workplace in Halifax is congenial and supportive, and not as politically charged as the more high-powered company in Kitchener. Finally, Nani's fiancé was unable to find a position in Kitchener that was a match for the one he held in Halifax.

Despite the prestige and apparent opportunities offered by the Kitchener position, Nani decided to stay in Halifax. She made her decision in part because of the cost–benefit analysis she and her fiancé undertook. It turns out to have been the right decision: among other positive outcomes, the planned expansion has brought Nani a small promotion, and the recent surge in housing costs that has hit most cities in the country so far has not touched Halifax, so Nani and her fiancé will be able to realize their dream of purchasing a house.

The social exchange model, though useful for analyzing certain kinds of dilemmas like the one that faced Nani, seems too limited to fully explain the dynamics of interpersonal relations. Any theory that reduces human behaviour to a formula or mechanistic process must of necessity overlook not only the element of human will and choice, but the human potential inherent in acts of selflessness, generosity, or love.

The Life Cycle of Interpersonal Relationships

Research suggests that relationships, like other human activities, develop through discernible stages: an initiation or **integration** phase, a more or less **stable middle period**, and an ending or **disintegration** phase.[17] Acquaintanceships that depend on context may run through all the stages in a short time: for instance, Jana develops a friendly acquaintance with one of her profs; she visits the woman's office regularly during the term, but when the class ends, so does the acquaintanceship. Allan interacts regularly with the people at work, but when he or they change jobs, this interaction based on context will end. Because acquaintanceships are often created and maintained by the context in which they occur, and they tend to begin and end when, with changes in that context, they may vary somewhat in the extent to which they conform to the pattern.

THE LIFE CYCLE OF INTERPERSONAL RELATIONSHIPS

- An initiation or integration phase
- A stable middle or 'maintenance' phase sometimes lasting for years
- An ending or disintegration phase

By contrast, friendships and intimate relationships that are not dependent on a specific setting more closely exhibit the patterns that researchers have noted. Such relationships, unlike acquaintanceships, create their own context: that is, we actively seek out the company of friends and companions rather than waiting for the context to bring us together. While no two friendships or intimate relationships follow an identical path, each seems to display recognizable characteristics in the three primary stages of initiation, stability or maintenance, and disintegration.

The initiation phase of friendship is one of 'coming together', of discovery and identification. The small talk that marked the early stages of acquaintance gives way to the more personal conversation that signals the beginning of a closer relationship: we no longer limit our comments to facts and observations about the physical context, but instead begin to reveal more about our feelings, beliefs, and thoughts. The initiation stage may be described as a kind of 'honeymoon' phase that may involve heightened emotional intensity and a flurry of activity. Like all beginnings, it is marked by discovery and sharing as we learn more about the other person and disclose more of ourselves.

As the friendship develops, our activities may become more interdependent and intertwined, and we learn more about the daily routine of the other person's life. We exchange invitations into each other's home or private space. Through this sharing of the details of our lives we develop a deeper level of trust and closeness, and we learn to expect and to reciprocate understanding and emotional support. If the friendship develops into intimacy, we may start to depend on each other as good friends do. The initiation phase, then, is period of integration, during which two separate 'I's become a 'we'.

The stabilizing or maintenance period of a relationship begins when each person feels comfortable with the level of interpersonal closeness that has been achieved. There is no formula to determine at what stage of intimacy a relationship will stabilize; some will remain casual friendships, some will turn into close friendships, and some will become more intimate. Relationships, even intense ones, can also last for various lengths of time, from only a few weeks to as long as years, even, perhaps, a lifetime, coming to a close only with the death of one person. It is also possible for a relationship that has stabilized at a level of friendship to move to a more intimate plane, as when long-time friends decide to become romantically involved. Friends who become romantic partners may experience a second initiation phase that signals the beginning of an entirely new and different interpersonal dynamic.

Relationships that are in the stable middle period are distinguished not by the excitement of discovering another person, but by the more comfortable sense of knowing where you stand with each other. This is not to say that such relationships aren't intense or deep; they are frequently both. But they are usually not so prone to emotional highs and lows as relationships in the discovery or initiation phase.

In the maintenance phase, relationships display predictable and often profound levels of trust and genuine pleasure in the other's company. The relationship is likely to be experienced by both participants as satisfying, comfortable, and reliable. They have established a mutually acceptable level of disclosure, trust, and vulnerability. In closer relationships there will be a sense of commitment to the other, and a willingness to make sacrifices to ensure the other's well-being.

Unfortunately, relationships sometimes end, even if we don't intend them to. Even close, intimate relationships may begin to undergo a disintegration that, if not addressed in the early stages, will inevitably lead to their ending. The disintegration, or deterioration, phase of a relationship has its own distinct stages: the beginnings of dissatisfaction, the process of drifting apart, and some kind of distinct, even formal, ending.

The beginning of dissatisfaction is felt when two people who have formerly been close start to become aware of, and perhaps irritated by, small differences between them. They may begin to feel bored or distracted in the other's company, or to become annoyed by little things about their friend or partner that used to pass unnoticed. They may start to focus more on their differences than on their shared interests. This early part of the 'coming apart' process may be marked by arguments and

Photo: Mark Duffy/World of Stock

struggles over issues that would once have been no big deal. The partners are not yet ready to call it quits or end the friendship, but if the deterioration is to be halted, some kind of concerted effort on both sides will be necessary.

Once dissatisfaction has begun to take hold, the partners or friends enter the 'middle period' of relational disintegration: the process of drifting apart. Without some intervention or concerted effort to rejuvenate the flagging relationship, the partners or friends may find that they are no longer able to sustain the same level of involvement in the other's activities or experiences. While they may argue less frequently, there is a growing feeling of resignation as the sense of 'we-ness' that had characterized the relationship during the maintenance period begins to devolve back into a separate sense of 'I-ness' for both members of the relationship.

While they may continue in this form for months or even in some cases years, they will likely find that they are less and less interested in spending time together. Self-disclosure becomes guarded and reveals less and less personal information; it is marked by a withdrawal to relatively low-risk facts and impersonal information. Friends who had been close begin to call less often; eventually they will stop calling altogether. Partners begin to find excuses to avoid each other, and may prefer to spend time together only when others are around. Spouses may start to take separate vacations or to enjoy more and more activities that take them away from their significant other. They may begin to spend more time at work than at home. The partners may not yet be able to formally end the relationship, but they may both become aware that it is stagnating.

Relationships disintegrate for many different reasons. It is fair to say that in all cases, however, some emotional distance has come between the two people. In some cases the distance may also be literal: a friendship fades because one of the friends moves away, and the physical distance makes it difficult to remain involved in each other's daily lives. After three years at college in another city, for instance, Demetrice finds that she no longer fits in so readily with her friends back home. It's hard to explain to them what her life is like now, and she has a whole new circle of friends that they don't know.

Sometimes the distance is simply one of context; Betsy and Tacy, for example, have been inseparable since childhood, and their friendship continued right through to high school graduation. They both got jobs after high school, Betsy in an insurance office and Tacy at the local department store, and they remained as close as ever. After two years, however, Tacy left her department store job and went to university. The two women still get together once a month for supper, but they find that they have less and less in common. Five years out of high school, married with two kids of her own, Betsy just can't identify with Tacy's talk about classes and teachers and studying. It seems incredible to her that, at 24 years old, her friend is still engaged in what, from Betsy's point of view, is a childhood pursuit.

Tacy finds it just as difficult to identify with Betsy's worries over toilet training and teething, or to tolerate the pettiness that seems to dominate office politics in the small insurance agency where Betsy still works. The two women aren't ready yet to abandon the friendship they've had since childhood, but it is no longer the same. Unless they can establish a footing that includes more than nostalgia for a shared past, a day may come when they will give up even these monthly suppers.

The distance that can develop in a relationship can also be the product of new interests, a new job, or a new circle of friends from which the partner feels excluded. Distance can be the result of some significant life event, such as a religious conversion; of a death in the family; or of an achievement that changes the direction of a person's life. Consider Phyllis and Vlad, who met and married while in university. Phyllis was working on an MA in psychology and Vlad, already a successful electrical contractor, had returned to school to study engineering. They graduated together, Phyllis with her MA and Vlad with his BEng; then Phyllis decided to continue on to the Ph.D.

Now that Phyllis has graduated and secured a faculty position at the university, Vlad suddenly finds himself resenting the unanticipated demands of her academic career. Like many people, he had expected that being a professor would be a pretty easy ride, what with the four months he imagined she would have off every summer. All through Phyllis's post-graduate grind he had sustained himself with dreams of the leisurely vacations they would take when she had completed her degree.

However, instead of being free during the summers, Phyllis is even busier than she is during the school year. And far from having the whole summer off, most of the time she doesn't even have time to take her allotted holidays. Vlad had not understood or anticipated the amount of time Phyllis would have to devote to research, writing, and conferences during the summers, when he had imagined she would have hardly any work to do. His dreams of enjoying some free time together have had to be put on hold.

If that's not bad enough, Vlad finds many of Phyllis's faculty colleagues insufferably pompous, especially when they talk down to him because he has only an undergraduate degree. Such condescension infuriates Vlad, whose contracting firm has become so successful that he could buy and sell them all twice over if he wanted to.

It's clear that a distance has come between Phyllis and Vlad, but in this case it has nothing to do with geography. What threatens to estrange them from each other is the profound change in Phyllis's circumstances. Such changes don't have to spell the end of a relationship, but unless Phyllis and Vlad can manage to stay connected and continue to share their experiences and feelings, it is likely they will start to drift apart emotionally. It's not distance by itself that compromises intimacy and brings a relationship to an end; it's the lack of meaningful contact and the withdrawal of willing disclosure that precipitates the breakdown.

The final step in the deterioration phase is the actual ending of the relationship, which may be accomplished by a simple cessation of contact, by a final argument, or by a formal process of some kind. For instance, once Vicki moved to England, she and Michael, who have been long-distance friends for years, gradually stopped talking on the phone and finally ceased sending even the yearly greetings they used to exchange on each other's birthday.

Similarly, Nancy and Margaret move to different cities, but continue to visit as often as they can. A day comes when Margaret notices that she has been doing most of the visiting; she begins to resent it, but doesn't break things off. For her part, Nancy has begun to begrudge the expense of continuing to exchange gifts for holidays and birthdays, but she doesn't move to stop the practice. Then, during one of their increasingly rare phone conversations, the two have an argument that leaves both with ill feelings. In the past they would have worked out their misunderstandings for the sake of their friendship, but this time they just leave things unresolved. Over a year has gone by, and neither of them has called the other since that last heated exchange.

Although it may end with an argument like Nancy and Margaret's friendship did, the ending of a relationship may instead be marked by some sort of declaration or formal process: Zoster and Denise decide to break up, and they formalize their decision by returning the tokens that each has given the other: a special ring, a medallion. Chris and Mark obtain a separation agreement, followed by a formal divorce. Artie and Paul sever their musical partnership and their friendship by means of a formal contractual dissolution. In all these cases, the partners are simply making official what they have both known for some time: that their relationship has been coming to an end.

Summary

Although a knowledge of theory by itself will not guarantee improvement in our interpersonal communication, it can provide a foundation for greater understanding, which is the first step towards more effective judgement and practice. This chapter has presented several theoretical models intended to help us understand the nature and rhythm of relationships, and the motivations that influence our interpersonal communication behaviour.

We began by defining interpersonal communication as an emotional association or involvement between two people that extends over several encounters. These associations can remain as acquaintanceships, or can develop into friendships, which may in turn evolve into close or intimate relationships. All interpersonal relationships involve contact and disclosure, but acquaintanceships are relatively low-risk encounters in which we exchange primarily factual information. Acquaintanceships typically depend on context; they begin and continue primarily because we are brought together through work, community involvement, or group memberships, and they generally end when those contexts change.

Friendships and intimate relationships, however, are different from acquaintanceships in both the quantity and the quality of our interaction. First, our contact increases in quantity: we actively seek out the other person's company and willingly choose to spend a greater portion of our discretionary time with the person. Second, the quality of our contact increases as we choose to disclose not only factual information but also more private opinions and thoughts, and finally—if the relationship progresses to a level of intimacy—our personal feelings. As a relationship becomes

more intimate, we can expect greater levels of self-revelation and deeper levels of trust; the increased intimacy of friendship also poses both greater interpersonal risk and greater opportunities for emotional support and fulfillment.

Theorists have offered a variety of models to explain what motivates us to seek out interpersonal relationships. Three of the four models we considered confirm that our interpersonal interaction fulfills fundamental human needs. Abraham Maslow's hierarchy of needs was intended to explain not only our interpersonal motivation but the reasons for all human behaviour. Maslow's theory locates human motivation in five essential levels of human necessity: securing basic physiological survival; maintaining safety and security; establishing social connectedness; obtaining ego satisfaction and self-respect; and finally, realizing our fullest human potential through self-actualization. Because our immediate physical survival depends on fulfilling the first two levels of need, which Maslow called 'deprivation' needs, he theorized that they must be fully met before an individual experiences the pressure of the psychological and interpersonal needs that occupy the remaining levels of his hierarchy.

Like Maslow's hierarchy of needs, William Schutz's interpersonal needs theory makes human motivation a function of what Schutz considers to be fundamental human needs. Focusing on the reasons for our interpersonal interactions, Schutz argues that our relationships are shaped by our need for affection, inclusion, and control. He explains that each individual's unique pattern of needs is established early in life, and is so strong as to be a reliable indicator of the person's future behaviour. Finally, the psychiatrist Murray Banks popularized the concept of interpersonal needs as motivation with his theory of the 'four basic wants': I want to live, I want someone to love me, I want a feeling of importance, I want a little variety. His treatment confirms the importance of love and belonging to human experience.

As a departure from the needs paradigm, John Thibaut and Harold Kelley's social exchange theory posits that human interaction is analogous to an economic transaction in which we incur costs in order to obtain desired benefits. However, the economic metaphor that provides the foundation of social exchange theory has been criticized as reductionist, since it seems to assume that human beings function much like computers, processing incoming information and calculating an appropriate solution. Such a simplification not only overlooks the element of human choice, but is inadequate to account for the generosity and self-sacrifice of which humans are also capable.

Whatever our motivation for engaging in them, interpersonal relationships are dynamic processes rather than static entities, and like other human activities, they go through discernible stages of development. Although every relationship is unique in its specific pacing, the general pattern of integration–stability–disintegration appears to be consistent across the spectrum of human interaction. For all relationships, the integration phase is marked by a process of 'coming together', during which two separate 'I's become a 'we'. It is a process of discovery and affirmation, and may be highly emotionally charged.

Eventually the excitement of the integration phase is replaced by the comfort and security of the stable middle phase. Relationships in this phase display predictable levels of disclosure, trust, and vulnerability; they involve genuine pleasure in the other's company. In this phase, the relationship is likely to be experienced by both participants as satisfying, comfortable, and reliable. The middle phase can last from a few weeks to months, years, even a lifetime.

Finally, a disintegration stage may develop, beginning with a growing sense of dissatisfaction that leads to a gradual drifting apart and eventually to a severing of the connection between people. The sense of 'we-ness' established during the integration phase and maintained through the stable maintenance period begins to devolve back into a separate sense of 'I-ness' for both members of the relationship. The relationship may simply be allowed to drift towards an end, or it may be terminated with some kind of formal gesture: a final argument, a return of gifts, a separation and divorce. For some, it may end with the death of the other person.

Interpersonal communication, like all human communication, is conditioned and influenced by a variety of factors that may not always be evident to those who are communicating. The theoretical insights of this chapter are intended to provide a foundation for the remainder of our discussion of interpersonal communication behaviour.

Key Terms

acquaintanceship	friendship	interpersonal relationships
basic wants model	growth needs	peak experiences
close friendship	hierarchy of needs theory	self-actualization
deficit needs	integration	social exchange theory
disintegration	interpersonal needs theory	stable middle period

Suggested Readings

Murray Banks, *How To Live With Yourself . . . Or, What to Do Until the Psychiatrist Comes*, sound recording (New York: Murmil Records, 1960). A good place to begin, if you can find a copy of this record, is to listen to Banks's entertaining discussion of his 'four basic wants'. Though some of the humour is dated, the principles Banks articulates are still relevant today.

Stephen Duck and Robin Gilmour, *Studying Personal Relationships* (New York: Academic Press, 1981). Duck is one of the foremost theorists of interpersonal relationships, and this readable text explores more fully the ideas presented in this chapter.

Matthew Kelly, *The Seven Levels of Intimacy: The Art of Loving and the Joy of Being Loved*

(New York: Simon & Schuster, 2005). Kelly's is a popular treatment of the 'levels' of relational intimacy, moving from the exchange of clichés, facts, and opinions through the revelation of hopes and feelings, to the disclosure of faults and 'legitimate' needs.

Sarah Trenholm, *Human Communication Theory*, 2nd edn (Englewood Cliffs, NJ: Prentice-Hall, 1991). Trenholm's book is a survey of social scientific theories of communication, including interpersonal theories and models. Intended as a textbook for senior undergraduates, it is easily readable by the average layperson.

Exercises and Assignments

1. In Chapter 1 we learned to distinguish between 'pragmatic' communication and 'symbolic' communication. We also learned, as Axiom #9 points out, that 'you cannot not communicate.' With these points in mind, what relationship appears to exist between the 'needs' theories advanced by Maslow, Schutz, and Banks and the functions of communication discussed in Chapter 1? Present your analysis in writing or as part of a class discussion, as directed by your instructor.

2. This chapter presented some theoretical models for understanding human motivation. With this in mind, take another look at the brief case studies of Martine, Victor, Lena, and Dr Krabb, provided as part of assignment #6 in Chapter 1. Do any of these theories of interpersonal communication help us to understand these four people? Have these theories in any way changed your views of the people in the case studies? Present your analysis in writing or as part of a class discussion, as directed by your instructor.

3. Songs and poems often deal with interpersonal relationships, especially love and loss, relational disintegration, longing for identification, and so forth. Paul Simon's 'The Dangling Conversation' (see Appendix B) dramatizes a relationship that appears to be in the late stages of coming apart. Drawing on what we have so far learned about interpersonal communication, and in particular in this chapter on the life cycle of relationships, analyze the state of the relationship revealed in Simon's song, using the following questions as a guide. Your instructor may ask you to present your findings in written form or in class discussion.

   a. These lyrics give us a kind of snapshot of two people whose relationship, apparently, is not what it once was. What kind of relationship was it? What is it like now? How do you know?

   b. What kind of mood seems to prevail in this dramatization? What is the speaker's tone? Does it change over the course of the story? What has happened, or is happening, to the relationship?

c. What do you think is the significance of the time of day? Why is the conversation described as 'dangling'? Would that also be an appropriate description of the relationship itself? Why do you think the speaker calls the person spoken to a 'stranger'?

d. Do you think the speaker has actually spoken his thoughts aloud to the other person? Why or why not?

4. Discuss the communication process as it is dramatized in Robinson's 'Richard Cory' (Appendix B), focusing on any of the concepts discussed in the course so far. Those that suggest themselves include the building of the self-concept; the gap between the private self and the public image; the differences between how we perceive ourselves and how others see us; the need for affection and inclusion; and the influence of the perceptual process of selection/classification/interpretation. Your instructor may ask you to present your findings in written form or in class discussion. Here are some questions to guide your analysis:

a. The case study describes Richard Cory's public image, rather than his private self-concept. What kind of public image does he display? How do 'we people on the pavement' view him? Do you think that we still 'wish that we were in his place'?

b. We are not told very much about Richard Cory's private self-image, though we can guess at it from his actions. Why do you suppose Robinson chose not to make it explicit? Do you think Richard Cory could have made it explicit?

c. Kenneth Burke suggests that any deliberate action—including violence—is a form of communication. If he is correct, what might Richard Cory be communicating through his suicide? Who do you think is his intended audience?

5. Turn again to the Personal Icons created by the class as directed in Chapter 3. Do any of these theories of interpersonal communication help to explain the choices you made as you constructed your Icon? Do they provide any insight or assistance in understanding the Icons of others? Have these theories in any way changed your views of the Icons? Is there any danger in approaching others' self-presentation using theories like these? Present your analysis in writing or as part of class discussion, as directed by your instructor.

Chapter 5

Verbal Communication

Learning Objectives

- To understand language as both a system of symbols and a rule-governed activity.
- To understand the power of abstraction.
- To understand the relationship between language, perception, and meaning.
- To learn the characteristics and uses of language.
- To learn ways to improve verbal skill.

A child sits on the bed with a book in her lap. A breeze wafts the curtains in the open window behind her, through which can be heard distant neighbourhood sounds. It is a summer day, and the child is about eight years old. She picks up a pen and begins to write on the front flyleaf of the book. 'Elaine Reid', she writes. Then: '57 Rigby Road', followed by 'Sydney' and 'Cape Breton Island'. She adds 'Nova Scotia'. Still not satisfied, she writes in quick succession 'Canada, North America, Northern Hemisphere, Planet Earth, the Milky Way, the Universe'.

Does this picture have a ring of familiarity? Certainly it has been replayed by millions of children, and replicated many times in stories and films. But maybe it is familiar for another reason: chances are, except for the details, it could be an episode from your own childhood. Elaine's action is a nearly universal human experience, because the act of placing the self in connection to the rest of existence is one of the functions of language.

Language—the medium of verbal communication—is the subject of this chapter. The term 'verbal communication' in fact refers to communication that is carried out through language; hence, it includes writing and sign language as well as speech.[1]

Although written language has been with us for about 6,000 years, no one knows with certainty how old spoken language is, or exactly how it originated. The question has intrigued thinkers for many thousands of years, because language is a complex kind of behaviour that, as far as we know, is unique to humans. Animals can and do communicate, sometimes in quite sophisticated ways, but although recent studies suggest that their communication may be more complex than we have previously understood, the specific features that set human language apart do not seem to be true of animal communication. The uniquely human ability to think abstractly and to communicate in symbols remains central to most of our understanding of human culture, including religion, philosophy, psychology, and politics.

When measured by numbers of native speakers, the English language is the third most common in the world (Mandarin Chinese is the native language for the largest segment of the world's population and Spanish is second). However, in geographic distribution, English is far more widespread than all other spoken languages. It is understood or spoken, at least to some degree, by between 25 and 35 per cent of the world's population, and is an official language in some 52 countries. English is also the dominant language in mass communication: about 75 per cent of the world's mail, telexes, and cables, 60 per cent of the world's radio programs, and 90 per cent of all Internet traffic are conducted in English. As a result, English is now the most useful language to learn for international travel, and has become the de facto language of diplomacy. In fact, when asked in 2001 what language should be used for communication with foreign embassies, more than 120 of the 189 member countries of the United Nations chose English.[2]

No matter what language, or languages, we speak, its role in our lives is the same. Language provides most of our knowledge of the world we live in; although we often think otherwise, relatively little of what we know comes through our own direct observation or experience. Instead, we obtain most of our understanding of ourselves, nature, culture, and human experience through the words of others. Even what we directly observe for ourselves is structured and organized for us by our language.

Language can be characterized in several ways. It is a symbolic process; it is a complex activity; it is both arbitrary and highly conventional; it operates according to systematic rules; it is the medium of thought, understanding, and identity. This chapter is concerned with exploring these ideas in greater detail.

Language as a System of Symbols

First, and most important, language is a system of symbols. In order to understand what this means and how important it is to human beings, we need to begin with an understanding of what a symbol is. A **symbol** is any object or item that can be used to stand for some meaning beyond itself: roses and chocolates symbolize love and affection, a policeman's badge represents his legal authority, the Canadian flag stands for Canada, an engagement ring signals betrothal, or a brand new sports car suggests prestige. Symbols like these have been used so often that their meanings have become conventionalized and are widely understood by all of us. Other symbolic meanings hold true only in specific circumstances or for a small group of people. For example, a memento from childhood may mean something special to you and your best friend, but have no special meaning for anyone else. If you have made the Personal Icon as directed in Chapter 3, you probably made use of such private symbols.

Symbols are said to be arbitrary. What this means is that the association between the symbol and the meaning it stands for is something we assign; there is no connection in nature that dictates that a symbol must point to a specific referent. And because there is no necessary connection between the symbol and the meaning it stands for, literally anything in our environment can be made to stand for any meaning that we wish it to have. This capacity for endless substitution and flexibility is the real beauty of symbolism.

The flexibility of symbolizing is easy to demonstrate. You can test it for yourself and have likely taken advantage of it in the past, as Brenda and Roxanne have recently done. Dan, who works in their office, is friendly and co-operative, but he is also a gossipy time-waster who is hard to discourage. The two friends have discovered that a ringing telephone is the one thing that will cause Dan to stop talking and withdraw, so they have arranged to 'rescue' each other if either sees Dan venture into the other's cubicle. Anytime you and a friend agree that a certain word or object or sign will have special meaning shared by the two of you, you are taking advantage of the symbolic capacities of language.

Humans are symbol-users by their nature, and symbolic meanings permeate human life at all levels. In fact, for many philosophers and communication theorists, it is this ability to use symbols—indeed, the compulsion to do so—that actually defines what a human being is. Certainly symbolic meanings are inescapable in our experience, so much so that nearly everything in our surroundings, even mechanical or biological things, accrues symbolic significance for us: consider the meanings associated with the house you live in, the furniture you choose, the car you drive, the brands of clothing you wear. What kinds of symbolic value, for example, do things like suntans, hairstyles, tattoos, or certain kinds of food have for you?[3]

Symbols are so important to us, in fact, that in some cases the symbol has come to be more important than the meaning it originally stood for. In nearly all cultures, the symbols of civic virtue, patriotism, erudition, piety, and affluence come to be more valued than the realities they stand for. For example, people will go deeply into debt in order to impress the neighbours with a show of wealth, will put on a show of moral superiority by going to church regularly even when their actions are corrupt, or will pronounce on civic duty even when their businesses are destroying the local water supply. Consider your own circle of acquaintances: how many do you know who value the degree or diploma they hope to receive more than they value the learning that it supposedly represents? Can you think of other status symbols that matter more to people than the achievement they are meant to stand for?

The sounds that make up our language are also symbols—that is, they stand for something more than themselves. Take the sound 'cat'. Make the sound, out loud or merely in your head. The sound you have made, and the animal that the sound stands for, have no necessary relationship. There is no logical or natural reason that this sound and that animal should be paired in your mind. That is, any sound *could* have been made to stand for the animal that we know as a cat.

In this sense, the association between words and their meaning—like that of other symbols—is said to be arbitrary. We could, if we wanted to, select some other sound combination to represent the animal, or we could assign some other meaning to the sound 'cat'. However, there are some complications associated with doing so, since the point of a language system is that it enables us to communicate with clarity and exactness to other speakers.

For this reason, although the association between a word and its meaning is arbitrary in the sense just described, individual speakers of a given language experience it as mostly stable and fixed: the sound-meanings of the language into which we are born are not invented by us; we learn both words and syntax from the adults around us, and it is mastering this symbol system that enables us ultimately to share in human culture and history. That is, although presumably any sound could have been selected to mean 'cat', I am not free, as a speaker of English, to choose my own combination of sounds to represent that animal. I must, if I wish to be understood by others, conform to the accepted practices of the language community.

Thus, while language is arbitrary in the way that all symbolic relationships are arbitrary, it is also highly conventional, which is to say that there is widespread and long-standing agreement among a community of users about what sounds and sound combinations will stand for what meanings. Because there is a multiplicity of these correspondences, we say that language is a *system* of symbols, which contains both a set of parts (the vocabulary of the language) and a set of rules for putting those parts together into meaningful units (the syntax of a language).

To say that language is conventional and that most users experience it as more or less fixed is not to say that word meanings do not shift over time; clearly they do. Language is influenced by its users, in both intentional and accidental ways. Every language can create new words to describe new situations and objects, and as a result no language is static. They all evolve over time in response to new social, cultural, and environmental situations.

New words and expressions come into the language to name new concepts, particularly in the areas of technology and political correctness (for example, 'nanotechnology', 'Internet', and 'google', or 'caregiver', 'parenting', 'letter carrier', and 'firefighter'); old words may fall into disuse (for instance, 'thee', 'kine', 'quoth' or 'mailman', 'policeman', 'fireman'). The words may be coined deliberately or imported from other languages; English in particular has benefited from extensive borrowing, which helps to explain the large number of words in its lexicon. Slang creates new usages, most of which are short-lived (consider 'hepcat', 'groovy', 'far out'), and formerly neutral words can be appropriated for more specific, sometimes political meanings (such as 'gay'). Such shifts in meaning are usually gradual and not generally the result of a single user deciding, for example, that 'cat' will suddenly mean something other than the animal it now signifies.

All natural languages—and computer languages, too—involve systematic structures of vocabulary and syntax, so there is no such thing as a 'primitive' language. Human languages, of which there are thought to be some 5,000, vary greatly in their grammatical and syntactic organization, but all involve sophisticated systems of sounds, words, and sentences that are effectively adapted to communicating the culture in which they arose. Interestingly, there is no apparent correlation between a culture's grammatical complexity and its technological sophistication.

However, cultures with complex economic structures and advanced levels of technology do tend to have larger vocabularies. For example, the English language has an enormous vocabulary of technical words, estimated at about 1.4 million and growing. Non-technical English words number around 600,000, for a total vocabulary of approximately two million words. This is a relatively large number (compare the estimates for German—about 185,000 non-technical words; French—perhaps 100,000 non-technical words; and Spanish, with fewer even than this). The available vocabulary in English is much larger because it has borrowed freely from more than 240 other languages, including French, Hebrew, Italian, Celtic, Norse, and several Native North American languages.

Estimating the number of words in a language is notoriously difficult, in part because it's hard to know how to count them. For instance, should a word be counted twice if it is used as a noun and again as a verb, as in 'I always address my professors as "Dr"' and 'I had to provide the delivery driver with my address'? Should each of the meanings for a single word listed in a reliable dictionary be counted separately, as in 'The sun set early tonight', or 'I have a set of books on language'? Should a word be counted separately for each of its inflections, as in 'I regularly walk to the store', but 'Yesterday I walked more slowly than usual'? Calculating the size of the average vocabulary is even trickier, and estimates of the average English-speaking North American's vocabulary vary widely, from a high of between 40,000 to 50,000 words (including both technical and non-technical vocabulary) to a low of around 1,000 words (non-technical vocabulary only). What is certain, however, is that few speakers of English have command of more than a fraction of the available vocabulary in English: even a high estimate of 40,000 represents only about 2 per cent of all the words in the language.

Interestingly, some nations have strongly resisted the acquisition of new words from other languages. France is one such country, with a tradition of resistance to the influx of words from other languages, especially in recent years with the intrusion of English words in the areas of popular culture and technology. However, whatever their governments' attempts to retain 'linguistic purity', young people in most developed nations tend to embrace new words readily.

When we speak of language change, we are more often speaking of alterations in vocabulary rather than changes in the syntactical or grammatical structures of the language. All linguistic evolution is gradual, but changes in vocabulary happen much more quickly and readily than changes in the rules that govern sentence construction and grammatical function. The syntax of a language, as a set of rules, is typically more systematic and less arbitrary than the words, and thus less subject to change.

Language Is an Activity

In addition to being a system of symbols, language is an activity in which we participate. In this respect it is similar to music. Like language, music in some sense exists separately from us as a system of harmonics, or in compositions and scores, but it doesn't become music as we usually think of the term until someone plays an instrument or sings. In the same way, language exists as a conventionalized symbolic system, but it also exists in the performance of its speakers.

As an activity, language use follows game-like rules. As in any game, there are two kinds or levels of rules: **constitutive rules** that determine which game is being played, and **regulative rules** that let you know if you're playing the game correctly or incorrectly. To understand the difference, consider an arena where a group of people in costume are skating on an iced surface. They are holding long, slightly curved sticks with which they are chasing after and hitting a small rubber disk. How do you know this game is hockey, and not football, soccer, or chess? The rules and conventions of costume, equipment, and permissible actions are what make the game hockey rather than something else. If someone came onto the ice wearing cleats or carrying a tennis racket, we would be likely to say, 'I don't know what game he's playing, but it's not hockey.' Rules that define for us what the game is are called 'constitutive' because they constitute, or define, the activity. In the same way that we can tell hockey from football or chess, we can tell English from other languages such as French, Arabic, Cree, or Mandarin.

Once we have determined what game is being played, we find another layer of rules that tell us how *well* the game is being played. In hockey, rules against icing, high-sticking, and roughing are all regulative rules; although these actions are technically forbidden, players who perform them are still recognizably playing hockey. Regulative rules also determine the difference between defence and offence, and tell us what actions can and can't be undertaken by the goalie. In general, a breach of constitutive rules is more serious than a breach of regulative rules, because it can cause the whole game to break down. Because regulative rules govern how the game is progressing rather than define what game is taking place, breaches are less serious.

As in any game, the choices a speaker can make in using language are limited by the structure of that language: you play by the rules that are in place when you join the game. 'I seen John at the store last night,' or 'I have went to the movies every weekend this month' are breaches of the regulative rules of English; they sound unlearned, but they are still understandable. But when many such breaches combine to produce a construction such as 'Very often the negative side of this equation is compounded when writing is not accompanied by action is the only action taken' or 'This failed employer/employee relationship is often due to a misconstrued advocate of one position or stance on either the part of the employer or the employee', communication may break down completely.

The Power of Abstraction

Language enables us to accomplish some extraordinary feats that we are fairly certain animals cannot perform. The most important of these is the ability to think abstractly. The symbolic nature of language enables us to detach our understanding of a thing from the thing itself, and manipulate that meaning on its own. In other words, we can talk about 'cats' and imagine a quality of 'catness' even if there are no cats in the room.

There is no evidence that animals can do this. A cat, for instance, may make a particular vocal sound—a sort of gagging cackle—when it sees a bird. This sound is familiar to every cat owner, and when you hear it you can be sure that your cat has its eyes on a bird. It is not clear whether this sound is a reaction only, or if it is meant to signify to other nearby cats that a bird is present. What is certain, however, is that cats do not make this sound when no birds are to be seen. There is no evidence that they have a conception of 'birdness' that can be considered separately from real birds, or that can be called to mind when no bird is in sight. Researchers who study animal communication have discovered some fairly sophisticated systems of signs, but have not yet found animals with the ability to abstract.

THE BENEFITS OF ABSTRACTION

- We can talk about things when they are not present.
- We can isolate qualities from objects that display them ('two-ness' or 'yellow').
- We can conceptualize abstract ideas such as 'peace' or 'patriotism' or 'loyalty'.
- We can study ourselves and our communication.

There are four important implications of the unique human ability of **abstraction**. First, unlike cats and other animals, we are able to think and talk about things that are not immediately present. For instance, the planet Mercury is not in the room, but we can refer to it and discuss its features. We can talk meaningfully about a vast range of objects and creatures, and we do not need to bring them into the room to bring them to mind: planets, cats, motor cars, bridges, microbes, books, movies, food, friends—all of these can be discussed even when they aren't here with us. This gives us enormous scope for learning and for understanding. To take one example, we can develop an understanding of a buffalo hunt such as might have taken place at Head-Smashed-In Buffalo Jump in southern Alberta prior to 1900, even though many of us may never have seen a buffalo, or may never have heard of such a method of hunting before, or may not have seen the prairie landscape in which it took place. We need not actually have experienced these things directly in order to conceptualize them or develop an understanding of them.

The second benefit of the ability to abstract is that it allows us to isolate qualities independent of the objects associated with them. That is, we can conceptualize a quality of 'two-ness' and work with it without needing to have two objects in front of us; we can think and talk about 'green' or 'yellow' even if we aren't currently looking at anything green or yellow. We can conceive of any number of qualities—tallness, attractiveness, shyness, and so on—without having to see examples of tall, attractive, or shy people right in front of us every time we talk about them. This capacity, taken so much for granted by us in ordinary daily life, is really quite remarkable, and it is what has allowed us to develop some of our more arcane fields of knowledge, such as mathematics, physics, philosophy, harmonics, and so on. In fact, humans would not have been able to develop any theoretical understanding in any field, or establish any general principles in any area of knowledge, without abstraction. Even basic arithmetic would be beyond us.

The third product of abstraction is that we can speak about qualities or ideas that have no correspondence to any concrete object: we can conceive of peace, order, and good government; we can talk about love, or politics, or patriotism, or friendship, or humour. We can recognize and prize honour, honesty, integrity, courage, and self-discipline. We can think and talk about ethics, values, and morals. These and other abstractions don't 'exist' in any concrete sense, because they are behavioural or relational or political processes or practices, but they are nevertheless very powerful forces in our experience. They can move us and provoke us to action, and they can shape a nation or a culture. Nevertheless, they exist primarily as conceptions available to us by our ability to abstract through language.

Finally, the capacity to abstract enables us to turn ourselves and our communication (including language itself) into an object of study. When we study the 'self' and when we study our communication, we necessarily use language as the medium of study. In this sense, the study of ourselves is the study of our language: we exist mainly in what, and how, we speak. The ability to abstract—a quality unique to symbolic systems—is what enables us to use language reflexively to study itself and its uses.

Language enables us to conceptualize in all fields of knowledge, but perhaps its most remarkable quality is its application to the study of itself: we use language to study how we use language, and when we study how we use language, we are in fact involved in the study of our own nature as human beings.

Language and Perception

In addition to its other features, language is interrelated with the process of **perception**. We know already that perception takes place in three stages—selection, classification, and interpretation. Our language plays a role in at least two of these stages, if not in all of them. The way we name the things or people or events that we perceive is the first step in classifying them. It is known that the simple act of naming by itself can have a powerful persuasive impact,[4] and that naming can deliberately be used to sway a hearer's opinions for good or ill.[5] When we name something, we automatically assign it a value and a place in the order of things. In other words, the mere act of labelling something is a means of classifying it.

Interpretation of the meaning of something, which is the step that follows naming, is already largely decided by the classification we assigned when we named it. This is especially important when we are dealing with people, and has implications for our interpersonal communication. For example, what view of Nancy do you have if she is described as a new mom? Would your interpretation change if she were introduced instead as a fully qualified dentist (DMD)? As a middle-aged woman? How do you think of Sheena if she is introduced as a professional dressmaker? Would your view change if she were instead described as a computer programmer? As a new homeowner? As it happens, each of these 'namings' is accurate, but each is incomplete, focusing on only a limited view of the complex human beings known as Nancy and Sheena. Each name that we assign to some phenomenon or some person is necessarily incomplete in this way.

Kenneth Burke explains how this process works in an essay called 'Terministic Screens'.[6] According to Burke, the names we give to things when we try to accurately represent reality act as a kind of screen, or filter, for meaning. First, the words we use are a partial *reflection* of reality—for example, Nancy really is a new mom, and Sheena really is a dressmaker. However, though these words do reflect reality, they are *selective*: in this case, only one feature of Nancy's or Sheena's experience is highlighted by our introduction. Finally, Burke emphasizes that the words we use also *deflect* or de-emphasize other aspects of the same reality. Thus, Sheena's computer programming or Nancy's DMD training are left out of our initial description.

Recall from Chapter 1 how, when we first encounter someone, we tend to infer entire personalities based on a single trait. If we had done so based on our initial introduction to Nancy and Sheena, do you think that our inference of their personalities would have included even the possibility of the dental or computer expertise? What misunderstandings might have been produced by these inferences? Try this exercise for yourself with some of the people you know. You will quickly see that the same phenomenon can take on a different meaning depending on how we name it.

Try another example. Imagine that, as you walk across campus one day, you spot a man dressed in a shabby overcoat rooting through a garbage barrel. What inference do you make about what you see? Would you assume you are seeing a homeless person? An actor in the current production of a college play? A professor who has accidentally dropped his keys in the bin and now is trying to retrieve them? A detective investigating a crime? What you see is the same, but your understanding of the event changes with each label you apply. So it is that how we understand what we see is shaped in large part by the language we use to name it.

To see how naming can colour our interpretations, consider the following lists of terms, compiled by the *Manchester Guardian* regarding press coverage of the 1991 war in Iraq:

> The press said that British forces launched 'first strikes, pre-emptively.' In contrast, they said Iraqi forces 'launched sneak missile attacks, without provocation.' British soldiers were described by the press as 'cautious, loyal, resolute, brave, Young Knights of the Sky'; whereas Iraqi soldiers were 'cowardly, blindly obedient, ruthless, fanatical, Bastards of Baghdad.'[7]

Identical actions and behaviour sound dramatically different depending on how they are named, and the naming is a function of the writer's attitude towards them rather than the actions themselves.

Language and Meaning

The relationship between word and thing is said to be arbitrary, but this relationship is not the only 'big question' in the study of language as a system. Also particularly fascinating is the relationship between word and thought.

Many theorists have debated whether thought, as a mental activity separate from feeling, reacting, or visualization, can even exist independently of the language in which it is expressed.[8] Most argue that it cannot, since it is impossible to separate thought and language; you can't get 'outside' of thought to consider language separately, and you can't get outside of language to some kind of 'pure' thought. Language is not only necessary for the formulation of thought, but is itself part of the thinking process. Thinking is always *about* something, usually something recalled from past experience, and that experience has been classified or organized for us by our language.

The process of thinking consists of making statements or propositions, which depend in turn on language. Without language, we would have mental processes of some kind, but they could not properly be called thought in the sense that we usually use the term. The most primitive act of thought is to distinguish an object from the blur of experience that surrounds it. As we learn language, the words we apply to sensory experiences become part of our understanding of them, and it is difficult or even impossible for us to separate the word from the concept it stands for.

The language we use defines how we think about the world we live in, just as the press coverage reported by the *Guardian* helped shape the public's view of the war. In other words, we experience the world in the terms that are set down by the structure of our language, which segments reality in ways that aren't necessarily required by reality itself. This assertion, known as the **Sapir-Whorf hypothesis**, is named for the linguists Edward Sapir and Benjamin Lee Whorf. As Sapir famously wrote in 1929:

> Human beings do not live in the objective world alone, nor alone in the world of social activity as ordinarily understood, but are very much at the mercy of the particular language which has become the medium of expression for their society. It is quite an illusion to imagine that one adjusts to reality essentially without the use of language and that language is merely an incidental means of solving specific problems of communication and reflection. The fact of the matter is that the 'real world' is to a large extent unconsciously built up on the language habits of the group.[9]

Whorf added that 'We dissect nature along lines laid down by our native languages. . . . We cut nature up, organize it into concepts, and ascribe significances as we do, largely because we are parties to an agreement to organize it in this way—an agreement that holds throughout our speech community and is codified in the patterns of our language.'[10] In English, experience is categorized into things and actions (nouns and verbs): wind blows, light flashes, snow falls. It is hard for an English speaker to imagine a world of experience where this is not so, where instead of saying 'I am eating my food', we might say instead 'With regard to the food unto me, there is an occasion of eating.'[11] In such a construction things happen, but there are no agents who act. If we could speak, and thus think, in only this manner, how different would our understanding of the world be?

That our language shapes our thinking and our understanding of external reality is no longer contested by semanticists, philosophers, and other theorists of language. But what is interesting to us as students of interpersonal communication is how it shapes our relationships and ourselves. The ability to use language is part of what defines the human being; it is also part of what makes each individual unique.

Characteristics of Language

There is no human society without some form of language; thus, linguists refer to language as both 'species universal'—meaning all humans participate in some speech community—and 'species specific'—meaning that language is an exclusively human phenomenon. Language is a system of sound-meanings producible and receivable by some single group of organisms. Thus, the communication that takes place, for example, between a rider and a horse is not 'language' in the sense that linguists use the term.

The first characteristic of human language is that it is learned rather than innate. However, human beings are actually *designed* to acquire speech: while language itself is not innate, the mental structures needed to learn it are, and the physical apparatus needed to produce speech sounds are present in every human being. However, though humans have an innate ability to produce some form of speech, each of us learns the particular language, accent, and speech patterns of our culture and our family.

A second important characteristic of human languages is that they all originate in sound.[12] Although we are both genetically programmed and physically equipped for speech, we do not have the same physical imperative to learn reading and writing. For this reason, although it has developed its own conventions and practices, writing is considered by linguists to be secondary to speech, or an 'overlaid function'.

Some people think of writing as a simple substitution for speech. However, although there would be no writing without speech, it's not simply a 'mummified' version of speech. The technology of writing likely was initially an attempt to represent speech in some permanent, portable way, but the two are now independent systems that run more or less parallel. Writing has developed conventions of its own and communicates in a manner of its own, sometimes making distinctions that cannot be discerned in speech. For example, 'my sister's friend's investments', 'my sister's friends' investments,' and 'my sisters' friends' investments' sound identical in speech but appear as clearly distinct in writing. As a result, we can sometimes use writing to clarify what has been spoken.

In other cases, we may use speech to clarify what has been written. For example, the first time you see the words 'pinochle' or 'picturesque' or 'Worcestershire' in writing, you may not recognize them as the words you've been pronouncing as 'pea-knuckle', 'picture-esk', or 'Wurster'. Sign languages, too, have developed their own independent conventions, so much so that signing is now considered by some to be a richer system of communication than writing, since it takes place in six dimensions: in sign language, separate meaning is created by the positioning, location, and movement of each of the right and left hands.

Despite the ways in which our experience seems dominated by visual stimuli, the presence of sound and speech is in some ways more fundamental to human experience. It is through sound that language first comes to you, and it is through language that you become a member of a human community.[13] Finally, you can't shut off sound the way you can shut out vision: you can close your eyes or look away, but you cannot close off your ears. Unless you are hearing-impaired, you cannot choose to 'not hear'.

The study of human symbolicity involves many approaches—from the scientific to the cultural, from the psychological to the rhetorical—but whatever the approach, the study of language is the study of what it means to be human.

The Uses of Language

According to the linguist S.I. Hayakawa, communicating through language is the 'fundamental cooperative act by which higher animals survive'.[14] Hayakawa argues that the notion of 'survival of the fittest' depends not on competition, as Darwin encouraged us to believe, but on the ability to join with others to achieve our goals and fulfill our needs. For Hayakawa, cultural and intellectual co-operation is the great principle of human life, and this co-ordination of function is achieved through language—or not at all.

 THE USES OF LANGUAGE

- To make reports.
- To forge judgements.
- To draw inferences.
- To categorize, specify, distinguish, clarify.
- To evoke emotion.
- To build relationships.

Our words perform a variety of actions and fulfill a variety of functions. The basic act we perform with language is to report or make factual statements about the things we experience, such as 'It's raining', or 'I saw Tony at the grocery store', or 'I got an "A" on my test.' Reports are typically verifiable through observation, and exclude, so far as it's possible, interpretation and judgements. Our reports can, although they don't always, reduce uncertainty by providing additional information and by limiting the possible conclusions we draw about things and people.

However, not everything that looks like a report is one. Reports must be distinguished from judgements, which are expressions of approval or disapproval of events, persons, or objects. Making this distinction is sometimes more difficult than it sounds. Because the act of naming itself sometimes includes an interpretation, judgements are often disguised as or confused with reports, both by the person making them and by the person hearing them.

In fact, though making reports is the most basic function of language, little of what we say is actually neutral, as we have already seen. Some theorists believe that all words—even the seemingly most innocuous nouns—are perceived to have some level of emotional loading that can be measured using a technique known as a **semantic differential test**,[15] which asks people to rate the emotional values of ordinary words along several bipolar scales.

For example, a word like 'knife' might be rated using three general attitudinal categories: evaluation (for example, good/bad, hot/cold, nice/awful), potency (for instance, strong/weak, big/little, powerful/powerless), and activity (such as active/ passive, fast/slow, noisy/quiet).

Although the semantic differential approach is now used widely in questionnaires such as course evaluations, and is commonly employed in advertising and marketing research, it has been criticized for producing shallow and sometimes misleading results.[16] A forced choice between two prescribed alternatives can tell us only that, in these restricted circumstances, a respondent preferred X over Y. It says nothing whatever about this same person's absolute preference for X, about her attitudes towards Y, or about her priorities in general. For this reason, some researchers recommend supplementing such quantitative approaches with open-ended items that tap participants' own language use, a qualitative approach that provides 'a richer context for understanding'[17] how people actually respond.

However, what the semantic differential approach does confirm is that words that sound like reports may not be: the statement 'Ian is childish' is the same in *form* as 'It is raining', but it is very different in kind, since it renders a judgement about Ian's behaviour rather than reporting what was observed. We need to be alert to when a statement is a report of fact or observation and when it is an interpretation.

In addition to making reports and rendering judgements, we also use language to express inferences, which, as we saw in Chapter 1, are statements that draw conclusions from observable data. In other words, inferences are statements about what we don't know based on what we do know. Like any kind of interpretation or judgement, inferences may be careful or careless, reliable or unreliable. The quality of an inference depends in part on the quality of the report on which it is based and in part on the interests, attitudes, agenda, and skill of the person making the inference. Murray Banks relates the story of a student whose biochemistry prof dropped a worm into a flask of water and another worm into a flask of alcohol. While the worm in water continued to wriggle about, the worm in alcohol died instantly. When the professor asked for an explanation, the student replied, 'I see that if you drink alcohol, you'll never have worms!' This was not, of course, the inference that the professor was looking for.

Our words can also perform a variety of interpretive and persuasive functions that would be impossible if we had to rely on non-verbal means alone: they allow us, for instance, to categorize, specify, distinguish, and clarify. Unlike our facial expressions, body movement, or manner of dress, words can express complex abstract ideas; in fact, they are the *only* means we have to do this. We can also use our words to evoke emotions and to induce action. Even if we didn't see an event, the words we receive about it can make us angry, sad, joyful, frustrated, or even nauseated.

The story is told of an anthropologist who was visiting the Inuit. One evening he was served whitish mounds floating in broth: blubber. After choking down a generous helping, he was overcome with nausea and ran outside, where he retched into a nearby snowbank. When the cook followed him outside to ask if he was all right, he replied that he just wasn't used to eating blubber. 'That wasn't blubber', she told him in disgust. 'It was only dumplings!' His nausea was the result not of what he had eaten—he was fond of dumplings—but of what he had *named* them. The words themselves had provoked his physical revulsion.

Beyond their capacity to make factual statements or to evoke powerful responses, words are also understood to perform certain kinds of social acts. In fact, there are some kinds of actions that we can perform *only* with words. For instance, we use words to make promises or wagers, to threaten or warn others, to forgive transgressions, or to pronounce vows. We use words to enact legal and social states, as when a clergy member pronounces someone married, a judge sentences someone for a crime, or a physician pronounces someone dead. The study of such uses of language is known as **speech act theory**.[18]

By now it should not surprise you to learn that prevention of silence is also an important function of speech, mainly because, as we have already learned, the togetherness that is achieved by talking with others is more important than the exchange of information. No matter what their practical intentions, our interactions always involve some attempt to establish communion.

We use language to make things happen, to establish co-operation, and to forge the relationships that sustain us. More than this, the way we use language is a direct reflection, and a clear indication to others, of who we are. In the words of Canadian actor, playwright, and teacher Brock Shoveller:

> Your language is you. It is you every bit as much as your five o'clock shadow, your sweat, your smudged eye-liner, your hair colour, your fears, your hopes, your habits, are you. . . . Your words—and they *are* yours—brand you just as obviously as the glowing iron brands the steer's rump. A glimpse at your brand and anyone can identify which corral you've escaped from.[19]

We need to understand our language not as something separate from us, but as the window into our selves. According to Hayakawa, having command of our language means understanding a central aspect of the 'complicated business of being human'.

How Can I Improve My Verbal Communication Skill?

There are several things you can do to make your language use more precise, vivid, engaging, and proficient. The first step to improving verbal skill is to build a more extensive vocabulary. Listen and watch for new words in conversation and reading. Look them up in a dictionary so you know what they mean. Use a thesaurus to develop your range of options and practise different ways of saying similar things. Do crosswords. *Read.* Above all, use the new words you learn until you are comfortable with them.

Second, watch out for language traps. The first, as we have already learned, is **labelling**. Our responses to people are shaped by the labels that we or others have applied to them, and when we accept those labels as reports rather than recognizing them as judgements, we condition our behaviour and our reactions. If we are to improve our verbal usage we need to be sure to distinguish between judgement and mere description.

LANGUAGE TRAPS TO AVOID

- Labelling
- Reification
- Bypassing
- Inappropriate euphemism
- Faulty generalizations
- 'Proper meaning' fallacy

Related to labelling is the process of **reification**, a kind of reductionism in which we mistake words for reality, treating them as if they are things with a life of their own. Reification is a language trap because it is a kind of depersonalization that denies people individuality and treats them as things or commodities, and it reduces complex human phenomena to a single dimension. For instance, when we sum people up with an IQ measurement, a GPA, or an SAT score, we are guilty of reification. When we speak of people as things or reduce them to a number, we deny them their humanity and thus abrogate our responsibility towards them. For example, when a physician refers to a suffering patient by the name of his disease ('the kidney failure in room 412' instead of Mr Johnson), when a soldier is taught to think of the enemy as 'vermin', when the military speak of 'collateral damage' rather than the horrible deaths of human beings, when corporations think of their customers as a 'market segment', they are all guilty of reification.

Reification can even happen when we persist in defining someone else according to outdated information. For example, when David Jr was a baby, it seemed cute to distinguish him from his father by calling him 'little Dave'. He's an autonomous adult now, but his nickname continues to deny him that independence by casting him in a subordinate role. It's not only incongruous now that he's a strapping six-footer, but also potentially demeaning.

A third language trap is **bypassing**, or assuming we and others are using words in exactly the same way without checking to be sure. The most serious cases of bypassing occur when we are dealing with values. Most of us approve of 'fairness', 'honesty', 'integrity', and 'loyalty', to name only a small number of positive value words. But the fact that we agree on the abstractions doesn't mean that we agree on a course of action.

Consider the case of Professor Benedetti and Professor Rolfes, who are designing a course together. Both value 'fairness' in assignments and grading, so they do not expect to encounter any disagreements over standards. But imagine their surprise when they discover that Benedetti interprets 'fair' to mean 'consistent', 'uniform', and 'identical', whereas Rolfes interprets 'fair' as 'pertinent', 'equitable', and 'judicious.' Benedetti concludes that Rolfes is inconsistent and sloppy; Rolfes interprets Benedetti as rigid and lacking in judgement. Of course, even if they agreed on terms like 'equitable' or 'consistent', they might still run into difficulties when it comes to translating these values into actual assignments.

It's easy to see how such disagreements can happen. For example, Bryan and David are best friends who both claim to enjoy well-made films. But they can't go to the movies together because David's idea of a good movie is one that includes lots of action and special effects: car chases, gun battles, pyrotechnics. He's not much interested in nuances of plot or character, and he rejects anything that is shot in black and white. This means that the classic films that Bryan enjoys are boring to him. David dismisses Bryan's taste as pretentious, and Bryan privately thinks David's taste in films is immature. It's just as well that they have other interests in common.

The use of euphemisms is a fourth potential language trap. **Euphemisms** are 'nicer' words, such as 'powder room' for 'toilet' and 'passed on' for 'died', that stand for words that have come to be regarded as impolite or too blunt. A physician asks you to 'provide a urine sample' rather than to 'pee in this cup'; a mortician (itself a euphemism) speaks of 'Mr Johnson' or 'the deceased' rather than 'the body' or 'the corpse'. Such polite evasions are harmless, and can help to make certain realities a little easier to bear.

However, some people are obsessively circumspect, and their linguistic squeamishness can make communication difficult, as is the case with Darlene, who recently consulted her physician about a bladder infection. To her annoyance she was prescribed an anti-diarrheal medicine. Was the physician incompetent? Possibly, but before you condemn him for the error, consider that in the consultation what Darlene told him was that she had pain 'down there' and was having to 'go to the bathroom' frequently.

Euphemisms can also be used perniciously to disguise a harmful or dangerous reality. So it is that the layoff and firing of employees becomes 'downsizing' or even 'right-sizing', landmines become 'non-lethal barriers', or lying becomes 'misstatement'. While it is sometimes socially appropriate to employ euphemisms, we must also be wary of allowing them to cloud our meaning and impede communication.

Generalizations can be another linguistic trap because they are, by nature, faulty—even when there is a grain of truth to them. We are in danger when we use generalizations about groups of people to make inferences about individuals, or when we allow our experience with one or two individuals to cloud our perceptions of entire classes of people.

Here are some common generalizations about various college disciplines: medical students are haughty and self-important; political studies majors are pushy and opinionated; engineering students are loutish and arrogant; computer science students are nerdy and uncommunicative; philosophy majors are argumentative and disconnected from reality; social work students are condescending and preachy; drama majors are attention-seeking and shallow. Did you find any of these generalizations offensive? How do such generalizations affect the way we interact with individuals? Can you think of other examples like these?

Generalizations can also be faulty because what was once true may be so no longer: 'Red Deer has only one or two good restaurants'; 'Housing costs in Saskatoon are really low'; 'Everyone in Sydney works at the steel plant.' Although no generalization is completely accurate, all of these statements once had a grain of truth to them. However,

they are no longer even partly correct. We can improve the quality of our verbal communication by taking care with generalizations, being sure to date them ('When I lived there in 1990, Red Deer had only one or two good restaurants.') and to qualify them ('Up until the 1960s, it seemed that nearly every family in Sydney had someone who worked at the steel plant.').

The final linguistic trap is something known as the **'proper meaning' fallacy**, which is the assumption that every word has only one 'pure' meaning exclusive of its context, or that words with similar meanings (synonyms) can be used indiscriminately in all situations. In fact, many of our social struggles are struggles over the meaning of words. Consider, for example, the struggles and public outcry in the early 2000s over the meaning of the word 'marriage'.

This isn't the only such controversy: during the late 1990s, the Association of Professional Engineers and Geoscientists of Newfoundland fought a court case over who could properly use the designation 'engineer'.[20] Americans struggle over what is meant by the phrase 'the right to bear arms' in their Constitution. Legal battles, particularly at the Supreme Court level, often depend on the interpretation of a word in law.

The 'proper meaning' fallacy is complicated by two factors. First, words can have more than one legitimate or 'dictionary' meaning. For example, if you consult your dictionary, you will find at least 16 distinct meanings for the word 'set', 9 different meanings for 'check', 11 for 'book', 5 for 'moon', 9 for ' walk'—and these do not include common expressions such as 'set-up' or 'moonwalk' in which such words appear.

Second, words 'mean' on more than one level. The *denotative* meaning is the simplest level of meaning, referring to the conventional, literal, 'dictionary' meanings associated with a word. The *connotative* value of a word adds another layer of meaning; connotation is the emotional, qualitative impact of a word. Some words have more emotional clout than others: for example, 'death' has more emotional impact than 'desk'. Connotation may also be positive, neutral, or negative: 'dog' is fairly neutral, whereas 'mongrel' has a definite negative value. As real estate agents know, 'home' has a more positive connotation than 'house'. 'Childlike' is more positive than 'childish', though both literally mean 'like a child'.

Sometimes connotation depends on the context in which a word appears. For example, the word 'little' can mean delicate or dainty, as it does in phrases like 'Your little mouth, / Oh, God, how sweet!' and 'Your little voice, / So soft and kind.' But see how praise turns to scorn when the same word is used in a different application: 'Your little soul, / Your little mind'.[21] Or consider the statement, 'You are a stranger to me', which would have a neutral connotation for most of us if it were spoken by an actual stranger. But how does the connotation change if it's said by your best friend or romantic partner?

Words can also accrue a positive or negative connotation for individuals through personal association. The word 'dog', which is neutral for most people, may be positive for those who love the animals and negative for those who have had bad experiences with them. These private connotations can affect both the way we understand others and the way we are understood by them. We should keep in mind that private connotations, so powerful to us, may not be recognized or shared by others, and that connotation can change dramatically with a change in circumstance or context.

To communicate more effectively, we must pay attention to how we use language, to its interrelationship with perception, and to the various traps we can fall into if we're not paying attention to what we and others are saying.

Language, Culture, and Gender

Language is inescapably bound up with culture; in fact, it is widely thought to be impossible to understand the subtle nuances and deep meanings of another culture without knowing its language well. Not only do vocabulary and idiom sometimes suffer in translation, but the cultural assumptions and values they encode may be difficult or even impossible to translate at all.

To illustrate this point, linguistics professor Hubert Spekkens used to tell the story of a scientist who developed the first computerized translation device.[22] The inventor envisioned his machine as contributing to international co-operation, intercultural understanding, and world peace. At the unveiling, he invited members of the public to step forward to try this miraculous device. Several people did so, and each success brought oohs and ahs from the crowd.

However, the last offering came from a linguist, who wished to underscore that translation is not simply a matter of substituting one vocabulary for another. He submitted the following proverb: 'The spirit is willing, but the flesh is weak.' The machine, lacking the judgement of a human speaker and unable to work with metaphor, produced the following answer: 'The wine is very good, but the meat is tasteless.' As the linguist's example shows, because language use is often figurative and is always embedded in cultural assumptions, mere word substitutions are not sufficient to prevent cultural misunderstandings. When we are interacting with someone whose first language is not English, or when we are attempting to communicate in our own second or third language, we need to be very careful to attend to the context as well as to the vocabulary we are using.

Surprisingly, cultural misunderstandings do not necessarily disappear when two cultures speak the same language. In fact, the challenges of linguistic bypassing may even be increased, since we may take for granted that another person who speaks the same language will automatically share the same values and attitudes. This is not necessarily so; in fact, surface impressions of similarity can be quite misleading.

Consider, for instance, an American in Canada who keeps running into situations that remind her that her new country is not the same as her former home, despite the ubiquitous presence of American stores, American magazines, and American television programming. Differences in vocabulary that show up, for example, in Canadianisms[23] like 'chesterfield', 'toque', 'cutlery', 'serviette', and 'snarky' are only the most visible difference.

More important than vocabulary are the systematic differences in values, culture, politics, and public life that underlie the way the two cultures express themselves.[24] These can be both pervasive and profound,[25] as is the case, for example, in the central philosophies of the two cultures, which also differ significantly; Canada's original Constitution, the British North America Act of 1867, established 'peace, order, and good government' as the central aims of the society that would become Canada,[26] in contrast to the 'life, liberty, and happiness' that shaped the American ideal.

Such features of a culture, which may be as invisible to its inhabitants as the air they breathe, nevertheless shape our attitudes and traditions and influence the way we interpret and report on what we experience. Thus, Canadians are likely to interpret certain kinds of situations much differently from the way an American might see them. By way of illustration, here is Pierre Berton's response (as reported by Margaret Atwood) to the Texan who proposed that Canada become part of the US:

> Berton retorted that he thought this would be a dandy idea. The Americans could get back the Queen, whom they've always coveted, and revert to constitutional monarchy, and do away with the FBI and receive the much more colourful Royal Canadian Mounted Police in return, and change to a three-party system and become officially bilingual. Well, that wasn't exactly what the Texan had in mind.[27]

Another example shows how even values that appear to be shared may be expressed and thought about differently in different cultures. For example, Canadians and Americans alike deplore and fear crime and lawlessness, but our attitude to violent crime, our perception of its causes, and our notion of appropriate solutions to the problem differ significantly, as does our direct experience of crime.[28] As a culture, Canadians have traditionally perceived violent crime, especially involving firearms, as an aberration rather than as a cultural pattern,[29] and even (a fact that might surprise their American cousins) as an unwanted side effect of American cultural influences.[30] In fact, the fear that 'violence may come to our cities from across the border' has been a part of Canadian culture since its counter-revolutionary beginnings.[31]

To see how such differences in cultural assumptions might affect our individual interpersonal interactions and attributions, consider the following example. Some years ago, as a professor at a Canadian regional college, I was shocked to hear that one of my colleagues—an American—was rumoured to keep a handgun in her office desk. Apparently another faculty member had spotted the weapon when the woman opened the desk drawer to retrieve a file. The story spread quickly, with everyone speculating on how disturbed she must be and wondering how much immediate danger she posed to the rest of us.

Five years later, when I was teaching in the US, I recounted the story of the woman with the gun in her office desk. None of my American colleagues found this odd. Far from considering the woman disturbed, most saw her as prudent! The conversation revealed that several of my colleagues owned handguns, and that they saw nothing unusual about doing so. Two kept a gun in the nightstand, one slept with a gun under her pillow, and another frequently carried hers *with her*—in her purse. The behaviour that in my Canadian workplace had seemed to indicate derangement was simply a product of a different—in this case, American—set of cultural assumptions.[32] How we interpret the meaning of what others say and do, and the attributions we make about them, can be deeply affected by both language and culture.

Considering culture from another level entirely, some researchers even argue that there is enough difference in the way men and women talk that their distinctive patterns can almost be considered another form of 'cultural' difference.[33] These differ-

ences aren't so much a matter of vocabulary, although men reportedly use more profanity than women, as much as they are patterns of language use—the rhythm of
talk, the directness of it, the number of topic changes, the functions it performs.
According to many researchers on male and female patterns in language use,[34] male
talk is typically competitive, hierarchical, and task-oriented, while women's talk is
more likely to focus on building community, providing emotional affirmation, and
supporting the feelings of another. These researchers have suggested that, generally,
men's talk is more direct, women's more polite; men interrupt, dominate conversational exchanges, and offer more advice, while women speak less frequently and use
more qualifiers. For example, males are believed to establish social bondedness
through mutual involvement in activities, while females are thought to rely to a
greater degree on self-disclosure and other strategies of emotional intimacy.[35]

Although these expressive versus instrumental patterns have been widely regarded
as characterizing female–male distinctions in values[36] and ethical orientation[37] as well
as language use, they have not been entirely without challenge. At least one group of
researchers suggests an alternative explanation to the issue of language differences,
arguing that anyone who feels relatively powerless in a situation will tend to employ
patterns that have been regarded as typically 'female', while those who are confident
of their status or power in a given interaction are more likely to use the patterns of
talk allegedly typical of males.[38]

An interesting corollary to the question of the perceived deference of women's talk
and the assertiveness of men's is the question of whether women are naturally more
compassionate than men,[39] an assumption that appears to underlie the interpretation
of the linguistic features noted by the researchers. Two issues must be considered
here: first, whether such patterns of difference hold across a wide sample of women
and men, and second, what such differences actually mean. For instance, if it is true
that men's communication tends to be more instrumental and less social in focus,
more task-oriented, more blunt and direct than women's, does that mean that men
are more competitive, less concerned with others, and more inconsiderate, or does it
simply mean that men use different means to establish relational intimacy? And if it
is true that women communicate in a more supportive, socially approved, and polite
pattern than men do, does it mean that women are in fact more gentle and consid-
erate? Or does it simply mean that their struggle for power or control is more covert?
Certainly the practices observed in male talk tend to be *perceived* as primarily competitive rather than as, for instance, an alternative form of co-operative behaviour,
and female practices are read as essentially co-operative rather than as, for example, a
kind of veiled competition.[40]

Researchers interpreting these findings have tended to privilege female patterns
for their greater levels of 'agreement and other positive social behaviours (e.g., reliev-
ing group tension and displaying group solidarity)',[41] while at the same time regarding male patterns as more authoritative, forceful, and believable.[42] However, much of

the research on such differences was developed in the 1970s, and speech patterns—as well as the political and cultural climate in which interpretations are made—tend to evolve in keeping with other social developments. At least one researcher argues that such gender stereotypes have weakened over time, although women's speech is still perceived to be less direct and more emotional than men's.[43]

What are the implications of such findings for our practice of interpersonal communication? It is well to remember that these characterizations of male and female patterns, even when they are statistically warranted, are still generalizations. As such, they may not be sufficient to explain, or even be relevant to, the dynamics of any given situation or individual. Thus, although women's talk is thought to be 'typically' more polite, gentler, less direct, and more emotional, Barbara or Nancy or Kaye or Debbie may speak directly, forcefully, and dispassionately, as the situation demands. And although the norm for men's talk is thought to be aggressive, boastful, and combative, Ian or Jeff or Paul or Bruce may speak politely, sensitively, and supportively, as required by the context. It may be that Ron's communication style doesn't conform to the stereotype at all, being *typically* co-operative, intimate, and emotionally supportive, while Vera is habitually blunt and direct, her speech filled with slang and profanity. In short, we should not assume, just because women's talk is thought to be more genteel and men's talk is believed to be rough around the edges, that a specific woman's or man's style will conform to type.

Generalizations, no matter how statistically accurate they may be, do not explain the dynamics of a specific relationship or circumstance. If we are to communicate more effectively in interpersonal contexts, we still need to learn how to pay attention to the details of the situation we're in, and to respond appropriately to our friends and intimates, taking relevant information into account.

Summary

Language, that uniquely human ability to think abstractly and to communicate in symbols, is central to most of our definitions of what it means to be a human being; it is also part of what makes each individual unique. Language defines us by shaping our relationships and our sense of ourselves.

Language is also what provides most of our knowledge of the world we live in; although we may think otherwise, relatively little of what we know comes through our own direct observation or experience. Instead, we obtain most of our understanding of the world through the words of others. Even what we directly observe for ourselves is structured and organized for us by our language.

Language has several important characteristics and functions. It is at once a symbolic process and a complex activity that operates according to systematic rules. As a symbolic medium, it bears an arbitrary relationship to physical experience. However, for the individual user, language is highly conventional: we do not ourselves invent the correspondences between sound and meaning that make up our language. Instead, we learn from others the conventions of meaning, usage, syntax, and grammar. Nevertheless, our language is the medium of thought, understanding, and identity, none of which would exist outside of language.

Language use is deeply embedded in culture. Not only does the specific language—English, French, Cree, Italian, or Gaelic—carry cultural codes and shape our understanding and interpretations, but the assumptions embedded in our speech can differ significantly even when we are speaking the same language. Many researchers have noted significant differences, for example, in the way Canadians and Americans understand and interpret some situations and issues; others have focused on the differences between the patterns in and expectations of the way women and men use language to achieve their interpersonal goals.

We use language to serve a variety of purposes, both practical and symbolic. It is one of the ways in which we accomplish the tasks necessary to living, and it is *the* way in which we obtain the co-operation of others in achieving our goals. Language is what allows human beings to organize into societies and cultures. Through its power of abstraction, language frees us from the here-and-now world, enabling us to learn the lessons of the past and dream of possibilities for the future. It is what has enabled advances in human understanding and technology.

More than endowing us with these remarkable capacities, however, language enables us to fulfill our deepest human need, the need for identification and belonging. It allows us to connect with each other and to aspire to be more than we are. It gives us a sense of community and a sense of self. More than any other human trait, language defines us and gives us to ourselves.

Key Terms

abstraction
bypassing
constitutive rules
euphemisms
generalizations
labelling
perception
'proper meaning' fallacy
regulative rules
reification
Sapir-Whorf hypothesis
semantic differential test
speech act theory
symbol

Suggested Readings

Bill Casselman, *Canadian Sayings* (Toronto: McArthur & Company, 1999) and its two sequels, *Canadian Sayings 2* (Toronto: McArthur & Company, 2002) and *Canadian Sayings 3* (Toronto: McArthur & Company, 2004). Wordhound Casselman's books offer a wealth of examples of uniquely Canadian linguistic inventiveness, and they're also very funny. You can sample Casselman's work at: <www.billcasselman.com>.

Norman Fairclough, *Language and Power* (New York: Longman, 1989). Fairclough offers an analysis of the way in which power is embedded in language use—who gets to wield it and how it is maintained, and how we are all complicit in its use. Though scholarly in its approach, the book is accessible to an undergraduate reader, and offers many case studies and examples.

S.I. Hawayaka and Alan R. Hayakawa, *Language in Thought and Action*, 5th edn (San Diego: Harcourt Brace Jovanovich, 1991). First published in 1939 as *Language in Action*, and updated in this edition by Senator Hayakawa's son, the book has never been out of print. Geared for the lay reader, it is a readable and fascinating study of language as a system of symbols that influence every facet of our lives. This book is highly recommended.

Jennifer MacLennan and John Moffatt, eds, *Inside Language: A Canadian Language Reader* (Scarborough, Ont.: Prentice-Hall Canada, 2000). This reader contains many interesting selections on language, and explores issues of personal and cultural identity, politics, persuasion, and linguistic play. Selections include George Orwell's classic 'Politics and the English Language', as well as uniquely Canadian selections such as Brock Shoveller's 'Your Language is You'.

John McWhorter, *Word on the Street: Debunking the Myth of a 'Pure' Standard English* (Cambridge, Mass.: Perseus Publishing, 1998). McWhorter's lively book is a discussion of the whole issue of 'standard' English.

Beulah Parker, *My Language Is Me: Psychotherapy with a Disturbed Adolescent* (New York: Ballantine Books, 1962). This classic work explores the relationship between language and the sense of self, through a case study of Parker's adolescent patient. The book is a readable and compassionate treatment.

Susan Schaller, *A Man without Words* (Berkeley: University of California Press, 1995). Schaller's book details her experience teaching English to a languageless man who had been deaf from birth. It is a thoroughly engaging and dramatic story with a shattering revelation when Ildefonso finally breaks through to language. I assigned this book to my English Language class; it is the only book I have ever assigned to any class that several of the students read twice.

Richard Weaver, *Language Is Sermonic: Richard Weaver on the Nature of Rhetoric*, ed. Richard L. Johannesen, Rennard Strickland, and Ralph T. Eubanks (Baton Rouge: Louisiana State University Press, 1970). This study of the inherent persuasiveness of language is geared to a more philosophical readership, and is challenging reading for a layperson. However, Weaver's discussion of the way in which naming itself is persuasive is worth a look.

Exercises and Assignments

1. As we have learned so far, the labels we apply to others can have a profound effect on how we communicate with them and how we experience their communication with us. Read 'How to Tell a Good Professor from a Bad Professor' in Appendix B and be prepared to discuss with the class what this passage shows about how judgements and interpretations can masquerade as reports, and what this means for our interpersonal communication.

2. Last month, Gwen invited Jordie, her visiting big-city cousin, for lunch at

Simeon's, the newest restaurant in town. Gwen and her friends really like the food, and Gwen believed that, for once, her cousin wouldn't be able to find anything to criticize about this small-town venue. On her arrival, however, Jordie strode up to the table and announced, in ringing tones that could be heard by everyone nearby, 'When you said we were eating at *Simian's*, I thought maybe I'd find you at the zoo! What's on the menu, bananas?' Gwen has been unable to enjoy a meal at the restaurant since. Drawing on everything you have learned about communication, and in particular about language, discuss with the class exactly what happened here.

a. What is the effect of such labelling on interpersonal trust, face, self-concept, and disclosure?

b. From the point of view of interpersonal needs theory, suggest what might have motivated the interaction: why Gwen took Jordie to the restaurant, and why Jordie might have said what she did.

3. In his letter to Roger Ebert's 'Movie Answer Man' column (Appendix B), James T. Cook laments how a friend's name-calling has changed his view of the movies he used to enjoy. Explain this event from the point of view of language, and, if you can, provide a similar example from your own experience.

4. It is fair to say that, no matter what discipline you are studying, your training in university or college is largely a matter of mastering a new vocabulary—and thus a new way of thinking. Choose any course you are currently taking or one you have already completed and explain how this is true.

5. Drawing on what you have learned in this chapter, explain what is meant by the following quotations, taken from a variety of scholars of language:

a. Kenneth Burke: 'Can we bring ourselves to realize . . . just how overwhelmingly much of what we mean by "reality" has been built up for us through nothing but our symbol systems?'[44]

b. Ludwig Wittgenstein: 'The limits of our language mean the limits of our world.'[45]

c. Northrop Frye: 'A person must learn words before any other kind of learning is of any use to him, must be articulate before he can be a real person, must know more than his native language to live with any awareness in a world like ours.'[46]

d. S.I. Hawakawa 'To perceive how language works, what pitfalls it conceals, what its possibilities are, is to comprehend a crucial aspect of the complicated business of living the life of a human being.'[47]

e. Charles Barber: 'Language itself is the most remarkable tool that man has invented, and is the one that makes all the others possible. The most primitive tools, admittedly, may have come earlier than language: the higher apes sometimes use sticks for digging, and have even been observed to break sticks for this purpose. But tools of any greater sophistication demand the kind of human co-operation and division of labour which is hardly possible without language. Language, in fact, is the great machine tool which makes human cultures possible.'[48]

6. Reread Edwin Arlington Robinson's 'Richard Cory', in Appendix B, this time focusing on its language use. As an experiment, replace Robinson's language with the following alternatives: 'sidewalk' instead of 'pavement', 'head to toe' instead of 'sole to crown', 'good-looking' instead of 'clean-favoured', 'thin' instead of 'slim', 'dressed' instead of 'arrayed', 'courteous' instead of 'human', 'wonderfully' instead of 'admirably', 'trained' instead of 'schooled', 'good manners' instead of 'every grace', 'in short' instead of 'in fine'. What happens to the impact and the meaning of the poem (apart from any effects on the rhyme) when you make these substitutions? Why did Robinson choose his wording rather than the alternatives? What did the original word choice contribute to the poem's meaning?

7. Without telling those around you what you're doing, see how long you can go through a normal day without making a single verbal utterance. (Give it up if you find the experiment causes interpersonal conflicts.) Be prepared to report your findings either in class discussion or in written form, as directed by your instructor

a. How long were you able to last without speaking? Was it a longer or a shorter time than you had expected?

b. How frustrating was the experiment for you? How frustrating was it for those around you?

c. How did people around you respond to your reluctance to speak? What was the effect on your interactions with others?

d. Did anything in this experiment surprise you?

8. Among the functions of language that we learned in Chapter 1 is the capacity to evoke strong emotions. Take another look at the form-letter e-mail 'Mark C is Caught in the Middle' (Appendix B). What emotions are evoked, or intended to be provoked, in the target audience? Why? Is the provocation contained purely in the words, or does the interpretation of this message depend just as much on social convention? If the latter, what does this fact tell us about language use?

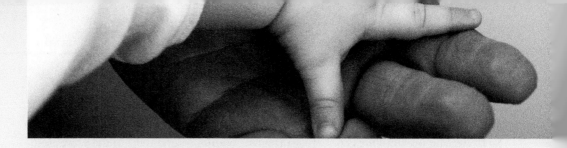

Chapter 6

Non-verbal Communication

Learning Objectives

- To understand the influence of the non-verbal in all communication.
- To learn the characteristics of non-verbal communication.
- To recognize the various channels or types of non-verbal communication.
- To learn strategies for better reading non-verbal cues.

So far we have been dealing primarily with verbal communication—the messages we create through language and other symbolic systems. Most of us recognize the importance of such verbal skills as public speaking, writing, listening, or reading; most of us, too, know that we can work on improving these skills since they are to some degree under our conscious control. However, even if we are already as skilled as possible in these areas, we would still lack some important understanding of human communication.

In addition to our speech and writing, humans also communicate in ways that do not require words and that are less available to conscious control and improvement. The term **non-verbal communication** is used for those aspects of our interactions that take place without words.

What Is Non-verbal Communication?

Non-verbal communication, sometimes called 'body language', isn't really a language at all because it's not systematic and is not always a matter of choice. Non-verbal communication refers to such features as facial expression, tone of voice, body movement, and gesture; it also includes the way we dress, the company we keep, and the way we decorate our living space. It encompasses all of our actions and gestures, and as we will see, it is a very powerful influence on how we are seen and received by others.

Most of us don't spend a lot of time thinking about the impact of the non-verbal cues that accompany our communication. Nevertheless, the kinds of expressions that flit across our faces, the ways we move our hands, or the very posture we adopt in an interaction can all have an impact on how our messages are understood.

In spite of our general lack of attention to the non-verbal in our interaction, we nevertheless often tacitly recognize that we can learn a lot from others' non-verbal cues. We tell someone whose story we doubt to 'look me in the eye and tell me that again.' We use metaphors that capture the power of non-verbal communication: 'I stared him down'; 'She should stand up for herself'; 'I wasn't going to take that lying down'; ' I gave him the cold shoulder'; 'He has turned his back on us'; 'She elbowed her way into the discussion.'

Non-verbal communication occurs on several levels and has several characteristics. It may come to us through sound in the form of vocalizations that are not words—that is, it includes grunts, sighs, tone, pacing, and pitch. It may be made up of visual cues that are communicated through appearance, movement, and grooming. It may also have to do with the way people use space: the arrangement of furniture in a room, the architectural layout, the positioning of people during an interaction.

Non-verbal cues may stand on their own, but more often they accompany verbal communication such as speech, sign language, or writing. Language is said to be embedded in gesture, the role of which is to reinforce the verbal by both audible and visible means. When we are uncertain how to interpret the meaning of what someone says, we often look to the accompanying non-verbal cues for help in deciphering the message. But because non-verbal communication is not systematic, we can some-times run into difficulty. The goal of this chapter is to develop greater understanding of how body language contributes to our interpersonal interactions.

Characteristics of Non-verbal Communication

The first important characteristic of non-verbal communication is how influential it is. Although our facial expressions, gestures, and other aspects of non-verbal commu-nication may seem inconsequential, they can have a greater impact than most of us consciously recognize. In fact, some researchers have estimated that as much as 93 per cent of what is communicated in any face-to-face interaction is communicated through facial expression (55 per cent) and vocal qualities such as tone (38 per cent), with what you actually say accounting for only 7 per cent of what others experience.[1]

Without even realizing it, each of us is continually 'reading', assessing, and respond-ing to the non-verbal cues of others, just as they are reading and responding to ours. Some people are more adept than others at reading non-verbal cues and tend to think of this as their communication 'radar'. In cases where the non-verbal cues fail to match the verbal ones, we tend to accept the non-verbal cues as more reliable. How often have you found yourself not quite trusting something someone was saying to you but not being sure quite why that was? Perhaps you were responding to something in the person's non-verbal behaviour that contradicted what was being said in the verbal message.

Despite its power to influence our interpretations of a verbal message, non-verbal communication is itself mostly ambiguous. While some of our non-verbal cues are learned gestures with fairly clear meanings, such as dismissing someone with a wave of the hand or inviting someone closer with a crooked finger, much of our non-verbal communication is made up of instinctive responses such as blushing, blinking, smil-ing, or laughing. While we can learn to control other non-verbal cues such as eye con-tact, facial expression, posture, and gesture, most of us have only minimal to moder-ate control over these instinctive responses, which may occur for a variety of reasons.

In spite of the many books that purport to tell you how to precisely interpret what someone's body language 'really' means,[2] non-verbal communication is notoriously indefinite in its meaning. While it is certainly worth paying attention to non-verbal cues as a way of becoming more sensitive and insightful communicators, we need to bear in mind that there can be several explanations for non-verbal behaviour, and that it is high-ly ambiguous. In the absence of corroborating evidence, we should proceed with cau-tion when we set out to interpret the non-verbal behaviour of others. For example, Devora, a new teaching assistant, was recently unnerved by Stephen, a student in her class who frowned and glowered throughout the first week of class meetings, so much so that she dreaded the thought of having to deal with him. When Stephen stopped her after class to ask a question, however, Devora discovered that the expression she had read as hostile was instead a look of intense concentration. When John joined his girlfriend Sarah and her best friend Jane for coffee last week, he noticed that their conversation abruptly halted when he entered the café. Certain that Sarah was divulging confidences to Jane, he has been sulking angrily all week. Imagine his embarrassment to discover that they had been planning a surprise party for his birthday.

Although non-verbal cues are pervasive and influential, the information they carry is somewhat limited. Non-verbal behaviour expresses emotional reactions rather than discursive thought. You can communicate your approval or disapproval with gestures and facial expression; you can express happiness, sadness, anger, fear, or surprise; you can transmit confusion, bewilderment, frustration, or doubt. But you cannot, for example, articulate your understanding of how advertising contributes to cultural materialism, or explain your theory about why Stephen Harper won the 2006 federal election, or describe the way your grandmother's influence has profoundly affected your life, or even declare your deep and abiding concern for animal welfare.

You can express feelings and emotional reactions non-verbally, but without language you cannot make statements, perform analyses, or interpret data. The articulation of thoughts, as opposed to the display of reactions, requires verbal communication. This is not to say that verbal communication doesn't benefit from the enrichment of non-verbal reinforcement—certainly non-verbal cues add colour and intensity to the things we say. But the making of statements requires detail and nuance available only through verbal utterance.

Since so much of our non-verbal communication is involuntary and automatic, it resists our conscious control. Well-trained actors can learn to exercise greater command of their bodily cues, as can expert card players, whose 'poker faces' give away little of what they are feeling. But such mastery comes only with years of concentrated effort and practice that most of us have not undertaken. An experienced actor, for instance, can cry or even, in some cases, blush on command during a performance. Few of the rest of us ever achieve that level of self-mastery, and even actors may not have such control over themselves when it comes to their own interpersonal interactions.

In addition to its power and its resistance to being controlled consciously, non-verbal communication is also pervasive. As we learned from the Nine Axioms, it is impossible to 'not communicate', and our non-verbal communication means that, even when silent, we are still making meaning. Our very presence, our every look and gesture, our clothing, our possessions, and even, under some circumstances, our absences, are interpreted by others as messages. These messages may be ambiguous, they may be unconscious, they may be limited in scope, but they are influential and always present.

Finally, if our language use is shaped and constrained by culture, non-verbal communication is even more so. Although non-verbal communication cannot be absolutely codified, cultural values and orientations can have a profound effect on such factors as the distance we maintain when interacting with others, the way we view and experience time, the importance we assign to qualities like individualism, fate, or social and professional hierarchies.[3] Because we rely on non-verbal cues to help us clarify meanings when verbal cues are absent or ambiguous, and because non-verbal information is highly rooted in cultural assumptions and values that may be taken for granted by each participant, the potential for misunderstanding can be magnified by non-verbal elements.

CHARACTERISTICS OF NON-VERBAL COMMUNICATION

- Influential
- Ambiguous
- Communicates emotion, not thought
- Resists conscious control
- Pervasive
- Rooted in culture

Types of Non-verbal Communication

Non-verbal messages are communicated by everything from our physical appearance and body movements to our use of space. They include our facial expressions, our tone of voice, our use of touch, our display of power. How these things are interpreted can depend on the context, the nature of the relationship between us, and the values of our society or culture. Non-verbal communication arises from cultural common sense—our ideas about what is appropriate, normal, or effective in an interaction with someone else. But cultures not only attach different relative value to verbal and non-verbal communication, they may also employ different systems of gesture, posture, spatial relations, and physical appearance that may or may not conform to the cultural patterns we are used to. The information in this chapter deals primarily with English-Canadian norms of behaviour; you can expect some variation in these principles across other ethnic and cultural groups.

TYPES OF NON-VERBAL COMMUNICATION

- Appearance
- Face
- Kinesics (movement and gesture)
- Proxemics (management of space)
- Paralanguage
- Chronemics (management of time)
- Touch
- Power

Appearance

When we encounter another person, we look for cues to the person's status, attitude, or purpose; we try to assess what kind of response will be appropriate in this situation, and how we ought to receive the person. Some of this information comes to us in verbal form, but much of it is communicated non-verbally. The first line of non-verbal communication is someone's appearance, which includes everything from general attractiveness to level of grooming and dress.

Remember that, as we perceive the person, we are looking for cues that will help us to categorize and interpret the encounter. Sex, ethnicity/visible minority status, and age are among the first things we notice about someone. It should be emphasized that, though we should be on guard against bigotry, the mere act of noticing such distinctions is not prejudice. Racism, sexism, and ageism are about how we *behave* towards others. Only when we treat someone unjustly as a result of such differences could we be said to be behaving in a bigoted manner. However, simply registering the fact of difference is inescapable.

Colleen, teaching English in Japan, reports that the sight of another 'Western' face came to seem very startling to her. On her return to Calgary after five years overseas, she found that the now relatively rare sight of a Japanese face struck her with a strong sense of comfort and familiarity, despite the fact that she is not Japanese. It is natural that these features of her social surroundings would affect Colleen strongly, and her notice of them is not at all racist.

Much of our initial contact with any person involves figuring out a protocol for how to conduct ourselves in the interaction. Dealing with the unexpected or the ambiguous can be unsettling because it causes us to have to rethink our approach. Consider David's recent embarrassment at a friend's wedding, where he expected to meet the bride's mother, along with her brother and two of her sisters. When he spotted a white-haired, fiftyish woman speaking to the bride, he strode over confidently to introduce himself. 'You must be Valerie's mother', he declared. 'I've heard so much about you.'

Unfortunately for David, the woman he had approached was Val's sister, not her mother. David had misread the non-verbal cues provided by her **appearance**. Is David being 'ageist'? Not in this case. His mistake is understandable: at 25, David is the oldest child in his family, and his parents are in their late forties. Val, by contrast, is at 30 the youngest in her family; her sister, the eldest, is almost 15 years older, making her a near-contemporary of David's parents. David had simply drawn on his own experience—in this case mistakenly—to interpret the meaning of the sister's white hair.

If unexpected differences are unsettling, even more unsettling is ambiguity, since it creates uncertainty about how to act, or react, in a given encounter. This fact was famously exploited for its humour by a character known as 'androgynous Pat' from the television show *Saturday Night Live*,[4] whose uncertain gender became the one-joke core of a recurrent skit. Because most people interact in slightly different ways with men and women, and some interact in markedly different ways, the uncertainty represented by 'Pat', while amusing on television, could be quite stressful in real life. It is in part for this reason that the 'transgendered' sometimes encounter difficulty. Such unsettling reactions aren't necessarily the result of bigotry, as is sometimes assumed. Instead, they are natural responses of ordinary people to ambiguous or unexpected situations. Real bigotry and racism, ageism, or sexism, are about how we treat others on the basis of these perceptions.

Height and weight are other factors that affect how we perceive and respond to others. Evidence suggests that taller than average people may be more successful and better regarded than those who are shorter than average,[5] although those who are exceptionally tall may also suffer from some stigma. The overweight have always suffered from ill treatment by others,[6] but the current hysteria regarding the obesity epidemic[7] has further legitimized such attitudes.[8] Many people currently respond more favourably to slender people than to the obese, attributing to them greater self-control and social value.

Clothing and grooming are also sources of non-verbal information about others, as is their general overall attractiveness. Not surprisingly, we tend to assess the well-groomed, well-dressed, attractive person more favourably than the generally untidy or poorly groomed. Such an assessment is not always accurate, of course, but most of us assume that good grooming and an overall confident and attractive manner suggest greater self-respect and command of the situation.

The matter of how to 'read' someone's appearance as a non-verbal cue is complicated. Appearance norms can vary significantly across cultures, particularly in matters of dress and hairstyle. Living in a multicultural or ethnically diverse context, such as in many of Canada's larger cities, thus requires greater care and vigilance in the way we assess and assign meaning to the non-verbal behaviour of others, and we should try to keep in mind that a form of dress that seems odd to us may be entirely normal to the person so attired, while we are the ones who appear strange to them. At the same time, it is just possible that the person whose ethnic dress or appearance renders him an outsider is just as uncomfortable among a majority whose norms are so different from his own.[9]

The question of appearance is further complicated by the fact that people have for centuries used dress codes to establish social identities, to distinguish in-groups and out-groups, and to otherwise set themselves apart.[10] Because clothing and appearance are a matter of choice, and because they remain chief among the ways in which we encode our social memberships, someone whose clothing is different from that of the mainstream is going to be seen as making a much larger statement than a simple fashion preference. Differences in clothing or headgear or hairstyle will inevitably be read as symptomatic of other, more profound, differences. As a result, we can find ourselves feeling uncomfortable or unsure of how to interact with someone whose manner or dress marks him as an 'outsider'.

It may be that the person is deliberately attempting to provoke a reaction, as Sylvana is when she dresses in the extreme Goth outfits that her parents hate so much, or as Linden is when he wears traditional Scottish kilts to his college classes.

Or it may be that the person is respecting norms of dress appropriate to his or her religious or ethnic affiliation.

What is striking from the perspective of interpersonal communication, however, is that the matter of appearance—hairstyle, clothing, headgear, and so on—is an extremely provocative, even explosive, issue for most of us. Consider, for example, the controversy over RCMP officer Baltej Singh Dhillon's 1989 campaign to have the ban on turbans lifted for Sikh members of the force. Dhillon was eventually successful, but not before a firestorm of protest erupted from people who saw the move as a threat to the integrity and symbolism of the RCMP.[11]

Face and Eye Contact

Following a person's general appearance, the face is the greatest source of non-verbal information, accounting for as much as 55 per cent of the relational content of any interaction. In general, a calm or smiling expression is more appealing and attractive than a scowl, and we tend to respond better to a genuine smile than to a forced expression. An animated expression is more compelling than a deadpan one.

We read emotions from a person's facial expression, and there are six that are universally recognized across all cultures: happiness, sadness, anger, fear, surprise, and disgust. Human faces can, of course, express far more subtle emotional distinctions, but some of these may be differently interpreted according to culture. All of us, however, can accurately read the six listed expressions on every other human face, irrespective of differing customs or physical characteristics. However, the meaning of such facial expressions can vary according to the context; in some Eastern cultures, for instance, it may be unacceptable for a host to show disapproval to a guest, so he or she may wear an expression of delight rather than disgust. Members of the culture who are more attuned to situational cues might be able to read the situation accurately, but a visitor might not understand. For this reason, we need to be cautious about how we read the meaning of facial expression when dealing with a culture other than our own.

By far the most powerful of the non-verbal cues we receive from the face is eye contact, and many of us believe that we can read a lot from what we see in the eyes of others. Because it is so powerful, however, eye contact must be handled with delicacy, and it can have startlingly different meanings in different cultures.

Eye contact can represent engagement, openness, involvement, and intimacy, or it can signal confrontation and intimidation. It can express a variety of emotions from amusement to confidence to dislike to passion. In mainstream North American culture, an unwillingness or inability to make initial eye contact may be read as dishonesty or evasiveness. However, in some Eastern cultures and in many Aboriginal cultures, direct eye contact can constitute a direct face threat and is often avoided, particularly with strangers or with those of greater social status. For members of these cultures, dropping the eyes is a sign not of evasion but of deference and honour. Even for mainstream North American culture, dropping the eyes after initial contact can be a sign of reserve, deference, and respectfulness.

When we find ourselves distrusting someone who can't or won't meet our gaze, when we assume the person to be dishonest or evasive, we may be misreading the situation, particularly if the person is from a different cultural background. In fact, even within our own cultural context, it could be that a person who avoids eye contact is not deceitful, but simply nervous or shy.

Although we generally approve of those who can meet our eyes, even in North America we do not want to be stared at, or stared down. In addition to helping us establish connection and intimacy, eye contact can also signal aggressiveness, even threat. Too much eye contact, or holding eye contact for too long, can be uncomfortable, unpleasant, even intimidating. A bold stare can be interpreted as arrogant, presumptuous, even hostile or threatening. It can be seen as indicating grandiosity or even psychopathology. This is why part of the skill of using eye contact well is knowing when to disengage.

Appropriate use of eye contact is a social skill that most of us learn early. Parents admonish their children not to stare at others, and we learn this lesson thoroughly. Too much eye contact, or too little, will brand you as inappropriate or uncertain, unskilled or unsophisticated, socially aggressive or socially inept. Eye contact is extremely potent, but it must be handled with care.

Kinesics: Movement, Posture, and Gesture

In addition to general appearance and facial expression, we communicate emotion through bodily movement, posture, and gesture. The study of these things is known as **kinesics**. We can read general mood, bearing, or state of health from the way someone moves; we can assess confidence and command of self and situation from how much someone fidgets; we can get a sense of attitude and co-operativeness from someone's positioning in a space.

If Gregory shuffles along slowly with his head down, he is likely to be read as unhappy or worried, particularly if he normally walks jauntily with his head held high. A habitual slouch, excessive fidgeting, or ungainly movement may be read as social discomfort or a lack of confidence. Someone who gestures dramatically will be perceived as more confident and more sociable than someone who rarely uses gestures to amplify points; if the gestures are too over-the-top, however, the person may be perceived as overly excitable or out of control. Someone who must be constantly on the move and can't seem to sit still for five minutes may be seen as energetic and exciting, or perceived as restless and inattentive. The impression that we make on others through our body language helps to condition how they respond to us and may influence not only their judgement of us but also the way the interaction unfolds.

Positioning can also make a difference to our interpersonal interactions. For instance, standing up when others are sitting can be a sign of authority, formality, or distance, as when a public speaker stands to address a crowd. In a personal situation, if we remain standing when someone else is sitting, we may signal a desire for greater emotional distance or a more formal interaction, as perhaps when we are seeking a raise from the boss or telling an intimate that the relationship is over. However, to stand over someone who is already sitting down may make us come across as overbearing, intimidating, even threatening.

Frequently, when people are communicating interpersonally, they demonstrate the phenomenon known as postural echo, in which each tends to take a posture similar to the posture of the other. This is particularly true if they are getting along well and find that they share attitudes and opinions. Postural echo is not usually a deliberate choice, but an unconscious reaction to perceived like-mindedness and similarity. A disharmony in body positioning can signal some disagreement in the interaction.

Proxemics: The Human Use of Space

We also communicate by means of our use of space, or **proxemics**, as the anthropologist Edward T. Hall established.[12] The most obvious ways that distance influences communication has to do with how much space we like to keep between ourselves and others during different kinds of interactions. These norms vary greatly by culture; for example, North Americans typically prefer greater distances than their European, Middle Eastern, or South American counterparts. Hall defined four different comfort distances that individuals employ during social interactions:

- intimate distance: 0–18"
- personal distance: 18"–4'
- social distance: 4'–12'
- public distance: 12'–∞

These norms are for mainstream North American culture; those from other cultures might be expected to prefer shorter distances for the same interactions.

The first of Hall's categories is **intimate distance**, which ranges from the skin outward approximately as far as you can extend your arm around someone—for most of us in Canada, this distance is about 18–20 inches. Normally, entry into this 'bubble' of space is reserved only for our closest friends and intimates. These distances are approximate, of course, since there is some variety among individuals regarding how much distance they need to feel comfortable. For example, Joanne won't ride an elevator if there's anyone else on it, and when she visits someone she doesn't know well, she always chooses an armchair rather than a seat on the chesterfield, to avoid the risk of a stranger sitting close to her. It's likely that Joanne's personal space bubble is larger than average. Not just for Joanne but for all of us, intrusion into this space without consent is acutely uncomfortable, and may even be experienced as a threat or as a form of harassment. Our need for this 'bubble' of intimate space is the reason that, when people are crowded into an elevator or other enclosed space, everyone avoids making eye contact, which would increase the discomfort and threatening nature of this unwelcome contact.

The second comfort space is known as **personal distance**, which begins where the first bubble ends and continues out to approximately four feet. Personal distance is suitable for conducting most of our interpersonal interactions, such as conversing in public. The closer range of personal distance is where most couples stand in public; the further range is where most of us are comfortable conversing with strangers. Generally speaking, the more intimate the relationship, the closer people stand.

As you can imagine, people whose cultural norms have accustomed them to stand much closer to non-intimates may be perceived by a Canadian as pushy or even threatening; conversely, a Canadian might be regarded by someone from South America or Europe as emotionally cold, distant, and standoffish. It's hard to imagine what such a visitor might make of Joanne, who keeps even her intimate friends at a distance. Even within a culture, preferences will vary somewhat, and people in conversation will automatically adjust the distance between themselves and another person to a distance that they find appropriate. Thus, when Joanne finds herself in conversation with Franco, who is Italian, they might find it very difficult to achieve a distance that is comfortable for both of them, since each time Franco moves closer, Joanne backs away. I once saw such a dance at a cocktail party; a man who shared Joanne's preference for distance was effectively backed right around the room by his conversational partner, who kept advancing on him as he kept retreating.

The third comfort zone is **social distance**, in which slightly more formal interactions take place. This distance ranges from approximately four feet to about 12 feet. Interactions between colleagues at work or between customers and salespeople, which are not especially personal, would normally take place within this distance. For example, if you visit your boss's office to ask about an upcoming project or to seek a raise, you would expect a distance of at least four feet would be maintained, frequently with a desk in between. When you are approached by a sales clerk in a store or showroom, you expect that the interaction will take place at a similar distance of at least four feet. You would likely feel uncomfortable, even pressured, if the salesperson moved in too close.

Of course, the friendlier the relationship, the less distance you would feel compelled to maintain. Generally speaking, however, the greater the level of formality in the interaction, the greater the distance we feel is necessary. Choosing the optimal distance can influence how we experience an interaction, how comfortable and satisfying it is, and we can 'personalize' some of our interactions by slightly reducing the amount of distance that we maintain.

Interestingly, visitors to Canada from Europe, the Middle East, or South America may be surprised to find Canadians reacting negatively or defensively to their friendly overtures. If so, it could be because they are standing too close and thus presenting an implied threat to their hosts. A little consideration on both sides can help to prevent such misunderstandings.

Finally, **public distance** is anything from 12 feet to infinity. This is the distance that is used for public performances or speeches, and most of us feel slightly uncomfortable if a public interaction is pushed closer to us. Consider, for instance, if your professor circulates and stands over your desk as she lectures. Many students, feeling their space slightly invaded, will cease taking notes or, if it is an exam, will stop writing until the professor moves away.

Most classrooms are arranged for teaching to occur at the closer range of public distance, though in that situation we have some ability to modify the distance to suit our own level of comfort. We can reduce interaction, and thus interpersonal pressure, by increasing the distance or the number of obstacles between ourselves and the speaker. Take note of the way your classmates have positioned themselves in the room; assuming that the seating arrangement is voluntary and that there are no other reasons that constrain people's choice of seating, those who wish to increase their interaction with the instructor are likely sitting close to the front of the room, or near an aisle where the instructor is likely to pass by. Those who wish to minimize interaction will likely be positioned towards the back of the room or near a wall where the instructor is unlikely to come near. Others whose preferences are more moderate will position themselves somewhere in between.

In every culture, there is a correlation between distance and the kind of interaction that can take place. We do not conduct intimate conversations at a public distance; likewise, most of us would find it weird or uncomfortable if someone in a formal, public role moved in too close. Generally speaking, the closer the space, the more intimate and informal the interaction; introducing more space tends to impose not only physical distance but also interpersonal distance and a greater level of formality. Thus conversations with good friends take place within our personal or even intimate distance; social interactions with acquaintances, such as conversations at a party, occur at personal or social distance; formal exchanges on the job or in a business setting likely occur within our social distance; and public events—speeches or classroom instruction—take place typically at a public distance. At the further reaches of public distance—30 feet and beyond—the possibility of two-way communication becomes as remote as the space between the participants. You will have noticed, if your college or university has very large classrooms, that the larger the distance at which you must operate, the less personal the contact.

Another feature of how we use space that affects our communicative dynamics is the arrangement of the physical layout. We can select and arrange furnishings and other objects in the room to emphasize comfort; we can organize them to establish and manage power; we can arrange a space to maximize efficiency; or we can structure the surroundings to encourage or discourage interaction. Through our arrangement of space, we can establish attitude, formality, intimacy, or authority. We do this to reflect our personal preference and interaction style, of course, but we may also arrange different spaces to emphasize different values. A kitchen may be arranged with efficiency in mind, or it may be made an inviting and homey gathering space. A family room emphasizes comfort in its selection and arrangement of furnishings, whereas in the same home a living room or parlour may have an untouchable quality. An office might provide an intellectual or business-like atmosphere that minimizes distractions, whereas a game or hobby room might present a riot of colour or 'fun' accessories. The company boardroom emphasizes the firm's success through its expensive good taste, whereas the boss's office reinforces his authority.

As an example, consider the differences in the offices of Professor Hautch and Professor McLaren (Figure 6.1). The offices are identical in size and furnishings: they are longer than they are wide, with a door at one end and a large window at the other. There are bookshelves along one side. The offices contain a desk, a filing cabinet, and two chairs, but the profs are free to arrange these items in any configuration they prefer.

Professor McLaren's office shows the desk against one wall with a chair positioned at one corner of the desk for student consultations. The office space itself is quite open. Professor Hautch has divided his room in two by placing the desk across the space so that the window is behind him. The student's chair faces him across the desk.

You may also notice that Professor Hautch's office contains an extra feature that

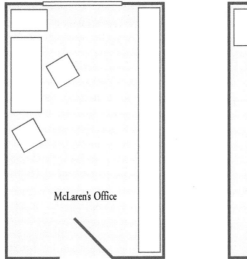 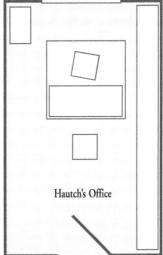

McLaren's Office   Hautch's Office

Fig 6.1
Office Layouts for Professors McLaren and Hautch
What difference do you notice? What does each layout emphasize?
What is communicated to the students who enter?

doesn't appear in Professor McLaren's office: his desk and chair sit on a raised dais or platform. A student sitting in the chair opposite Professor Hautch finds himself peering over the top of the desk, which now comes nearly to chest height. The professor is backlit by the window. While it may be that this dais was already in the office when Professor Hautch moved in and that he therefore has no choice but to arrange his office in this manner, there is no such platform in any other faculty office in the building.

Which office would be more inviting and conducive to student–professor interaction? Why? Which professor do you think is visited more often by students? What does each of these office layouts say about the professor who works there?

The arrangement of space affects the kinds and quality of interactions that take place within it. Consider, for instance, what is contributed to the interactions that occur there by the design of a cathedral, a court room, a theatre, or a tennis court. Consider, too, a time when you have deliberately chosen a setting for a special occasion or interaction: a romantic dinner, a late-night poker game, a wedding ceremony or reception, a picnic, a pub crawl. Why did you choose, or arrange, the venues as you did? What did they contribute to the kind of interaction that took place?

Paralanguage

We know already that our speech and writing are interlaced with non-verbal information that can intensify, qualify, amplify, or even contradict and undermine our verbal messages. Although non-verbal influences are present in all our communication, including written messages,[13] they are most influential in our face-to-face communication and have an impact on our interpersonal effectiveness. When we speak, our verbal communication is accompanied by other vocal qualities that are not considered part of the language but that nevertheless influence what we say. These vocal additions to our verbal communication are known as **paralanguage**, and they carry considerable information about such things as the speaker's attitude to the listeners, her commitment to the content of what she is saying, or her general confidence.

Paralanguage includes such features as volume, rate, pitch, articulation, tone, voice quality, rhythm, and accent; it also involves the lack of sound, as in hesitation, pauses, or breathlessness. Finally, it includes vocal fillers such as 'um' or 'uh'. Paralinguistic elements can also vary with a speaker's native language; some languages use tonal cues much more extensively than we typically do in English. The elements of paralanguage discussed here are those associated with English as it is spoken in Canada.

Paralinguistic qualities can reinforce or undermine our impression of a speaker's confidence: perhaps she speaks too softly to be heard, says 'um' so frequently that the coherence of her words is destroyed, or engages in 'uptalk'—a raised pitch at the end of statements as if she is asking a question. All of these habits can be heard as uncertainty or lack of confidence.

On the other hand, a loud voice can suggest excitement or anger, engagement or belligerence, enthusiasm or unruliness. Someone who habitually speaks more loudly than average may inadvertently communicate overexcitement, arrogance, or an inability to govern himself appropriately. The rate at which you speak and the clarity of your articulation can also affect how intelligent others think you are, irrespective of what you are talking about. If they can't understand you easily or have to work too hard to make out your meaning, they may dismiss your point of view without even having had a chance to consider it seriously.

Have you ever had the experience of speaking up about something you know about, only to have your opinion discounted by others present? Have you wondered why it is that, even though you are knowledgeable about the subject, you couldn't win a hearing from those around you? If so, perhaps it has something to do with your paralanguage. Listen carefully to those who make their living with their talk—broadcast journalists on radio and television are a good example—and, whether you agree or disagree with the *content* of what they are saying, pay attention to how clearly they enunciate their words, how rarely they use vocal fillers, and how effectively they modulate their voices. You will notice that most of these professional speakers have developed a pleasing, mellifluous sound—no screechy or nasal qualities, no constant throat-clearing, no noisy breathing or wheezing, no 'ums'. There is simply no mistaking the sound of a voice that has been trained to establish authority, to communicate enthusiasm and engagement, and to win listeners' confidence through careful articulation, fluent modulation, and effective use of pauses.

One of the trickiest components of paralanguage is accent. Some communication scholars claim that it is sounding different, even more than looking different, that marks someone as 'other' and that may cause difficulties in communicating.[14] People who speak English as a second language, native English speakers from other parts of the world, or those who come from regions of our own country where speech patterns vary from what is considered the norm, frequently carry evidence of their original speech patterns with them in the form of marked accents. An accent in itself is not a bad thing, of course—it is part of the music of speech, particularly in a multicultural society. Nevertheless, people who hail from St John's or Glace Bay may have trouble being understood in Toronto or Calgary; Canadians whose first language is Cree or French or Gaelic may speak English with a noticeable accent or use expressions that others do not understand; English speakers who come to Canada from Australia or Scotland will always sound foreign to Canadian ears. And, of course, new Canadians from non-English-speaking countries have the greatest challenge of all.

Should those who speak with a nonstandard accent seek to eliminate the sound from their speech? There is no easy answer to this question; some will want to sound more like the people around them and will seek accent modification training, as Alfred, a Chinese acquaintance of mine, has chosen to do. Others will reject such an idea, since the accent is part of their origins and hence part of their self-definition.[15] Still others may find themselves automatically adjusting their speech to remove what they experience as a stigma. When I moved to Ontario from Cape Breton, and again when I moved to Washington state from Ontario, I found myself unconsciously moderating my accent and my way of talking, not because I had difficulty making myself understood, but because it made me uncomfortable to have others comment on my unusual speech patterns. Now, although I can still hear the rhythm of Cape Breton in my voice, I find that my habitual speech pattern bears marks of all of the regions where I have lived.

Paralanguage—pacing, tone, articulation, and rhythm—accompanies all our speech, and communicates to others how intelligent we are, how engaged we are with what we are saying, whether we 'belong' in a given group. It can help establish or undermine credibility, build passion, or inspire confidence. Great speakers can use their voices in nearly magical ways to invoke powerful responses in their audiences. Preachers can stir their audiences spiritually, comedians can contribute to the humour of their routines, and sports announcers can generate part of the excitement of watching a hockey game. When a hypnotist lulls you into a trance, it is through the management of her voice—quiet, concentrated, intimate, comforting. When we speak it is the attitude, tone, and mood of how we communicate rather than the content of what we say that makes the greatest impact on others.

Chronemics: Time as Communication

If everything we do conveys a message, and if all of our communication is accompanied by non-verbal communication, even our use of time constitutes a means of communicating with others about such matters as status, power, and importance. We do this through the timing of meetings or gatherings, punctuality and lateness, and who waits for whom. The study of time as communication is known as **chronemics**.

Interestingly, conceptions of time have been among the most significant factors in cross-cultural misunderstandings. According to one analyst, 'time is one of the most central differences that separate cultures and cultural ways of doing things.'[16] Western cultures, including North American and European cultures, view time very differently from how it is conceived in Eastern cultures such as India. Aboriginal cultures, too, tend to understand time differently from the predominant Western view, which typically sees time as a progression—linear, logical, and sequential. It is also present-focused, since the past is seen as over and done with, behind us, while the future is a distant goal not yet achieved.

By contrast, non-Western cultures are reported to see time as repeating itself in an eternal cycle in which past and future are nearby, contained within the experiences of the current moment. Time is fluid, something in which we are immersed, rather than a commodity that we use up.

Neither of these views of time is *wrong*; they are simply different, and interactions that are heavily influenced by issues of time—appointments at a certain hour, meetings of a certain duration, deadlines that must be met—can be difficult if the two parties bring very different understanding of the shape, importance, or role of time. Mainstream Canadian society operates very much by a 'Western' conception of time, in which time is linear and is measured, like inches, in incremental units.

Naturally, none of us lives in a vacuum; every group or culture in the world has now had some experience of the other's ideas of time and space, thanks to the impact and influence of mass media. Our Aboriginal cultures are no exception, whatever their original experience of time may have been. Nevertheless, cultural values can remain a potent force in how we communicate, and can contribute to interpersonal, cultural, and even political misunderstandings on both sides.

The important point here is that management of time, like other non-verbal behaviour, can itself be a message that communicates either respect and regard for the interests and needs of others, or an utter disregard for them. Even cultural differences such as those surrounding time can be used in exactly this way. Consider some of the cultural differences implicit in a land-claims dispute, especially as they were conducted in the past. A team of government negotiators insist on tight time frames, arguments based on bare facts and figures, flow charts and rationally founded claims; meanwhile, the Aboriginal representatives take time to tell stories about the interconnectedness of the people and the natural world, to celebrate their links to past and future, to honour the ancestors who are with them in spirit. Both groups may be acting in good faith, simply proceeding on the assumptions that come most naturally to them. Or each may be deliberately exploiting their cultural differences, cloaking a power agenda in the trappings of culture. The bureaucrats, perhaps, hope to confound the other side with incomprehensible charts, diagrams, and reams of reports written in impenetrable bureaucratese. For their part, the Aboriginal leaders perhaps hope to befuddle their opponents with long, drawn-out narratives that don't seem to go anywhere or have any bearing on the issues at hand. Perhaps the situation involves a bit of both—genuine expressions of a cultural perspective *and* a deliberate tactic to help their side seize the advantage in a negotiation.

What is most important for us to consider from an interpersonal perspective, however, is that whenever the management of time is used to the discomfiture of others it is an expression of power and control. Consider Cheryl, who works as a junior administrator in the policy management office of a large organization. Because policy issues touch every department in the organization, a policy representative—Cheryl—must be present at any meeting in the organization where the issues are likely to affect policy or procedure. Thus, she has a finger in a wide range of projects and units, and must attend meetings across every department.

In the 10 years since she joined this organization, and out of the hundreds of such meetings that she has attended, Cheryl has been on time exactly twice. Cheryl is not Aboriginal, nor is she from an Eastern culture, but even if she were, it would be disingenuous for her to claim that the rest of the company is working with a different conception of time than she is used to. She has worked there long enough to be well aware of the protocols in the company and in the culture at large. Thus, we can suspect that there is some other reason for her persistent tardiness.

Although she sits ex-officio in most of these meetings and thus doesn't have a vote in their proceedings, Cheryl represents the policy management office and, technically, the meetings can't get underway until she arrives. Although she is a minor functionary in her own department, she nevertheless has found a way to inflate her organizational importance through her manipulation of time, since others cannot go about their business without her. The fashion of her entrance to each meeting also seems to be intended to inflate the importance of her position—her bustling manner suggests that, unlike the others, she has so much to do that she can't possibly make it on time to every little meeting.

As Cheryl's example shows, people who wish to display or exert power can sometimes use time to do so. Not all such gestures are as self-serving as Cheryl's, however. Tobias, a manager who wants to keep meetings short and on topic, routinely schedules them late on a Friday afternoon. Everyone in the department is obliged to attend, so in order to get out of there and not delay the start of their weekend, his subordinates stick to business and come to agreement quickly, without wasting time in pointless haggling. Although they hate the timing, everyone agrees that at least their meetings seem to accomplish the tasks that need doing, and they never drag on overtime, as meetings in other divisions do.

Power in interpersonal relations can be expressed by who gets to control the duration of an interaction and who has to wait for whom. Karen is dearly loved by her friends for her generosity and willingness to help out in a crisis, but when she phones, they dread seeing her number come up on their caller ID, since once she gets talking they can't get her to stop. No amount of hinting seems to bring the call to a close. Pam has even on occasion 'accidentally' hung up on Karen.

Chronic disregard for others, as expressed in the abuse of their time, can have many causes—it may not always be as strategic as Cheryl's. But if it happens repeatedly it may nevertheless suggest that the other person's time, and therefore the other person, is not as valuable as your own, or as you yourself are. On the other hand, some people use a fanatical obsession with punctuality as an expression of superiority. Allan and Kayla have invited a few friends in for dinner. Kayla has set the time for 'seven-ish', meaning that most of the guests will arrive between seven and seven-thirty. But Nancy shows up at five to seven and sits fuming for the next half-hour as the others trickle in.

The management of time, like other non-verbal behaviour, can encode meaning, displaying our attitudes towards ourselves, the situation, and the other participants. It can establish and maintain respect and good will, or it can be used indirectly as a form of aggression.

Touch

Touch is essential to human survival. It is known, for example, that infants who are otherwise well cared for can die without human contact.[17] Adults, too, suffer from a deep loneliness without the comfort of touch.

Touch is one of the richest and most fundamental forms of human communication. It provides security and solace, establishes and expresses intimacy, and can even be therapeutic. As a form of communication, touch encompasses everything from a handshake to a pat on the back to a caress. Touch communicates affection, approval, and encouragement; it can signal pride in a job well done. It can also, of course, indicate sexual interest.

Touch creates and maintains the bond between people: between mother and child, between friends, between lovers. Touch builds, and requires, trust with others. The touch of a supportive friend, an approving dad, a devoted mom can inspire confidence as we set out on a difficult task.

But touch, like all non-verbal communication, is complex and somewhat ambiguous in certain circumstances. Because it is such an intimate thing, social uses of touch can be highly charged. For example, in Canada strangers do not usually touch each other except in highly prescribed ways, such as shaking hands. You may also be touched by your physician, your dentist, your hairdresser, your tailor, or your massage therapist in the performance of their work. But it is unlikely that you would be touched by your mechanic, your veterinarian, your plumber, your dry cleaner, or your cab driver.

In our culture, touch between those who are not intimates is also highly restrict-ed and codified as to the level of intimacy it signifies: a touch on the arm is less inti-mate than on the back; a touch on the back is less intimate than one on the front of someone's body; a touch on the upper back is less intimate than on the lower back. To catch the attention of a stranger you might touch him lightly on the arm or the shoulder. To greet a new acquaintance you might shake hands, perhaps even gripping her hand in two of yours. Someone may extend you a hand to help you up or down from a vehicle or other awkward place. Occasionally, someone who is showing you around might lightly touch your arm or upper back in the course of guiding you.

Touch can be a display of affection or politeness, but it can also be a display of power, since in general those of superior social status can touch subordinates more freely than subordinates can touch their superiors. You may, for example, receive an encouraging pat on the back from a teacher, a coach, a supervisor at work. But it is less usual for a subordinate to touch the boss or a supervisor as a form of encourage-ment. Canadian men and women show different patterns of social touch; women can touch others, including men, more freely than men can. But because uninvited phys-ical contact, whatever its intention, may be read as harassment, we are all likely to be circumspect in our touching behaviour, particularly in a work context. Because touch is such a potentially intimate thing, it can also be threatening, and men especially are inclined these days to touch less.

In general, we in Canada, and in North America generally, are far less culturally 'touchy' than Europeans and South Americans. Thus visitors from those areas may experience Canada as an emotionally cold culture, while Canadians living in these cultures may feel uneasy about the unaccustomed physical contact.

Improving Your Non-verbal Acuity

While non-verbal communication is ambiguous and difficult to interpret with any exactness, it is nevertheless possible to become a more sensitive and acute 'reader' of the non-verbal cues of others. The first step in that direction is to keep firmly in mind the fact that a given non-verbal expression could have a variety of possible meanings, some of which may not be immediately evident to you, and some of which may be compounded by differences in culture. Despite the promises of those who hope to sell us dictionaries of non-verbal signs,[18] there is a huge range of personal and cultur-al influences that shape the meaning of an individual expression or action. Instead of jumping to an immediate interpretation, note what you saw and continue to pay attention to other signs of what a person may be feeling.

You can do several things to become more sensitive to others' non-verbal commu-nication. First, you need to learn to attend to subtle cues, not just obvious ones. Watch others' facial expressions while they are speaking; it is particularly good practice to do this when they are speaking to others and not to you, as for example when you are watching someone speak in a meeting. The pattern of eye contact is another cue to the person's emotional state. Tone and other paralinguistic features can also provide insight, as can stance, posture, and movement.

In particular, as you begin learning how to observe, pay attention both to the habitual non-verbal patterns of others and to any exceptions to these habitual patterns; both will tell you something about your colleague's sense of self, her place in the order of things, her attitude to the subject under discussion, and her general bearing. Make it a habit to observe the non-verbal panorama around you when you're sitting in a coffee shop, making your morning commute, or strolling along the mall or through the student centre. People will reveal a lot about themselves to those who are patient and observant enough to learn how to see it. Such observations can even improve your sensitivity to the non-verbal cues of other cultural groups.

The second thing you need to attend to if you are going to be a better reader of non-verbal cues is to recognize the role of context in shaping how we all interact. The physical setting, the circumstances of the interaction, the balance or imbalance of power can all have an impact on how each of us behaves. For example, we are all likely to interact differently at a funeral than we are at a garden party, even if we are among the same people. The history of the particular kind of interaction we're involved in, as well as the history of our relationship, or our own previous experience with the same kind of circumstances, can also shape what takes place. For example, Donna is very shy and is unnerved by job interviews. She's already had a number of unfortunate interview experiences that have only made her difficulties worse. Thus, in a new interview situation, her nervousness may create non-verbal reactions that could miscue the interviewers.

In paying attention to context you need to keep in mind the personal stakes of the various players in the interaction. The more someone has to lose, the more uneasy he will be, whereas the more in control someone feels, the more confident he can appear. Try to take these things into account as far as you are able to do so in assessing the unspoken communication that takes place in a given interaction.

The third step in improving your non-verbal acuity is to consider the ways in which your own non-verbal signals may be affecting the interaction. Just like the other person or persons, you bring with you issues of power, context, and personal stakes. Like them, you may have an agenda for the interaction that affects what you are communicating. Keep in mind that your own interaction style may also influence how others respond to you.

Finally, remember that your assessments of others' non-verbal communication are always provisional. All non-verbal communication is ambiguous, and may be the result of a variety of influences you can't see right way. Don't stop observing once you think you've got it all figured out; look for additional cues that may confirm or contradict your tentative conclusions. Pay attention not just to one or two individual expressions but to a person's overall interaction pattern in order to gain as accurate an understanding as you can. Consider, too, how culture may affect what you're observing.

Improving Non-verbal Skill

Finally, although you will never bring your non-verbal communication completely under conscious control, it is possible to become more skilled in managing your own cues. Try to keep in mind the communicative power of even subtle expressions and gestures and the way they can influence an interaction. Others may be very sensitive to the subtle elements in your tone, bearing, or expression that you aren't aware of yourself. Try to be more observant and learn more about your own style.

If non-verbal mastery is important to you, you might arrange with a friend to videotape you during an ordinary interaction, when you are not conscious of the taping. Study the tape to learn how you appear to others. If you think you can handle the honest feedback, ask a close friend to provide you with an analysis of your non-verbal behaviour. Be aware, however, that you may be inviting insights that will make you defensive or uncomfortable.

Most of all, pay attention to little things that you say or do. When you've interacted with someone else, especially when you feel that the interaction didn't go as well as you had hoped, reflect on how you presented your message. Would you want to be addressed in the manner that you used with the other person? Was there anything you did that may have contributed to the way the interaction turned out? Watch others whose communication skill you admire. What non-verbal features of theirs seem particularly effective? Can you learn to incorporate similar skills into your own interactions? Finally, as a general rule, try to communicate genuine interest in the other person as you interact, and try to maintain—and communicate—a positive attitude.

Non-verbal communication accompanies all of our interactions, tempering, contradicting, enriching, and amplifying the things we say. Even our silences contribute to what we communicate non-verbally. With non-verbal communication even more than with any other medium, the truth of Axiom #9 is everywhere evident: *Remember: you cannot not communicate.*

Key Terms

appearance

chronemics

intimate distance

kinesics

non-verbal communication

paralanguage

personal distance

power

proxemics

public distance

social distance

touch

Suggested Readings

Haig A. Bosmajian, ed., *The Rhetoric of Nonverbal Communication* (Glenview, Ill.: Scott, Foresman & Co., 1971). Bosmajian's edited collection, now unfortunately out of print, is available second-hand from on-line bookstores, and is worth a look for those who are curious about the political and rhetorical implications of non-verbal behaviour. The reader, part of the Scott, Foresman College Speech Series, is geared to an undergraduate audience, and includes essays on everything from how to read body language to the communicative function of rhythm, touch, music, picketing, even Nazi marching.

Julius Fast, *Body Language*, rev. updated edn (New York: M. Evans and Company, 2002). Fast's book, first published in 1971, has become a classic, and covers all of the major forms of non-verbal communication, from posture and facial expression to body movement and use of space. Addressed to a popular audience, it's highly readable and entertaining.

Valerie Manusov and Miles L. Patterson, eds, *The Sage Handbook of Nonverbal Communication* (Thousand Oaks, Calif.: Sage, 2006). A scholarly rather than popular treatment, this reader includes essays on every facet of non-verbal communication research, from types of non-verbal expression to descriptions of research approaches. It's excellent reading for those who are serious about the study of non-verbal behaviour from a social scientific perspective.

Barbara Pease and Allan Pease, *The Definitive Book of Body Language* (New York: Bantam, 2006). Pease and Pease follow in the track initiated by Fast. Although the book draws on research in psychology and neuroscience, it should be read more for its entertainment value than its scholarly depth. The authors claim to provide a 'basic vocabulary to read attitudes and emotions through behaviour', a somewhat dubious claim given the notorious ambiguity of non-verbal communication.

Virginia P. Richmond and James C. McCroskey, *Nonverbal Behaviour in Interpersonal*

Relations, 3rd edn (Boston: Allyn & Bacon, 1995). Richmond and McCroskey's book is an in-depth scholarly treatment of the types of non-verbal communication outlined in this chapter. Intended for a university course in non-verbal communication, the book is accessible to an undergraduate audience, and covers such topics as physical appearance, gesture and movement, face and eyes, space and territory, and vocal behaviour.

Exercises and Assignments

1. Spend 15 minutes watching a TV drama or sitcom, with the sound turned off. Carefully observe the use of non-verbal elements in the program, including in the commercials. Focus on facial expression, body positioning, and gesture. What kinds of cues predominate? What sort of information do they convey? Are you able to glean much about the plot from the non-verbal cues? Keep a record of your observations for class discussion.

2. Your instructor will divide the class into pairs. Sitting or standing about two feet from your partner, and without speaking, try to maintain eye contact for a full two minutes. Discuss the experience with the class. How uncomfortable was the experience? Was it difficult to maintain contact for the full time? Is there any face threat associated with this activity? If so, in what way? What reaction did you experience at being stared at for so long? What reaction did you experience at having to stare at someone else for so long? What was communicated to you by your partner? What do you think you communicated?

3. Consider the contribution of non-verbal communication to the effectiveness of the Personal Icon exercise. How much were people able to communicate through non-verbal means? Did anyone include verbal elements in the Icon? If so, why might people have chosen to do so? What did the addition of verbal elements contribute?

4. What is the connection, if any, between non-verbal and symbolic communication? How does the symbolism of non-verbal communication differ from the symbolism inherent in verbal communication? Is the linguist Roy Harris correct in arguing that non-verbal communication is not language? Write your answer in a brief essay of about 500 words.

5. Consider again Rose De Shaw's 'Guilt, Despair, and the Red Pottery Pig' (Appendix B). The pig is not language, but it is clearly symbolic. Is its meaning private among the members of the group, or is its symbolism more broadly social or cultural? To what extent does it incorporate both? What is the connection, if any, between non-verbal and symbolic communication? How does the symbol-

ism of non-verbal communication differ from the symbolism inherent in verbal communication? Present your analysis in writing or as part of class discussion, as directed by your instructor.

6. Your instructor will divide the class into pairs. Sit facing your partner with the list below in front of you. Each one of you in turn should consult the list and choose an emotion to portray using non-verbal cues, while the other attempts to identify the emotion in question. As your partner portrays the selected emotion, you should record your guess on paper. Repeat until each of you has portrayed five emotions, then briefly compare notes to see how accurately you portrayed, and interpreted, the other's emotions.

   Rejoin the group for a class discussion. What was the overall success for the class in 'reading' the emotions that others attempted to display? Or, to think of it in another way, what was the overall success for the class in accurately portraying their emotional states to others? Were some emotions harder to portray, or to read, than others? Does this exercise confirm or challenge the idea that non-verbal communication is ambiguous?

aggressive	confused	frightened	puzzled	unco-
agitated	curious	happy	sad	operative
angry	defensive	hostile	shocked	unhappy
apprehensive	depressed	impatient	shy	upset
bored	disgusted	insecure	smug	withdrawn
caring	eager	interested	surprised	welcoming
comfortable	energetic	intimidated	timid	
concerned	enthusiastic	irritated	trusting	
confident	friendly	nervous	uncertain	

In a variation of this exercise, your instructor may ask members of the class to portray their selected emotions in front of the entire class and allow the class to 'read' the body language together.

7. Study the ad parody 'Gluttony' (see Appendix B). Although the ad does contain a verbal tag line, much of its impact is visual—that is, non-verbal. How does this ad strike you? Is it funny? Is it offensive? Why or why not? What cultural attitudes does it exploit? What do the verbal elements add to the meaning of the message? What does the ad teach us about the interconnectedness of verbal and non-verbal communication?

8. In Chapter 4 we learned that the life cycle of interpersonal relationships falls into discernible stages of integration–stability–disintegration. In the integration

phase (the 'coming together') and in the disintegration phase (the 'coming apart'), people are likely to express their state of mind towards each other, and towards the relationship itself, in their non-verbal behaviour patterns. Drawing on the discussion of non-verbal communication in Chapter 6, describe and explain, based on the life-cycle theory, the types of non-verbal behaviour patterns you would expect to see in these two phases of the relationship. Be as specific as you can, and discuss at least three different types of non-verbal behaviour for each phase. Fully justify your answer using material from both this chapter and Chapter 4. Present your findings in writing or as part of classroom discussion, as directed by your instructor.

9. At the websites listed below, you will find three different 'body language' quizzes. Visit each site and try the quiz.

   a. The quiz at <www.kent.ac.uk/careers/interviews/nvc.htm> is about non-verbal skill in a job interview.

   b. The quiz at <www.bbc.co.uk/radio1/onelife/fun/personal/confidence/body/index.shtml> gives some general observations about non-verbal gestures and posture.

   c. The quiz at <www.johnboe.com/people_skills_quiz.html> is intended for those interested in a sales career.

   Drawing from information contained in this chapter, assess whether these quizzes are useful for the purposes claimed. What is the purpose of each quiz? Is any of the three 'better' than the others, from an interpersonal communication perspective? Why? What would you have to believe about non-verbal communication to take such quizzes seriously? Your instructor may ask you to present your findings in writing or in class discussion.

10. The Personal Icons created by the class were intended to symbolize each individual's self-presentation. Drawing from your experience in creating your own Icon and in reading the Icons of others, consider the meaning of such symbolic representations. If language is symbolic, does the deliberately symbolic nature of the Icons make them a form of language? Why or why not? To what degree is all non-verbal communication symbolic? Is there such a thing as non-verbal communication that is *not* symbolic? Be prepared to discuss your analysis with the class, or to present it in writing, as directed by your instructor.

Chapter 7

Listening and Responding

Learning Objectives

- To understand the interpersonal functions of listening.
- To recognize poor listening habits.
- To learn the components of listening.
- To understand the challenges of giving advice.
- To develop strategies for more effective listening.

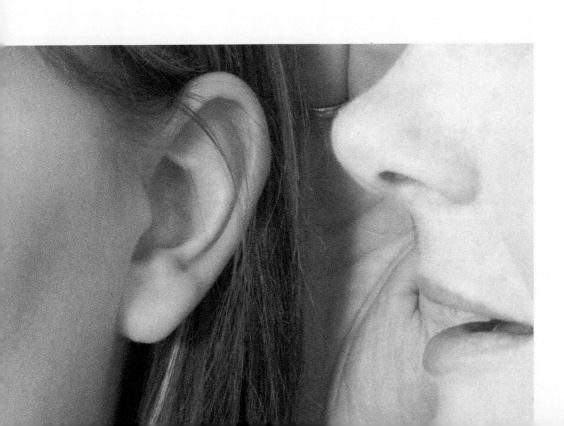

Listening may be defined as giving one's attention to a sound or making the effort to hear something. In interpersonal communication, however, listening is much more than simply attending to a sound, which is only the first stage of the perceptual process. Interpersonal listening involves paying attention to the relational content of messages as well as to their verbal meaning; it means connecting with others. It means providing support and recognition to those who communicate with us.

How important is the act of listening? According to some estimates, we spend 70 per cent of our total waking time communicating in some way, and nearly half of that is spent listening. In other words, we listen to messages that are equivalent to an average book's worth of information each day. Unfortunately, although we spend a lot of our time listening, we often don't do it very well, especially when it comes to interpersonal contexts.

PURPOSES OF LISTENING

- To obtain information
- To fulfill relational goals
- To provide affirmation and emotional support to others
- To help others gain perspective
- As a form of 'crap detection'

The Purposes of Listening

We listen for a variety of reasons. First, of course, since much of what we know comes to us from others, we listen in order to understand and retain information that we need to function in our daily lives. This level of listening is adequate for instances where content is most important, for example, if we are receiving directions to the nearest shopping centre or instructions on how to replace a spark plug, or even if we are learning factual information such as the names of Canada's prime ministers. In such cases, we will want to pay attention to ensure that we have got all of the details correct or all of the steps in the right order, but we need not be so very concerned about the relational subtext of the interaction.

However, as we have already learned, relatively little of our communication is purely informational. Most of it contributes in some way to building and maintaining the relationships that are central to a healthy, satisfying life. Thus, in addition to listening for information, we also listen in order to fulfill our relational goals. As we know from previous chapters, one of the main things people want from others is to feel that they are really being heard, that what they have to say is significant, that their existence is affirmed by the attention of someone else. Listening, therefore, is at least as important a skill of interpersonal communication as talking is, and perhaps more so.

At times, we listen to help others as well as ourselves. We listen in order to provide affirmation as others share their joys and achievements, their sorrows and disappointments. The ability to share these things with someone else makes them more meaningful or easier to bear, and we provide that emotional support to those around us.

We also listen at times to provide perspective to someone else, just as our friends do for us. When we get all wound up with a problem we need to talk it out, and it's important to have somebody to listen while we figure out what's going on. Listening is one of the ways our friends and intimates provide support to us, and one of the ways we provide similar support to them.

Finally, we may listen as a form of what Neil Postman and Charles Weingartner describe as **'crap detecting'**.[1] That is, we can listen for the ways in which messages are inconsistent, insincere, deliberately manipulative, or misrepresented. We listen to test our own assumptions and beliefs against those of others.

The Challenges of Listening

The first thing to keep in mind about listening is that it is not the same as hearing. Unless we suffer from some degree of hearing impairment, we cannot shut our ears against sound as we shut our eyes against light and images, so we cannot easily avoid hearing. But we can certainly manage to avoid listening.

Listening, unlike hearing, does not happen automatically. It is also not easy, since there are so many demands on our attention that may make it difficult to concentrate on what is being communicated. One of the things that might prevent us from listening effectively is **information overload**—we are presented with so much information that it is difficult to know what to attend to. And if we are not *attending* to what is being said, we will not be able to listen to it.

We may also be unable to concentrate on what is going on around us because we are preoccupied by concerns of our own. Our lives seem to be increasingly busy, overscheduled, and overextended, and it may be that we just don't have any mental space left to devote to information coming in from outside. As well, when too many demands compete for our attention, we may not be able to listen with care to everything or everyone we need to hear. Distractions can interfere with our ability to listen.

As well, our own thoughts move at a faster pace than speech, and we may find ourselves racing ahead of what is being said without hearing it all. We can have too much 'free time' and allow our minds to wander. As well, noise in the environment may prevent us from even being able to hear what's being said: poor phone reception, loud music playing, contractors jackhammering, kids shouting, a cat yowling can all compromise our listening.

Our perceptual process of selection, classification, and interpretation also means that not all listeners will hear a message in quite the same way. What we hear is affected by a range of factors that influence what we attend to and how we interpret what we hear. Our own emotional responses can cloud what we hear, as can our interests and priorities. We may be distracted by superficial elements of a person's message and miss the substance of what's being said—poor grammar, for example, or an unfamiliar accent. Sometimes we stop listening to avoid overload—we can't take in everything, so we just stop paying attention.

Poor Listening Habits

One of the greatest barriers to effective listening is poor listening habits. We may find ourselves victim of TV syndrome, expecting everything that we encounter to be entertaining so that we can remain passive. When it's not, we indulge in **pseudo listening**, pretending to listen while daydreaming and allowing our thoughts to spin off in another direction.

Some people listen only in order to find a segue they can use to jump in and take over the conversation. Such **stage-hogging** isn't really listening; instead, it is looking for an opening so the conversation can be turned to your own interests. A stage hog typically comes off as self-centred and self-absorbed, and uninterested in what anyone else has to say.

A related habit of poor listening is **gap-filling**, when we may think we have the gist of what someone is saying, so we don't have to pay close attention; instead, we fill in the gaps ourselves with our own inferences and examples. We may, in effect, be putting words in someone's mouth. Trevor, a computer technician at a large organization, has for months been frustrating the people he serves because of this habit. Trevor knows a lot about computers, but he's not very good at listening, so he often fails to pay attention to the details when someone calls about a computer breakdown. After listening only for a brief moment or two, he believes that he already knows what the person is going to say and so doesn't pay attention to the details of their reports. As a result, the solutions he proposes are often inappropriate and wrong.

Selective listening is another bad habit. We have all encountered someone who pays attention only long enough to confirm his existing opinion, and we all do it ourselves from time to time. We listen for things that substantiate our own point of view without taking into account the whole message. Conchita, for instance, has taken a strong dislike to her brother's new girlfriend. When Carlos brings the girl over to the house for supper, Conchita listens only enough to confirm her own attitude.

Insulated listening is a similar practice that we all indulge in from time to time. It involves hearing only what we want to hear and ignoring the rest, emotionally insulating ourselves from what we would prefer not to know. Garfield has just had this experience after his breakup with Madison. When they met in the weeks after the breakup, Garfield found himself listening for indications that she wanted to get back together. Madison seemed friendly, so Garfield convinced himself that she, like him, was planning to drift back into their romantic relationship. Garfield's friends told him that Madison was moving on and not to read too much into her friendliness, but he was sure he was not imagining a renewed interest. He disregarded completely anything that contradicted what he wanted to hear, and as a result he was devastated when Madison started dating Lal.

Listening can even be used aggressively, in ways that are designed to discredit or lash out at others. For example, a **defensive listener** looks for comments that can be interpreted as an attack, and then responds defensively, setting up the other person for an argument. **Ambushing** is another form of aggressive or hostile listening. Instead of genuinely listening with understanding to what someone else has to say, we listen only for cracks or holes in their argument so that we can pounce on what they say and catch them in a mistake. Both of these approaches use listening in aggressive and interpersonally damaging ways.

POOR LISTENING HABITS

- Pseudo listening
- Stage-hogging
- Gap-filling
- Selective listening
- Insulated listening
- Defensive listening

The Components of Listening

Listening, like all perceptual activity, takes place in several stages. The first of these, of course, is actually being able to hear what is being said. If something interferes—an impairment in my hearing, ambient noise, or too low a volume from the speaker—I will be unable to listen effectively because I can't hear what's going on.

COMPONENTS OF LISTENING

- Hearing
- Attending
- Understanding
- Remembering
- Responding

The second stage is akin to the selection process we have already discussed—in order to listen I must pay attention to what is being said. If my mind wanders, or if I am daydreaming or only half-attending, I will also be unable to listen in a meaningful way.

The third stage of listening is understanding. My ability to understand what someone is saying depends on a number of factors, including my familiarity with the language being used. If the speaker is using specialized vocabulary that I don't know, or if English is unfamiliar to me, I may be unable to grasp more than the gist of what is being said. I will also be less able to pay attention. To listen with understanding I must also be familiar with the context of the message. For example, if I attend a lecture in a field outside of my major, I may be unable to understand very much of what's going on because I lack sufficient context to grasp the message. We have all felt this kind of frustration from time to time when we have begun to study a new subject and discovered that we lack sufficient context to understand something being covered in class.

The fourth stage of listening, remembering, has to do with how well we retain what we have heard. Researchers estimate that we retain relatively little of the informational content of what we hear if we don't take specific steps to commit it to memory. Immediately following an interaction, our recall of content is about 50 per cent. After eight hours, we will remember only about 35 per cent of it, and after a couple of months have passed we will be lucky to recall 25 per cent of what we have heard. Effective note-taking can help recall by helping us remain actively engaged with what is being said, and by providing a record of our impressions.

Our memories of what we hear are strongly affected by the emotional impact of a message. Though we tend to forget the details of content, what we do retain is an overall impression of the person who spoke and of the quality of a relational interaction. Generally, we retain information that has come to us with higher intensity, intimacy, trust, or commitment. As a result, our retention of any message is strongly affected by the bond a speaker has forged with us, and by the connection we feel with the message. If we don't feel any identification with the speaker or her message, we are less likely to remember what she had to say. On the other hand, our recall of the message is dramatically improved if the speaker has established a strong bond with us or has made clear the connection between the message and our needs and interests.

The final stage of listening is responding. There are a variety of listening responses we can perform if we are genuinely attending to what someone else is saying. We may listen silently in an engaged way, absorbing the details and even, perhaps, taking notes. This is the sort of listening behaviour you would employ, for example, during a class lecture.

Interpersonal Listening Responses

To be effective, interpersonal listening often requires more active strategies, such as questioning or paraphrasing. These techniques, known as **active listening**, can help to ensure both that you stay engaged with what the other person is saying and that you are clear on what she means. Using questioning, you can obtain clarification as you go along, while paraphrasing or restating what you have heard allows you to check for misunderstandings and lets you be sure you've got things right. When paraphrasing, your aim is to restate in your own words what you think the person means; doing so offers an opportunity to verify what you think was said. You can also ask for an example, or offer one yourself, as a way of confirming that what you thought you heard is what you did hear.

Questioning and paraphrasing are effective if used with a genuine interest in developing your understanding. However, it is well to be aware that, if they are used carelessly, both these strategies can backfire. Questioning without a real commitment to developing a positive and supportive relation can seem aggressive and condescending; paraphrasing, too, can be used manipulatively to make another person look foolish. Like any of the techniques of interpersonal communication, if these are employed without good will, they can provoke defensiveness and anger, and can permanently damage the relationship. You must be very careful when you apply these strategies that you are not attempting to one-up the other person or to show off your superior communication skill. The minute you start thinking in those terms, you will have stopped listening actively and reverted to defensive, selective, or insulated listening. In short, active listening is not simply applying the techniques of questioning and paraphrasing. It is attending with sensitivity and care to what someone else is saying, and must focus on seeking genuine understanding.

Active listening strategies, if used well, can help us to better understand what's behind someone else's communication. However, there is still another pitfall to be avoided. We can run into trouble in interpersonal relationships when we perceive someone's communication as a request for information or advice, when what is wanted is actually something more, or even something else entirely. Frequently, even when someone makes a request for information, what is being sought is empathy or emotional support, rather than facts or a solution to a problem.

Why does this happen? We know already that, for a variety of reasons, people don't always make explicit what is really bothering them, and it is up to us to attend not only to the content of the message but to the implicit signs. When you are **listening interpersonally**, you are often listening for the '**message behind the message**', an unspoken request for affirmation, emotional support, and community. In such a situation, you need to be relation-centred rather than task-centred, paying extra attention to verbal/non-verbal inconsistencies—these can leak unintended or implicit messages. In such situations what gets said really isn't as important as the support that is being offered or sought.

Empathizing is a form of listening response that respects and affirms someone's feelings, irrespective of what the circumstances or factual information might be. Empathy is about acceptance and understanding, not of the content of a message so much as of the feelings that underlie it. It means feeling with someone else—sharing that person's sadness, embarrassment, anger, or even joy. **Supportive listening** goes a step further, not only reinforcing the feelings, but actively taking the person's side. You may not always be able to do both of these things, but you can at least offer some comfort and understanding of how the person feels and why.

Listening and Advice-Giving

When you are confronted with someone who is in turmoil over some personal difficulty, you may be tempted to try to analyze the person's reactions and feelings, to evaluate what you are hearing, or to offer advice. While there are times when these responses can be helpful, you have to be very careful in employing them, since the act of analyzing someone else's feelings and reactions inherently assumes a level of superiority. Before you give advice, you need to be certain that such guidance and instruction are what is called for.

Even when people request it, you should be wary about handing out advice. For example, for the past five years, Mohsen and his sister Hanyeh have been primary caregivers for their elderly father, who, though in failing health, still lives in his own home. Mohsen and Hanyeh visit him three times a day, and make sure he is eating well and taking his required medications. Although the burden is heavy, they have resisted placing their father in a nursing facility and are hopeful that he can live out the rest of his life at home. This has been their dad's expressed wish, and they view it as their responsibility to carry through no matter what the inconvenience to themselves.

Nevertheless, the stress of caring for him day in and day out is taking its toll. Talking to his cousin Ranjit on the phone last week, Mohsen remarked, 'I don't know what to do about Dad.' Ranjit, reading this comment as a request for direction and advice, responded quickly and decisively: 'Don't you think it's time to put him into a home?' Mohsen, offended, reacted with anger, and now the cousins are not speaking.

What went wrong here? There are likely several factors at issue. First, what appeared to be a request for advice was in fact more likely an expression of feeling—of the anxiety, the guilt, the frustration, the sadness, and the heavy burden of responsibility that Mohsen and his sister are carrying. The fact is, Mohsen does know what he and Hanyeh plan to do about their dad; as things currently stand, they mean to continue caring for him as they have been doing, for as long as he lives. They don't really want to alter this plan, but they both feel the need for some acknowledgement of the demands of their situation. What Mohsen sought was not advice, but recognition and support.

On a deeper level, it's even possible that Ranjit's remark posed a face threat, since in the midst of his exhaustion and frustration Mohsen has secretly entertained the idea of consigning his dad to a home. He has no intention of actually doing so, of course, and he feels horribly guilty for having thought about it for even a moment, so his cousin's comment has likely touched a nerve, causing Mohsen to react defensively.

A more sympathetic and supportive response might have been for Ranjit to acknowledge the effort Mohsen and Hanyeh are making for their dad, to honour their commitment and their sense of duty, and to recognize their stress and exhaustion. He might simply have said something like, 'It must be very difficult for you. Your father is very lucky in his children.' Notice that this response targets the feelings beneath Mohsen's comment rather than the apparent comment itself. It is a gesture of affirmation, and it would have enabled Mohsen to feel that his efforts are recognized and understood. In this situation, even a question about Mohsen's own well-being—such as, 'How are you and Hanyeh holding up?'—would have been preferable to advice.

As a listener, Ranjit heard the words, but he completely failed to hear or acknowledge the feelings behind them. Thus he misread his cousin's plea for understanding, interpreting it instead as a request for advice and instruction, and in so doing contributed to a rift that may well, due to the emotionally charged situation, become permanent.

Here is a principle that you can pretty much rely on: people in emotional turmoil generally don't want to be told what to do, even if that's what they seem to be asking for. What they often really want instead is to be heard, understood, and validated. To give unwanted advice is to provide instruction in place of sympathy and support, and is likely to lead to defensiveness, frustration, even anger, as it did for Mohsen and Ranjit.

How can you determine the difference between a situation where advice is appropriate and one where it's not? The best thing you can do is to assume in the first place

that advice is probably *not* what is called for. Offer emotional support first, and employ active listening techniques such as questioning and paraphrasing to help clarify the situation, both for your friend and for yourself. Avoid making judgements or offering evaluations, especially at first. Instead, listen to the person's feelings and reactions. If, after some discussion and clarification, it becomes clear that the person really does need some additional help in deciding on a course of action, you might then provide whatever insight you can, but even then it's better to let the person come to his own decision. You can help to outline options and you can offer your support, but in the end the choice must remain with the other person.

Giving advice in an interpersonal context is never easy, since most interpersonal interactions are not really about seeking advice, even if that's what the person said she wanted. Before giving advice, you need to recognize that doing so means you are automatically assuming a superior position of judgement and evaluation. You need to be certain that offering instruction or guidance is the appropriate response to the situation, and you need to be sure that you have the footing to offer these things to the other person. If these conditions are met, you can proceed with care; if they are not, it's better to listen and support your friend than to plunge ahead and possibly harm your relationship.

INTERPERSONAL LISTENING RESPONSES

- Silent listening
- Questioning
- Paraphrasing
- Empathizing
- Supporting

Summary

Listening is a fundamental skill of interpersonal communication—it enables us to understand others' feelings and concerns more completely. Although it is through listening that we obtain much of our information about the world, we also listen to fulfill relational goals, including providing affirmation and emotional support to others.

Listening occupies approximately 35 per cent of our waking time, but we don't always do it very effectively, particularly on an interpersonal level. In order to listen effectively, we need to engage with what is being said, set aside our own preoccupations and agendas, and bring a genuine willingness to understanding the other person's point of view. If we listen in order to segue into our own pet topic, or to trap the person into saying something amiss, or to pick a fight, we are likely to engender defensiveness and hostility in place of understanding. Listening well on an interpersonal level requires a commitment to building an effective relation rather than one-upping the other or establishing our own agenda.

Like all perception, listening takes place in stages. If we are to understand, recall, and respond appropriately to what someone is saying, we need to pay attention to what is being said. Listening effectively in an interpersonal context frequently involves active listening techniques such as questioning and paraphrasing. Both of these techniques, if used as genuine attempts at understanding, can help cement a positive relation and ensure that you are not misunderstanding the other person.

As an interpersonal function, effective listening aims at understanding the relational level of the interaction rather than focusing only on the explicit content. Since people don't always make their relational needs or motives explicit, we need to pay close attention to what is implied by what they say. In general, it is a mistake to treat someone's interpersonal disclosure as a request for information or advice; usually, it is safest to assume that what is being sought are comfort, affirmation, and support. Although giving advice is sometimes an appropriate response to such a situation, more often it is likely to harm the interaction because it automatically imposes an air of superiority on the advice-giver and casts the recipient into a subordinate position.

In order to respond appropriately to someone else's interpersonal communication, you need to pay close attention to the situation you're in, the relationship you have with the person, the reason she may have sought you out in the first place. You need to consider the 'message behind the message', whether the person is seeking affirmation or real advice. You also need to consider your own comfort level and your own agenda for the interaction.

Key Terms

active listening
aggressive listening

ambushing
'crap detecting'
defensive listening
empathizing
gap-filling
information overload
insulated listening
interpersonal listening
message behind the message
paraphrasing
pseudo listening
questioning
selective listening
silent listening
stage-hogging
supportive listening

Suggested Readings

Madelyn Burley Allen, *Listening, The Forgotten Skill: A Self-Teaching Guide* (New York: John Wiley and Sons, 1995). Allen's book explores the link between listening and overall interpersonal effectiveness, and includes material on non-verbal listening behaviour and on the relationship between influence and non-verbal communication. Allen emphasizes the importance of exhibiting a genuine interest in others as the key to effective listening, and provides tips on improving listening skills.

Wayne C. Booth, *The Rhetoric of Rhetoric: The Quest for Effective Communication* (Boston: Blackwell, 2004). Booth, a celebrated theorist of rhetoric, argues in this manifesto that communication in every corner of life can be improved if only we study rhetoric more closely. The book is addressed to a lay audience, and is a thoughtful exploration of human communication, but it is the final chapter that is of greatest interest in this context. Here he advocates what he calls 'coduction', a rhetoric that depends on deep listening by both sides.

Mark Brady, ed., *The Wisdom of Listening* (Somerville, Mass.: Wisdom Publications, 2003). Brady's approach to listening is founded on Buddhist practices, and his collection of essays treats listening as a therapeutic activity, with an emphasis on 'healing' and obtaining a sense of personal peace. It isn't precisely a self-help text, and it lacks the brisk boosterism of the Allen and Donoghue and Siegel books, but it does provide guidance for those who wish to approach listening on a more spiritual plane.

Paul J. Donoghue and Mary E. Siegel, *Are You Really Listening? Keys to Effective Communication* (Notre Dame, Ill.: Sorin Books, 2005). Donoghue and Siegel begin with the premise that nobody listens well—or at least, not well enough—and they hope to provide the solution. Their book focuses on listening in interpersonal relationships—between parents and children, between professionals and clients, between managers and staff, between friends and siblings—thereby covering most of the significant relationships in any person's life. Their book covers much of the same territory as this chapter, including basic forms of non-listening and the dangers of giving advice, and offers suggestions for listening more effectively.

Krista Ratcliffe, *Rhetorical Listening: Identification, Gender, Whiteness, Studies in Rhetorics and Feminisms* (Carbondale: Southern Illinois University Press, 2005). As her title indicates, Ratcliffe treats listening as a rhetorical activity, arguing that rhetorical listening is that which facilitates conscious identifications with the 'other'. Ratcliffe's treatment is challenging and rather radical, and establishes eavesdropping, listening metonymically, and listening pedagogically as approaches to rhetorical listening. The book is readable by an undergraduate audience, but is geared for scholars and teachers of composition.

Exercises and Assignments

1. Read the excerpt from Margaret Laurence's *A Jest of God* or Edwin Arlington Robinson's *Richard Cory* in Appendix B. To what extent is either story about a failure to listen? To what extent does it appear to be something else? Would a change in listening practices have made either of these relationships more effective? To what extent are they ineffective now? As important as listening is, can it be considered separately from other interpersonal concerns (such as self-concept, face, interpersonal needs, relationship dynamics, defensiveness, and conflict)? What does this analysis teach us about the relationship between listening and our overall interpersonal effectiveness? Present your analysis in writing or as part of a class discussion, as directed by your instructor.

2. Read 'A New Student Evaluation Form' (Appendix B) and participate in a class discussion on this reading. This article is likely to produce strong reactions and heated debate. How challenging is it to listen well in such circumstances? When defensiveness rises, what happens to listening? What does this experience teach us about the role of listening in interpersonal conflict?

3. Listening well means paying attention, not only to the words that people speak but to the emotional or relational content that may be unspoken in a given

encounter. What role did 'listening' play in the reception of the Personal Icons? How effectively were we able to pay attention to, and interpret, the meaning that others expressed through their Icons? What lesson can be learned from the Icon experience for our overall listening effectiveness?

4. The instructor will ask for volunteers from the group to speak to the class for two or three minutes about the most interesting thing they've so far learned about interpersonal communication.

   a. While the first person is speaking, the members of the class should do their best *not* to pay attention, and should communicate their inattention using whatever non-verbal means are available.

   b. While the second person is speaking, the members of the class should *pretend* to listen, but should allow their thoughts to wander elsewhere. As a listener, do your best to appear attentive but without paying attention to the speaker's meaning.

   c. While the third person is speaking, the members of the class should pay attention but do their best to communicate no reaction at all—no eye contact, no laughter, no smiles, no nods or supportive gestures.

   When the speakers have finished, discuss your reactions to the behaviour of the class. As a speaker, which audience was most challenging? What reactions did you experience? As a member of the audience, what challenges did you face in participating in this disconfirming behaviour? What was it like to be part of a group of non-listeners? What does this exercise teach us about the power of listening as an act of communication? Present your analysis in writing or as part of a class discussion, as directed by your instructor.

5. Considering the functions of listening as interpersonal communication, what is the relationship between listening and the various 'needs' theories described in Chapter 4? Choose any one of these theories and discuss fully. Present your analysis in writing or as part of a class discussion, as directed by your instructor.

6. What, if any, was the role of listening in the Personal Icon experience?

Chapter 8

Managing Defensiveness and Interpersonal Conflict

Learning Objectives

- To understand the nature and causes of defensiveness.
- To learn to distinguish the different causes of interpersonal conflict.
- To learn how to better manage interpersonal conflict.

Conflict is an inevitable part of interpersonal relationships, since we each bring a variety of face needs, values, attitudes, habits, and interpersonal skills to our interactions. We all seek affirmation and affection, a sense of approval and belonging, and a chance to be heard and understood. It is inevitable that our needs and values will sometimes come into conflict with those of others. Although we all wish to minimize the harmful effects of conflict in our relationships, the measure of our interpersonal skill is not in the extent to which we are able to avoid conflict; rather, it is in the way we respond to it. This chapter is designed to help us to understand interpersonal conflict a little better, and to develop skills that will aid us in reducing the negative consequences when conflicts do arise.

Conflicts are sometimes caused, and always aggravated, by defensive responses, and a defensive posture from one person generally evokes a like response from the other. Defensiveness thus breeds defensiveness, which escalates a climate of conflict. One of the most effective ways of defusing conflict is to minimize defensive reactions as far as possible. But before we can do that, we need to understand what defensiveness is and how it arises in interpersonal interactions.

What Is Defensiveness?

Defensiveness is the attempt to fend off or protect ourselves from an expected or perceived threat or attack. In interpersonal communication, it refers to the protective reaction we make when we perceive or experience a threat to the 'face' we have presented to the world.

Face, you will remember, refers to the social affirmation and approval that we all seek and normally are able to obtain through our interactions with others. We all want to be seen as worthy, we want acceptance and respect, we want others to think well of us. In order to obtain these positive affirmations, we invest in a pattern of behaviour that we hope will establish the face we wish to maintain.

As long as others respond positively to important parts of this self-projection, we will be unlikely to feel defensive. But when others' reactions to us seem to threaten the image we want them to approve, we will respond with embarrassment, irritation, resistance, even anger. Depending on the situation, we may feel faint or ill or sick with humiliation; we may shout, cry, or stomp out and slam the door; we may withdraw into sullen silence, refusing to participate further in the interaction; we may find ourselves unable to speak or to meet the eyes of people around us. If the message has been an overt face attack, we may respond with an attack of our own.

Whatever the specific behavioural response, once defensiveness has been aroused, two things are likely to occur: first, trust will evaporate, so that meaningful communication becomes difficult or impossible. Second, a defensive reaction is likely to breed a like reaction in the other person, so that defensiveness actually escalates and can spiral out of control, damaging the interaction and possibly compromising the relationship permanently.

We experience face attacks in many forms. The most obvious kinds of face attack are overt acts of criticism, rejection, or ridicule. Your boss criticizes the quality of your work; your mother gives you her famous lecture on irresponsibility; your prof returns a paper on which a lower grade than you expected is accompanied by a stinging comment. Smart-mouth Ernie claims your ears are too big and starts calling you 'lobes'. Others overhear it, and the name sticks for the whole school year. Closeted in a cubicle in the washroom, you overhear two of your friends making cruel fun of your performance on the dance floor last night. You ask out the attractive person who sits beside you in biology class, only to have the person retort, 'What, go out with *you*? I don't get it—is this some kind of joke?' while classmates snicker in the background.

A threat to face doesn't have to be overt, however, and implied criticisms can be just as face-threatening. As Axiom #8 suggests, 'Communication is frequently ambiguous: what is unsaid can be as important as what is said.' Consider Steve, who runs his own small renovation company, and who is currently remodelling a basement. When some friends of the homeowner drop by to check out the progress, Steve overhears the guy praising the electrician and plumber, but notices that he says nothing at all about the work Steve is doing. Like Steve, Betty has felt the same kind of indirect face attack. After two years as a lab assistant for first-year chemistry, Betty has been showing the ropes to Veronica. Imagine Betty's reaction when their supervising professor stops by to praise Veronica on her excellent performance so far in her first term of work, something she has never done for Betty. Even on this occasion, while she's full of praise for Veronica, she makes no mention of Betty's contributions.

No overt criticism has taken place in either of these situations, but it's likely that Steve and Betty both feel some loss of face. Ben, too, recently had a similar experience when he auditioned for the drama department's upcoming play. Confident he's going to be cast, he has talked a lot to everyone about how he plans to approach his anticipated role. The cast list was posted this morning, but Ben's name is not on it. You run for student council and are standing on stage in the auditorium when the results are announced; out of the entire student population, you received only 27 votes. Public incidents such as these are likely to engender a feeling of humiliation and face loss, and to make us react defensively if anyone points them out to us.

It is obvious that people may become defensive over undeserved or unjust criticism, and it's easy to see why: Ben did perform really well at his audition, and you had a very good policy platform for the elections, so naturally you both feel the sting of these symbolic rejections. But what is interesting is that defensiveness is just as likely to occur—perhaps more likely—when the criticism is justified. Your mother is right about your recent irresponsible behaviour; your prof's impression of your paper was dead on; your boss is correct to suspect that your work hasn't been up to scratch lately. So how come you feel such a need to justify yourself?

The answer, perhaps, is that your good view of yourself is being compromised. Although your critics aren't actually wrong, you had hoped for a better reckoning of your abilities. You want very much to be seen as a responsible adult, an intelligent and thoughtful writer, a capable and competent worker. Secretly, though, you sometimes fear that you are a disappointment to your parents, that you are less intelligent than you wish to be, or that you are not worthy of the faith your boss has placed in you. When you are called on a mistake that comes close to these secret concerns, it is as though your private fears are being exposed. The face loss and the resulting defensive reaction are thus that much greater.

Not surprisingly, defensiveness is likely to arise during conflicts, particularly when they involve a face investment or when deeply held values are at stake. Defensive reactions range from embarrassment and resistance to irritation or out-and-out anger. Defensiveness is a response to the sensation of being attacked, and when we feel under attack we may react with anything from an angry outburst to sullen silence. We may even go on the offensive, responding to the perceived slight with an attack on the person we feel has injured us.

As defensiveness breeds defensiveness, conflict can be escalated. Once a cycle of defensiveness is initiated, it is unlikely to recede unless one of the parties makes a concerted effort to bring it to a halt. Since defensiveness is in large part an anger response, it can be defused in the same way anger can: with laughter, with affirmation of the other's feelings, or with a suitable apology. A story is told of a team of negotiators who were involved in a particularly tense union–management contract dispute. In a brief break during an especially strained bargaining session, one union negotiator set a box of gingerbread men on the table. The others looked at him quizzically. 'At this point in the proceedings', he said, 'I figured we'd all be ready to bite someone's head off!' The resultant shared laughter defused the tension and established a bit of good will, so that the group seemed more prepared to negotiate a compromise agreement.

A genuine acknowledgement of the other's point of view can also help to defuse a defensive situation. Most of us need to feel, especially in moments of frustration and defensiveness, that we are being genuinely heard, listened to, and acknowledged. We may be defensive because we feel that we are not receiving a hearing; in such a situation, if the other person can offer a genuinely supportive response that acknowledges the legitimacy of our feelings and our reactions, we may find that our defensiveness evaporates almost on the spot.

For example, Pearl reports an incident that happened to her at work recently. She was copied on an e-mail regarding a project she is directing, sent to her new supervisor from the head of another division in the company. In it, Pearl was horrified to read the following: 'If your staff can't cope with the intricacies of this project, then I would be happy to assign one of my own staff to ensure procedures are followed correctly.' Furious at this implied insult to her competence, and worried about what her new boss must think of her, Pearl immediately went to her supervisor's office to try to defend herself and her team against the implications of the e-mail. But before she got very far, her supervisor said, 'Don't worry. I know exactly what kind of games he's playing, and I have no intention of letting him take over this project. You and your team are doing exactly what you should be doing, and you have my complete confidence.' As soon as she heard that, Pearl felt her anger and worry vanish, replaced instead by a renewed sense of respect and good will towards her supervisor.

A heartfelt apology can also help to calm someone's defensive reaction by acknowledging and helping to repair the face loss. When Calvin had just picked up his tray at the local burger joint, the clown in line ahead of him jostled his arm, upending a large soft drink over his brand new shirt. Calvin's immediate response was to get mad, but the guy was so apologetic and embarrassed that Calvin's anger was immediately defused. However, when a similar incident happened to Tim, he wasn't so lucky: instead of apologizing, the jerk turned around and pointed a finger at him, laughing. His friends Devon and Shawn had to restrain Tim from knocking the guy's block off.

These strategies offer possibilities for defusing defensive situations, but even they are not guaranteed to do so all the time. For example, laughter only works if the joke is shared. However, if a defensive person perceives that he is being laughed at or made the butt of a joke, his defensiveness will only escalate. He may feel that his genuine concerns are being trivialized, and his frustration and anger will increase. For these strategies to work, both parties in the conflict must be equally committed to resolving the dispute; if for any reason one of them prefers to maintain or even escalate the hostilities, a gesture of good will may be perceived as weakness, and may even provoke further levels of aggression.

In order to get defensiveness under control and defuse the situation, we will need to break the cycle of escalating defensiveness with strategies that help to re-establish the connection between the two parties. To do this, we need to understand what kind of conflict we are dealing with and where it is centred.

Types of Interpersonal Conflict

Interpersonal conflict arises when the needs, interests, or ideas of one person are, or appear to be, at odds with the needs, interests, or ideas of another. Conflict in some form is an inevitable part of interpersonal relationships, but many of the conflicts we experience can be managed if we understand what's driving them and take steps to minimize the damage they can do.

Conflict can arise for a variety of reasons and in a variety of forms. Some of these can be resolved relatively easily, but others can escalate out of control, particularly if we respond defensively or if we fail to recognize the central issues. What follows is a brief outline of various kinds of interpersonal conflict.

TYPES OF INTERPERSONAL CONFLICT

- Facts
- Values
- Policies
- Ego or face conflicts

Although the specific circumstances of any given conflict may be unique, interpersonal conflicts can be classified into four general types: conflict over facts; conflict over values; conflict over policies; and ego conflicts. Resolving each requires strategies unique to that type; the strategies required to resolve a simple disagreement over facts are quite different from what would be required to resolve conflicting ego needs. And the challenge to dealing with conflict is that it's sometimes difficult to discern when the real issue is an ego investment. It is also true that even simple conflicts over facts, if mishandled, can quickly escalate into face or ego conflicts.

A truly **fact-based conflict** is one in which the primary issue is merely the truth or accuracy of a particular assertion. Conflicts over such things as who won a particular sporting event, who made a famous remark, who sang that golden oldies song, or who directed a famous film are fact-based and relatively easy to resolve, so long as there are reliable records to consult, and so long as the person has not made the accuracy of his or her claim into a face issue. If fact is the only concern, checking a reliable source for information to verify or disprove the assertion can suffice.

Conflicts are relatively easily resolved when they involve simple disputes over objective facts; they become somewhat more complicated when interpretations, values, and face needs enter the picture. Sometimes conflicts that appear to be fact-based are actually of another kind. For instance, conflicts over personal information, such as the date of an appointment or the order of a series of events that happened in your shared past, may be a little more difficult to resolve unless you have some means of checking the information. For example, Peter and Jenna have scheduled a lunch meeting. Jenna is in her office on Tuesday when Peter phones from the restaurant to ask where she is. She tells him that their meeting is scheduled for Wednesday, but Peter's calendar shows that it is scheduled for today and Jenna is already late. Unless the two have recourse to a more reliable record—for instance, the e-mail exchange in which they made the appointment—the conflict may remain unresolved, especially if the relationship has a history of misunderstandings or missed appointments.

A second form of conflict involves a struggle over values. **Values conflicts** are rooted in people's deeply held convictions or beliefs regarding what is good, what is moral, what is desirable or acceptable, or what is important. These beliefs may be so completely taken for granted that we aren't even aware of them until they come into conflict with the equally strong convictions of someone else.

A values conflict may be expressed as a struggle over meaning, such as marked the recent debates about same-sex unions, in which the meaning of the word 'marriage' was a central issue. The struggle over the federal gun registry was also rooted in a conflict over values and the meaning of concepts like 'freedom'.[1]

Interestingly, in a values conflict both sides may even lay claim to the same fundamental value: respect for the sanctity of life, regard for the institution of marriage, concern for individual freedom. For example, in arguments over such issues as abortion or even capital punishment, both sides may advance arguments rooted in the sanctity of life. Opponents of legalized abortion claim that their position is fundamentally one that respects the sanctity of life, specifically that of the unborn, while defenders of legalized abortion claim just as strenuously that it is *their* position that respects the sanctity of life, since they are defending the interests of an actual life over the claims of a life that is merely potential.

Similarly, the relatively small percentage of Canadians who seek to reinstate capital punishment for convicted predators such as Clifford Olson or Paul Bernardo may lay claim to the same foundation of respect for human life that underlies their opponents' arguments. Opponents of capital punishment argue that we should not allow the state itself to become a murderer, no better than those it would put to death; to do so is to compromise the sanctity of life. Proponents of the practice, however, argue that in fact we disrespect and devalue the lives of the innocent people who were murdered when we fail to seek the ultimate sentence for their killers.

The same kind of contradiction informs arguments over the federal gun registry. Opponents of gun registration may argue that freedoms are being curtailed by the policy; they point to the expense, to the increase of state control, to the cumbersome burden of regulation. Defenders of the same legislation may start from the same value—individual freedom—but argue in contrast that the individual is most free when society is most secure, and that the expense is small in exchange for increased public safety, and thus the freedom to walk safely on the streets of our large cities.

Because values conflicts involve deeply held and often unquestioned convictions, they are much more difficult to resolve than simple conflicts over facts. We have no recourse to a 'correct' answer, since conflicts over values typically involve our interpretations, ideals, and beliefs rather than purely fact-based information. The best we may be able to hope for is to recognize a values conflict for what it is, to state our case as persuasively as possible, and at times, to accept each other's differences.

Values conflicts occur not only when fundamental values are at odds, but also when the hierarchy of value is different. For example, both Raymond and Hadih are strong proponents of human rights; both also deeply value personal autonomy and freedom of conscience, and recognize at the same time that those who cannot speak for themselves, such as children or the mentally infirm, should be defended and protected. They have become friends through their volunteer work with the local Fetal Alcohol Syndrome Resource Society.

Raymond has been appalled by the devastating effects of fetal alcohol syndrome on individuals and their families, as well as the social and economic costs to society. He knows that FAS is easily and completely preventable; all that would be required is that a woman not consume alcohol during pregnancy. However, his research on the subject has convinced him that appealing to individual conscience has been insufficient to prevent this heartbreaking—and socially expensive—condition. For Raymond, it's pretty clear that what's at stake is not only society's best interests, but also the health and well-being of defenceless children who have a right to society's protection. It seems clear to him that the need to protect newborn infants from serious, and completely preventable, lifelong impairment is more important than the freedom of any woman to drink during pregnancy. He argues that this position isn't inconsistent with his belief in individual freedom; after all, society already imposes other limitations on our freedoms in order to ensure public safety, and to Raymond this is no different. Although in principle he is committed to individual freedom of choice, Raymond has come to believe that serving any form of alcohol to pregnant women should be made a criminal offence, as should the consumption of alcohol by any woman who is or who may be pregnant.

Hadih is equally committed to eradicating the ravages of FAS, but he deeply disagrees with his friend's position on the issue. Hadih argues that a civil society must respect and defend individual autonomy, particularly in matters involving a person's own body. He cannot condone the selective criminalization of an activity that is not normally illegal, since such a policy would clearly be discriminatory. It would also be regressive; Canadians have progressively repealed or struck down laws and policies that target specific groups on the basis of sex or race. Would we wish, he asks, to return to the days when the minimum wage for women was lower than that for men, or when immigrants of Chinese descent were forced to pay a 'head tax', or when it was illegal to sell alcohol to Aboriginal people? All of these discriminatory policies are offensive to a Canadian of today, but Hadih points out that when they were current, they were all justified using some form of the same social welfare argument that

Raymond uses to defend his position. Hadih is convinced that, though it is imperfect, the best way to deal with the FAS issue is through advocacy and education.

Who is right here? In some sense, the answer is both of them, since Raymond and Hadih can each offer persuasive arguments to bolster their cases. But which one we are likely to find more convincing depends on our own hierarchy of values with respect to whether society's interests should win out over individual autonomy.[2] The issue is complex, and the two sides won't easily be brought to a compromise, since both have legitimate concerns. What is most interesting for our purposes, however, is that even people whose values are generally congruent can differ strongly on an issue because of the priorities that they give to different values in individual cases. Values conflicts are hard, sometimes even impossible, to resolve. At times the parties just have to agree to disagree, as Raymond and Hadih have ultimately done. They still argue good-naturedly over this issue, but each knows that he has little chance to sway the other.

Policy conflict is a third kind of conflict. People can agree about the facts, and even concur on values, but disagree over what they should do about their situation. For example, Becca has been volunteering long enough at the local phone-in Suicide and Depression Help Centre that she has recently been made assistant director. Except for the director, which is a paid position, the Centre runs entirely on volunteer efforts. When they complete their training, volunteers commit to doing a minimum of four four-hour shifts per month. However, Becca is aware that many of the volunteers are failing to live up to this commitment, with some spending as little as one shift a month on the phone lines.

Whatever the cause, though, the logistics are daunting. The Centre's phone lines are supposed to be open 24 hours a day, with two volunteers scheduled for every four-hour shift. Becca calculates that, even if every volunteer fulfills his or her minimum shift commitment, the Centre needs an active field of approximately 90–100 volunteers to adequately cover the six shifts a day. She has discussed the issue with Mahmood, who co-ordinates scheduling, and the two agree that right now they are barely able to cover the shifts, and then only because some dedicated volunteers are doing far more than their minimum commitment. If the people who are doing extra were to stop, the phone lines would have to shut down at least part of the time, and what's a phone-in help line if nobody's there to take the calls?

Becca and Mahmood approach the director, Scilla, to discuss the looming volunteer crisis; as long-time volunteers themselves, they believe the problem stems from the sense of alienation among the volunteer staff. Volunteers work only in pairs, and have no real opportunity to feel like part of a team or to meet or share experiences with other volunteers. Becca and Mahmood believe that the Centre should make an effort to build a sense of community, and plan to suggest that they create an e-mail newsletter and some face-to-face gatherings so as to build morale and encourage a stronger sense of identification among the volunteers.

When they meet with Scilla, she readily agrees that there is a logistical problem, and that the low participation rate among volunteers must be addressed. However, she is not particularly enthusiastic about the solutions proposed by Becca and Mahmood, because she has a policy of her own. First, Scilla proposes to make the four-shift-per-month commitment into a binding contract that volunteers will be asked to sign at the same time that they complete the confidentiality agreement; those who refuse will be expelled from the Centre. Second, those who do not live up to their minimum service agreement in a given month will be 'sentenced' to a double shift during the subsequent month. If they do not complete that commitment, they will be expelled from the Centre.

Becca and Mahmood are horrified by Scilla's idea. They argue that her proposed policy will only aggravate the problems they are already experiencing, destroying whatever good will already exists. They reason that the Centre cannot afford to expel volunteers who do not comply with the policy, since they are already stretched to the limit as it is. Besides, those who are unable, or unwilling, to meet a 16-hour-per-month commitment are not likely to agree to do 32 hours. In any case, because the staff of the Centre are all volunteers, the director has no means to enforce such punitive measures, and in fact, Becca and Mahmood argue, the policy is likely to further alienate those who already give their time to the Centre.

Becca, Mahmood, and Scilla agree that there is a problem with their volunteer staff and recognize the looming shortfall in shift coverage; they even agree that something must be done to address it. But they differ markedly in their ideas of what would be an appropriate solution.

This conflict is policy-based to the extent that it is a dispute over what action should be taken. However, as in most disagreements over policy, there appears to be an underlying difference in how the opposing sides have defined the problem. Scilla apparently believes that people should honour their promises, and that those who renege on their commitments should face the consequences. For her, the main issue appears to be compliance with the rules of the organization, and her proposed solution is therefore rule-based.

Mahmood and Becca see the situation from a completely different point of view. For them, the issue is a lack of identification or sense of belonging. They believe that the volunteers need affirmation and a sense of community, and that the Centre should provide these things as a way of acknowledging the gift of their time. These philosophical differences also point to differences in the way the two sides think about the Centre itself. To Scilla, it's primarily about a structure whose policies must be respected; the volunteers are simply one part of the overall scheme of things. To Mahmood and Becca, however, the volunteers are the central issue, since they believe that the real heart of the Centre is not its organizational structure but the people who answer the calls.

The real dispute here is not which definition of the organization is the 'right' one, though from the perspective of interpersonal relations Mahmood and Becca may appear to offer a more humane reading of the situation. The question, though, is which of these conceptions will provide the more satisfactory solution to the problem. Scilla thinks that her new policy will drive out the uncommitted volunteers so they can be replaced with those who are more likely to fulfill their obligations. Mahmood and Becca, however, believe that volunteering is a gift that must be willingly given, and that punitive measures will drive out even those who are committed.

Can such philosophical differences be bridged? It's possible that neither side will be able to help the other to see the problem from such a different point of view. But if the conflict is to be resolved in a satisfactory way, three things have to happen. First, both sides will have to try to keep their disagreement from escalating into a face conflict. This will involve a concerted effort, since at the outset each party probably believes that the other's judgement is faulty.

Second, they will have to approach the other's argument with a genuine willingness to listen and to try to understand the other person's point of view. Scilla likely has her reasons for believing as she does; for example, she has a Board of Directors to answer to, and their expectations may be helping to shape her view of what should be done to resolve the problem of lax volunteers. Mahmood and Becca have obtained their understanding and experience of the Centre exclusively from the other side of the table, as volunteers, so they identify most strongly with those dedicated people

on the phones, and they are not familiar with some of the issues or perspectives that Scilla has to accommodate.

Third, they must all have more invested in resolving the problem than in proving the other person wrong. All three want the volunteer crisis to be settled, and all three are committed to the continuation of the Centre. If they can keep that commitment foremost, it will be easier for them to come to some kind of compromise that allows all of them to feel that they've achieved their ends.

Like all conflicts, though, this one has the potential to escalate (or deteriorate, depending on your point of view) into the fourth type of conflict, one of face or ego investment. **Ego conflict** is the most difficult form of conflict to resolve because it involves the potential for public humiliation of one or both parties. Face, as we know, is a kind of public commitment to a course of action or a point of view; it is an emotional and psychological investment that involves the person's entire definition of self.[3]

Sometimes what looks like a conflict of fact or policy is actually an ego conflict. For example, when two people argue over who said what in an earlier dispute, what is at issue may relate more to face than to fact. For example, Nancy's recollection of her last argument with Margaret differs quite radically from Margaret's memory of the same interaction. They were too irritated to pay close attention to what they were saying, and each accurately recalls only her own hurt feelings, for which she blames the other. It's unlikely that this disagreement will ever be resolved unless they are willing to compromise. Similarly, if Scilla, Mahmood, and Becca allow their dispute over the Suicide and Depression Help Centre to become an argument over whose judgement is better instead of one over what policy will be most effective, the disagreement over policy may reinvent itself as an ego conflict.

Once an issue becomes tied to self-concept, it is difficult for a person to back down or compromise without feeling a loss of face. For example, Bonita has a summer job as counter clerk in a local fast-food restaurant, a mom-and-pop operation with only a few employees, including Bonita's supervisor, Reid, who has recently been promoted into the position from the job Bonita now holds. In the short time she's been there, Bonita has established herself as reliable and conscientious, so much so that the owner has already entrusted her with signing for incoming orders from suppliers; there has even been talk of allowing Bonita to open once a week.

On Tuesday, Bonita is overseeing the receipt of a large delivery of paper goods—food boxes, serviettes, plastic cutlery, and paper cups. Since the small building has no separate receiving door, orders are delivered to the front counter. Reid has impressed upon her how important it is to maintain a neat front shop; he is adamant that it creates a good impression and gives customers confidence in the general cleanliness of the restaurant. Thus, deliveries are to be moved to the storage area as soon as the paperwork has been signed.

Bonita is about half-finished putting the paper goods away when she is distracted by a phone call from a customer who is placing an enormous pick-up order for early afternoon, including several individual cole slaws, potato salads, and pasta salads, which have to be made up from the large containers in the back. Bonita knows there will be no time to do this once the lunch rush begins, so as soon as she gets off the phone, she sets about packaging the individual salads. It isn't until she hears Reid enter and start calling for her that she remembers the half-finished order of paper goods that she's left cluttering up the front shop.

Embarrassed to admit that she simply got distracted and forgot about the delivery, and fearful that such an admission might compromise her status with the owners, Bonita makes a critical mistake that escalates the incident into an ego conflict. Instead of accepting responsibility for her oversight, she instinctively attempts to save face by arguing that the boxes cluttering up the front shop are 'no big deal', and that an extra half-hour's delay doesn't matter.

Unfortunately for Bonita, Reid hears in her remarks an implied disregard not only for his explicit instructions, but also, by extension, for his authority and his judgement. In other words, Bonita has been so caught up in her own attempt to save face that she has inadvertently attacked Reid's face, causing him in turn to respond defensively.

To his credit, Reid manages not to launch an attack of his own, but it is clear from his icily polite and suddenly officious manner that he has been offended. The incident ends with Bonita doing what she now realizes she should have done in the first place: apologizing and stowing the rest of the delivery in the storage room. But although the conflict has ended, it isn't really resolved. Bonita keeps her job, but there is no more talk of giving her additional responsibilities. Saddest of all, the friendly relationship she had begun to establish with Reid has disappeared under a cloak of frosty politeness.

Making an Effective Apology

It is best, if you can, to keep your conflicts from escalating to this level. However, for a variety of reasons, it may not always be possible to avoid finding yourself in an ego conflict. Ego conflicts are the most difficult of interpersonal conflicts to resolve, because they usually involve a high level of defensiveness, and defensive people are less likely to listen to others or to want to resolve differences. You may have little hope of resolving an ego conflict unless you are able to defuse the bitterness and return the interaction to a more stable footing, one in which each party can commit to finding a reasonable solution.

De-escalation, however, will not happen on its own. Hard feelings have already been created and expressed; both parties are likely to have experienced face loss, to be upset, disappointed, angry, or hurt. What is required is for one party—why not you?—to take responsibility for whatever hurt may have been caused to the other person and to apologize willingly and genuinely, even in situations where you feel you're not entirely to blame. A half-hearted or insincere apology will not only fail to correct the situation, it may even escalate it by hardening attitudes even further. An apology thus requires careful attention to the relational element of the interaction—if the other person's feelings of hurt or frustration are ignored, the situation may be further inflamed.

COMPONENTS OF AN APOLOGY

- Acknowledge the wrong done to the other person.
- Recognize the legitimacy of feelings of hurt, anger, frustration, disappointment, or betrayal.
- Take responsibility for any damage inflicted, even if you don't think you did anything wrong.
- Sincerely apologize, on a personal level.

In order to de-escalate an ego conflict, you must be more interested in resolving the problem than in retaliating for a face attack or proving the other person wrong. You must find a way to stop the cycle of defensiveness and return the interaction to a level of trust. This will likely require you to make yourself vulnerable to the possibility of additional face attacks, since the other person will initially remain hurt and angry. A sincere and effective apology recognizes these feelings and supports the other person's expression of them. When that has been sincerely achieved, compromise may be possible.

An effective apology always avoids placing blame on the other person. A statement like 'I'm sorry you got the wrong impression' or 'I'm sorry you misunderstood me' is not likely to be effective, since it implies that the fault lies with the other's ability to understand or communicate. Instead, 'I'm sorry I didn't make myself clear' or 'I'm sorry I gave you the wrong impression' would be more likely to gain the other's trust. For your apology to be effective, you must personally express regret, and must explicitly acknowledge the actual or potential pain the other person has suffered. Without these gestures, sincerely given, rifts may not be healed and divisions may be increased and irrevocably entrenched.

Summary

Conflict is inevitable in interpersonal relationships, since people necessarily bring different value systems, experiences, and points of view to their encounters. Interpersonal conflict is generally considered to fall into four categories: conflicts over facts, values conflicts, policy conflicts, and ego conflicts. However, though it is easy to create such classifications, in practice conflict is more complex and nuanced than the neat categorization suggests. Conflicts are rarely 'pure' in type, but are more likely to overlap these categories. It may even be fair to say that most of our conflicts, with the possible exception of the simplest conflicts over issues of fact, involve elements of ego and face risk, and that many of them are informed by or arise out of underlying values that we are not even consciously aware of.

Interpersonal conflicts, even simple ones of fact, can be escalated by defensiveness. When we are challenged, we may respond defensively to what we experience as a threat to face. Defensiveness in one participant tends to breed defensiveness in the other, which in turn escalates the conflict, turning even the simplest disagreement into an ego battle. The only way to break the escalation of defensiveness is for one party to defuse the situation with humour, a gesture of affirmation, an apology, or even an offer of compromise. Depending on the level of trust in the relationship, even these may fail to achieve peace, and they can actually escalate the dispute if they are not genuinely expressed or tactfully handled.

Not all conflicts can be resolved; in some cases, the best we can hope for is to agree to disagree, but we can maintain good will if we can genuinely accept that the other person's position, though different from our own, is nevertheless legitimate.

Key Terms

defensiveness
ego conflict
fact-based conflict
policy conflict
values conflict

Suggested Readings

William R. Cupach and Daniel J. Canary, *Competence in Interpersonal Conflict* (Prospect Heights, Ill.: Waveland Press, 2000). Cupach and Canary begin with the premise that conflict between people is a natural part of human interaction that can have positive as well as negative consequences—provided it is handled effectively. As communication scholars, their interest is in the role played by communication in both the emergence and the resolution of conflict. This undergraduate text is intended to build skills on a foundation of theoretical principles, and provides plenty of case studies and reflective discussion questions to help students develop greater command of interpersonal conflict management strategies.

Kathy Domenici and Stephen W. Littlejohn, *Mediation: Empowerment in Conflict Management*, 2nd edn (Prospect Heights, Ill.: Waveland Press, 2001). Littlejohn and Domenici are professors of communication, and theirs is an introductory textbook intended for an undergraduate audience. Although relatively brief, it provides an adaptable theoretical model that focuses on managing power issues between disputants, and approaches the study of mediation from a communication perspective.

Wendy Grant, *How to Resolve Conflicts: Turn Conflict into Cooperation* (London: Collins & Brown, 2007). A more popular and less scholarly treatment, Grant's self-help guide focuses on reducing conflict in interpersonal relationships, with the promise that doing so will lead to a better and more peaceful life. Written for a general audience, the book includes exercises and visualizations, along with 'inspirational' case studies. Its approach, however, tends to oversimplify, attributing interpersonal conflict to a 'basic lack of self esteem', and in response offering strategies aimed at 'confidence-building'.

John Hoover, *Best Practices: Conflict Resolution: Working Effectively with Prickly Bosses, Coworkers, and Clients* (New York: HarperCollins, 2007). Like many popular books on interpersonal conflict, Hoover's self-help guide focuses on the workplace rather than on personal relationships. It is specifically addressed to getting along with 'difficult' people, and offers suggestions for creating a 'harmonious work environment'. However, in place of in-depth analysis, it offers a pre-set list of difficult personality 'types', with cookie-cutter responses to each. It's unlikely to encourage a deeper understanding of interpersonal conflict or its causes.

Ken Lawson, *Successful Conflict Resolution* (Hauppauge, NY: Barron's Educational Series, 2007). Promotional material from the publisher showcases the 'concise answers to problems' approach of Lawson's book. Billed as a 'fast-read' with lots of 'do's and don'ts' and checklists, its emphasis on efficiency over understanding suggests that it can't possibly deliver on its promised insight into the causes of conflict or the means of nurturing genuine trust in the workplace.

Stephen W. Littlejohn and Kathy Domenici, *Communication, Conflict, and the Management of Difference* (Prospect Heights, Ill.: Waveland Press, 2007). Littlejohn and Domenici approach the study of interpersonal communication from the perspective of understanding and managing conflict. The authors survey scholarly theories and models for understanding the dynamics and causes of conflict, and introduce various alternative dispute resolution methods, including negotiation, mediation, facilitation, collaboration, and public engagement. The emphasis throughout the book is on how effective communication skill can minimize the occurrence and the escalation of conflict in social and interpersonal relations.

Christopher W. Moore, *The Mediation Process: Practical Strategies for Resolving Conflict*, rev. edn (New York: John Wiley & Sons, 2003). First published in 1986, Moore's book is regarded by many scholars and practitioners as a classic in the field. In addition to practical guidance, the book provides an overview of contemporary scholarship and theoretical models of mediation practice. Intended as a textbook, it is accessible to undergraduates and a valuable resource for those who wish to understand the theory and practice of mediation.

Exercises and Assignments

1. Read the case study 'Facebook Face-Off' in Appendix B and the comments that follow it (more of these are available on-line) and answer the following questions, either in class discussion or in written form, as directed by your instructor.

   a. What is the central conflict as it's outlined in the article itself? Is this a conflict of fact, value, policy, or ego? How do you know?

   b. What are the primary positions articulated by the respondents? What kind of conflict appears to be taking place in the responses?

   c. As we learned in this chapter, interpersonal conflict (and political conflict, too) frequently arises out of a struggle over meaning. To what extent is that true in the 'Facebook Face-off' case?

2. What connection can be drawn between conflict and the human needs described in any of the theories discussed in Chapter 4? Is conflict an expression of need? If so, how? Is conflict therefore inevitable in human interaction? Be prepared to discuss this idea with the group or to present your analysis in writing, as directed by your instructor.

3. Throughout this chapter, and this book, we have emphasized the importance of a sense of belonging, of social connectedness and inclusion, to our well-being and happiness. However, as Kenneth Burke[4] and others theorists[5] have observed, our sense of belonging depends as much on who is 'included out' as on who is

'included in'. To what extent could it be argued, then, that conflict between ourselves and others, or between our group and another group, is actually necessary to the formation of individual and social identity? Draw on as much of the course material as you can in answering this question. Present your analysis in writing or as part of a class discussion, as directed by your instructor.

4. Assume that the different points of view articulated in 'How to Tell a Good Professor from a Bad Professor' (Appendix B) represent two sides of a conflict. To what extent is it a conflict over fact? Over value? Is there any way in which such differences in perspective could lead to ego conflict? What does this suggest is the relationship between conflict and the perceptual process outlined in Chapters 1 and 3?

5. What is the nature of the conflict at the heart of George Orwell's 'Shooting an Elephant' in Appendix B? With whom is Orwell in conflict? Explain your answer.

6. The chapter suggests that conflicts of all types can be understood as potentially ego or face conflicts. Use William Schutz's interpersonal needs theory to fully explain why this might be so. Fully justify your answer using material from this chapter and Chapter 4. Present your analysis in writing or as part of a class discussion, as directed by your instructor.

7. John Malaprop is about to graduate from civil engineering at Western Plains University. Like many students, he has sometimes been frustrated by what he perceives as a mismatch between the theory taught in his courses and what he believes actual engineering practice will be like. Last summer, between his third and fourth years, John spent three months on a professional internship and was surprised to find out that he didn't know as much about engineering practice as he had thought. Bolstered by the internship experience, he thinks he knows why this is, and has decided to write this unsolicited e-mail message to his former professor, Dr Harding ('Hardline') McAlister. You can see it below, exactly as he sent it.

Date: Fri 9/9/05
From: map333@mail.wpu.ca
To: hmcalister@wpu.ca
Re: coarse advise

Dear Hardling,

I don't know if you remember me but I took that class you taught about three years ago. I didnt do very good in it, and now I think I know why. Since I'm graduating in a couple of months, and I spent last summer on an internship, I have a lot more expierence with what Engineers really need to know, and I figure you would be greatful for some advise.

Your coarse, and expecially the textbook, could of been a lot better. I've tried to figure out why you might of picked that book, but I cant see any reason. The problem being is that you didnt really cover the kinds of current computer applications that most Engineers need when their in the work force. I looked in ur book for how to use PowerPoint, but I didn't find anything on it. I know that your just a prof, not a real PEng, so I thought you would appreaciate some help to know what your studnets really need to learn. I feel that you should choose a better text book that doesn't waist students time with irrevalent theories that real Engineers never need to know.

I trust that this feedback will prove constructive. Furthermore, any further questions you might have about how to pick a book can be directed to me at map333@mail.wpu.ca. If you send an email, it might take a few days for me to get back to you.

Sincirely,

John Malaprop, PEng.

Apparently, to John's complete surprise, the message has angered his professor, who has responded with a curt e-mail of his own. John feels that Professor McAlister has completely misunderstood and overreacted to his message.

a. Drawing on all that you have learned about interpersonal communication, including face, footing, self-concept, defensiveness, advice-giving, and conflict, explain why John's e-mail might have caused a conflict with Dr McAlister.

a. What kind of conflict is it? Do you think it can be resolved?

a. If he hopes to resolve the conflict, what should John do now? Justify your answer.

Chapter 9

The Dynamics of Influence

Learning Objectives

- To recognize the pervasive role of persuasion in everyday life.
- To understand the relationship between influence and trust.
- To learn what an enthymeme is and how it functions.
- To understand the psychology of influence.

It's near the end of the spring term; you have two big reports and a major presentation due next week, and you're wondering how you're going to get them all done. It's at times like this that you kind of envy your best friend Norm. Unlike you, Norm got himself out into the 'real' world after high school. He took an apprenticeship and now nearly has his electrician's ticket. With construction booming, he's much in demand and can pretty much name his own price. Norm works hard, but when Friday comes along, he likes to cut loose and party.

You usually take Friday night off yourself, to spend some time with friends and have a little fun. But this weekend the crunch is on, and you just *have* to devote the time to working on those reports. You're well into it when Norm arrives at your apartment, revved up and ready to go out. Good old Norm, he really knows how to put the pressure on.

'Don't be a wuss', he tells you. 'What's one night? Anyway, you've got the whole weekend to do the stupid reports, and besides, one of them isn't due until Friday. You could even skip class next week if you need extra time to finish it up—that's what I always used to do when I was in school.

'Plus, Bill's in town and the whole gang's getting together. You don't even know when you might see Bill again, because he's in the military now and might be sent to Afghanistan. Anyway, you're only young once, and your friends are all expecting you; it'll be a blast. And when you're on your deathbed, you can bet you won't be wishing you'd spent more time writing reports. C'mon, I'll make sure to get you home before you turn into a pumpkin.'

You give in, as you usually do with Norm. It is nice to see Bill, and it's fun to hang out with your old friends. But when midnight rolls around, Norm's in full swing and you don't want to break his stride. And frankly, staying here is a lot more appealing than going back to your empty apartment to work on a bunch of dull reports. Besides, Monday's a long way away, and you can put in some good time on the rest of the weekend.

One thing leads to another, and Saturday you wake up on the floor in an apartment belonging to some friend of Norm's. It's two o'clock in the afternoon, and you have to figure out how you're going to get home, since you spent all your money last night and you don't have a car. After a bit of scrambling, you finally score a bus ticket from somebody; by the time you get home, it's ten to five. Naturally, you're not in fit shape to get right at those reports, so you end up vegging in front of the TV for a couple of hours before settling down to work. Then your mom calls, and before you know it, it's 10 o'clock.

You suddenly realize that you don't have a single clean shirt for the presentation you have to give on Monday, so on top of everything else you now have to do tomorrow, you will have to go to the laundromat. Meanwhile, Norm has no worries; all he has to do is show up at work, just the way he always does. You don't know for the life of you why you let him talk you into these things. But one thing is sure: you're gonna be paying all week for slacking off this weekend.

What Is Persuasion?

The goal of this chapter is to explore the meaning of persuasion as an interpersonal phenomenon, to understand what makes it effective, and to determine why our efforts to persuade sometimes fail. In order to answer these questions, let's begin with a standard definition, taken from *The Canadian Oxford Dictionary*, which tells us that to persuade is 'to cause to believe; to convince; to induce'.[1] Persuasion, then, refers to the intention or attempt to shape others' attitudes or beliefs, to mould their thinking in some way, and most especially to influence their actions or behaviour.

Influence is a pervasive part of the give and take of all human interaction, as we have already learned. As Kenneth Burke teaches us, wherever there is communication, there is some kind of invitation to a shared way of seeing the world, and thus to persuasion.[2] We know from the Nine Axioms (Chapter 2) that even interpersonal communication relies on persuasion just as other forms of communication do, and that we are continually subject to influence from others even as we exert our own influences upon them.

Consider the ways, large and small, that you experience interpersonal influence during a typical day, and the similarly pervasive ways in which you seek to influence others. Influence is present, for example, in ordinary situations such as when you ask someone seated next to the window if she would mind opening or closing it, or if you request a second helping of the casserole your roommate made for supper. It is present, too, in interactions like attending classroom lectures or receiving a party invitation. Admonitions from parents, advice from dentists or physicians, guidance from teachers, or instructions from police officers at a traffic accident are all forms of persuasion, as are writing a resumé, interviewing for a job, petitioning for a change of grade, or approaching your boss for a raise. Even writing an exam is an act of persuasion in which you hope to convince the prof that you've mastered the course material.

Persuasion is present, too, in our interpersonal interactions, as we present a face to the world, negotiate our sense of self in interactions with others, establish and maintain relationships, and seek to fulfill our need for affection and inclusion. Although such interactions may not seem to be matters of persuasion, interpersonal influence is inherent in all of them.

Some persuasion is obvious and easy to spot: advertisements, appeals from charities, sermons, and newspaper editorials are explicitly aimed at influencing what we believe or how we act. But what is more interesting about persuasion is that it is at its most powerful when it is not explicit. For example, you may be able to recognize persuasion lurking in the product placements that appear in movies[3] or in promotional pieces disguised as magazine or newspaper articles.[4] What's more difficult to see is how the *format* of a magazine you read, not just its content, can exert influence on your attitudes and behaviour.[5] It might surprise you to learn, as well, that the television programs you watch—not the ads, but the programs themselves—are forms of persuasion.[6] Even the way you're taught to see the world as you study a particular academic or professional discipline can influence your assumptions and values.[7] At this level, you are often being persuaded without even realizing it.

Thus, although we may not be fully aware of it, we are surrounded by persuasion. Unfortunately some people mistakenly believe the word 'persuasion' refers only to deliberate and often unwelcome attempts to influence us, such as the messages of commercial advertising. We may tend to think of such messages as manipulative, even unethical; certainly it is true that, because advertising messages are driven by a desire for profit rather than by a concern for our welfare, they can sometimes be employed in devious ways, using clever strategies to entice or cajole us into buying things we don't need or even want. It seems only a short step from there to the kinds of manipulative messages contained, for instance, in spam e-mails that offer huge rewards in exchange for your help in rescuing funds from some oppressive political regime or that purport to be from your bank, warning about irregular activity on your account and asking for your personal information and personal identification number (PIN).

Such appeals are certainly attempts at persuasion, and they are clearly duplicitous. However, although it's well to be on guard against unscrupulous attempts at persuasion, there is some danger in assuming that all persuasion is manipulative or unscrupulous. Much of the persuasion we encounter, especially at the interpersonal level, is harmless, even benign; much of it is even in our best interest. In fact, the qualities of leadership that we admire are really skills of managing interpersonal influence. Understanding how persuasion works can help us to distinguish the harmless from the manipulative, the beneficial from the unscrupulous.

As we have been discussing throughout this book, the ability to exert influence and to benefit from the influence of others is a critical part of our life experience and happiness. It's pretty clear, then, that not all persuasion is created equal. It may be overt and explicit, or it may take place below the surface of our conscious awareness, but one thing is certain: persuasion of some sort, on some level, is present in pretty much every interaction. When it occurs on an unstated, implicit level, persuasion is sometimes harder to detect, but it is also far more powerful. The rest of this chapter is devoted to explaining why this is so.

The Foundation of Persuasion: Aristotle's Enthymeme

Maybe you really do have a friend just like Norm, someone who can always talk you into taking part in his schemes—even when you know deep down that going along with him may not always be in your best interest. Likely you have simply resigned yourself to the fact that Norm can really push your buttons. But what exactly does that mean?

It means that Norm instinctively knows how to adapt his messages to suit his audience—in this case, you. Chances are Norm can't explain how he knows just what to say to have the desired effect, but there's no doubt that he's a very shrewd and successful observer of people. He understands intuitively what every rhetorician since Aristotle has taught: that effective persuasion depends on an understanding of the audience's psychology.

Not all efforts to persuade are as successful as Norm's. Sometimes they work, but just as often they fail, sometimes quite dramatically. In order to understand fully how the process itself actually works, rhetoricians focus their study not only on successful persuaders like Norm, but also on failed attempts to persuade. Through this study, they hope to better understand why people behave as they do, how they are motivated, and in particular, how the dynamics of influence are created.

One of the secrets of persuasion lies in what is known as **common sense**. Aristotle was the first, though not the last,[8] to observe that the things people accept as common sense can contribute to what kinds of arguments influence them. In other words, people are persuaded in part by what they already believe, and if what they take for granted can somehow be incorporated into a persuasive appeal, they will find it easier to accept.

For Aristotle, the key to this process is something he called the **enthymeme**, which is a kind of reasoning pattern or way of structuring an argument. An enthymeme contains two statements that are connected by some belief or attitude, some common sense, that is relied upon but not explicitly stated. It works, in effect, by leaving something out. Consider the following examples:

> Commerce can't be that hard; Jonathan got straight A's last term.
> Of course Bradley's good at drama; he's gay.
> Sharla and Rodney must have broken up. I saw her bingeing on
> fast food yesterday.
> My cousin is an arrogant know-it-all. But then, he's from Toronto.
> You can tell by how flaky she is that Aretha's from the west coast.

Did any of these statements affirm your view of the world? Did any of them oppose your beliefs? Did you find any of them irritating? Amusing? Can you identify the unexpressed assumptions that underlie them?

Note that you do not need to agree with the statements to be able to interpret them; all you need is to be familiar with the 'common sense' values or attitudes they rely on. But the more you agree with the assumptions they take for granted, the more readily and easily you will be persuaded. The enthymeme works by engaging the audience in the reasoning process; the speaker doesn't supply the information that links one statement to the other. Instead, as Aristotle explained, 'the hearer adds it himself.'[9] In order to even understand the examples, you have to be able to import the unstated connections from your own experience, attitudes, or beliefs. When you do that, you're already half way to be being convinced.

In structure, the enthymeme resembles a pattern in formal logic called a **syllogism**, which consists of three explicit statements: two propositions and a conclusion. For example:

Stewart is a German shepherd.
All German shepherds bite.
Therefore Stewart bites.

Note that it is the *structure* of the syllogism, and not its content, that makes it valid or invalid. Whether the statement is factually true isn't the point; not all German shepherds bite, and Stewart might in reality be a gentle dog. But the structure of the syllogism is such that, if the first two statements are true, the conclusion has to be true as well.

The enthymeme works in a similar way, but in an enthymeme, the general proposition about what 'all' such dogs do would be left to the audience to fill in. Thus, Dave might tell you, 'Of course Stewart bites. He's a German shepherd.' As listeners, we would have to be able to fill in the implied generalization that all German shepherds bite, or at least that Dave thinks they do and expects us to think the same way.

Consider how much more difficult it is to challenge the second example than the first. When the major premise—the generalization about '*all*' German shepherds— is made explicit, it's easier for the audience to resist or argue with. It's obviously not true that *all* German shepherds bite, and stating the belief explicitly makes it available for us to examine, challenge, and ultimately reject. However, when a generalization is not explicit, we're less likely to notice it or to see it as requiring a challenge, and the whole argument is harder to refute.

The enthymeme gains its power from the fact that the audience actually helps to construct the speaker's argument by supplying the 'missing' information from their own common sense. Consider that, in order to even make sense of Dave's statement, we have to agree, even for a moment, that German shepherds are likely to bite. We typically find enthymematic arguments more convincing than syllogistic ones simply because we participate in them ourselves, especially when the common sense that underlies them is something we ourselves share.

The fact that these common-sense assumptions are unstated does not mean that they are unimportant or that they have no influence on the meaning that is being shared. In fact, the reverse is true. At this point, you may recall Axiom #8, which states that 'what is unsaid can be as important as what is said.' In discussing this Axiom, I referred to the unexpressed and often unacknowledged 'subtext' of communication—its underlying and usually unstated common sense. It is this common sense that provides the foundation for enthymemes.

The embedded assumptions shared by a culture or group are accepted by them without question, and as members of that group we make our common-sense arguments by an **associative process** rather than an explicitly logical one. We tend to group ideas or qualities together generally without making the connections explicit, since everyone in our circle can be assumed to share similar attitudes. In some cases, the assumptions we are making are so deeply embedded in common sense that it doesn't even occur to us to question them. In fact, it may not even occur to us that we are *making* assumptions. We believe we are simply reporting on how the world really is. When they are grounded in the way the listeners already see and interpret the world, enthymematic arguments are very persuasive, as Aristotle recognized when he called them 'the most effective of the modes of persuasion'.[10]

We may find it difficult at times to unearth the common sense that informs someone's communication, but we can learn to improve our understanding if we remember to consider what underlying beliefs, attitudes, or values may be shaping a given message. When considering how someone succeeds in influencing and persuading others, ask yourself this: what would you, as a listener, have to believe about the world, or about the situation, or about yourself, in order for the other person's message to make sense to you?

Go back now and take another look at Norm's appeals. What would you have to believe for his entreaties to persuade you? Can you identify any of the 'common sense' that he relies on you to share? If you find Norm's line of argument convincing, it's probably because you agree with the things he *doesn't* say as much as with the things he does say. The better Norm knows you, the better able he will be to align his arguments with the things you take for granted, and the more successful a persuader he will be.

The Trouble with People

To persuade effectively, we need to understand what our listeners want, need, or believe, and bring our appeals into line with those beliefs, values, and expectations. Some people assume that the easiest way to discover what other people want or what they believe is simply to ask them. Once you have surveyed their interests, needs, and expectations, you will be able to adapt your messages effectively to your listeners and every interaction will meet with success. This is a very good approach, in every way except one: *it doesn't work*.

The reason for this is that some of what motivates us is hidden, even from ourselves. As you will recall from Chapter 1, while some of our motivations are practical and obvious, others are more deeply embedded in our symbolic nature. This is true even for highly self-reflective people who have achieved a good understanding of themselves, and it is why everyone's Johari window contains a pane or quadrant marked 'blind'.

Perhaps surprisingly, one of the best explanations of human motivation comes from the study of advertising. In the 1950s, the journalist and social critic Vance Packard advanced an influential conceptualization that he called '**The Trouble with People**'.[11] Packard was particularly interested in why and how people are influenced by advertising messages, but his theories also tell us about motives in general, and about why people interact as they do.

Packard explained why it is so difficult to motivate people and even to understand them. First, he argued, you can't simply ask people what they want, because they don't always really know. Our real motives for what we do—our psychological or symbolic reasons—are often embedded in values and assumptions we take for granted without even knowing they exist. While our practical motivations are readily available to us, and easy to articulate, these symbolic motivations reside in those areas of the psyche that the Johari window calls 'hidden' or 'unknown', where they are either unrecognized or completely unavailable.

Nevertheless, although they aren't always available for us to articulate, our symbolic motivations, as we have seen, remain powerful influences in shaping our communication and our action. As we learned from the theories covered in Chapter 4, we are all motivated by the need for identification, for belonging, for acceptance and

love; but we are also motivated by fear of loss, by a need for status, by a sense of pow-
erlessness over our lives, by the knowledge of our own mortality and frailty. We know
that everybody has such fears from time to time, but when it comes to thinking about
our own reasons for doing what we do, we are unlikely to identify these symbolic
needs as playing a part in our everyday actions.

Here is just one example: Pat saves every issue of all the magazines to which he
subscribes, and has been doing so since childhood. His parents have urged him to sell
them or donate them to charity, but he has stubbornly resisted doing so, even though
they now sit in boxes in the garage. If he is asked why he keeps these boxes of magazines, Pat will say that he just doesn't like to throw away something that he spent so
much money to acquire. But those who know Pat believe that the issue isn't really
about money. If it were, Pat could recover some of his investment by selling the collection, or he could cut the expense altogether if he started reading his favourite magazines at the library. He doesn't like to have the question raised, and becomes irritated if his parents push him to get rid of his collection. It's thus more likely that Pat's
packrat tendencies spring from some kind of symbolic motive.

Possibly these remnants of his childhood are a hedge against growing older; perhaps they represent an attempt to exert control over his life; or maybe cluttering up
his parents' garage is an act of rebellion, or a way of keeping them from selling the
house Pat grew up in and moving into a condo. We can't know for sure without
knowing more about Pat's situation and his other habits, but it's probable that some
explanation like this underlies the obsessive collecting of the magazines. Whatever
the reason, the symbolic motives that prompt his behaviour are not immediately
available to Pat.

But even if Pat has an inkling of what the underlying reason is for his growing collection of magazines, it's unlikely that he would share his intuitions with us. As
Packard points out, the second challenge of dealing with people is that even if they
do recognize their deeper motives, they often won't, or can't, acknowledge or admit
to them. This reluctance arises because our deeper motivations often reveal us as
imperfect: vulnerable, frightened, desperate for status or recognition, even in some
instances selfish. They make us susceptible to criticism, rejection, and face loss. Even
if we could admit them to ourselves, the face risks of sharing them with others would
be enormous.

Consider Inderjit, who has recently been short-tempered with her best friend
Salma. Things just seem to be going Salma's way lately, while everything Inderjit
touches seems to fall apart: she has just broken up with Paul, she is struggling to keep
up her grades in her courses this term, and to top it off she's gained 10 pounds. In
contrast, Salma's relationship with Bryan is still solid, her course grades this term are
in the A range, and she seems to find it easy to keep trim.

Inderjit genuinely cares for her friend and is glad things are going well for her, but
deep down she suspects that her frustration with Salma is fuelled partly by jealousy.

However, she will likely avoid acknowledging these motives, even to herself. Certainly she will never publicly admit to these feelings for fear of exposing herself as petty, mean-spirited, or disloyal. To announce such base motives would cause her to feel guilty and to lose face, and would possibly destroy the relationship.

So, even if she recognizes these motives, it is likely that Inderjit will attribute her impatience to other causes. She may even find a way to blame Salma for her feelings. Does Inderjit sound like a mean-spirited, petty person? In fact, she's not—at least not more than any of the rest of us. Her reactions are typical of how we behave in situations where exposing our real motivations would tend to discredit us or diminish us in our own eyes and in the eyes of others.

Packard's third observation is that, while people are *capable* of rational behaviour, they often don't behave in rational or logical ways. Theorists of influence from Aristotle to Robert Cialdini[12] have long recognized, for example, that it is people's feelings or passions, rather than their reason alone, that move them to action. We may see the merits of a position that someone else takes on an issue, we may even agree that the ideas are sound, but if the person's words don't stir our emotions, it's unlikely that our actions or beliefs will be affected. Facts alone do not persuade or influence; what we believe those facts mean, their relevance to us, and their power to move us emotionally are what matters.

It is true that we can sometimes offer some sort of logical-sounding reason for our actions after the fact, but often the real motivation resides in our need to belong, our need for status, our fear of losing face, or our desire for identification. We may not recognize the source of these motivations, or be willing to articulate it if we do recognize it, but we often behave in ways that do not seem logical to an observer because doing so fulfills some emotional or psychological need that is more important than reason. While we don't always perceive these emotional needs or admit to them, and while we are adept at hiding them behind a screen of seemingly logical rationalizations, we are moved to action more by passion than by facts.

THE TROUBLE WITH PEOPLE

- People often don't know what they want.
- People can't, or won't, admit to their deeper motives.
- People don't act logically.

The Psychology of Interpersonal Influence

The study of influence is usually carried out in the context of public rather than interpersonal communication. However, persuasion takes place between intimates just as frequently, and with at least as much effect, as it does in the public domain. The insights into human motivation and the dynamics of influence that have been gained from the study of public communication can also contribute significantly to our understanding of what happens when persuasion is practised between individuals.

Theorists and researchers in the area of influence are interested in what I have termed the '**Big Question**'.[13] That is, in any given message, 'who is saying what, to whom, and for what purpose?' This question operates on three levels: first, who is speaking? In other words, what face is this person presenting to the world, what self-image seems to be informing the way the message is being positioned, what footing has she established, and how is she inviting others to respond to her?

The second part of the question focuses on the negotiation itself, on how the listeners are being imagined or addressed, how they are regarded by the speaker, how they are being invited to see themselves. Finally, the Big Question asks us to think about the purpose and motive behind the message, about its positioning, and about its 'common sense'. Influence research has identified a number of principles that help to answer these questions and to explain why people are persuaded by the appeals of others.[14] Such 'principles of influence' are intended to uncover the psychology behind influence and the engendering of commitment between people. As you read about them, consider what you have already learned about face, self-concept, and perception. As well, you may wish to think again about Norm. Do any of these principles help to explain his success as a persuader?

SIX PRINCIPLES OF INFLUENCE

- Reciprocity
- Scarcity
- Authority
- Commitment
- Liking
- Social proof

Reciprocity

The first principle of influence is **reciprocity**, which refers to a mutually beneficial exchange of some kind.[15] Psychologically and interpersonally, reciprocity refers to a feeling of obligation when someone makes a kind gesture or offers a gift. Reciprocity identifies the expectation, both on the part of the giver and on the part of the receiver, that we should respond to a kind or generous gesture with a similar gesture of our own.

Thus, reciprocity suggests that people tend to feel some commitment to 'return a favour', to give something in exchange for a benefit or favour that they have received from someone else. For example, when you feel it is appropriate to invite people for dinner after you have had a meal at their house, you are experiencing the social or psychological pressure of reciprocity. Similarly, consider the discomfort you might feel when you receive an unanticipated gift from someone for whom you cannot reciprocate or with whom you have not been on 'gift-giving' terms.

Reciprocity is evident in interpersonal communication in a variety of ways. For instance, most of us feel it appropriate to return the compliment when someone makes a flattering or generous remark. Self-disclosure and the building of trust also depend on the principle of reciprocity. As you will recall from Chapter 4, self-disclosure invites a reciprocal level of disclosure from the other person, which in turn contributes to building intimacy. Respect, too, is mutual, as is liking. The more we believe that someone holds us in esteem, the more we tend to view the other in a positive light.

In interpersonal and social terms, however, reciprocity runs even deeper than this sense of obligation. You will recall that, in social interactions, we all have an investment in the face needs of everyone who is taking part: we not only move to protect ourselves from the threat of face loss, but we also move to protect the face of others. Normal people do not wish to see others humiliated or socially discomfited, and will sometimes even '**give face**', taking pains to ensure that others' gaffes are not cause for too much loss of social approval. In this sense, our investment in the face of the group, and the interaction, is a reciprocal one.

Even defensiveness operates by a kind of reciprocal process; as we saw in Chapter 8, an expression of defensiveness from one person breeds defensiveness in the other, and can escalate conflict. The effects and pervasiveness of reciprocity as an interpersonal principle can also be felt in non-verbal communication: we return someone else's smile, wave at someone who waves at us, or 'mirror' someone else's body position through postural echo.

Reciprocity is a way of expressing both identification and trust. Both of these, as we know, are essential for effective interpersonal communication. Reciprocity reminds us that we can create or affirm a bond between ourselves and others by making gestures that they are socially or psychologically obliged to return. When others have made such gestures to us, we feel some pressure to respond in kind. Reciprocity, then, is one of the ways in which we establish connectedness, which in turn makes us more likely to be influenced by the actions or words of the other person. In part because of the effects of reciprocity, someone we have come to like and trust holds more influence over us than a stranger. Reciprocity is simply a reflection of the mutuality involved in interpersonal communication: a shared investment in the relationship and the desire for identification.

Commitment

A second principle that helps to explain how people are influenced in interpersonal interaction is **commitment**. We can think of this principle as a kind of interpersonal inertia; we are more easily persuaded to continue with a course of action that we have already chosen than we are to choose a different approach. If you have ever rejected a new way of doing things on the grounds that 'we've never done it that way before' or argued that things should continue as they are because 'that's the way it's always been', you have experienced the effects of commitment as a principle of influence. Humans are creatures of habit, and once they have made up their minds about what to do, they typically do not change direction without a very good reason to do so.

The principle of commitment is pervasive, in part because we find routine comforting. Even small children express this principle when they demand that a story be read in exactly the same way as the last time they heard it, or that their sandwiches be made in precisely the way Mommy makes them at home. You shop at your favourite stores, sit in your own special seat in class, or take the same route home in part because of the principle of commitment.

Commitment is a principle of influence because it affects the way we behave and the choices we make. Remember Shirley, whose job interview experience we encountered in Chapter 3? She continued to answer the interviewer's inappropriate questions because once she had answered the first one, she felt committed to following through on her chosen course of action. Even though the subsequent questions made her increasingly uncomfortable, she nevertheless felt unable to change her mind, even when doing so would clearly have been in her best interest.

Commitment has an impact on all aspects of our interpersonal communication, not least because it affects both our self-concepts and our judgements of others. You'll

recall, for instance, that both of these things tend to resist change. Commitment as a psychological principle helps to explain the aging beauty queen who continues to dress like a teenager, or the former high school athlete who sustains serious injury when he tries to repeat the feats of strength that came so easily to him when he was in regular training.

As well, once we have made up our minds about another person, we tend to resist new information that might serve to challenge our initial assessment. Parents may continue to treat their adult son as a child, or the son may even find himself falling into childhood habits when he comes home for a visit from university. The psychological persistence of commitment in part explains why snap judgements are so influential and why prejudices can be so difficult to remove. We tend to stay 'married' to the ideas and attitudes that we have picked up first.

Commitment in this sense is also connected to face. Once we have committed to a 'line' of action, we may feel that we have to follow through, since to discontinue what we have begun would be to invite the risk of significant face loss. Consider Mark and Chris, who got married last August after dating since high school. Chris described to friends how they arrived at the decision to wed: 'we thought five years was long enough, and it was time to either break up or get married.' And besides, their friends and families more or less expected their relationship to culminate in marriage.

Chris and Mark threw a huge party to celebrate their formal engagement, and then set about planning a lavish and costly wedding. As the big day grew closer, both of them began to experience doubts about the wisdom of making their shaky relationship permanent, and wondered whether, after all, they should just have broken it off. However, at this late date, neither could face the public humiliation of cancelling their expensive and complicated arrangements.

So Mark and Chris went ahead with the wedding despite their misgivings. The celebration was everything they could have hoped for, but the marriage itself was something else. After two tumultuous and miserable months, they were forced to call it quits. Mark moved out of their apartment, and they have since filed for divorce. Since this happened to them, they've observed a similar pattern among several other couples in their circle of acquaintances—Heather and Jim, Geoff and Leah, Nana and Steve, David and Kathy.

The pressure to carry through with an action just to avoid public embarrassment is achingly familiar to most of us. No one wishes to court humiliation or loss of face. This phenomenon has been explored in detail by some of the language's greatest writers; for instance, in his essay 'Shooting an Elephant', the celebrated English essayist George Orwell provides a vivid case study of how a person may be driven to continue with a course of action, even when he has come to understand that it is an error, simply because he has publicly committed to it and does not wish to lose face. As a young member of a British security force in Burma, Orwell was responsible for helping to maintain order. Receiving a report that an elephant was on the rampage, he set out, gun in hand, to destroy the animal if it turned out really to be dangerous. By the time he located the elephant, it was grazing quietly in a field and posed no further threat to anyone. But a huge crowd had gathered, and Orwell reports feeling a growing sense of public pressure to carry through with the shooting, despite his conviction that the animal was now harmless. The shooting itself is depicted with sickening realism, and Orwell's reaction as one of deep shame. He reports that he shot the animal, against his own better judgement, 'solely to avoid looking a fool' in front of the gathered multitude.

Face is a commitment to a kind of self-presentation, and to be forced to abandon the line to which we have committed is to invite public humiliation. Once people have made a public commitment to an idea, a position on an issue, or a course of action, they are more easily influenced to take actions that bolster the original commitment than they are to do something that would contradict it. This can be true even if they have come to see the original choice as a mistake. Like Mark and Chris, and indeed like all of us at one time or another, the young George Orwell was impelled by his fear of face loss to carry through with an action that he himself had already begun to regret.

Scarcity

Scarcity is a third principle of influence that has an effect on our interpersonal interactions. While most theorists of persuasion focus on the role of scarcity in business negotiations, making objects and results more desirable, this same principle can also be seen at work in our interpersonal interactions. Interpersonally, the principle of scarcity speaks to the human fear of loss: we fear losing intimacy, trust, or social prestige, in part because we see them as difficult to attain. The interpersonal principle of scarcity means that we place a higher value on relationships, memberships, or status that we perceive to be unique or comparatively unattainable.

Most fundamentally from an interpersonal perspective, we cannot bear the idea that those we love might be taken from us or betray us. This potential for loss is the most fundamental and most influential of our interpersonal concerns; thus, 'rare' or 'scarce' become synonymous with precious or treasured. Consequently, the more unusual a relationship or quality is thought to be, the more cherished it becomes, and the more precious a relationship is to us, the more likely we are to think of it as a rare achievement. As a result, we tend to describe our own most important interpersonal relationships in terms that emphasize uniqueness and rarity.

The proverb 'absence makes the heart grow fonder' expresses the principle of scarcity in interpersonal terms. The intensity of our feelings for someone else is magnified by the recognition that the person may be taken from us by circumstances, or even, eventually, by death, and the theme of how love is intensified by the knowledge that a loved one may not be with us for much longer is a common one in songs and poems, such as Shakespeare's 'Sonnet 73' (see Appendix B).

Scarcity also can be seen as an operating principle in our concerns with identity and status, particularly in our fears that we may lose our place in the order of things or fail to achieve the position in life that we had hoped for. On some level, each of us longs to feel special, to achieve distinction or exclusivity. These desires are fuelled in part by the notion of scarcity—after all, a longed-for or hard-won status is treasured because it is available only to those who have distinguished themselves in some way or who are otherwise considered special.

Thus we are inclined to respond more favourably to, and be more easily persuaded by, those who make us feel remarkable or treasured than to those who make us feel like simply one of a crowd. Consider the number of advertising pitches that exploit this principle by assuring us that this or that special offer is available to 'only a select few'. The quality of distinction conferred by identification with something that we regard as exclusive is very appealing to us. Scarcity, therefore, increases our perception that a thing is special and desirable, and its very rarity helps to make it so.

Liking

A further principle that influences our interpersonal as well as our public communication is something known as **liking**. The power of liking as a source of influence seems obvious: not surprisingly, researchers have found that we are more apt to be persuaded by those we like than by those about whom we have no positive feeling. For this reason, liking is linked to ethos—we are more inclined to respond positively to those who project the Aristotelian qualities of good will, good judgement, and good character than to those who do not display these attributes. We not only like and respect them more readily than those who lack ethos, but we also find them more credible.

The role of liking in the success of interpersonal persuasion also derives in part from the centrality of identification to our social and psychological well-being. As we have already learned, identification—the creation of a sense of connectedness and intimacy with others—motivates much, if not in some way all, of our communication. As social beings, we need the approval and affirmation that we obtain from interacting and achieving identification with others; in general, the more people appear to have in common with us, the more comfortable we feel with them and the more favourably we tend to view them. And, of course, the more influential we find them to be.

Like so many other aspects of interpersonal interaction, liking is also reciprocal: we are more inclined to like those who have expressed or displayed liking for us, and are more susceptible to their influence. In other words, those who like us, and whom we like in return, have a greater chance of persuading us than do those with whom we have not forged a relationship.

Authority

Authority is a fifth principle that affects our interpersonal interactions. In general, we are likely to defer to those we perceive to be credible or authoritative; we are generally more inclined to model ourselves on these people, to submit to their guidance, or to follow their lead. Authority derives from a number of sources: from earned credentials; from experience; from institutional affiliation or sanction; or from personal skill or demeanour. For example, Burton's MA in communication (a credential) and polished presentation style (a skill) give him authority to lead a workshop on public speaking; John's years as a lighting technician (experience) and his knowledgeable way of speaking (personal demeanour) give him authority to win a contract with the local concert hall as a lighting director; Jeanie's association with the university's Ron and Jane Graham Centre for the Study of Communication (institutional affiliation), her imminent PhD (a credential), and her lively teaching style (personal demeanour) give her the necessary authority to deliver a course in communication for a technical Master's program; Vicki's DMV and PhD degrees (credentials), along with her specialization in epidemiology (experience) give her authority to conduct animal health research with the Veterinary and Infectious Disease Organization; Deb has been made team leader by her boss (institutional sanction), and that, along with her greater experience, gives her the authority to set policy for her working group.

Authority is not the same thing as 'authoritarian', which suggests a bossy, hierarchically driven person who delights in making others follow rules. Instead, authority refers to a person's credibility and self-assurance, and to that person's command of self and situation. A person with authority is likely to be looked on by others as a leader, and is able to inspire confidence in others. As with liking, authority is linked to the Aristotelian concept of ethos, which as we know involves the projection of good will, good judgement, and good character.

As an interpersonal principle, and as a principle of influence, authority is also connected to the concept of footing, which provides a foundation for any speaker's credibility. To speak with authority on a given issue, a person must possess not only an understanding of the subject, but also a pertinent role in the situation and an appropriate relationship to the listener. For instance, imagine receiving advice on your love life from a friend you know has been cheating on her long-time boyfriend, being instructed in how to study by an acquaintance who flunked out of college, or having your driving criticized by a cousin who had to repeat the road test three times before receiving his driver's licence. These comments would rankle most of us, in part because the people involved lack the footing to make their remarks, and thus lack authority. Someone with authority has both the credibility and the social sanction to address a given issue.

Finally, authority depends to some extent on both social role and context. Remember Adrian, who is team leader in his part-time job at a local fast-food restaurant? On the job, he has the authority to tell co-workers what to do and how, and they willingly accept his direction. However, when Adrian assumes the same level of authority with the same people in one of their classes at college, he faces significant resistance. His role in the situation is now one of equals, not one of authority, and it is no longer his place to give direction to the others. Similarly, a communication instructor is given authority, by virtue of her professional role in her students' education, to comment on grammar and sentence structure in their writing and speech. By enrolling in her class, the students have implicitly requested her guidance and advice. But in her private life, that same instructor would be overreaching her authority if she began to criticize, without being asked to do so, the communication of friends and acquaintances. They would, quite rightly, begin to doubt her good judgement. Thus, authority is not necessarily portable across situations; like all ethos, it must be re-established, or established on a different basis, for each new situation.

Social Proof

The final principle of influence that has a role in our interpersonal lives is something known as **social proof** or consensus.[16] Social proof refers to our increased readiness to accept or approve of ideas, attitudes, or actions if they have already been accepted by others.[17] Likely you're already familiar with social proof; no doubt as a child you argued that your parents should give you permission to participate in some activity because all your friends were doing it. More recently, you may have concluded that a test was unfair because everyone in the class did poorly, or perhaps you tried to discourage a friend from some action on the basis that 'nobody does it that way.' If you have done any of these or similar things, you have exploited the principle of social proof.

Like so many other of these principles of influence, social proof is a reflection of our need for social and interpersonal identification. We need to find our place in the social world, and to do so we may model ourselves and our behaviour on the actions and expectations of selected others. We derive our sense of belonging, as well as our sense of self, from such identifications. As a result, it can sometimes be carried to extremes of blind conformity, as with those who slavishly follow social trends and fads. You can probably recall your parents warning you about the dangers of taking social consensus too far: 'If everyone else jumped off a cliff, would you do it, too?'

But while there is folly in simply following the crowd, social proof also serves important interpersonal and social functions. It is from our sense of social proof that we learn to understand what the norms of a situation might be. As a principle of influence and of interpersonal communication, social proof helps us to improve our reading of unfamiliar contexts and serves as a kind of guide to appropriate behaviour: we learn what to do in an unfamiliar situation by watching the behaviour of those who are more experienced.

Because we all need some form of social affirmation to satisfy face needs and to provide a sense of identification and belonging, we are subject to the influence of social proof. How much social proof each individual needs will of course vary, not only from person to person but across different situations. In general, however, very few of us want to venture completely outside the bounds of what is acceptable to our community. Most of us choose to act in ways that confirm our membership in a community, and so we need to feel that our behaviour and our attitudes, no matter how adventurous, fall somewhere within the bounds of what our shared community considers to be 'normal'.

Consider what your reaction might be to Victor, who could be in one of your classes. One afternoon last week, two of his classmates discovered him waiting at the bus stop outside of the main college building—wearing a large cardboard carton that completely covered his upper body. It was raining rather heavily, and Victor explained that the carton was intended to keep him dry while he waited. What is your initial impression of Victor? If you had been one of the classmates who encountered him wearing the box, what would your reaction have been? Would you wish to become friends with him? If so, would you have joined him under the box?

There's no denying the *logic* of Victor's action; from a purely logical point of view, it's wiser to stay dry than to get drenched by a cold rain, but—as we have learned already—people's actions are not driven by logic alone. It's fair to say that most of us would probably choose to get rained on rather than to be discovered wearing a cardboard box, and the reason for this can be found in the concept of social proof.

Does Victor's behaviour set him apart from his classmates? Undoubtedly it does, though ironically it has nevertheless gained him a form of social acceptance: some of his classmates have started to collect stories like this one and repeat them to others, with a certain degree of indulgence and pride. But there are dangers to being this unconventional; although Victor's classmates have learned to accept his eccentricities, and some have even become genuinely pleased to be able to say they are acquainted with him, his membership in their circle remains limited. While they interact with him in a friendly way at school, he is rarely included in the group's social activities, and he has not really become friends with any of them. Victor seems mainly content with the lot he has chosen, but most of us would probably require a greater degree of social acceptance than he seems willing to tolerate.

Photo: Tannis Toohey/Toronto Star

Social proof shows up in less dramatic ways as well. Marguerite, for example, is regarded by her friends as a real risk-taker, mostly based on her preferred activities: mountain climbing, kick-boxing, and snowboarding. But as much as she thrives on such challenges, the truth is that Margie is actually daring only in situations where physical prowess and skill are the key. In social situations, for instance, she is far less courageous than her friend Albrecht, whose favourite pastime is belting out tunes at karaoke night. Unlike Albie, Margie would literally rather jump off a mountain than sing in front of a crowd. In fact, anything involving public performance makes her uncomfortable: giving a speech, going to an interview, calling a stranger on the phone. Albie, on the other hand, says that karaoke is just fun, whereas Margie's extreme sports are a form of death wish!

The contrast in their personalities carries over into their choice of major: they're both studying nursing, where Albie is one of only two guys in their whole year. Margie can't imagine being in classes where she would be the only woman, and she doesn't know how Albie puts up with some of the snide comments he gets, mostly from the boyfriends of their classmates. But he seems to take it all in stride, including the digs and unfounded assumptions about his manliness. Margie is the one with the physical courage, but Albie has a level of social confidence that she can't quite match.

Interestingly, though both of these people have chosen to push the social envelope, their choices, though daring and somewhat unusual, remain within more reasonable limits than Victor's simple action. After all, lots of people enjoy physically challenging sports, and male nurses, while still somewhat unusual, aren't completely unheard of. However, wearing a box as protection from the weather would be considered odd in all but the most extreme situations. Despite their willingness to embrace risk and express their individuality, Margie and Albie are—like most of us— treading pathways that have been forged by others before them.

Margie's and Albie's stories, and Victor's too, illustrate the extent to which we are all shaped to some degree by the force of social proof, and show that we are constrained by the need for social approval. While we prize the idea of originality and unconventionality, we are apt to view with suspicion, or even scorn, those whose originality marks them as weird or unpredictable. As a source of interpersonal influence, then, social proof can be one of the most powerful forces in our experience.

Summary

Although some people tend to equate the word persuasion with manipulation, not all persuasion is bad. In fact, all of us engage in persuasion as part of our everyday interpersonal interaction, and are, often quite willingly, influenced by others. Sometimes our attempts to influence others are for their own good: parents warn their children away from things that might endanger their safety; a supervisor encourages an employee to upgrade his skills; a dental hygienist demonstrates how to properly floss your teeth; a pharmacist cautions you about the medicine prescribed by your physician. All of these are explicit attempts to exert influence, and all of them are in our best interest.

In addition to our overt acts of persuasion, however, we also implicitly persuade each other in order to obtain the social co-operation, affirmation, and identification that we seek. As many theorists have maintained, and as we learned in Chapter 5, our language itself is inherently 'sermonic' or persuasive;[18] that is, in naming and in making statements we rely on interpretations and classifications that shape the way others will understand and react to what we are discussing. Some theorists, most notably Kenneth Burke, have maintained that *all* communication—all attempts to make meaning—inescapably involve persuasion.[19] Thus, just as we cannot 'not communicate', we also cannot 'not persuade'.

Persuasion, or influence, can be overt or it can be implicit, but it is an unavoidable part of human experience. It is embedded in human symbolicity and psychology, and in our need for relation. Theorists of influence, among them psychologist Robert Cialdini, argue that people are more readily influenced in accordance with a number of psychological and social principles, including the spirit of reciprocity, the binding nature of commitment, the urgency that arises from scarcity, the power of liking and authority, and the confidence that comes from social proof. In general, the more we have emotionally invested in a person, an object, or a course of action, the more we are likely to be influenced by it.

Persuasion is also more powerful when it doesn't declare itself, as is the case with most of the influence we experience. The most effective persuasion is thus implicit, as Axiom #8 points out: what is unstated can be as important, and often is more important, than what is explicitly stated. Such implicit arguments, which Aristotle called enthymemes, rely on associations, which in turn depend on principles already embedded in our attitudes and cultural belief systems.

Enthymemes, the linking of a premise to a conclusion by way of an unstated association, rely on a shared foundation of 'common sense'—attitudes or beliefs that speaker and hearer already hold in common. Since the common sense foundation is already accepted by both parties, the links in reasoning do not need to be made explicit. Needless to say, the more we already agree with the underlying common sense of a message, the more likely we are to be influenced by it. Most of the persuasion we experience in our daily lives is of this implicit, associative sort, and thus may pass almost unnoticed. Nevertheless, although we are often unaware of being persuaded, we are quite routinely convinced by arguments in which the links are supplied from our own fund of common knowledge and attitudes.

Key Terms

association
authority
Big Question
commitment
common sense
enthymeme
give face
liking
reciprocity
scarcity
social proof
syllogism
trouble with people

Suggested Readings

Pierre Berton, *The Big Sell: An Introduction to the Black Arts of Door-to-Door Salesmen and Others* (Toronto: McClelland & Stewart, 1963). Berton's book is out of print now, and that's a shame, because it is a fascinating and entertaining look at con games. Although there was no Internet when Berton wrote his book, many of the scams he describes are identical to ones now circulating via e-mail: they are just old techniques in a new guise. Berton's a master storyteller, and along with stories of the hapless victims of the scam artists, the book offers an impressive analysis of the dynamics of influence, from the persuasive power of story to the emotional impact of the highball-lowball technique. If you can find a copy second-hand, it's well worth picking up.

Daniel Joseph Boorstin, *The Image: A Guide to Pseudo-Events in America*, reissue edn (New York: Vintage Books, 1992). Boorstin's book may be a challenging read for an undergraduate audience, but it's an important book for anyone who wants to understand the persuasive function of electronic media. Although it was originally published in the 1960s, Boorstin's analysis of the inauthenticity of life in the media age has, like Packard's work (below), more relevance than ever today. Boorstin's central thesis is that the advent of photography—a quick way to capture, reproduce, and manipulate images—fundamentally changed cultural values and our sense of the value of actual events and interactions. This absorbing book ranges widely through popular culture, covering everything from travel to Hollywood films to news reportage, and argues that the dominant feature of contemporary culture is the 'pseudoevent', an event deliberately staged primarily so as to be reported in the media.

Robert Cialdini, *Influence: Science and Practice*, 4th edn (New York: William Morrow, 2000). Highly praised by marketing and sales practitioners, Cialdini's book is an analysis of why and how people are persuaded. Though it does not treat influence as an interpersonal dynamic, it does explore the six principles outlined in this chapter from a practical point of view. Aimed at a general audience and augmented with examples, it was not intended specifically for use as a textbook, but it has proven popular with undergraduates in business and marketing courses.

Vance Packard, *The Hidden Persuaders*, new edn (Brooklyn, NY: Ig Publishing, 2007). Packard's classic analysis of public persuasion, originally published in 1957 and out of print for decades, has just been released in this new edition with an introduction by Mark Crispin Miller. Packard, a journalist and social critic, was a pioneer in the analysis of how advertisers use motivational research and other psychological techniques to manipulate the public and create mass desire for consumer goods and products. In addition to consumer advertising, the book also looks at advertising in politics, and laid the groundwork for contemporary media analysts and critics such as Neil Postman and Michael Moore. Reading this work in the media-saturated world of 2007 reveals the keenness and prescience of Packard's perceptions, since many of his assertions about how image and personality would come to overshadow substance have come true in ways, and to an extent, that might even have surprised Packard. The publisher of the new edition correctly bills the book as 'more relevant than ever in today's super-saturated media world'.

Exercises and Assignments

1. In addition to being the foundation of associative arguments, the enthymeme—a logical structure in which the major generalization remains implicit—frequently provides the foundation of the jokes we tell. Consider the following jokes and identify the unstated assumption that links the opener to the punchline.

   a. How do you tell the difference between a doctor and God? God doesn't think He's a doctor.

b. How can you tell if a lawyer is cold? He has his hands in his own pockets for a change.

c. How can you tell if an engineer really likes you? When he's talking to you, he looks at your feet instead of his own.

What would you have to believe in order to make sense of jokes like these? What cultural attitudes do they represent? Did you find any of these jokes offensive? Why or why not?

2. The following statements may appear to be reports, but they are actually interpretations and judgements, based on implicit assumptions that are never overtly stated. For this reason, they perhaps tell us more about the person who is speaking than about the subject they address. What assumptions or values underlie them?

a. I can't do math—I'm an English major.

b. People should automatically lose their drivers' licences at age 65.

c. I do business with that firm because their sign says they are Christians.

d. I would never work for a female boss.

e. It's a guy thing.

f. Don't bother seeing that movie; it's a chick flick.

g. Gay men understand what it's like to be a woman.

h. John would have had that job, except he got 'skirted'.

3. What is the connection between the enthymeme as it is described in this chapter and the values conflicts studied in the previous chapter? What does this relationship tell you about the connection between persuasion and conflict?

4. Consider the story of Norm, as told at the beginning of this chapter, and answer the following questions, either in writing or as part of class discussion.

a. Can you identify any of the underlying 'common sense' that Norm relied on to persuade his friend?

b. Did any of Norm's appeals find their roots in the six principles of influence detailed in this chapter?

c. Is there any connection between Norm's appeals and the needs discussed by any of the theorists in Chapter 2. If so, what is the connection? What does it suggest about how persuasion operates?

5. The 'sermonic' nature of language—its power to exert influence and shape our understanding through labelling—is one of the most pervasive strategies of the propagandist. After reading Clyde Miller's 'How to Detect Propaganda' (Appendix B), discuss what the relationship is, if any exists, between Miller's seven propaganda devices and the six principles of persuasion described in this chapter.

6. Consider again the Personal Icons of the group constructed in Chapter 3. To what extent do the Icons, as deliberate self-representations, function persuasively. Do the principles of influence discussed in this chapter help us to better understand our own Icons or the Icons of others? To what degree is all self-presentation an act of persuasion? Present your analysis in writing or as part of a class discussion, as directed by your instructor.

7. The 'sermonic' nature of language—its power to exert influence and shape our understanding through labelling—is one of the most pervasive strategies of the propagandist. After reading Clyde Miller's 'How to Detect Propaganda' (Appendix B), discuss what the relationship is, if any exists, between Miller's seven propaganda devices and the six principles of persuasion described in this chapter.

8. Is Rose De Shaw's 'Pig of Shame' a form of persuasion ('Guilt, Despair, and the Red Pottery Pig', Appendix B)? Why or why not? If so, who is saying what, to whom, and for what purpose? To what extent is the red pottery pig an expression of control? Present your analysis in writing or as part of a class discussion, as directed by your instructor.

9. Look once more at the form-letter e-mail 'Mark C is Caught in the Middle' (Appendix B). This spam advertisement is clearly a form of persuasion. How effective is it? What kind of 'common sense' does it rely on? Can you reconstruct any of its enthymemes? Is it propaganda, according to the principles outlined by Clyde Miller ('How to Detect Propaganda')? Present your analysis in writing or as part of a class discussion, as directed by your instructor.

Chapter 10

Leadership as Interpersonal Communication

Learning Objectives

- To understand leadership as an interpersonal and rhetorical skill.
- To learn the principal qualities of leadership.
- To understand the traits of an effective leader.
- To distinguish between 'person-centred' and 'task-centred' leadership styles.

As we have learned so far, we communicate for a variety of reasons: to fulfill our most fundamental needs; to establish and maintain a sense of identity; to express our dreams. Most of these aspirations are fulfilled through the meaningful relationships we experience and establish throughout our personal and professional lives.

In addition to the acquaintanceships, friendships, and intimate relationships discussed in Chapter 4, there remains one more significant kind of relationship that can have profound effects on our lives: that between a leader and followers. Though leadership has traditionally been treated primarily as an aspect of organizational behaviour, there is a growing body of theory that treats this important dynamic from an interpersonal perspective.[1] There are at least two reasons to consider leadership as an interpersonal interaction. First, like all interpersonal relationships, the relationship between leader and followers is built on a foundation of trust. Second, the skills and traits that have been identified as essential for effective leadership are the very skills of communication discussed in this book.[2]

From a practical point of view, it is also worth considering leadership as part of the study of interpersonal communication because the skills of leadership are more and more frequently required in all our work relationships, whether or not we formally act in a managerial or supervisory capacity. The ability to engender trust and to demonstrate genuine respect for others—abilities we associate with good leaders—are valued traits for all employees, and indeed are important traits for all of our interpersonal interactions.

Leadership, like all interpersonal communication, also involves questions of ethics. The issue of trust is especially important in understanding and practising leadership, because of the ways in which leaders must influence the options and behaviour of those they lead. As soon as we are in a position to constrain or affect the choices of others or to influence their actions or attitudes, as leaders are expected to do, we confront issues of ethics.

This chapter explores this important interpersonal relationship in greater detail, with the twin goals of greater understanding and increased skill. While we cannot hope to cover every aspect of the scholarly study of leadership in a single chapter, we will explore the points of overlap between leadership and interpersonal communication.

Leadership as a Skill of Communication

Leadership is a communication phenomenon that combines the interpersonal and the rhetorical through the medium of trust. On an interpersonal level, leadership is best understood as a relationship, rather than as a purely organizational function in which one individual oversees the work of others. Leadership, as we will see, involves much more than ensuring that procedures and protocols are followed and tasks completed 'by the book'; it is also more involved than simply overseeing project assignments and workflow.

Effective leadership, like all interpersonal relationships, is built on trust and commitment. As a rhetorical activity, leadership is the ability to engage and influence others, to motivate them and to build a strong sense of dedication to common objectives. The study of leadership is therefore also the study of persuasion. Not surprisingly, the collection of skills and traits that we label 'leadership' describes, in large part, the characteristics of an outstanding and persuasive communicator: the ability to inspire commitment, communicate a vision, create enthusiasm, and help develop the potential of others.

Leadership has been defined in various ways; some theorists focus on the interactional process itself,[3] others on the context in which leadership emerges,[4] and still others on the traits, skills, and behaviour of various leaders,[5] but nearly all agree on a few key points: leadership involves influence and, as such, is aimed at particular ends.[6]

In keeping with the Nine Axioms set out in Chapter 2, we will treat leadership as involving a combination of these factors: first, we will assume that leadership is, like all communication, the product of interaction and not simply something imposed by one individual on others. Second, we understand that leadership is situated, as all communication is, and that, while the qualities of a leader are consistent across various contexts, the authority to lead is not necessarily portable from one situation to another. Third, and in keeping with our rhetorically grounded approach, we will treat leadership as a function of ethos: the character a leader displays and the relation that he or she can establish with others.

QUALITIES OF LEADERSHIP

- Leadership combines both interpersonal and rhetorical skill.
- Leadership involves influence.
- Leadership is a product of interaction.
- Leadership is situated.
- Leadership is a function of ethos.
- Leadership involves trust.

Leadership can be defined as the capacity to exert influence over what others do or believe. This does not mean simply forcing your will on others, however, or abusing the authority of your position. In fact, most contemporary theories specifically distinguish between coercion and leadership, just as rhetorical theorists have always drawn the line between force and persuasion; someone who leads by threats and coercion is considered by most people to be a tyrant rather than a leader.[7]

True leadership involves more than an application of policy or positional authority; it also involves obtaining the assent and co-operation of those being led. As we know already from our study of interpersonal influence, people are much more likely to accept the direction of someone they trust and respect and who has shown them respect in return. Not surprisingly, this same principle is at work in the dynamic between leader and followers (or as some theorists prefer, collaborators[8]). As the physician and authority on military leadership, Jonathan Shay, explains, 'the persuasive power that comes when a leader appeals to reason comes more from the degree to which it provides evidence for the leader's respect toward the troops than from the power of reason to compel assent, or having compelled assent, to guide or restrain behavior.'[9] In other words, even appeals to reason are convincing only because the leader has already established a bond of trust with his or her followers.

This kind of influence can be accomplished only through communication that is both interpersonally effective and rhetorically sound, building strong relationships and successfully motivating others. In fact, according to leadership experts Boyd Clark and Ron Crossland, 'the ability to communicate powerfully is the leverage leaders need.' Unfortunately, they also note that it is the very skill that workplace supervisors and managers 'most lack'.[10] It seems clear that improving your interpersonal and rhetorical skills is the first step toward becoming an effective leader.

Much has been written about the specific traits and qualities that make an effective leader, but all theories reinforce the principle articulated by behavioural psychologist Kurt Dirks: 'trust is a crucial element of effective leadership.'[11] Leaders may emerge naturally or they may be appointed; they may be naturally gifted with the drive and commitment to succeed or they may be called forth by a particular set of circumstances; but they will be successful and effective leaders only if they can command the trust of those they hope to lead. To do this, they need to demonstrate the kind of authority and footing that are granted by an understanding of the subject, a pertinent role in the situation, and an appropriate relationship to the listener.

Jonathan Shay agrees, arguing that, if we are to understand the nature of the relationship between a leader and followers, 'we must understand . . . what it means for a leader to seek trust: It's about dealing with fellow-citizens, where each looks the other in the eye and says, "you are part of my future, no matter how this turns out."'[12] Shay thus defines leadership as a 'shared binding commitment in the face of uncertainty'. Shay's characterization of leadership as a deep personal commitment makes clear the connection between the qualities of leadership and interpersonal communication, and he anchors his discussion explicitly in the good character, good will, and good judgement that Aristotle made central to effective communication. At the heart of Shay's characterization is the necessity for respect between leader and followers.

The Traits of Leadership

The single most important quality required of leaders is **credibility**, the characteristic that leadership gurus James Kouzes and Barry Posner describe as 'the foundation on which leaders stand . . . [their] most important asset'.[13] For Kouzes and Posner, credibility entails 'trustworthiness (honesty), expertise (competence), and dynamism (inspiration)'. Similarly, well-known leadership specialist Stephen Covey articulates a 'principle-centred' model of leadership that shares Kouzes and Posner's emphasis on credibility, since it is founded on 'such basic principles as fairness, service, equity, justice, integrity, honesty, and trust'.[14]

The focus that these theorists place on credibility, integrity, and trust is echoed in nearly every contemporary leadership model. But what is most interesting is that what they're saying is not entirely new. You may already have noticed that these models are restatements of that same quality that Aristotle insisted was 'the most effective means of persuasion' any speaker—or leader—possesses: ethos.[15] With its emphasis on good judgement (seen in these contemporary models as competence and justice), good character (represented as integrity, honesty, and trustworthiness), and good will (shown in the characteristics of fairness, equity, service, respect, and inspiration), Aristotle's conception of ethos[16] is the essence of an effective leader, as Jonathan Shay explicitly shows in his application of Aristotelian rhetoric to leadership in a military context.[17]

In addition to the reconfiguring of these essential Aristotelian virtues, the characteristics that contribute to a person's capacity to lead effectively have been clustered into four general areas of competence: ability, sociability, motivation, and communication.[18] Successful and effective leaders generally show greater levels of these qualities than are shown by those they hope to lead. Although some theorists, such as John Gardner, have itemized as many as 14 qualities,[19] most of them can be understood as arising from these key four.

THE TRAITS OF LEADERSHIP

- Ability
- Sociability
- Motivation
- Communication

A leader's superior **ability** in this context means something akin to Aristotle's conception of good judgement, since it includes appropriate assessment of the situation, a degree of insight and understanding greater than that of the followers, and sufficient verbal adeptness to articulate those judgements in a suitable fashion. In most contexts, 'ability' can also be construed as a superior level of practical skill at a specific task or set of tasks: for example, the head chef should be more skilled than the line cook, the journeyman electrician should be more able than the apprentice. In addition to practical skill, 'ability' may also be interpreted as more extensive theoretical or scholarly knowledge: the tutorial leader should know more than her first-year charges, for instance, and the Ph.D. supervisor should be more knowledgeable than the Ph.D. candidate.

Leaders are expected to demonstrate a fuller understanding of the issues at stake than is required of those to whom they would give direction; they must bring a foundation of good assessment and skill in making informed and thoughtful judgements. They are also expected to project a quality of practical wisdom and willingness to make difficult decisions. In short, as followers we are inclined to assign a greater degree of trust and allegiance to those we regard as intellectually and professionally capable than to those whose understanding, skill, or intelligence we have cause to doubt. In the first instance, then, leaders are those whose knowledge, experience, and skill are greater than our own.

However, a greater degree of knowledge by itself is not sufficient to establish someone as a leader. The second desirable quality that a leader must possess, and demonstrate, is a greater degree of what might be called **sociability**. Good leaders are typically seen as more approachable, more person-centred, and both more active and more co-operative than those they would lead. They are dependable and worthy of respect and regard, and they are also seen as genuinely respectful of others.

Leaders are also more interpersonally observant than average; they can demonstrate understanding of the needs and expectations of their followers, and they bring skill in dealing effectively with people. Such leaders are able to attract others by virtue of their commitment, not only to the task at hand but also to the team members. Good leaders are able to make their followers feel that their contributions are genuinely valued and that they themselves matter to the success of the venture. Such leaders are viewed as accessible to their team, and while they are able to wield the necessary authority and to act decisively, they are also seen as capable of recognizing and rewarding the efforts of others, and they are able to foster a sense of loyalty and unity among the group.

Third, leaders are also effective by virtue of their greater degree of **motivation**. They seem to have a higher than average need for achievement, and the drive necessary to pursue and achieve their goals. They are rarely satisfied with the status quo; instead, they are goaded by possibility, perceiving not only what more can be done, but also how to bring it about. They are willing and confident enough to follow through on their vision of what might be, in spite of the risks that doing so might entail. That said, however, they do not place their followers at unnecessary risk; instead, they are able to take responsibility for mistakes and willing to share responsibility for the team's successes.

Effective leaders are highly self-disciplined and not easily discouraged by setbacks, showing persistence and initiative both in starting projects and in following them through. Their attitude and behaviour are marked by both courage and resolution, and they show a degree of self-confidence (not arrogance) that is founded on ability and on a willingness to work as hard as is necessary to bring their plans to reality.

However, despite their greater degree of motivation and commitment, effective leaders understand that they can't realize their goals on their own. They are also adept at motivating others to join them; their enthusiasm for what they do is both evident and infectious, and they have the ability to motivate others as well as themselves. An effective leader's commitment to the project, task, or course of action is typically highly visible to collaborators and followers, and is unwavering. This visible commitment is in part what inspires a like commitment in others, and it is in this sense that good leaders are able to lead by example.

In addition to their greater degrees of ability, sociability, and motivation, effective leaders must be adept communicators, both interpersonally (in forming and nurturing effective relationships) and rhetorically (in their ability to engage and persuade others). Effective leaders typically have a good understanding of themselves and others, are perceptive and skilled listeners, and are verbally adept. They treat others with fairness and know not only how to save face, but how to give it when required. They take responsibility for the work of their team and can adapt their interactional style to suit the particular situation. Good leaders recognize the shared commitment of everyone on the team and are able to give credit for everyone's contributions. In short, effective leaders are powerful and ethical communicators.

Styles of Leadership

Leadership style generally refers to a person's pattern of interaction or behaviour in leading others. Numerous leadership styles have been described using different terminology,[20] but most seem to concur with the pioneering work done by Ralph White and Ronald Lippit, who posited two general categories or patterns that they labelled 'autocratic' or 'task-oriented' and 'democratic' or 'person-oriented'.[21] Leaders who take a **task-oriented** approach are more focused on problem-solving: they are concerned with identifying what needs to be done and finding a means of making it happen. This approach generally tends to express itself in a greater degree of control over situations and people. At the extreme, a leader adopting this strategy may even tend to micromanage others. Task-focused leaders will likely be more directive and unilateral in their interactions, and are less inclined to ask for others' input, trusting their own instincts and judgement. Task-oriented leadership is typically decisive and efficient, like a sports coach, a captain of a fire brigade, or a military team commander. Taken too far, it is likely to be perceived as overbearing or tyrannical.

By contrast, **person-oriented leadership** focuses more on what is known as the 'maintenance' or relational dynamics of the group. While getting the job done still matters in this approach, it is less important than getting everyone 'on board'. A person-oriented approach invites the input and commentary of everyone on the team, and a leader who habitually takes such an approach is less inclined than a task-focused leader to issue strong direction, preferring to allow solutions to arise collaboratively from the whole group. A leader taking a person-oriented approach may serve more as a guide and sounding board than a director or boss. Work gets accomplished more slowly with this emphasis on consensus; at its extreme, a person-oriented approach may even be perceived as indecisive.

In his study of the interpersonal dynamics of advice-giving, George Dillon offers a useful insight into these seemingly incompatible leadership styles through a parallel construct that he characterizes as 'hard' and 'soft' rhetoric.[22] According to Dillon's configuration, an advice-giver or leader employing a **hard-rhetoric** style may emphasize 'contention, competition, and combat' as the dominant mode, portraying interactions as a kind of struggle in which the leader must triumph. Such hard rhetoric, like White and Lippit's autocratic style, is directive and task-focused. The typical hard-rhetoric stance is relatively impersonal and formal; it tends to favour directness over tact. It is likely to be emotionally distant but may be quite forceful, even confrontational, in its language and tone. Because a hard-rhetoric approach tends to make decisive pronouncements, it assumes and encodes a level of superiority over the rest of the group.

A **soft-rhetoric** footing, by contrast, is more like White and Lippit's 'democratic' or person-oriented style. Emphasizing 'cooperation, conciliation, and the enactment of social bondedness',[23] a soft-rhetoric approach tends to be more personal and less formal than the hard-rhetoric footing; it tends to emphasize equality between leader and team. Soft rhetoric typically avoids confrontation and promotes solidarity. The language of this approach is likely to be less decisive or directive and to place tact ahead of directness.

At first glance, especially in the context of interpersonal relationships, it would appear that the 'person-oriented', soft-rhetoric style would be generally preferable to a hard-rhetoric, task-oriented approach. However, several things must be said about this apparent superiority of one style over the other. First, the two categories of leadership style or footing are extreme characterizations. It's rare that any single interaction falls completely into one or the other style; usually, messages fall somewhere between the two poles, with some features that would be considered 'hard' rhetoric and some that would be considered 'soft'.

Second, the success of a particular approach is determined not by whether it is 'person-oriented' or 'task-oriented'. Rather, the effectiveness of an interaction is measured by how appropriately it is adapted to the demands of the situation and the needs and expectations of those it is intended to influence. It's easy for most of us to think of situations in which soft rhetoric would be superior to a harder approach, but there are also many situations in which the reverse is true. For example, in a situation that requires speed and efficiency—a fire chief giving instructions at the scene of a fire, a sergeant leading troops into battle, a surgeon at an operating table, an air traffic controller talking a pilot through an emergency landing—the soft rhetoric of conciliation and democratic leadership would be inappropriate and possibly disastrous, whereas a more decisive, directive approach is clearer and easier to follow, saving precious minutes in an emergency situation. Similarly, in a situation in which a clear chain of responsibility is important—such as a judge sentencing a convicted criminal or a military commander giving the order to fire weapons—the clarity and singularity of responsibility represented by hard rhetoric are more appropriate than the diffusion of responsibility that arises from the 'democratic' approach of soft rhetoric.

Even in everyday situations, soft rhetoric may be inadvertently obstructionist: we would rarely use it, for instance, in replying to a direct request for information when an unadorned, clear response would be preferable. For instance, if I'm in a hurry to complete some research for a project due on Monday and I ask the librarian where to find the books on the subject I'm researching, I would prefer a harder, more directive approach over a softer query that asks how I *feel* about the topic matter; if I need to locate Malcolm and I ask Brenda if she's seen him, I may experience Brenda's attempts to 'enact social bondedness' as an impediment to the work I have to get done. In situations where time is limited and deadlines or reputations or even lives are at stake, it's likely that a somewhat more task-focused approach is the better choice because it's more effectively adapted to the constraints of the situation.

At the same time, of course, in a situation that requires conciliation and social affirmation, the task-centred, directive, confrontive approach of hard rhetoric could be disastrous. As we discussed at length in the chapter on listening, someone who is feeling the need for connection and affirmation or who needs a shoulder to cry on

may respond angrily or defensively to your task-focused, directive comments. Remember Mohsen, whose cousin Ranjit mistook his comments about his ailing father as a request for advice and problem-solving? The rift between the two has still not been healed.

Finally, since the key to the effectiveness of a communicative or leadership style is its appropriateness, good leaders—and good communicators in general—need both skills in their communicative repertoire. Someone who can adopt a style suitable to the situation is a more effective and skilled communicator than one who has only one style of response. A leader who is person-centred when a task-centred focus would better serve his purpose is likely to be regarded as weak-willed and indecisive, a pushover. He may be seen as a nice enough person, but generally ineffectual in managing the day-to-day challenges of the workplace.

Similarly, someone whose responses are always couched in competition and combativeness, or who consistently puts processes ahead of people or tasks ahead of everyone's feelings, is likely to be considered an aggressive bully—and she may be one in fact. Thus, rather than thinking of these labels as categories into which people can be slotted, you would do better to think of them as skill sets that can be applied according to what is best for a given situation.

This discussion may call to mind the distinction between 'typically female' and 'typically male' communication patterns, as identified by Deborah Tannen and others, that we discussed in the context of verbal communication in interpersonal relations. If we compare the characterizations offered by Dillon and by other theorists of leadership, such as White and Lippit, with the views of these scholars, it would appear that a hard-rhetoric, task-centred style is more 'typically male' and the soft-rhetoric, person-centred style is more 'typically female'. Indeed, some theorists have argued that women bring different values and communication patterns to leadership and organizational structures generally.[24] As with generalizations about how men or women 'typically' interact, it is problematic to assume that these patterns hold for all women at all organizational levels, or indeed for all men, though it is interesting to consider them as part of the overall study of leadership and interpersonal communication.

What is certain is that effective leaders, female or male, are those who can combine a sensitivity to people with an ability to get the job done, and who bring the good judgement to know which emphasis is appropriate to the specific situation. A good leader stands on principle when principle is what counts, and focuses on the task at hand when it is necessary to do so, but also builds team loyalty and commitment by bringing an appropriate commitment of her own, not only to the job but to the members of the group. A good leader gets the job done, but also supports the team as necessary.

An important component of a leader's effectiveness, then, is judgement. Effective leadership isn't simply a collection of traits or a 'typical' pattern of behaviour or style of interaction. Like all interpersonal communication, it isn't a cookie-cutter formula or a matter of simply following a set of rules or routines. Instead, good leadership is the product of sensitive and thoughtful assessment and judgement. As Jonathan Shay explains, in cases where 'everything can be done by formula, by the book, what's needed is a supervisor, not a leader.' A supervisor in Shay's sense is simply someone who oversees procedures and ensures that regulations are followed. Such a supervisor doesn't need to apply any judgement or make any decisions; he or she is simply a functionary whose decision-making authority has been replaced by a collection of ordinances.

A leader, however, is someone whose judgement can be trusted in situations that are not readily predictable, who can act decisively and take responsibility for those choices, and who has committed to the welfare of the team. As Shay notes, 'many critical decisions cannot be solved by the book, because they involve competing, incommensurable goods and uncertainty,'[25] and it is in such situations that real leadership is needed.

Mentoring as a Form of Leadership

Mentoring is a special kind of leadership function, with its own interpersonal and ethical imperatives. Typically a mentor is someone senior in experience and status who provides guidance and advice to a protege, an associate with less experience. Ideally, a mentor's counsel is given one-on-one and is completely voluntary. It is normally also a confidential relationship characterized by a high level of trust, in which both mentor and acolyte can speak freely. The benefits to the associate are obvious: he or she can grow in skill and understanding by learning from someone who is successful and well respected, and gains from the benefits of years of experience that are handed down. For mentors, the rewards are intangible: they act mainly for the satisfaction of passing on wisdom and knowledge, and for the gratification of seeing another person develop under their guidance.

Like all our interpersonal relationships, of course, each mentoring relationship is unique, but all instances of mentoring share some general qualities. For example, because it is a relationship entered voluntarily, because it is a one-to-one interaction, and because it depends on a high level of trust between mentor and protege, mentorship is characterized by a greater degree of interpersonal intimacy than other leader–follower relationships. Although it is qualitatively different from friendship because of the definite disparity in experience and status, a mentorship is nevertheless as much a personal as a professional relationship, and it can involve the same high degree of commitment and disclosure that characterizes any other intimate friendship.

Although some schools and workplaces have developed 'mentoring programs' in which an inexperienced newcomer is paired with someone more seasoned, the relationship doesn't become a true mentorship until the participants voluntarily develop the requisite trust and intimacy. While formal structures can help to foster and facilitate the development of mentoring relationships, they cannot generate true mentorship without the willing investment of self from both mentor and protege.

Not all of us will be fortunate enough to experience the guidance and advice of a supportive mentor in our lives. Those who are lucky enough to participate in one of these remarkable encounters will know that they have experienced a truly special form of human bond with someone who genuinely cares about their welfare, and who does so without thought of reward.

Communicating Effectively in a Leadership Role

Along with possessing superior abilities, leaders, we are told, are more effective communicators than the rest of us: more articulate, more perceptive, better listeners, and more acute judges of characters and situations. They are adept at forming effective relationships and at balancing task- and people-centred functions. Assuming that we meet the criteria of knowledge and experience required for leadership in our own fields, how can we become more adept at the communication skills required of leaders?

According to Boyd Clark and Ron Crossland, ineffective leaders typically make four 'fatal assumptions' about their communicative effectiveness: that those they lead have understood what has been communicated, that the subordinates agree with the message, that they care about what has been said, and that they will take appropriate action.[26] Thus, the authors claim, the biggest problem with leadership communication is 'the illusion that it has occurred'.

Despite what is promised by the many leadership books in the self-help section of your local bookstore, good leadership isn't simply a question of mastering a specific skill set. Instead, it involves improving your communicative judgement so as to avoid Clark and Crossland's 'fatal assumptions'. Nevertheless, although good leadership (like interpersonal effectiveness generally) isn't simply about mastering a set of strategies, you can hone your ability to assess and respond to the demands of various situations in which you find yourself. As you develop your interpersonal effectiveness, there are some things you can do to prepare yourself to take on a leadership role.

First, in order to be a more effective leader, and to communicate more effectively in that role, you will need to be knowledgeable about the particular tasks your team needs to accomplish. Since leadership is a matter of judgement and you can't reasonably assess what you don't fully understand, you will need to learn as much as you can about what you propose to do. Take Davin, for instance. He has just finished an MBA after completing his undergraduate degree in mechanical engineering, and has accepted a supervisory position in industry where most of those he oversees are journeyman machinists who never went to university. When Davin first joined the company four months ago, he couldn't help swaggering a bit. He was proud of his two degrees and saw them as granting him the necessary authority to lead those who had little or no higher education.

However, despite what he initially viewed as his superior training, Davin has already run into some difficulty. The plain fact is that, while he learned about management principles in his MBA and took plenty of engineering courses as part of his engineering degree, he has no direct experience of the industry where he now hopes to lead others, and he's beginning to realize that he doesn't really have the depth of understanding of those who have worked for years on the front lines.

Instead of being given the respect and deference that he initially expected his newly minted MBA would earn him, Davin finds himself encountering resistance. Those on the shop floor are highly skilled, with years of experience in the industry; several of them are older than Davin. His lack of technical mastery and his inexperience caused him to make foolish pronouncements in front of the machinists during his first few weeks on the job. He suspects that they now view him with scorn and ridicule him behind his back.

To Davin's credit, he now recognizes that he made some mistakes in the way he tried to establish his authority. He sees that his MBA is not sufficient to give him the footing to lead a group for whom expertise arises from hands-on skill. It's going to be hard to revise his standing with the skilled trades people in his department, but Davin is determined to learn from his mistakes and to treat this experience not as a fiasco but as an opportunity to develop his leadership skills. He has already learned something important about leadership: people are more willing to follow those they judge to be competent, and part of competence is a fullness of understanding of the situation and the task at hand.

Davin has been humbled by his initial mistake and has vowed to do better. But in making the initial error, he's not alone. Notice that what matters is not just any knowledge or expertise, but *relevant* expertise. Davin's MBA mattered to his superiors when they hired him to do the job, but to those on the shop floor it was irrelevant, and his ignorance in the areas that matter to his intended followers prevented him from establishing the kind of authority he needs to lead. If he is to be an effective leader, Davin needs to understand the world that his followers live and work in, to be able to share their perspective, and to know the challenges they face. He needs to build his credibility through mastery of the knowledge base that his followers see as central to their work.

Not surprisingly, then, the second thing you should do if you wish to become a more effective leader is to learn to listen to others with genuine interest and concern. As we have already discovered, what most people want is to feel that their issues have been heard and their interests taken into account. Even if their expectations cannot always be completely accommodated, most people will appreciate when a sincere effort has been made to include their input and will be more willing to compromise as a result.

Listening to others means more than paying attention to the content of their messages. Since people don't always make their relational needs or motives explicit, you need to pay attention to the unspoken assumptions, values, needs, and attitudes that their messages convey. As you hear their words, listen for what lies beneath the explicit message: what interpersonal, political, or ethical factors are at play? As a leader, you should learn to use effective techniques of active listening and paraphrasing, to distinguish, for example, between a request for advice and a plea for understanding and affirmation. You can develop your skills of listening by practising the strategies outlined in Chapter 7, but remember that what is most needed is a genuine interest in others, not a collection of strategies that enable you to 'fake' interest.

Third, learn to pay attention to non-verbal cues, both your own and those of others. Remember that more than 90 per cent of the information communicated in any interaction is communicated non-verbally. You will be more readily able to adapt your leadership style to suit the context if you are sensitive to what others are feeling, information that is frequently communicated through their non-verbal responses.

In particular, you should pay attention to the patterns that emerge in how others interact, since it is the patterns of behaviour, rather than individual instances, that reveal a person's orientation and attitude. As well, individual occurrences are given more meaning by an understanding of how those incidents relate to the person's overall attitudes and habits. For instance, the fact that Jack is shouting is more significant if he's normally calm and easygoing than it is if he's normally inclined to be a bit melodramatic.

Pay attention to the non-verbal dynamics of interactions, not only between yourself and other individuals, but among the rest of those you are leading. Being observant of the non-verbal patterns and aberrations will make you more effective as a leader and minimize the chance of your being caught off guard by some interpersonal eruption. Chapter 6 offers some suggestions for becoming a more sensitive observer and 'reader' of others' emotional states and responses, and this sensitivity to the general mood of your team's interactions will make you a more perceptive and able leader or group member.

A fourth step you can take is to be more conscientious in your language use. Developing greater mastery of both writing and speech will pay huge dividends, since it is through your words that you can best inspire others. Consider that being articulate and verbally polished are among the qualities considered essential for good leaders, and then recall that the average North American has a working vocabulary of under 2 per cent of the available words in English!

As a leader, you should be able to articulate ideas with precision and clarity; you should be able to create vivid word pictures to help others visualize your meaning. To inspire others, you need to be able to use language accurately, with passion and flair. You cannot do this if you're working with limited tools. One way to improve your articulateness is to work actively to enlarge your vocabulary and to make your language more concrete and vivid. Try to avoid buzzwords, clichés, and trendy jargon like 'thinking outside the box' or 'change events' or 'elephants in the room'. Instead, wherever possible, reach for original phrasing that captures your own meaning clearly rather than simply slotting in some pre-packaged phrase. Use concrete language in place of abstractions wherever you can, and help others to see your meaning in their own minds' eyes.

You can develop your vocabulary with any of the methods suggested in Chapter 5: actively listen and watch for new words in conversation and reading, and make note of them so you can look them up in a dictionary to verify the meaning. Consult a thesaurus to develop your range of options and practise different ways of saying similar things. You can also do crosswords or play word games like Scrabble or Boggle. Above all, you should read as much as you can, keeping watch for unfamiliar words that can be added to your own vocabulary. However, you do need to be careful if your reading focuses on management self-help books or leadership manuals: these tend to be packed with exactly the kind of fuzzy, trendy jargon that will deaden your ability to communicate your insights in fresh and powerful ways.

If you wish, you could make yourself a policy to add a new word to your vocabulary each day. You can do this by selecting words from a dictionary, from the books and reports you routinely read, or even from the television. Make sure you know exactly what they mean before you begin tossing them around, however; nothing can discredit you more quickly than misusing words that others around you may know. Once you are certain you have mastered the nuances of your new words, you should make a concerted effort to use them until you are comfortable with them and they have become a naturalized part of your vocabulary.

Another way to become more articulate and to engage others is to bring your vision to life with stories, anecdotes, or case studies. Such examples can be both informative and entertaining; certainly they offer a more vivid way to communicate your meaning than simply making pronouncements. In ancient times, parables and fables such as those of Aesop served exactly this purpose, and contemporary storytellers like Rick Mercer,[27] Stuart McLean,[28] Pierre Berton,[29] and Paul Connolly[30] demonstrate the persistent force of story to engage, entertain, and illuminate. Stories have great power to make your ideas real to your listeners, to help them visualize and identify with what you are saying. This is true in part because we are all storytellers—and hence listeners to stories—by our very nature.

Consider for a moment the story of Norm at the beginning of Chapter 9. The details of that story not only bring Norm to life, but also make vivid the dilemma that faces his overworked friend. What do you think would be lost from the chapter on interpersonal influence if the story of Norm were removed?

The case studies in that chapter and throughout the book serve a similar purpose: they engage the reader in a familiar and realistic scenario, make important points more vivid, and illustrate the theory that is central to the chapter. Stories like these make good use of the capacity of narrative to engage others' attention; they are memorable because they dramatize meaning in a form that most of us find easy to identify with, and they communicate much more forcefully than a declaration such as 'Sometimes we are persuaded against our better judgement by someone who knows us well enough to "push the right buttons."' Good leaders understand the power of narrative to communicate with their audiences, and you should try to develop your own storytelling abilities to help you make your own points more vividly and forcefully.

A fifth essential component of leadership is trustworthiness, since it is the fundamental ingredient of credibility. According to the leadership scholar Kurt Dirks, trust in the leader of a team has a greater impact on the quality of a team's performance even than the trust that teammates place in each other.[31]

If you wish to develop your leadership potential, you must make a habit of behaving in ways that make you worthy of the trust that others will place in you as their leader. Keep your word. Follow through on your promises. Support your team, especially in the face of opposition. Make sure that they are kept in the information loop by sharing details that they need to know. Build their loyalty by demonstrating loyalty to them. Keep your confidences. Treat others with respect and fairness. Maintain control of your temper, and avoid lashing out in anger or defensiveness. Try to get the full story before you act. Avoid making snap judgements, and be ready to adjust your assessments in the face of additional information. If you make an error, own up to it and take full responsibility for making it right. In all that you do, try to demonstrate the qualities of ethos: good and thoughtful judgement, good character, and respectful treatment of others. This is an extremely tall order, and you won't be able to manage all of these things all of the time. But it is important that you try, and keep on trying even when you occasionally fail, because through this effort you are building the habits that will make you an effective leader.

The final quality of an effective leader is a strong work ethic. Effective leaders cannot be lazy or uncommitted. To lead, it's not enough to direct others or tell them what to do; you must provide an example for them to follow. Good leaders are able to delegate effectively, but they are also ready to shoulder their share of the burden and are at least as involved in the success of the team effort as anyone else in the group, and usually they are more so.

Good leaders also take responsibility for the actions of the team, especially for their failures and setbacks. But the mark of a good leader is also the ability to share the credit for the team's successes. If you wish to be an effective leader, you must be prepared to work harder than anyone else, to take responsibility for setbacks, and to share successes with the rest of the team.

According to Jonathan Shay, who saw in Aristotle's *Rhetoric* a handbook for potential leaders, a team will more readily and willingly place their trust in someone who demonstrates '[p]rofessional competence and spirited personal integrity; intelligent good sense and practical wisdom; and good will and respect' for those who would be led.[32]

Summary

We have defined leadership as the capacity to exert influence over what others do or believe. Leadership is not only a particular kind of interpersonal relationship, it is also a specialized and highly valued form of influence anchored in a foundation of trust.

Leadership is more than mere supervision, which involves application of by-the-book rules; it is also not coercion, in which the will of one is imposed on others by threat or force. Instead, leadership is a function of ethos, and the character of the leader plays in integral part in how effectively that person can lead. Like all communication, leadership is given shape and meaning by the context or situation in which it occurs, and to be effective the leader must demonstrate a full understanding not only of the task but of the situation and of the people he or she will lead.

Although it is possible to produce long lists of desirable characteristics for effective leaders, most research points to four general clusters of traits that distinguish them from others. First, leaders typically are more adept and more knowledgeable than their followers about the task they are meant to perform; this knowledge and ability help to give subordinates confidence in their leader's judgement. Second, effective leaders must be socially adept, able to work and interact effectively with others; weakness in these traits is likely to be perceived by subordinates as ineptitude or a lack of authority, and will affect the ability of the leader to influence those who must be given direction. Third, because the leader is responsible for motivating and invigorating others towards the group's goals, he or she must exhibit higher levels of personal enthusiasm and motivation. Finally, good leaders must be articulate, inspiring communicators, since communicative skill is one of the measures by which we assess the overall competence of others. A leader who is unable to communicate effectively will not be able to maintain the footing necessary to effectively direct or inspire others.

The responsibilities and actions of a leader may be carried out in a variety of styles. Most of those who study leadership posit two general categories of leadership style: a predominantly task-oriented, 'autocratic' style characterized by the hard rhetoric of competitiveness and contentiousness, and a more person-oriented, 'democratic' style characterized by the softer rhetoric of co-operation and conciliation. Some researchers believe that the former is more typical of male communication and leadership styles, while the latter is more common to female communication and leadership styles.

However, we concluded that, rather than seeing these extremes as ways of looking at or classifying the habitual approaches of individuals, it is more productive and useful to see them as characterizing strategies that may be adapted by any leader as required to fit a particular situation. While the softer, 'democratic' style might appear to be universally preferable from an interpersonal perspective, in some situations a harder, task-focused approach is desirable. A skilled leader, then, is someone who can effectively adapt his or her style to suit the demands of the situation, employing a more task-centred approach when the context demands it and a more person-centred approach when that is what's required. Few interactions fall to the extreme end of either category, requiring instead an appropriate blend of person- and task-focused approaches.

Like all interpersonal relationships, leadership is not determined by a cookie-cutter formula. Instead, like all effective communication, it's the product of sensitive and thoughtful assessment and judgement. Leadership involves both influence and trust, and thus, like any other kind of interpersonal relationship, it is a dynamic process rather than a static condition that can be imposed on others.

Because it involves both influence and trust, the practice and study of leadership bring us squarely into the realm of ethical practice, which is concerned with our behaviour towards others. As we have learned throughout this book, all of our interpersonal interaction has the power to affect the interests and well-being of others, their understanding of themselves and their relationships, their sense of self-worth and identity. This is especially true when we are formally placed in a position to constrain or affect someone else's choices or to influence their actions or attitudes, as leaders are expected to do. For this reason, it's not possible to consider leadership without confronting issues of ethics.

To become more effective and ethical leaders, and more proficient communicators generally, we need to learn to listen to others, to consider the interaction from their point of view, to become sensitive to both verbal and non-verbal components of our communication, to recognize the relational components of each interaction. If we are to earn the trust and respect that we desire and need, we must learn to treat others with an appropriate level of respect—in some cases, even, a level of respect greater than what we hope to receive in return.

Truly effective leaders are more able and knowledgeable, more sociable, more highly motivated, and better communicators than the rest of us. They are also held to an even higher ethical standard than those of us who place in their hands our trust, our commitment, and our welfare. Good leaders are good communicators, both interpersonally and rhetorically; good communicators are those who acknowledge and honour, in every interaction, the humanity and well-being of others.

■ Key Terms

ability
autocratic
credibility
democratic
hard rhetoric
leadership
mentoring
motivation

person-oriented leadership
sociability
soft rhetoric
task-oriented leadership

Suggested Readings

Boyd Clarke and Ron Crossland, *The Leader's Voice* (New York: Select Books, 2002). In the tradition of management research, Clarke and Crossland offer a leadership model based on surveys of the practices of several hundred business leaders rather than a scholarly analysis. Based on the three 'channels' of communication employed by business leaders, Clarke and Crossland propose their 'FES model' of Fact, Emotion, and Symbol, which they argue will enhance leadership effectiveness in any situation. Geared for a lay audience of business practitioners, the book is more a practical self-help guide than a comprehensive theory of leadership communication.

James M. Kouzes and Barry Z. Posner, *The Leadership Challenge* (New York: John Wiley, 2002). Kouzes and Posner's best-selling book, originally published in the 1980s, revised in the 1990s, and updated for this edition, has been influential in the field of management studies. Originally intended as a practical manual of advice for business leaders, their book identifies five steps or 'keys' to effective leadership, famously formulated as 'model the way, inspire a shared vision, challenge the process, enable others to act, encourage the heart.' Although their methods differ from scholarly approaches used in the field of communication, and especially in rhetoric, astute readers will see in them elements of Aristotle's modes of persuasion, with particular emphasis on pathos appeals. Deriving their leadership principles by studying the practices of those they considered accomplished leaders, Kouzes and Posner have produced a work that has achieved significant status in management circles as a readable, inspiring approach to improving leadership practices in professional settings. Written for a general public, the prose is easily accessible for a lay audience.

Peter Guy Northouse, *Leadership: Theory and Practice*, 3rd edn (Thousand Oaks, Calif.: Sage, 2004). Northouse's book combines practical advice with the theoretical understanding that distinguishes a scholarly treatment from some of the facile self-help approaches so prevalent among titles on the self-help shelves. Northouse not only provides an overview on current approaches to the study of leadership, but considers the limits of treating this human process from a purely social scientific perspective, and raises important questions about ethics in leadership. The book is solidly grounded in research, but written in an accessible, readable style.

Exercises and Assignments

1. Brainstorm with your class a list of traits or qualities that mark a really good teacher and those that mark a really bad teacher (you should probably not name any specific professors as part of this exercise). How many of the items on your list are also qualities of a good leader, as articulated in this chapter? What does teaching have in common with leadership?

2. Make a list of influential people, those from whom you seek advice or from whom you take direction (for example, teachers, your parents, your physician, your clergy, and so forth). Why do you seek advice from these people? What is the source of their authority? Are they all authoritative in the same way? What does authority contribute to leadership?

3. What is the relationship between leadership, conflict resolution, listening, and ethical communication? What do these have to do with interpersonal interaction? Draw on at least four course concepts to support your argument.

4. Did any of the Personal Icons created by the class display indications of ability, sociability, commitment, or communicative skill? If so, how? Is it possible to symbolize such qualities as confidence, trust, dependability, integrity, or work ethic? If not, why not? If so, how might such things be suggested? Would you expect that the Icon of a leader would differ from those of the rank and file? In what ways? How, exactly, do the qualities of leadership get communicated as we present and establish ourselves through our normal interactions?

5. Read the following scenario carefully. Drawing on everything you have learned about leadership and about interpersonal communication generally, identify the leadership issues inherent in the situation and suggest what Melissa might have done differently. Prepare to discuss your analysis with the class, or submit your findings in writing as directed by your instructor.

Melissa recently started a new job after earning a master's degree. She's now an instructor at Waskasoo College, where her primary assignment is teaching professional communication and report writing for the college's Correctional Worker Program.

This is Melissa's very first job ever; as a scholarship student, she never had to work even part-time during her years in school. Nevertheless, Melissa is enthusiastic and prepared to work hard. She is confident that her literature degrees have provided the expertise she needs to teach communication to her correctional students, and even prides herself on being able to 'broaden their horizons' with fascinating details of post-colonial theory and deconstruction instead of focusing only on the dull subject report-writing. After all, how much can you really say about that? Melissa is also proud of another of her exceptional efforts as a teacher: she has put her lectures on computerized slides, and has posted them on her website for the students.

Lately, though, Melissa's enthusiasm has been dampened, because these students just don't get it. Their attendance is extremely poor, they don't seem to care about the innovative theories she's presenting, and to top it off their reports are just lousy. You'd think they would welcome some intellectual stimulation for a change, and that they would put some effort into their work. But no, they don't. So Melissa has concluded that she is simply throwing pearls before swine: these students aren't very bright or very serious about their studies. She can't wait until the college assigns her to a different group, who will surely be more motivated than this crowd.

In any case, though, she has more to think about right now. Each term, the Correctional Studies Department organizes tours to nearby provincial and federal correctional institutions. The students are required to attend, of course, and usually some of the faculty go along. Melissa has been invited, but she can't frankly see the point—why would she want to spend a whole day parading through some boring prison? It's bound to be dirty and unpleasant, not to mention dangerous, and it's not as though she's ever going to have anything to do with such places. So no, she's not going to go along. Now all she has to do is figure out how to politely turn down the invitation.

If you were Melissa's mentor, what advice might you give her?

Chapter 11

Ethics in Interpersonal Communication

Learning Objectives

- To understand the relationship between communication and ethics.
- To appreciate the role of ethics in interpersonal communication.
- To develop a code of ethics for interpersonal communication.

The idea of a communicator's ethical responsibility has been implicit in every topic discussed in this book, so why devote an entire additional chapter to the subject? The answer is simple: though we have been taking our ethical responsibility to others for granted in our discussions, the topic is too important to be left without more direct and comprehensive attention. Because our communication has such power to affect the interests and well-being of others, their understanding of themselves and their relationships, their sense of self-worth and identity, we cannot fully consider our communicative choices in an interpersonal context without considering their ethical implications and effect. For this reason, our interpersonal communication brings us directly into the realm of ethical responsibility.

What Is Ethics?

Ethics refers to the principles or values that guide our actions. Just as the traits of leadership find a foundation in Aristotle's principle of ethos, so does our understanding of ethical behaviour. In fact, the very word 'ethics' is derived from the Greek word 'ethos', or 'public character'.[1] We have already seen that Aristotle made ethos a cornerstone of his theory of communication. As the earliest theorist of communication, he well understood the relationship among communication, trust, and the qualities of character that he called good will, good character, and good judgement.[2]

For many of us, the word 'ethics' still carries some of the flavour of its original meaning; for example, we still recognize ethical behaviour as a key component of good character.[3] As it's used now, the word has at least two distinct, though related, meanings, both of which retain a clear relationship to its Greek origins.

First, 'ethics' refers to a branch of academic study that concentrates on how people make decisions between right and wrong, on how we choose between two conflicting values, and on how deeply held principles actually guide our choices and our actions. Although usually thought of as a specialization within philosophy or theology, the study of ethics may also take place in professional contexts, such as law, medicine, engineering, or business. In these contexts, ethicists not only study values and their sources, but also conduct analyses of various cases to identify the pertinent issues that shape decision-making in specific situations.[4]

Not surprisingly, ethics has a long tradition of association with the study of communication, and especially with the practice of influence, whether it occurs in public or in interpersonal interactions. Aristotle, for example, insisted that the study of persuasion could best be understood as 'an offshoot of ethical studies'.[5] The Roman rhetorician Quintilian, writing some 400 years later, made the link between communication and ethics explicit when he emphasized that, to be considered an accomplished communicator, a person must also be ethically good.[6] Much later, the distinguished eighteenth-century philosopher and rhetorician George Campbell saw persuasive communication—rhetoric—as indistinguishable from 'moral reasoning'.[7] Recent and contemporary theorists continue to explicitly recognize the essential link between persuasive communication and ethics,[8] since, as B.J. Diggs explains, 'ethics is concerned with human action . . . [and] when one attempts to persuade, he presumes to tell another what he *should* believe or how he *ought* to act.'[9] Thus, the study of communication inevitably involves the study of ethical decision-making.

The word 'ethics' is also used in a second, more practical or applied sense. In addition to referring to the formal study of the way people reason and choose between right and wrong, 'ethics' also refers to the systems of values or codes of behaviour that we have evolved to help us make reasonable and effective choices as we live, work, and socialize with other people. To act ethically is to act responsibly and with good judgement, taking into account not only our own wants, but the needs and the autonomy of others. To act ethically is to respect and interact with other people as beings, not as objects to be manipulated for our own benefit, and our ethical systems have evolved to help us to make decisions in keeping with this fundamental principle of respect for others as human persons.

It is important to understand that ethical systems do not originate with individuals. Although each of us is free to evaluate and respond to situations using our own judgement and values, ethics is not simply a matter of doing what you feel like, nor is it a matter of expediency or convenience or self-gratification.[10] These are all motives that from time to time drive our behaviour, but they are not effective interpersonal practice, and they are certainly not the result of ethical decision-making, which is a thoughtful, deliberative process and not an automatic, accidental, or unintentional outcome.

Individuals do not invent their own ethical codes. Instead, **codes of ethics** typically find their justification in some authority beyond the individual: the authority of religious belief, the sanction of society, the collective experience of a profession, the traditions of a culture, the wisdom of a distinguished individual. Whether based on religious, cultural, familial, or professional codes of behaviour, all ethical systems have a strong collective component; they are based on interests broader than those of the individual, and are not simply a matter of personal whim.[11] Thus, our interactions with others at all levels have an ethical dimension that is given its particular flavour by religious beliefs and cultural norms, by social custom, by church doctrine, by family tradition, by law, by the code of a profession, even by standards of conduct within a given workplace.

A sense of right and wrong, of appropriateness, of ethical conduct, permeates human interaction. For instance, Erving Goffman's study of face behaviour is in many respects a study of unspoken ethical codes that seem to transcend all cultures.[12] The many studies of leadership that we have considered, and many more that we have not explicitly discussed, also offer a code of ethical practice.[13] Religions, too, have creeds that include ethical precepts—the Ten Commandments of the Judeo-Christian tradition are one such example; the ancient admonition of Confucius that has come to be known as the golden rule is another. Most professions have developed explicit codes of ethics to guide their members in carrying out their responsibilities;[14] many organizations, including universities, have developed codes of conduct for their members that implicitly assume an ethical standard.[15]

Some Universal Ethical Principles

Interestingly, although there are variations in the specific precepts of different ethical systems, there are some universal principles that they all seem to share. At the heart of all ethical codes is some form of the principle that we have been calling respect: regard and honour for others with whom we interact. The philosopher Martin Buber characterized this as an **'I–Thou'** orientation for its recognition of the other as a human self, in order to distinguish it from what he described as an 'I–It' orientation, in which others are regarded and treated essentially as objects.[16]

This principle permeates all ethical codes, and is implicit in the **golden rule**, which is most frequently stated as 'do unto others as you would have them do unto you.' The best-known and longest-standing code of professional ethics, the **Hippocratic oath** of physicians, implicitly embodies this same principle in its admonition to 'first, do no harm.'[17] In interpersonal communication, this fundamental principle translates into a recognition of, and respect for, what might be called the 'selfhood' of the other.

A code of ethics is not a cookie-cutter recipe; it does not typically itemize rules of behaviour or set out specific regulations such as the 'pool rules' posted in the hot tub room at the neighbourhood condo. Its purpose is not to directly govern behaviour, but to provide a foundation for thoughtfully evaluating and judging the situations in which we must act. A true code of ethics (as opposed to a code of conduct) is meant to assist, and not replace, human assessment and choice, and thus offers general principles rather than a template for how to behave. The ultimate responsibility for choosing how to act remains with the individual.

As the ethicist Andrew Olsen explains, the purpose of a code of ethics is not to tell us what to do, but to give us a foundation for deciding for ourselves what we must or should do. According to Olsen, 'a code of ethics increases ethical sensitivity and judgement, strengthens support for individuals' moral courage, and helps to hone an organization's sense of identity.'[18] Because the situations in which we have to make judgements are not always clear-cut, because they are not entirely predictable, and because each is unique, we must draw on our understanding to make choices that will best fulfill our obligations to our listeners, our messages, and ourselves. A code of ethics is intended to help us do that.

If you study the ethical codes of a number of professions and organizations, you will be initially struck by the range of variation in the specific details each addresses. Some are closer to a code of conduct than to a code of ethics, since they address specific actions that must be performed or avoided, while others provide general principles to guide decision-making. But, as Cristina Sewerin has observed, one of the key issues of professionalism is responsibility to the public, and she notes that 'a key role of licensure and of licensing bodies is to set across-the-board standards on which the public can rely.'[19]

Despite their outward variations, the majority of such codes share some striking similarities. Two features in particular stand out: first, professional ethics codes focus not on the benefits to individual practitioners, but on their obligations and responsibilities to those they serve, to society, to the profession or organization of which they are a part, or to some other higher good. The language of the codes frequently emphasizes service, focusing on such values as duty, responsibility, and obligation. Sewerin, for example, points to the Canadian Medical Association's emphasis on 'the ethic of service' as a 'key feature of medical professionalism', and observes that, for physicians, '[t]wo relationships are considered crucial: the relationship between a physician and a patient, and the social contract between physicians and society.' Like the CMA, the Canadian Council of Professional Engineers also take seriously 'the overriding duty to serve and protect the public interest',[20] and their Code of Ethics reflects that fact. First among the values articulated in the Code is the principle that engineers must 'hold paramount the safety, health and welfare of the public and the protection of the environment and promote health and safety within the workplace.' They are also admonished to 'conduct themselves with fairness, courtesy and good faith towards clients, colleagues and others, give credit where it is due, and accept, as well as give, honest and fair professional criticism.'[21]

But it's not just the medical and engineering professions who understand their profession as a matter of duty or service. Virtually every profession, from accountan-

Photo: Dennis MacDonald/World of Stock

cy to nursing, from veterinary medicine to university teaching, espouses a code of ethics that emphasizes responsibility to a public and to the profession itself. The following excerpt from the Statement of Professional Ethics of the American Association of University Teachers is a typical example:

> As teachers, professors encourage the free pursuit of learning in their students. They hold before them the best scholarly and ethical standards of their discipline. Professors demonstrate respect for students as individuals and adhere to their proper roles as intellectual guides and counselors. Professors make every reasonable effort to foster honest academic conduct and to ensure that their evaluations of students reflect each student's true merit. They respect the confidential nature of the relationship between professor and student. They avoid any exploitation, harassment, or discriminatory treatment of students. They acknowledge significant academic or scholarly assistance from them. They protect their academic freedom.[22]

Similarly, the Purchasing Management Association of Canada's Code of Ethics emphasizes several core values, including 'Honesty/Integrity', which is defined as 'Maintaining an unimpeachable standard of integrity in all their business relationships both inside and outside the organizations in which they are employed'; 'Professionalism', which is described as 'Fostering the highest standards of professional competence amongst those for whom they are responsible'; and 'Serving the Public Interest', elaborated as 'Not using their authority of office for personal benefit, rejecting and denouncing any business practice that is improper'.[23]

Finally, even librarians, whose profession would seem to involve limited interaction with the public, describe their profession in terms of ethical obligation: 'Those who enter the library profession assume an obligation to maintain ethical standards of behavior in relation to the governing authority under which they work, to the library constituency, to the library as an institution and to fellow workers on the staff, to other members of the library profession, and to society in general.'[24]

The ethical codes of professions or public organizations may also speak of such personal qualities as honour, respect, honesty, and integrity, all in the context of obligation and service. As an example, consider these four 'core values' that inform the character-building focus of the Boy Scouts: 'personal honesty, fairness in one's dealings, respect for others, and the maintenance of a healthy self'.[25] A similar set of values underlies the description of fair play offered by the Canadian Curling Association:

> Fair Play begins with the strict observance of the written rule; however, in most cases,
> * Fair Play involves something more than even unfailing observance of the written rule.

- The observance of the spirit of the rules, whether written or unwritten, is important.
- Fair play results from measuring up to one's own moral standards while engaged in competition.
- Fair play is consistent demonstration of respect for teammates and opponents, whether they are winning or losing.
- Fair play is consistent demonstration of respect for officials, an acceptance of their decisions and a steadfast spirit of collaboration with them.
- Sportsmanlike behavior should be demonstrated both on and off the ice. This includes modesty in victory and composure in defeat.[26]

While most codes of ethics are not so explicitly aimed at character-building, they all, at least implicitly, encode the notion of Aristotle's 'good character'. Thus, one feature of all ethical practice is a pervasive sense of responsibility or obligation to others, to the profession or field, or even to a higher power.

Second, in addition to their emphasis on service and social obligation, ethical codes always presume a fundamental regard for the sanctity of human life. They are marked, both explicitly and implicitly, by respect for the integrity and autonomy of other people, for their safety and well-being, for their individual liberty, for their essential value as human beings.

A Communication Code of Ethics

Communication, like other forms of human choice and action, can be ethical or unethical; it can be honest or dishonest; it can be helpful or harmful. But because it is essentially social, effective communication places regard for others at the centre of ethical practice. This acknowledgement of the other is important to all forms of communication, but as we have seen it is especially critical for effective interpersonal relations.

A COMMUNICATION CODE OF ETHICS

1. I will take responsibility for my words and my actions.
2. I will take care not to misrepresent myself or my message.
3. I will avoid unnecessary hurt to others by my words or my tone.

Ethical interpersonal communication involves genuine respect for the other person, a sincere commitment to what you are saying, and respect for your own integrity. Aristotle's treatment of ethos—the character of the speaker—can thus be understood as essentially an ethical system for communicators. The principles of good judgement, good will, and good character that he articulated constitute an ethical stance because, like any code of ethics, they are both a manifestation of the social nature of human interaction and a result of personal choice. The ethical principles of communication—credibility, sincerity, and integrity—are anchored in the participatory process of building connections with other people. Let's consider the three principles of our ethical code in greater detail, along with examples of how they might translate into specific behaviour.

1. *I will take responsibility for my words and my actions.* I will acknowledge and honour my obligation to stand behind my words. I will do my best to ensure the validity of my interpretations. I will not present interpretations and judgements as if they are simple reports. I will keep my word. I will try to recognize and defuse defensive reactions before conflict escalates. I will try not to contribute to the escalation of conflict through defensive reactions of my own. If I do not know the answer to a question, I will acknowledge it rather than try to bluff my way through. I will focus on accommodating others' need for understanding, information, and support before indulging my own need for self-expression. I will hold myself responsible for how well someone else understands my message. When I am wrong, I will admit it. I will not divulge things said to me in confidence. I will offer advice only when it is asked for. I will do my best to listen genuinely in the spirit of understanding. I will keep in mind that my assessments are provisional and can be altered by subsequent information.

2. *I will take care not to misrepresent myself or my message.* I will strive to communicate clearly, simply, and tactfully. I will not pretend to be something I am not. I will not assume a footing I do not legitimately merit. I will use language with care and precision. I will label inferences and judgements as such, and not present them as fact. I will not distort or misrepresent issues in order to win a point. I will present my thoughts in my own language, and will not present the ideas or thoughts of others as though they are my own. I will pay attention to what I may be communicating nonverbally. I will know the source of information that I use and be able to explain how and why it's credible. I will not claim expertise I do not possess. I will recommend to others only actions that I have myself taken or genuinely would take. I will not make promises I cannot keep.

3. *I will avoid unnecessary hurt to others by my words or tone.* I will treat others as I would like to be treated if I were in their place. I will assume good will on the part of others and act with good will in return. I will listen to others as carefully as I expect them to listen to me. I will respect others as autonomous human beings and treat them with courtesy. I will follow through on my promises to others. I will give face when necessary, and will avoid causing face loss to others. I will make reasonable requests. If I must criticize others, I will speak with tact and generosity of attitude.

Where an apology is due, I will apologize to others genuinely and sincerely. I will avoid repeating unfounded gossip. If a conflict arises, I will do my best to avoid escalating it. I will try not to say things in anger that I may later regret.

Ethics in Practice

Practices that violate the fundamental ethic of respect and that deny the humanity of others, even when they are entrenched cultural practices or sanctioned by government, law, or religious custom, are at their root unethical. Apartheid, 'ethnic cleansing', slavery, head taxes, expulsion of whole groups of people from their homes, stripping others of their ethnic identity—all have at one time or another been in force somewhere on the globe, and several of these unethical policies have been pursued in Canada. The fact that such policies were sanctioned by various political or cultural regimes does not make them ethical, nor does the fact that hundreds, even thousands, of people subscribe to whatever system of belief support such acts of dehumanization.[27] Thus, when we deny the humanity of others, we behave unethically.[28]

Even though we cannot always fully accommodate the needs of others, we nevertheless have a fundamental obligation to behave in ways that respect their humanity and their autonomy. As Erving Goffman explains, 'participation in any contact with others is a commitment'[29] to others and to the social structure to which we belong.

However, because people have freedom of choice in their dealings with others, they sometimes behave in ways that violate their ethical obligations to those around them. This mistreatment of others may arise unintentionally, as it does when someone, in haste to save face, inadvertently issues a face challenge to another person, or it may be the product of deliberate acts of disrespect, such as the desecrating of the local mosque in the wake of 9/11. It may be a minor infraction, as when the clerk in the registrar's office places policy above the human interest, or it may be a criminal action, as when someone is made the victim of a hate crime.

Whatever the circumstances, however, we need to be very clear that whenever we choose to disregard the welfare, dignity, and integrity of others, when we treat others simply as things that can be used for our own purposes and then brushed aside, when we serve ourselves at the expense of others, when we attempt to influence others without regard to their well-being, we are choosing to behave unethically, just as much as when we lie, cheat, steal, or betray others. As individuals, we should regard any policy or practice that treats human beings as things to be manipulated for profit or other benefit as unethical to its core.[30] Indeed, disregard for the safety or welfare of others is in certain circumstances a criminal act.[31]

S.I. Hayakawa wrote that as a result of our participation in human society we reap many rewards, including a sense of belonging and the social co-operation that ensures our very survival. But our membership in human society also entails, along with these significant benefits, an equally significant obligation to those with whom we share its benefits. We are bound by our humanity to honour and respect the human dignity and worth of others. To do less than this, no matter who might sanction it or what short-term benefits it might bestow, is to behave unethically.

Summary

As we have learned throughout this book, all of our interpersonal interaction has the power to affect the interests and well-being of others, their understanding of themselves and their relationships, their sense of self-worth and identity. For this reason, in studying interpersonal interaction we must consider the impact of our actions and words on those with whom we interact.

All ethical systems have a strong collective component, and are based on interests broader than those of the individual. They are not simply a matter of personal whim or convenience or self-gratification. As well, whether they are derived from religious, cultural, familial, or professional codes of behaviour, all ethical systems have, as a central principle, some form of what we have been calling respect: the regard and honour for others that the philosopher Martin Buber characterized as an 'I–Thou' orientation.

Because our communication can have such a powerful influence on others' choices and attitudes, we have a responsibility to proceed with consideration and care. To act ethically is to respect and interact with other people as beings, not as objects to be manipulated for our own benefit. To act ethically is to act responsibly and with good judgement, taking into account not only our own wants, but the needs and the autonomy of others.

To this end, we articulated a three-part Communication Code of Ethics: I will take responsibility for my words and my actions; I will take care not to misrepresent

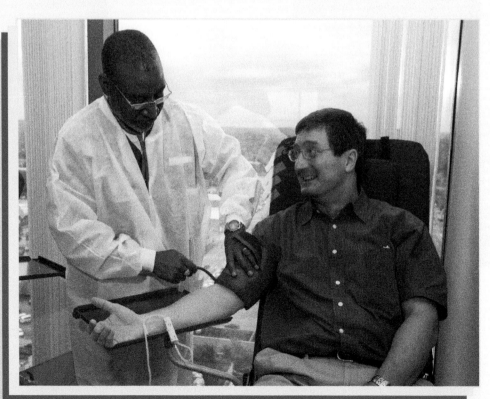

myself or my message; I will avoid unnecessary hurt to others by my words or my tone. While we may not always perfectly achieve the goals described by this Code of Ethics, we can make our own communication more ethical, and ourselves more worthy of others' trust, if we consciously strive to uphold these principles in all of our interactions, offering other people the same level of respect that we would like to receive in their place.

To become more effective, more ethical, and more proficient communicators generally, we need to learn to listen to others, to consider the interaction from their point of view, to become sensitive to both verbal and non-verbal components of our communication, and to recognize the relational components of each interaction. If we are to earn the trust and respect that we desire and need, we must learn to treat others with an appropriate level of respect—in some cases, even, a level of respect greater than what we hope to receive in return.

Good communicators, both interpersonally and rhetorically, are much in demand professionally and are valued as colleagues and friends. Good communicators are those who listen, those who respect others, those who can adapt their words and actions appropriately to the situation, but above all, good communicators are those who acknowledge and honour, in every interaction, the humanity and well-being of others.

Key Terms

codes of conduct
codes of ethics
ethics
golden rule
Hippocratic oath
'I–Thou'

Suggested Readings

Paul Babiak and Robert Hare, *Snakes in Suits* (Toronto: HarperCollins, 2006). A study of psychopathy in organizations, Babiak and Hare's book offers a completely different take on ethical behaviour. Hare is a world-renowned Canadian expert on the subject, whose work has produced the psychopathy checklist, a diagnostic tool for identifying predatory individuals who make their way in the world by taking advantage of others. As Hare and Babiak explain, such predators are not violent criminals, but all are exploitative and deceitful. Although Hare and Babiak emphasize that a diagnosis of psychopathy may only be made by a qualified professional, this book is intended to help the rest of us protect ourselves from exploitation at the hands of these superficially charming, but essentially self-serving, people. Written for a lay audience of non-specialists, it is a fascinating read.

William Kilpatrick, *Why Johnny Can't Tell Right from Wrong: Moral Illiteracy and the Case for Character Education* (New York: Simon & Schuster, 1992). Kilpatrick's book is a critique of the education system that has allowed ethical questions to be reduced to personal whim or preference. Along the way, it provides an interesting discussion of what it means to develop and possess 'good character', and considers the obligation of society, in particular its educational institutions, to instill respect for others and for the social order.

Martha Nussbaum, *Poetic Justice: The Literary Imagination and Public Life* (Boston: Beacon Press, 1995). Nussbaum, a lawyer, provides a spirited defence of literary and other narrative experience as essential to the development of an ethical sensibility. The essence of her argument is that literature, and especially the novel, expands our imaginative capabilities and our understanding beyond the limits of our own lived experience, providing us with a deeper and more thoughtful foundation upon which to make the judgements demanded of us in public life. It is worthwhile reading for anyone who values the role of storytelling in the formation of an ethical self.

Peter Singer, *Practical Ethics*, 2nd edn (Cambridge: Cambridge University Press, 1993). Singer's classic textbook, first published in 1979, is an accessible introduction to the study of applied ethics, and includes an extensive bibliography. The book has been controversial in some countries for its consideration of difficult and controversial social questions such as animal experimentation, abortion, and euthanasia. A superb and challenging read for anyone seriously interested in what it means to act ethically.

Margaret Sommerville, *The Ethical Imagination* (Toronto: Anansi, 2006). Sommerville's book consists of the lectures she gave in the CBC Massey Lecture series for 2006. Sommerville, a Canadian, has been a controversial figure for her stand on such questions as gay marriage (she's opposed to it on the grounds of its impact on families). More philosophical than strictly practical, the book thoughtfully explores some of the most pressing contemporary ethical issues, including personal responsibility, spirituality, and technology. The prose is clear and lucid, and easily accessible to an undergraduate audience.

Exercises and Assignments

1. Locate the Code of Student Conduct for your university or college and compare it with those from one or more other universities. Are there any significant dif-

ferences, or are the codes pretty much identical? What might this mean? Compare the collective standards for student behaviour with the Communication Code of Ethics provided in this chapter. What elements do the two have in common? Where do they differ? What do you think would account for these similarities or differences?

2. Gather the Codes of Conduct for several professions from the Center for the Study of Ethics in the Professions at <ethics.iit.edu/codes/>. Are these ethical codes or behavioural guidelines? On what did you base your answer?

3. Read the case study 'Facebook Face-off' (Appendix B). Based on the Communication Code of Ethics articulated in this chapter, evaluate the action of the four girls who created the website about their Writing 105 TA. Was their communication ethical? Why or why not?

4. From the perspective of interpersonal communication, one of the more disturbing trends associated with electronic communication is the apparent increase in willingness to inflict face assaults on others, simply because people do not have to take responsibility for the hurt they are causing. One indication of this state of affairs is the proliferation of websites that allow people to send anonymous messages to their co-workers. One such site is <www.secretmessage.com>, which, while recognizing that 'we may feel insulted to hear something negative about ourselves', nevertheless defends its practices as 'ultimately creating better relationships and a better world'.[32] Based on what you know about communication ethics, as well as about face, trust, self-concept, self-disclosure, advice-giving, and defensiveness, is such an action likely to create better relationships or will it cause a different result?

5. To understand the chilling effect that receiving such a message can have on relationships, you are asked to take part in an exercise that is high in face risk. Your instructor will provide you with the name and e-mail address of a classmate. Do not reveal whose name you have been given. In time for the person to read your message before the next class meeting, visit <www.secretmessages.com> and send a message to the person you have been assigned. In the next class, the group should discuss their reactions to receiving such a message from an anonymous sender.

6. Since the creation of a Personal Icon necessarily involves a degree of self-disclosure, it involves an element of trust, and thus imposes ethical imperatives on the audience. What ethical responsibilities did the class have as readers of each other's Icons? Why? How much risk was involved in the disclosures made by individuals in the class? What is the relationship between trust, disclosure, and ethics? Present your analysis in writing or as part of a class discussion, as directed by your instructor.

7. How ethical is the spam marketing e-mail depicted in 'Mark C is Caught in the Middle'? It appears to be a personal message, but it's not one. What is the purpose of this deceit? Why doesn't the author of the ad provide an honest pitch for the weight-loss product? Why is the ad presented as though it's from a colleague? How different is this advertisement from the anonymous messages discussed in the previous assignment? In framing your answer, draw as fully as you can on everything we've learned about interpersonal communication. Present your analysis in writing or as part of a class discussion, as directed by your instructor.

Appendix A

The Personal Icon Project

Learning Objectives

- To learn about the symbolic and ambiguous nature of self-presentation.
- To provide a common foundation for discussion of major course concepts, including self-disclosure, face, defensiveness, self-concept, relationships, ethics, and conflict.
- To lessen the risks associated with personal disclosure in a classroom setting, while providing a shared interaction that can form a touchstone for later disclosure and applications.

In keeping with their nature as symbol-users, and with their desire for identification, humans create and employ icons, insignia, heraldic symbols, or 'colours' to designate a whole host of group memberships. You may be familiar with some of these: coats of arms, totem poles, corporate logos, clan tartans or crests, national flags or symbols such as the Canadian maple leaf, tattoos, uniforms, military badges, and even national costumes serve to identify us as members of nations, ethnic communities, kinship groups, tribal councils, families, religious sects, professional organizations, military units, and so forth.

The impulse to symbolize our social and individual identity and affiliations can be seen everywhere we look. In the Middle Ages, a knight carried a shield on which he had created a symbolic decoration to represent himself. Contemporary pilots do the same thing during wartime. Graffiti artists develop a unique signature design, or personal logo, to identify their work. Modern athletes wear team colours; in the Olympics, they decorate their helmets or their bobsleds or their swimsuits with symbols that represent their country. Fashion-conscious teens acquire tattoos or wear name-label brands of clothing. Organizations like the Boy Scouts issue distinctive uniforms, insignia, and badges; motorcycle groups display their own identifying marks; even fast-food restaurants require their staff to wear recognizable uniforms. All of these are expressions of the human need to symbolize individual and social identity and to display marks of membership. Thus we come to know someone, in part, by the symbols he or she chooses to display as part of self-identification.

Within the first two weeks of the term, your instructor will ask everyone in the class to create just such a visual representation. You will be asked to make a 'Personal Icon'[1] that symbolizes *you* as you wish the class to see you—not simply as a member of an organization or kinship group, but as an individual. In constructing your Icon, you are free to choose how much or how little you wish to share with the group, and you may represent any aspects of your personality or social identity that you wish.

Although collage is one obvious approach to building such a self-representation, you are free to take another approach if you wish. You can use actual objects, scale models, photos, memorabilia, drawings, jewellery, cut-outs, or collections to construct or assemble your self-representation. The few restrictions on your creativity are outlined below.

As you prepare this Icon, you should concentrate on the overall message about yourself that you would like to communicate through your choice of symbols. Think of it as symbolizing your essence, as representing the qualities in you that you would like your classmates to attribute to you. Most likely, your instructor will also create and display a Personal Icon.

The Personal Icon assignment is an integral part of the interpersonal communication course, since it is designed to provide a shared experience for the class to draw from in applying and discussing many important course concepts, including public and private self, perception and communication, self-concept, negotiation of selves, conflict, face needs, interpersonal trust, intimacy, and self-disclosure. Since everyone will have taken part in the interaction and will have contributed to it in a meaningful way, the Personal Icon exercise also provides the foundation for group membership and identity as we return to the Icons to deepen our understanding of each subsequent course topic.

One of the basic tenets of interpersonal communication theory is recognition of the individual's freedom to choose how much personal information he or she wishes to disclose in a given encounter. However, at the same time, the teaching and study of interpersonal communication are very much up-close and personal experiences that require meaningful levels of self-disclosure from the participants in order to provide the necessary fodder for class discussion, analysis, and understanding. The Personal Icon exercise provides a means to accommodate both of these important concerns without resorting to forced disclosure[2]—a practice that threatens the trust and freedom of choice necessary to genuine interpersonal contact—or to confidentiality agreements of the sort that might be used for group therapy.[3] Because you can choose just how much you wish to reveal or withhold, the Icon exercise minimizes face risk at the same time that it allows the class to explore the course concepts in a meaningful way without violating their personal privacy.

Building the Personal Icon

Your Personal Icon will represent you in a symbolic way, as you would like to be seen or remembered by the class. You are free to choose nearly any medium that is portable enough to carry to class, that will not easily fall apart during transport, and that you are comfortable with displaying in public. To get the most benefit from the exercise, and from the course, you should participate as honestly and genuinely as possible. Since you will eventually be asked to explain the choices you made for your Icon, you should choose items or images that you will be comfortable discussing with the group, and you should present a self-image that you will be comfortable 'wearing' for the rest of the term.

The Icon may consist of collaged images or it may take some other form: it can be three-dimensional if you wish, and can be built out of actual objects that are significant to you (the Icon will be returned to you when the class is finished viewing it). Your Icon should be able to be viewed in a classroom setting without any special equipment: a DVD or CD is thus not an appropriate format for this project. You may decorate your Icon in any manner you please: photos, cut-outs from magazines or brochures, drawings, actual objects, scale models, scraps of memorabilia, jewellery, small personal articles, etc. Make sure that any such objects are securely attached and won't come loose when the Icon is moved.

While it doesn't matter what you use to create your Icon, please observe some rudiments of good judgement and situational appropriateness. Remember that this representation will become a permanent part of the impression that the class forms of you for the entire term. Choose your items with that standard in mind. Pornography or other obscene items are probably not appropriate.

While you may wish to incorporate some words into your Icon, you should not display your name anywhere on the piece. And, although your Icon will include visual and tactile elements, it should not include an easily identifiable picture of yourself. The group should be given the opportunity to read your Icon in as 'pure' a form as possible so that your classmates will be able to read and interpret the meaning of the symbolic representation on its own merits rather than making attributions based on what they may already know about you.

In creating the Icon, concentrate on symbolizing your essence, on representing the qualities in you that you would like your classmates to attribute to you. In brief, then, follow these guidelines:

- Create something that you can carry easily to class.
- Choose a format that is readable without special equipment.
- Make something you can display without discomfort.
- Observe standards of appropriateness.
- Do not put your name anywhere on the Icon.
- Try not to include photos of yourself or anything else that would immediately identify you.
- Don't reveal your Icon to anyone else in the class until the group has finished discussing them.

The exercise is more effective if the group does not know beforehand whose Icon is whose.

Submitting the Icon

On the day that the Icons are due, you should shroud your Icon in some sort of covering—a green garbage bag works well for most items. Bring your submission to your instructor's office before class begins so as to avoid any premature 'unveilings' that would compromise anonymity. Before revealing the Icons for class inspection, your instructor will ask you to reflect, from an interpersonal communication perspective, on the process involved in creating such a symbolic self-representation.

When the class has had a chance to consider the implications of symbolizing their self-presentation, the instructor will unveil the Icons, and the group will have the opportunity to observe and interpret them. Discussion will focus on interpretation and assessment, including the qualities of each Icon that are appealing, mystifying, beguiling, or repellent. As a group, the class will determine as best they can what each intends to communicate and what the self-representation says about its creator. Expect that there will be some misunderstanding and misattribution at this stage, but do not be tempted to give yourself away.

Once the discussion and interpretation process has been completed (this will take more than one class period), the owners will be asked to briefly explain their own Icons. Be prepared to have fun and to experience some revelations about your classmates and yourself.

Viewing and Recording Your Impressions

When the Icons are unveiled in class, your instructor will ask you to spend several minutes studying each Icon in turn. Make quick notes of your first impressions, as directed below, and complete a semantic differential assessment for each Icon. Add any additional observations you think would be helpful, particularly for any of the icons you find particularly compelling. For each Icon assigned to you, record the following:

- My initial reaction to the Icon was:
- I believe this to be the Icon of [ ]a male [ ]a female.
- One or two words that I feel capture the 'essence' of this Icon are:

The Personal Icon Exercise: Semantic Differential Rating

Assess each of the Icons by placing a mark where appropriate on the line between each of the following pairs of adjectives:

Warm ....Cool
Outgoing ....Reserved
Engaged...Resistant
Extroverted ....Introverted
Emotional ....Rational
Intense ....Low key
Informal ....Formal
Personal..Professional
Public ....Private
Explicit...Mysterious
Authentic ....Artificial

Interpretation and Attribution of Meaning

Your instructor will ask you to interpret one or more of the Icons and present your reading to the class. When it comes time for the group to interpret your own Icon, be careful not to give away your identity. Note any comments that you feel over misunderstandings of your Icon.

As you make your public assessment, keep in mind that, although you don't know who the creator of each Icon is, that person is still present in the room and will hear what is said about his or her self-presentation. While you are asked to be honest, you are also expected to be tactful and respectful of the face that someone else has presented. Remember, too, that your comments could have an impact on the atmosphere of the class for the remainder of the term. Your assessment should consider the following:

- What does the Icon mean? What impression do you believe the person wished to create?
- What attributions did you make about the Icon? What judgements did you make about the person who created it?
- Which of the Icons did you find most attractive/appealing? What qualities made it so? Did any of the Icons affect you negatively? What qualities caused you to react as you did?
- Did the group disagree over the interpretation of any of the Icons? Why might this have occurred? Were there any Icons in which the group was in complete agreement?

Confirmation and Challenge: Revealing Ownership of Your Icon

When the 'readings' and interpretations have been completed, your instructor will ask each member of the class to introduce and briefly explain his or her own Icon. When you are invited to do so, you should briefly explain its symbolism and comment on any misattributions you witnessed.

Conclusion

The presentation and negotiation of a 'self' in everyday life are often motivated by concerns that aren't immediately obvious to ourselves. We take for granted values and assumptions that we believe the rest of the world shares; we embed our deepest sym-

bolic motives in apparently pragmatic actions; we respond defensively to an innocuous act by someone else. We don't always see ourselves as the rest of the world sees us,
nor are our best intentions always evident to others. Misreadings can happen more easily than we have ever imagined, leading at times to conflict and hurt feelings.

The act of creating these Personal Icons and of 'reading'—or misreading—the
self-presentations of others provides a common experience that the class can use as a
source of examples and illustrations of many of the concepts that are central to a
course in interpersonal communication. The exercise demonstrates, in a relatively
safe way, how we can unintentionally miscue others about our sensitivities, our needs,
and our expectations. It shows how difficult it can sometimes be to interpret others'
manner or messages, and how easy it is to make faulty attributions.

The experience of having created a symbolic self, and of having that self-presentation studied, interpreted, and perhaps misunderstood, is also instructive. We learn
how snap judgements may be completely mistaken, how our good intentions may be
misguided, and how it feels to be utterly misunderstood. As the course unfolds and
you learn more about interpersonal dynamics, you will be asked to return to this
experience for additional analysis and insight.

Appendix B
Readings for Interpersonal Analysis

William Shakespeare

Sonnet 73

That time of year thou mayst in me behold
When yellow leaves, or none, or few, do hang
Upon those boughs which shake against the cold,
Bare ruin'd choirs, where late the sweet birds sang.
In me thou seest the twilight of such day
As after sunset fadeth in the west,
Which by and by black night doth take away,
Death's second self, that seals up all in rest.
In me thou see'st the glowing of such fire
That on the ashes of his youth doth lie,
As the death-bed whereon it must expire
Consumed with that which it was nourish'd by.
This thou perceivest, which makes thy love more strong,
To love that well which thou must leave ere long.

Paul Simon

The Dangling Conversation

(From Simon and Garfunkel, *Bookends*, Columbia Records, 1968.)

It's a still life water color
Of a now late afternoon,
As the sun shines through the curtain lace
And shadows wash the room.
And we sit and drink our coffee,
Cast in our indifference
Like shells upon the shore;
You can hear the ocean roar,
In the dangling conversation
And the superficial sighs,
The borders of our lives.

And you read your Emily Dickinson,
And I my Robert Frost,[1]
And we note our place with bookmarkers

That measure what we've lost.
Like a poem poorly written
We are verses out of rhythm,
Couplets out of rhyme,
In syncopated time.
And the dangling conversation
And the superficial sighs
Are the borders of our lives.

Yes, we speak of things that matter
With words that must be said:
Can analysis be worthwhile?
Is the theater really dead?
And now the room is softly faded;
I only kiss your shadow,
I cannot feel your hand.
You're a stranger now unto me,
Lost in the dangling conversation
And the superficial sighs
In the borders of our lives.

Edwin Arlington Robinson

Richard Cory

(From Edwin Arlington Robinson, *The Children of the Night* [1890–7], 35.)

Whenever Richard Cory went down town,
We people on the pavement looked at him:
He was a gentleman from sole to crown,
Clean-favoured and imperially slim.
And he was always quietly arrayed,
And he was always human when he talked;
But still he fluttered pulses when he said,
'Good Morning!' and he glittered when he walked.

And he was rich, yes, richer than a king,
And admirably schooled in every grace:
In fine—we thought that he was everything
To make us wish that we were in his place.

So on we worked and waited for the light,
And went without the meat and cursed the bread,
And Richard Cory, one calm summer night,
Went home and put a bullet in his head.

George Orwell

Shooting an Elephant (Autumn 1936)

(From George Orwell, *Shooting an Elephant and Other Essays* [New York: Harcourt Brace and World, 1950], at: <http://www.orwell.ru/library/articles/elephant/english/e_eleph>.)

In Moulmein, in lower Burma, I was hated by large numbers of people—the only time in my life that I have been important enough for this to happen to me. I was sub-divisional police officer of the town, and in an aimless, petty kind of way anti-European feeling was very bitter. No one had the guts to raise a riot, but if a European woman went through the bazaars alone somebody would probably spit betel juice over her dress. As a police officer I was an obvious target and was baited whenever it seemed safe to do so. When a nimble Burman tripped me up on the football field and the referee (another Burman) looked the other way, the crowd yelled with hideous laughter. This happened more than once. In the end the sneering yellow faces of young men that met me everywhere, the insults hooted after me when I was at a safe distance, got badly on my nerves. The young Buddhist priests were the worst of all. There were several thousands of them in the town and none of them seemed to have anything to do except stand on street corners and jeer at Europeans.

All this was perplexing and upsetting. For at that time I had already made up my mind that imperialism was an evil thing and the sooner I chucked up my job and got out of it the better. Theoretically—and secretly, of course—I was all for the Burmese and all against their oppressors, the British. As for the job I was doing, I hated it more bitterly than I can perhaps make clear. In a job like that you see the dirty work of Empire at close quarters. The wretched prisoners huddling in the stinking cages of the lock-ups, the grey, cowed faces of the long-term convicts, the scarred buttocks of the men who had been flogged with bamboos—all these oppressed me with an intolerable sense of guilt. But I could get nothing into perspective. I was young and ill-educated and I had had to think out my problems in the utter silence that is imposed on every Englishman in the East. I did not even know that the British Empire is dying, still less did I know that it is a great deal better than the younger empires that are going to supplant it. All I knew was that I was stuck between my hatred of the empire I served and my rage against the evil-spirited little beasts who tried to make my job impossible. With one part of my mind I thought of the British Raj as an unbreakable tyranny, as something clamped down, in *saecula saeculorum*, upon the will of prostrate peoples; with another part I thought that the greatest joy in the world would be to drive a bayonet into a Buddhist priest's guts. Feelings like these are the normal by-products of imperialism; ask any Anglo-Indian official, if you can catch him off duty.

One day something happened which in a roundabout way was enlightening. It was a tiny incident in itself, but it gave me a better glimpse than I had had before of the real nature of imperialism—the real motives for which despotic governments act. Early one morning the sub-inspector at a police station the other end of the town rang me up on the phone and said that an elephant was ravaging the bazaar. Would I please come and do something about it? I did not know what I could do, but I wanted to see what was happening and I got on to a pony and started out. I took my rifle, an old 44 Winchester and much too small to kill an elephant, but I thought the noise might be useful *in terrorem*. Various Burmans stopped me on the way and told me about the elephant's doings. It was not, of course, a wild elephant, but a tame one which had gone 'must'. It had been chained up, as tame elephants always are when their attack of 'must' is due, but on the previous night it had broken its chain and escaped. Its mahout, the only person who could manage it when it was in that state, had set out in pursuit, but had taken the wrong direction and was now twelve hours' journey away, and in the morning the elephant had suddenly reappeared in the town. The Burmese population had no weapons and were quite helpless against it. It had already destroyed somebody's bamboo hut, killed a cow and raided some fruit-stalls and devoured the stock; also it had met the municipal rubbish van and, when the driver jumped out and took to his heels, had turned the van over and inflicted violences upon it.

The Burmese sub-inspector and some Indian constables were waiting for me in the quarter where the elephant had been seen. It was a very poor quarter, a labyrinth of squalid bamboo huts, thatched with palmleaf, winding all over a steep hillside. I remember that it was a cloudy, stuffy morning at the beginning of the rains. We began questioning the people as to where the elephant had gone and, as usual, failed to get any definite information. That is invariably the case in the East; a story always sounds clear enough at a distance, but the nearer you get to the scene of events the vaguer it becomes. Some of the people said that the elephant had gone in one direction, some said that he had gone in another, some professed not even to have heard of any elephant. I had almost made up my mind that the whole story was a pack of lies, when we heard yells a little distance away. There was a loud, scandalized cry of 'Go away, child! Go away this instant!' and an old woman with a switch in her hand came round the corner of a hut, violently shooing away a crowd of naked children. Some more women followed, clicking their tongues and exclaiming; evidently there was something that the children ought not to have seen. I rounded the hut and saw a man's dead body sprawling in the mud. He was an Indian, a black Dravidian coolie, almost naked, and he could not have been dead many minutes. The people said that the elephant had come suddenly upon him round the corner of the hut, caught him with its trunk, put its foot on his back and ground him into the earth. This was the rainy season and the ground was soft, and his face had scored a trench a foot deep and a couple of yards long. He was lying on his belly with arms crucified and head sharply twisted to one side. His face was coated with mud, the eyes wide open, the teeth bared and grinning with an expression of unendurable agony. (Never tell me, by the way, that the dead look peaceful. Most of the corpses I have seen looked devilish.) The friction of the great beast's foot had stripped the skin from his back as neatly as one skins a rabbit. As soon as I saw the dead man I sent an orderly to a friend's house nearby to borrow an elephant rifle. I had already sent back the pony, not wanting it to go mad with fright and throw me if it smelt the elephant.

The orderly came back in a few minutes with a rifle and five cartridges, and meanwhile some Burmans had arrived and told us that the elephant was in the paddy fields below, only a few hundred yards away. As I started forward practically the whole population of the quarter flocked out of the houses and followed me. They had seen the rifle and were all shouting excitedly that I was going to shoot the elephant. They had not shown much interest in the elephant when he was merely ravaging their homes, but it was different now that he was going to be shot. It was a bit of fun to them, as it would be to an English crowd; besides they wanted the meat. It made me vaguely uneasy. I had no intention of shooting the elephant—I had merely sent for the rifle to defend myself if necessary—and it is always unnerving to have a crowd following you. I marched down the hill, looking and feeling a fool, with the rifle over my shoulder and an ever-growing army of people jostling at my heels. At the bottom, when you got away from the huts, there was a metalled road and beyond that a miry waste of paddy fields a thousand yards across, not yet ploughed but soggy from the first rains and dotted with coarse grass. The elephant was standing eight yards from the road, his left side towards us. He took not the slightest notice of the crowd's approach. He was tearing up bunches of grass, beating them against his knees to clean them and stuffing them into his mouth.

I had halted on the road. As soon as I saw the elephant I knew with perfect certainty that I ought not to shoot him. It is a serious matter to shoot a working elephant—it is comparable to destroying a huge and costly piece of machinery—and obviously one ought not to do it if it can possibly be avoided. And at that distance, peacefully eating, the elephant looked no more dangerous than a cow. I thought then and I think now that his attack of 'must' was already passing off; in which case he would merely wander harmlessly about until the mahout came back and caught him. Moreover, I did not in the least want to shoot him. I decided that I would watch him for a little while to make sure that he did not turn savage again, and then go home.

But at that moment I glanced round at the crowd that had followed me. It was an immense crowd, two thousand at the least and growing every minute. It blocked the road for a long distance on either side. I looked at the sea of yellow faces above the garish clothes—faces all happy and excited over this bit of fun, all certain that the elephant was going to be shot. They were watching me as they would watch a conjurer about to perform a trick. They did not like me, but with the magical rifle in my hands I was momentarily worth watching. And suddenly I realized that I should have to shoot the elephant after all. The people expected it of me and I had got to do it; I could feel their two thousand wills pressing me forward, irresistibly. And it was at this moment, as I stood there with the rifle in my hands, that I first grasped the hollowness, the futility of the white man's dominion in the East. Here was I, the white man with his gun, standing in front of the unarmed native crowd—seemingly the leading actor of the piece; but in reality I was only an absurd puppet pushed to and fro by the will of those yellow faces behind. I perceived in this moment that when the white man turns tyrant it is his own freedom that he destroys. He becomes a sort of hollow, posing dummy, the conventionalized figure of a sahib. For it is the condition of his rule that he shall spend his life in trying to impress the 'natives', and so in every crisis he has got to do what the 'natives' expect of him. He wears a mask, and his face grows to fit it. I had got to shoot the elephant. I had committed myself to doing it when I sent for the rifle. A sahib has got to act like a sahib; he has got to appear resolute, to know his own mind and do definite things. To come all that way, rifle in hand, with two thousand people marching at my heels, and then to trail feebly away, having done nothing—no, that was impossible. The crowd would laugh at me. And my whole life, every white man's life in the East, was one long struggle not to be laughed at.

But I did not want to shoot the elephant. I watched him beating his bunch of grass against his knees, with that preoccupied grandmotherly air that elephants have. It seemed to me that it would be murder to shoot him. At that age I was not squeamish about killing animals, but I had never shot an elephant and never wanted to. (Somehow it always seems worse to kill a *large* animal.) Besides, there was the beast's owner to be considered. Alive, the elephant was worth at least a hundred pounds; dead, he would only be worth the value of his tusks, five pounds, possibly. But I had got to act quickly. I turned to some experienced-looking Burmans who had been there when we arrived, and asked them how the elephant had been behaving. They all said the same thing: he took no notice of you if you left him alone, but he might charge if you went too close to him.

It was perfectly clear to me what I ought to do. I ought to walk up to within, say, twenty-five yards of the elephant and test his behavior. If he charged, I could shoot; if he took no notice of me, it would be safe to leave him until the mahout came back. But also I knew that I was going to do no such thing. I was a poor shot with a rifle and the ground was soft mud into which one would sink at every step. If the elephant charged and I missed him, I should have about as much chance as a toad under a steam-roller. But even then I was not thinking particularly of my own skin, only of the watchful yellow faces behind. For at that moment, with the crowd watching me, I was not afraid in the ordinary sense, as I would have been if I had been alone. A white man mustn't be frightened in front of 'natives'; and so, in general, he isn't frightened. The sole thought in my mind was that if anything went wrong those two thousand Burmans would see me pursued, caught, trampled on and reduced to a grinning corpse like that Indian up the hill. And if that happened it was quite probable that some of them would laugh. That would never do.

There was only one alternative. I shoved the cartridges into the magazine and lay down on the road to get a better aim. The crowd grew very still, and a deep, low, happy sigh, as of people who see the theatre curtain go up at last, breathed from innumerable throats. They were going to have their bit of fun after all. The rifle was a beautiful German thing with cross-hair sights. I did not then know that in shooting an elephant one would shoot to cut an imaginary bar running from ear-hole to ear-hole. I ought, therefore, as the elephant was sideways on, to have aimed straight at his ear-hole, actually I aimed several inches in front of this, thinking the brain would be further forward.

When I pulled the trigger I did not hear the bang or feel the kick—one never does when a shot goes home—but I heard the devilish roar of glee that went up from the crowd. In that instant, in too short a time, one would have thought, even for the bullet to get there, a mysterious, terrible change had come over the elephant. He neither stirred nor fell, but every line of his body had altered. He looked suddenly stricken, shrunken, immensely old, as though the frightful impact of the bullet had paralysed him without knocking him down. At last, after what seemed a long time—it might have been five seconds, I dare say—he sagged flabbily to his knees. His mouth slobbered. An enormous senility seemed to have settled upon him. One could have imagined him thousands of years old. I fired again into the same spot. At the second shot he did not collapse but climbed with desperate slowness to his feet and stood weakly upright, with legs sagging and head drooping. I fired a third time. That was the shot that did for him. You could see the agony of it jolt his whole body and knock the last remnant of strength from his legs. But in falling he seemed for a moment to rise, for as his hind legs collapsed beneath him he seemed to tower upward like a huge rock toppling, his trunk reaching skyward like a tree. He trumpeted, for the first and only time. And then down he came, his belly towards me, with a crash that seemed to shake the ground even where I lay.

I got up. The Burmans were already racing past me across the mud. It was obvious that the elephant would never rise again, but he was not dead. He was breathing very rhythmically with long rattling gasps, his great mound of a side painfully rising and falling. His mouth was wide open—I could see far down into caverns of pale pink throat. I waited a long time for him to die, but his breathing did not weaken. Finally I fired my two remaining shots into the spot where I thought his heart must be. The thick blood welled out of him like red velvet, but still he did not die. His body did not even jerk when the shots hit him, the tortured breathing continued without a pause. He was dying, very slowly and in great agony, but in some world remote from me where not even a bullet could damage him further. I felt that I had got to put an end to that dreadful noise. It seemed dreadful to see the great beast Lying there, powerless to move and yet powerless to die, and not even to be able to finish him. I sent back for my small rifle and poured shot after shot into his heart and down his throat. They seemed to make no impression. The tortured gasps continued as steadily as the ticking of a clock.

In the end I could not stand it any longer and went away. I heard later that it took him half an hour to die. Burmans were bringing dash and baskets even before I left, and I was told they had stripped his body almost to the bones by the afternoon.

Afterwards, of course, there were endless discussions about the shooting of the elephant. The owner was furious, but he was only an Indian and could do nothing. Besides, legally I had done the right thing, for a mad elephant has to be killed, like a mad dog, if its owner fails to control it. Among the Europeans opinion was divided. The older men said I was right, the younger men said it was a damn shame to shoot an elephant for killing a coolie, because an elephant was worth more than any damn Coringhee coolie. And afterwards I was very glad that the coolie had been killed; it put me legally in the right and it gave me a sufficient pretext for shooting the elephant. I often wondered whether any of the others grasped that I had done it solely to avoid looking a fool.

Margaret Laurence

From A Jest of God

(From Margaret Laurence, *A Jest of God* [Toronto: McClelland & Stewart, 1966], 66–8.)

Rachel Cameron, a 34-year-old unmarried elementary schoolteacher, lives with her aging, somewhat hypochondriac mother in the small Manitoba town where Rachel grew up. Rachel rarely dates, but on this occasion has been invited out to a movie by an old acquaintance who is back in town to visit with his parents. This scene dramatizes an exchange between Rachel and her mother while Rachel waits for her date to arrive.

'Where are you going, Rachel? Are you going somewhere?'
'Yes.' I should have told her before, I know. 'I'm going to a movie.'
'Oh. What's on? Maybe I'll come along.'
'I mean I'm going—with someone.'

'Oh. I see. Well, you might have said, Rachel. You really might have told me, dear.'

'I'm sorry, Mother. I just—'

'You know how glad I am, dear, when you go out. You might have mentioned it to me, that's all. It's not too much to ask, surely. After all, I do like to know where you are. I would have thought you could have said, Rachel.'

'I'm sorry.'

'Well, it's quite all right, dear. I'm only saying if you had let me know, it would've been better, that's all. I could have invited one of the girls in, maybe. Well, never mind. I shall be quite fine here by myself. I'll just slip into my housecoat and make some coffee, and have a nice quiet evening. I'll be just dandy. Don't you worry about me a speck. I'll be perfectly all right. If you'd just reach down my pills for me from the medicine cabinet. As long as they're where I can get them handily, in case anything happens. I'm sure I'll be fine. You go ahead and enjoy yourself, Rachel.'

I can never handle this kind of thing properly. What's behind it can never be brought out. She'd only deny, and be stricken and wounded. Maybe she really doesn't know what she's saying. She half convinces me, all the same, because it is true that something might happen when I'm away, and then what? All my fault. It worries me, anyway, even apart from whose fault.

'Maybe I shouldn't go.' Do I mean this?

'No, no. You go ahead, dear. It isn't so often that you—and I'll be perfectly fine. After all, you're young. I must expect to be a bit lonely sometimes.'

'I'm sorry.' We could pace this treadmill indefinitely.

'You never said who it was, dear. It doesn't matter in the least, but it does hurt me just a little when you don't even—'

'Nick Kazlik.'

'Who? I don't believe I—'

'I told you the other day that I met him on the street. Nick Kazlik.'

Mother, flitting around the living room, having suddenly decided that the pictures all need straightening, pauses with one small white mauve-veined hand on the autumn-coloured print of The Strawberry Girl.

'You mean the milkman's son?'

The milkman's son. The undertaker's daughter. But she wouldn't laugh. I must be very calm and careful. Anything else is useless.

'The same.'

An infant sigh bubbles from her lips.

'Well, of course—I mean, it's your business, dear. You go ahead and have a nice time.'

If only once she'd say what she means, and we could have it out. But she won't. Maybe it would be worse if she did. I don't know.

Doorbell. Quick—I must get her pills for her, first. They are on the top shelf of the medicine cabinet, so high that no one will take them by mistake. She can't reach that high.

'Here—they're on top of the TV. Is there anything else you need?'

'No, no.' She has moved on to the straightening of a simpering puce-mouthed Madonna. 'I told you, dear—I'll be quite all right. I may get started on the laundry.'

'Mother—you're not to! You know you mustn't lift things, or strain too much. I'll do it tomorrow morning.'

Doorbell again.

'Well, Rachel, dear, I only thought I might as well get going on it, as I haven't much to do.'

'*Please.*'

She glances at me with the innocent guile I've seen so often on the faces of my children [her pupils.]

'I'll see how I feel, dear. I only thought I might as well be doing something useful.'

'Promise me not to. Please.'

'We'll see. There are those blankets we've been meaning to wash all spring—'
'Mother!'

Why does she do this now? Why not half an hour ago, when I would have had the time to cajole. That's why she didn't then, of course.

'All right. All right. Wash them if you like. I can't stop you, can I?'

Going down the stairs, rapidly, my heels clattering, I can see again the astonished disbelief on her face. I can't believe, myself, that I could have said what I did. What an awful thing to say. I don't care. I don't give a damn. I'll care later. Not right now.

Clyde Miller and the Institute for Propaganda Analysis
How to Detect Propaganda

(From Records, Manuscripts, and Archives Division. The New York Public Library. Astor, Lenox, and Tilden Foundations.)

In 1937, the Institute for Propaganda Analysis was created to educate the public about the widespread nature of political propaganda. Composed of social scientists and journalists, the IPA published a series of books, including The Fine Art of Propaganda, *from which this selection has been taken. The IPA is best known for identifying the seven basic propaganda devices described below, which have been repeated so frequently that they are now understood to be synonymous with the study and analysis of propaganda. Although the IPA approach has been criticized as too limited, there is no disagreement about its goals of educating citizens in the methods and uses of propaganda techniques as a means of* *defending against the unscrupulous use of language to deceive and manipulate. Once you have learned to spot these seven techniques, you will be amazed at the frequency with which they are used all around you. More on these and other propaganda devices can be found at: <carmen.artsci.washington.edu/propaganda/contents.htm>.*

As generally understood, propaganda is the expression of opinion or action by individuals or groups deliberately designed to influence opinions or actions of other individuals or groups with reference to predetermined ends. Thus propaganda differs from scientific analysis. The propagandist is trying to 'put something across', good or bad, whereas the scientist is trying to discover truth and fact. Often the propagandist does not want careful scrutiny and criticism; he wants to bring about a specific action. Because the action may be socially beneficial or socially harmful to millions of people, it is necessary to focus upon the propagandist and his activities the searchlight of scientific scrutiny. Socially desirable propaganda will not suffer from such examination, but the opposite type will be detected and revealed for what it is.

We are fooled by propaganda chiefly because we don't recognize it when we see it. It may be fun to be fooled but, as the cigarette ads used to say, it is more fun to know. We can more easily recognize propaganda when we see it if we are familiar with the seven common propaganda devices. These are:

1. The Name Calling Device.
2. The Glittering Generalities Device.
3. The Transfer Device.
4. The Testimonial Device.
5. The Plain Folks Device.
6. The Card Stacking Device.
7. The Bandwagon Device.

Why are we fooled by these devices? Because they appeal to our emotions rather than to our reason. They make us believe and do something we would not believe or do if we thought about it calmly, dispassionately. In examining these devices we note that they work most effectively at those times when we are too lazy to think for ourselves; also, they tie into emotions which sway us to be 'for' or 'against' nations, races, religions, ideals, economic and political policies and practices, and so on through automobiles, cigarettes, radios, toothpastes, presidents, and wars. With our emotions stirred, it may be fun to be fooled by these propaganda devices, but it is more fun and infinitely more to our own interests to know how they work.

Lincoln must have had in mind citizens who could balance their emotions with intelligence when he made his remark: ' . . . but you can't fool all of the people all of the time.'

Name Calling

'Name calling' is a device to make us form a judgement without examining the evidence on which it should be based. Here the propagandist appeals to our hate and fear. He does this by giving 'bad names' to those individuals, groups, nations, races, policies, practices, beliefs, and ideals which he would have us condemn and reject. For centuries the name 'heretic' was bad. Thousands were oppressed, tortured, or put to death as heretics. Anybody who dissented from popular or group belief or practice was in danger of being called a heretic. In the light of today's knowledge, some heresies were bad and some were good. Many of the pioneers of modern science were called heretics; witness the cases of Copernicus, Galileo, Buno. Today's bad names include: Fascist, demagogue, dictator, Red, financial oligarchy, Communist, muckraker, alien, outside agitator, economic royalist, Utopian, rabble-rouser, troublemaker, Tory, Constitution wrecker.

Bad names have played a tremendously powerful role in the history of the world and in our own individual development. They have ruined reputations, stirred men and women to outstanding accomplishments, sent others to prison cells, and made men mad enough to enter battle and slaughter their fellowmen. They have been and are applied to other people, groups, gangs, tribes, colleges, political parties, neighborhoods, states, sections of the country, nations, and races. Use of 'bad names' without presentation of their essential meaning, without all their pertinent implications, comprises perhaps the most common of all propaganda devices. Those who want to maintain the status quo apply bad names to those who would change it. For example, the Hearst press applies bad names to Communists and Socialists. Those who want to change the status quo apply bad names to those would maintain it. For example, the *Daily Worker* and the *American Guardian* apply bad names to conservative Republicans and Democrats.

Glittering Generalities

'Glittering Generalities' is a device by which the propagandist identifies his program with virtue by the use of 'virtue words'. Here he appeals to our emotions of love, generosity, and brotherhood. He uses words like truth, freedom, honor, liberty, social justice, public service, the right to work, loyalty, progress, democracy, the American way, Constitution defender. These words suggest shining ideals. All persons of good will believe in these ideals. Hence the propagandist, by identifying his individual group, nation, race, practice, or belief with such ideals, seeks to win us over to his cause. As Name Calling is a device to make us form a judgment to reject or condemn, without examining the evidence, Glittering Generalities is a device to make us accept and approve, without examining the evidence.

For example, use of the phrases 'the right to work' and 'social justice' may be a device to make us accept programs for meeting the labour-capital problem which, if we examined them critically, we would not accept at all.

In the Name Calling and Glittering Generalities devices, words are used to stir up our emotions and befog our thinking. In one device 'bad words' are used to make us mad; in the other 'good words' are used to make us glad. The propagandist is most effective using these devices when the words create devils for us to fight or gods to adore. By his use of the 'bad words', we personify as a 'devil' some nation, race, group, individual, policy, practice, or ideal; we are made fighting mad to destroy it. By the use of 'good words', we personify as a godlike idol some nation, race, group, etc. Words which are 'bad' to some are 'good' to others, or may be made so. Thus, to some the New Deal is 'a prophecy of social salvation' while to others it is 'an omen of social disaster'.

From consideration of names, 'bad' and 'good', we pass to institutions and symbols, also 'bad' and 'good'. We see these in the next device.

Transfer

'Transfer' is a device by which the propagandist carries over authority, sanction and approval of something we respect and revere to something he would have us accept. For example, most of us respect and revere our church and our nation. If the propagandist succeeds in getting church or nation to approve a campaign in behalf of some program, he thereby transfers its authority, sanction, and prestige to that program. Thus we may accept something which we otherwise might reject. The cross represents the Christian church. The flag represents the nation. Cartoons like Uncle Sam represent a consensus of public opinion. These symbols stir emotions. At their very sight, with the speed of light, is aroused the whole complex of feelings with respect to church or nation. A cartoonist by having Uncle Sam disapprove a budget for unemployment relief would have us feel that the whole United States disapproves relief costs. By drawing an Uncle Sam who approves the same budget, the cartoonist would have us feel that the American people approve it. Thus, the Transfer device is used for and against causes and ideas.

Testimonial

The 'Testimonial' is a device to make us accept anything from a patent medicine or a cigarette to a program of national policy. In this device the propagandist makes use of testimonials. 'When I feel tired, I smoke a Camel and get the grandest lift.' 'We believe the John L. Lewis plan of labor organization is splendid; C.I.O. should be supported.' This device works in reverse also; counter-testimonials may be employed. Seldom are these used against commercial products like patent medicines and cigarettes, but they are constantly employed in social, economic, and political issues. 'We believe the John L. Lewis plan of labor organization is bad; C.I.O. should not be supported.'

Plain Folks

'Plain Folks' is a device used by politicians, business leaders, and even by ministers and educators to win our confidence by appearing to be people like ourselves—'just plain folks among the neighbours'. In election years especially do candidates show their devotion to little children and the common, homey things of life. They have front porch campaigns. For the newspaper men they raid the kitchen cupboard finding there some of the good wife's apple pie. They go to country picnics; they attend service at the old frame church; they pitch hay and go fishing; they show their belief in home and mother. In short, they would win our votes by showing that they're just as common as the rest of us, and therefore, wise and good. Business men often are 'plain folks' with the factory hands. Even distillers use the device. 'It's our family's whiskey, neighbour; and neighbour, it's your price.'

Card Stacking

'Card Stacking' is a device in which the user employs all the arts of deception to win our support for himself, his group, nation, policy, practice, belief, or ideal. He stacks the cards against the truth. He uses under-emphasis and over-emphasis to dodge issues and evade facts. He resorts to lies, censorship, and distortion. He omits facts. He offers false testimony. He creates a smoke screen of clamour by raising a new issue when he wants an embarrassing matter forgotten. He draws a red herring across the trail to confuse and divert those in quest of facts he does not want revealed. He makes the unreal appear real and real appear unreal. He lets a half-truth masquerade as truth. By the Card Stacking device, a mediocre candidate, through the 'build-up', is made to appear an intellectual titan; an ordinary prize fighter a probable world champion; a worthless patent medicine a beneficent cure. By means of this device propagandists would convince us that a ruthless war of aggression is a crusade for righteousness. Card Stacking employs sham, hypocrisy, and effrontery.

The Band Wagon

The 'Band Wagon' is a device to make us follow the crowd, to accept the propagandist's program en masse. Here his theme is: 'Everybody's doing it!' His techniques range from those of the medicine show to dramatic spectacle. He hires a hall, fills a great stadium, marches a million men in parade. He employs symbols, colours, music, movement, all the dramatic arts. He appeals to the desire common to most of us, to 'follow the crowd'. Because he wants us to 'follow the crowd' in masses, he directs his appeal to groups held together by common ties of nationality, religion, race, environment, sex, or vocation. Thus propagandists campaigning for or against a program will appeal to us as Catholics, Protestants, or Jews; as members of an ethnic minority; as farmers or school teachers; as housewives or as miners. All the artifices of flattery are used to harness the fears and hatreds, prejudices and biases, convictions and ideals common to the group; thus emotion is made to push or pull the Band Wagon. In newspaper articles and in the spoken word the device is also found. 'Don't throw your vote away. Vote for our candidate. He's sure to win.' Nearly everybody wins in every election—before the votes are in.

Propaganda and Emotion

Observe that in all these devices our emotion is the stuff with which propagandists work. Without it they are helpless; with it, harnessing it to their purposes, they can make us glow with pride or burn with hatred; they can make us zealous in behalf of the program they espouse. As we said at the beginning, propaganda as generally understood is expression of opinion or action by individuals or groups with reference to predetermined ends. Without the appeal to our emotions—to our fears and to our courage, to our selfishness and unselfishness, to our loves and to our hates—propagandists would influence few opinions and few actions.

To say this is not to condemn emotion, an essential part of life, or to assert that all predetermined ends of propagandists are 'bad'. What we mean is that the intelligent citizen does not want propagandists to utilize his emotions, even to the attainment of 'good' ends, without knowing what is going on. He does not want to be 'used' in the attainment of ends he may later consider 'bad'. He does not want to be gullible. He does not want to be fooled. He does not want to be duped, even in a good cause. He wants to know the facts and among these is included the fact of the utilization of his emotions.

Keeping in mind these seven common devices, turn to today's news and almost immediately you can spot examples of them all. At election time or during any campaign, Plain Folks and Band Wagon are common. Card Stacking is hardest to detect because it is adroitly executed or because we lack the information necessary to nail the lie. A little practice with the daily newspapers in detecting propaganda devices soon enables us to detect them elsewhere—in radio, news-reel, books, magazines, and in expressions of unions, business groups, churches, schools, political parties.

James T. Cook

Letter to Roger Ebert

(From Roger Ebert, *Questions for the Movie Answer Man* [Kansas City: Andrews McMeel Publishing, 1997], 111.)

Q. I am experiencing a crisis with a friend who insists on lowering some of my favorite films to the common denominator of 'hair movies'. I really liked 'Last of the Mohicans', as there have never been enough decent Revolutionary era films. My friend says the film was a failure because nobody had access to creme rinse in those days, as 'Hawkeye' must have, since his hair was too perfect. Now when I think of this film, I can only see Daniel Day-Lewis in curlers on the way to the set. It happened again with 'Legends of the Fall', where Brad Pitt's hair (according to my friend) had an unnatural luster that could not have been achieved without creme rinse.

Now it has gone too far. I am a history buff, Mel Gibson fan and Scotsman by descent. I am eagerly awaiting 'Braveheart', but my friend mischievously commented the other day, 'Oh, another hair movie, eh?' I have now lodged in my consciousness a picture of Sir William Wallace looking like Fabio on a paperback cover, replete with wind machines and unbuttoned shirt. All period movies now look like 'Dr. Quinn Medicine Woman' to me. What do you think about this, and do you have any remedial suggestions?—James T. Cook, Corpus Christi, Texas

A. As a corrective, I suggest you rent 'Roadie', and study Meat Loaf's hair carefully to see what the heroes of the movies you love would have looked like without modern advances in hair care.

Jennifer MacLennan

How to Tell a Good Professor from a Bad Professor

- A good prof has high standards; a bad prof marks too hard.
- A good prof is confident; a bad prof is arrogant.
- A good prof isn't afraid to speak out on important topics; a bad prof is opinionated.
- A good prof gives clear guidelines for assignments; a bad prof is hung up on rules.
- A good prof lets us express our opinions; a bad prof accepts any answer no matter how stupid it is.
- A good prof maintains control of the class; a bad prof acts like a tyrant.
- A good prof is witty in class; a bad prof is sarcastic.
- A good prof is passionate about the subject; a bad prof thinks this is the only subject we're taking.
- A good prof gives me an extension when I need one; a bad prof gives extensions to whiners when the rest of us got our work in on time.
- A good prof is cool enough to socialize with students; a bad prof needs to get some friends his own age.

Rob Capriccioso

Facebook Face-Off

(From Rob Capriccioso, 'Facebook Face-Off', *Inside Higher Ed*, 14 Feb. 2006, at: <www.insidehighered.com/news/2006/02/14/facebook>.)

Students at Syracuse University utilize Facebook.com's on-line networking groups to discuss a range of topics—the sexiest bodies on campus, the best hookah bars in the area, and even where to buy the most comfortable sweatpants. On plenty of occasions, students have added comments to such groups regarding educational issues. One group, for instance, devoted to distaste for a particular instructor, carries this description: 'This group is for those of us who have to sit through this woman's boring, non English-speaking lectures for 3 hours a week and put up with her flaming red hair and disgusting, leopard print outfits. Not to mention her teeth and bad breath!'

While thousands of students nationwide have added similarly outspoken language to on-line discussion groups and message boards, four students at Syracuse have learned the hard way that private institutions have the right to dole out punishments if they deem content expressed on Facebook.com, or any other online medium, to violate their official codes of student conduct.

Several students, including those who have never posted on Facebook.com, and some professors, including those who have had nasty comments made about them on-line, are questioning whether due process was afforded to the students.

The students in this instance—all female freshmen, three of whom attend Syracuse and one who transferred this semester to Drexel University—had created a group last fall called 'Clearly Rachel doesn't know what she's doing, ever.' The description of the group continued, 'and neither does Syracuse's Writing 105 program for hiring this loser grad student who loves to pronounce her Ws obnoxiously. Rachel, I'm sorry, you really suck.' Next to that description, the students posted a picture of a grinning Rachel Collins, an English doctoral student at the university.

The group had at least 16 members, with Amanda Seideman, Colleen Smith, Caitlin Womble and Madison Alpern taking on 'officer' roles in the group.

Each of the officers described their distaste for the instructor in sexually explicit or otherwise harsh ways. Seideman wrote, 'I'd rather watch my brother masturbate to midget porn with my mom than go to your class, Rachel.' (And that was relatively tame, and clean, compared to Womble's and Smith's comments, which can be found here: <website>.) Alpern's was the gentlest of all: 'I'd rather eat all the hair stuck in the drains of the showers than go to your class, Rachel.'

Last fall, one of Collins's colleagues happened to be perusing Facebook.com, found the group, and quickly alerted officials at the university. The Office of

Judicial Affairs, which handles matters regarding the code of student conduct, ultimately investigated this situation. The students say they were treated in an 'intimidating' manner, and that expulsion was brought up more than once by Juanita Perez Williams, director of the office. After several weeks of waiting, the officers of the group found out that they would face punishment for violating the school's Judicial System Handbook by 'threaten[ing] the emotional and mental health' of Collins.

The students were expelled from her writing class, and were placed on 'disciplinary reprimand' until next fall. They also had to create informational posters for distribution around campus 'about the dangers of Facebook and similar networks as well as online communications', according to Womble. Seideman also deleted the Facebook.com group. If the three students who remain at the university commit other violations of the student code, they could face expulsion from the university. Alpern did not leave Syracuse because of this incident, but for unrelated 'personal reasons'.

Womble said Saturday that no physical harm was ever suggested to Collins and that 'no threats of any kind were made.'

'I will have a reprimand on my permanent record for seven years,' she added, 'so if a grad school inquires into any interactions with judicial affairs or asks on an application if I had any violations that required punishment, this would apply.'

Williams would not comment on whether the students received due process, nor how the specific punishments were determined. She directed inquiries to Kevin Morrow, a spokesman for the university, who said that an 'appropriate process' was followed. 'The book is not thrown without an individual having an opportunity to defend himself or herself', he said Friday. He declined to offer additional details on the process used in this case.

'We do not think that their freedom of speech was infringed upon', said Morrow. 'These matters involved hateful, damaging and harmful remarks. The bottom line is that we're trying to protect the best interests of all our students.'

Collins also declined to comment for this article. She directed inquiries to Carol Lipson, director of the writing program, who, in turn, directed inquiries to Morrow.

Joel Kaplan, an associate dean for graduate professional studies at the Newhouse School of Public Communications at Syracuse, does not believe that anyone's best interests have been served. 'The comments are silly, juvenile, stupid and distasteful, but fully protected', he said. '[T]his is an incredible overreaction by those in power at this university.'

'If [the judicial office] wants to operate on a case-by-case basis, that doesn't seem like a standard process', Kaplan continued. 'What can and cannot be said on the Internet should be spelled out clearly.'

Alan Charles Kors, a professor of history at the University of Pennsylvania and a frequent critic of college policies on student speech, said that at least three of the students—Alpern, Seideman and Smith—seem to have received punishments that exceeded their crimes. But Womble's comment 'levels a crude and personal accusation of possessing an infectious disease, which, though meant hyperbolically, crosses a different line', Kors said. 'If Syracuse had excluded the student who made that specific comment from the class of the teacher, I, speaking for myself, would have not criticized the University for doing that.'

Womble said that she had little idea that posting such comments to Facebook.com could have resulted in such punishments. 'The student body needs to be aware of the [administration's] expectations and if Facebook is fair grounds for policing, they need to make us aware of it.'

Morrow said that the university will not conduct further investigations of Facebook.com groups unless someone draws their attention to them.

An *Inside Higher Ed* review reveals that hundreds of current and former Syracuse students are, in fact, members of Facebook.com groups similar to the ones that got the Rachel Collins crew in trouble. 'I Hate Writing 105', 'Deport Professor Hsiang', and 'Jay Wright Is the Devil Incarnate' are among current groups that may raise ire among administrators. Writing 105 is an introductory level English course, and Hsiang and Wright are professors at Syracuse.

For their part, three of the charged students have said, in retrospect, that they didn't intend to hurt Collins's feelings. 'I am horrified I had anything to do with what occurred and I still feel just horrible that I hurt another person's feelings', Alpern said Saturday. 'I really would like this all just in the past.'

'In this particular situation, I was in the wrong as well as the other girls involved', said Womble. 'I don't feel that the creation of the group was what provoked judicial proceedings, but more the content, which was unnecessary, and material that really shouldn't have been posted anywhere regardless of whether I feel judicial affairs and the administration have the right to take disciplinary action based on Facebook.'

Still, she believes that the situation could have been handled differently. 'I think that the group shouldn't have affected a mature educator confident in her abilities', she said. 'Had it been me I would have dismissed it. I wouldn't take some Internet group by a bunch of freshmen to heart, and yes, it's more than fair for me to have an opinion on her teaching style.'

Michele Weldon, an assistant professor in Northwestern University's Medill School of Journalism at Northwestern, who has been criticized by students on the Internet, said that all universities are dealing with similar issues. 'I think students and everyone else who blogs need to learn the lesson that you have an ethical responsibility not to intentionally and deliberate harm someone with words that you publish', she said. 'This is a cautionary tale that there is no such thing as privacy on the Web. If you have something critical and unkind to say about a professor or student, I suggest you do it the old-fashioned way: Say it to yourself.'

Kaplan thinks the opposite is true. 'What our university did will have a chilling effect on students', he said. 'We need some First Amendment training at this university.'

A sampling of the responses to 'Facebook Face-Off'. These have not been edited for grammar or spelling.

What a surprise!

Gee, there are actually students who don't like a teacher, and say so. All of the comments reported describe what the students would do in preference to attending this TA's class. So? Where's the meanness or the harm to the TA? Not every student will love you, or even like you. In my experieence as both a student and a teacher, the real question is—did the people attend class and do the required work? Particulary for an Intro/core course, there is no real 'bond/mentoring/advising' relationship built. I do credit the TA with (based on the reporting) not making a stink about the webgroup herself. But is her college going to retaliate when her first professional journal article is rejected, and they say 'Sorry, we have other pieces we's reather print?—Richard, East Coast University, at 8:55 am EST on February 14, 2006

Why is this Controversial?

Truly ironic; if the professors defending the comments had made any of those comments to each other in a staff meeting, THEY would have been fired. If those comments were made face to face in a local bar, they could have resulted in a fist fight. If the teacher had made similar comments, on a public website, about those very students, SHE would have been fired. If the students had made similar comments about OTHER STUDENTS IN THE CLASS, they would have been kicked out (statements about expectations of respect towards other students are standard in class itineraries handed out at the beginning of the semester). What is remotely controversial about treating 18 year old adults as adults (i.e. punishing them for behaving inappropriately)? I challenge anyone to go into his boss's office tomorrow, use the insults listed on the website, and still have a job at the end of the day. Being on probation is an onerous burden? Come on.—Steve, February 14, 2006

Freedom of speech or Freedom from consequences?

Maybe I'm just a little naive here, but I don't think that this is a matter of free speech. This is becoming a question of whether or not people should be protected from the consequences of free speech.

Communication is full of often unwritten rules of conduct and behavior. These rules are prescriptive and always allow for the freedom of choice, meaning that you don't have to follow them, but you should be prepared to accept the consequences if you engage in antisocial (mean) behavior. Often, the consequences of violating rules of 'good' communication mean that you can be 'punished' by individuals, institutions, and/or society. Interpersonally, this can mean lost friendships. Institutionally, this can translate to being fired. Societally, this can mean being made a pariah.

These young women freely chose to say cruel and demeaning things in a public webspace where anyone could stumble across them. This is the same as standing on a streetcorner and proclaiming their ideas to anyone who walks by to hear them. We would consider their remarks foul if they were said out loud. We should consider them equally unacceptable in an online context. . . . Just because you are free to say something, that doesn't mean that you should do it . . . or be protected from the consequences of it.—Jacob, February 14, 2006

Why do so many of these 'free speech crusaders' ignore the simple fact that this facebook group was HARASSMENT? Despite what the infamous Dr Kaplan might want to enlighten us with (without ever seeing the comments himself) this is NOT a free speech issue, as Steve has mentioned in comments above.

The [US] Supreme Court has rejected the notion that all speech has is speech without consequence. Let's do away with that foolish idea right now.

This facebook group is, without question, NOT at all a critique of teaching or teaching practice. This isn't dorm room chatter or notes passed in class. This is publicly published, malicious and obscene harassment. Nothing more.—Michael, February 14, 2006

The crucial point, I think, is not the fact that the students published these comments on the internet, but the fact that they chose to publish them in a forum specifically aimed at students and staff at Syracuse. By publishing their remarks in Facebook they clearly intended that these remarks would be read by other Syracuse students (and possibly faculty members), people Ms Collins might deal with in the course of her employment. Had they published their comments on a random website or on a personal blog with no connection to the university community there would not be nearly as strong a chance that Ms Collins' colleagues and other students would view the remarks. They clearly intended to belittle Ms Collins (in an unmistakably sexual way) in a forum which would be viewed by as many members of the Syracuse community as possible. This is not the same thing as a conversation in the corridor or in a dorm room. They wanted to do some damage.

. . . When I said that they wanted to do some damage, I didn't mean that they wanted to do damage by merely criticising the TA in a public forum in the way that a pundit would criticise a politician in a public forum. They wanted to do damage by degrading and humiliating the TA in front of other students (People in her workplace), who would then carry their collective little 'joke' at the TA's expense into the classroom, probably treating her with less courtesy and respect as a result and thereby creating a hostile work environment. It's actually a form of bullying and the use of Facebook allows the students involved to organise and to ensure that they have the numbers in a way that other websites wouldn't.—June, February 15, 2006

How long do you think it will be before employers begin looking into MySpace or FaceOff to see if a potential employee has posted comments about anyone or anything at anytime? These students will have more to worry about than the negative comments that will be part of their permanent transcripts for the next seven years. Not only have they made their opinions public (protected under the First Amendment) they put a face to a name.

In short, thinking before speaking is always a wise move.—Adrienne, March 7, 2006

Jennifer MacLennan

A New Student Evaluation Form

Student evaluation forms have become ubiquitous in college and university classes, despite the fact that they have been shown to be unreliable as meaningful measures of what goes on there.[2] Such forms suggest, in contrast to all that is known about group dynamics, that the group members themselves—the students—contribute nothing to the success or failure of a class experience. In fact, however, the students who make up a class can have a lot to do with how effective a course is.

The relationship between a good professor and a class is an interpersonal dynamic between leader and followers; at its best, it is a personal rather than an impersonal interaction. Unfortunately, the 'semantic differential' approach used by most evaluation forms can depersonalize the interaction and reduce it to a numerical result that, while it has the appearance of objectivity, is actually derived from subjective, even biased, assessments. The forms may feature anywhere from 15 to 30 items, including such favourites as:

- The instructor is well prepared for class
- The instructor has a thorough knowledge of the subject.
- The instructor communicated his/her subject well.
- The instructor stimulated interest in the course subject.
- The instructor is one of the best teachers I have known.
- The instructor clearly interprets abstract ideas and theories.
- The instructor demonstrates a favourable attitude toward students.
- The instructor is willing to experiment and be flexible.
- The instructor encourages students to think for themselves.

Administrators argue that such measures make it easier to compare instructor performance and that they are efficient and (despite evidence to the contrary) reliable. However, these very arguments sound like a good reason to use the same kind of assessment tool for other purposes—such as, for instance, the grading and ranking of student performance.

Imagine if your professors could use a time-saving, equally reliable measure for comparing student performance in a course and for arriving at final grades. With the implementation of such a system, the tedious work of grading assignments could be reduced, perhaps even eliminated, and grades would be arrived at more objectively and consistently. Eventually, students might even have to compete for entry to classes, based on their overall scores on the form. The uses of such a 'valid' measurement tool, it can be imagined, would be numerous.

If such a system were to be implemented, it might contain the items listed below, which were derived from a typical instructor evaluation form used at one Canadian university. Just as in the forms currently used to assess instructors, the respondent—this time a professor—would assess students by ticking a response from one of the following: Strongly Agree, Agree, Disagree, or Strongly Disagree. How do you think you would fare on such a measure?

- The student's written work was well-planned and clearly organized in a coherent, well-defended argument.
- The student read all the recommended reading materials on time, and with attention and understanding, taking notes on each.
- In general, the student was thoroughly prepared for class.
- The student was present at every class meeting and did not miss, except in the case of a medical emergency for which a doctor's excuse was provided.
- The student was able to answer, clearly and comprehensively, any questions on the readings that the instructor put forward in class.
- Generally, the student demonstrated interest in and motivation to learn the materials in the course.
- The student participated willingly, contributed in a valuable way to class discussions, and provided insightful comments on course readings.
- The student asked useful and challenging questions in class discussions.
- The student was more interested in learning than in grades.
- The student prepared all assignments with care and attention, and made use of previous comments and advice to improve subsequent assignments.
- The student consulted additional readings and journals, outside the course materials, to enhance learning in the course.
- The student completed all assignments promptly, beginning them as soon as possible after class was over for the day.
- The student made use of office hours to consult with the instructor, not only about material covered in class, but also about the discipline in general and about the instructor's own research interests and specialization.
- The student respected the classroom as a place to learn, and did not disrupt by whispering, passing notes, reading the student newspaper, doodling, or doing homework for another class.
- The student was open to new ideas, even and especially when they challenged the student's current world view.

- Overall, I am satisfied with the performance of this student and would willingly welcome the student into my class again.

Jarl Olson, Mike Lescarbeau, and Dean Hanson
Gluttony

(From Jarl Olson, Mike Lescarbeau, and Dean Hanson, 'Gluttony', *Harper's* (Nov. 1987): 44. The complete series can be seen in PowerPoint slides at <www.adbuzz.com/OLD/3 Abrands.ppt>.)

In the fall of 1987, Harper's *magazine attempted to demonstrate that it was possible to create a convincing advertisement for anything at all. In that spirit, they invited several top advertising agencies to prepare ads for the Seven Deadly Sins: sloth, lust, wrath (anger), pride, envy, gluttony, and avarice (greed). The ad below was one of the series. As you view it, ask yourself what such an ad, even as a parody, says about the culture we live in and the view we have of each other.*

Reprinted with permission of Fallon Worldwide

Anonymous

Mark C is Caught in the Middle

During the fall of 2006, the e-mail message below was received by a colleague of mine. Although it's intended to look like a personal message, it's actually a spam ad for a weight-loss product. It has not been edited for grammar or spelling.

Subject: Fwd
To: John Colleague
From: MarkC
Date: 10 20 2006

Listen, I am not sure whether you got my first message or not. I am sort of concerned. People are making me feel uncomfortable and I don't like being in the middle. Some of the staff are spreading rude jokes behind your back about your weight. I personally have no problem with you being you.

Please don't come back at me for informing. I just wish to help if anything. I thought about mentioning it to a boss but then to have something like this explode is silly and embarassing for everyone involved, including you being the center of attention. If you really want to make somewhat of a difference, I know my cousin and friend both used this and it worked very well for them. They grabbed it off the internet to keep a low profile & stay confidential. This was the site they got it from, if this helps any. <web site address for a weight-loss product>

Again, I don't like people insulting others behind their backs. I am only trying to help. Which I hope I am. Thanks for at least listening & I hope I am not out of line by writing this. I am only trying to help.

Mark

Rose De Shaw

Guilt, Despair, and the Red Pottery Pig

From 'Facts and Arguments', *The Globe and Mail* (Monday 20 May 1996): A14.

Guilt, despair and the red pottery pig

Big and strong go together: This is a lesson women of size learn, if they are lucky, before they waste their whole lives fighting a battle they can't win and feeling like failures.

By Rose DeShaw

"The essence of sexuality," it is said, "is being comfortable in your own skin." Sometimes, if that skin covers what might be called a large frame, the process of being comfortable takes on all the aspects of a journey.

"Woman of size" a friend has been calling herself as she comes to terms with the knowledge that her weight is not a temporary condition.

My grandmother was a large woman, my mother was a large woman and I, well, you get the picture. The mirror says I am no longer a mere slip of a girl but a substantial figure. "Built to last," the cartoonist Chon Day calls it.

More and more there are plusses to this size thing. The other day in the park with my dog, two young punks were harassing an older immigrant woman who was clearly terrified. As they yelled and jeered I drew myself up like a balloon inflating, slapped on my dignity and bellowed "HEY!" as I started toward them. "You boys know better than that." I tried to sound like all the disapproving mothers and grandmothers of the world as I waved my little plastic bag of dog poop. "Get away from that woman!" I commanded.

Then I tried to remember the body moves from my women's self-defence class in case that was the next step. But the boys took one look at me and beetled off, much to my astonishment.

After reassuring the weeping woman and trying to help her find the courage to do this for herself someday, I caught a glimpse of myself in a shop window on the way home. The rage had given me a Valkyrie look as I swooped down on those punks wielding my psychic axe. Mine is a bulk to take seriously, as Wagner did. Not some skittish skinny woman you might ward off with a fly swatter.

In a study group the other day, we talked about myths that surround big women: that we want to be thin; have no control, no lovers; aren't sexy or healthy æ and adore polyester. The word fat almost always has negative associations: fat chance, fathead. And there's "overweight" æ the confession. Insurance companies have gone to a lot of trouble to figure out the proper standardized tonnage for all women of specific height and years, never mind their genetic inheritance. So smarten up and pay attention, we are commanded.

The objective term "of size," on the other hand, is merely an observation with no attendant baggage.

Big and strong go together spiritually and emotionally, too: to find pleasure in the substantial frame you didn't choose, this vehicle of your mind and soul as you exploit he big bones to whack a golf ball farther than the other little ladies, slug a baseball, dig a trench in the garden, swim more lengths, and run the dog longer.

One issue we have little control over is clothes. Traditionally, camouflage has been the key to the larger sizes. Big splashy florals so that someone might mistake you for a sofa. Lots of black that should either be slimming or at least keep you depressed and quiet. Stretch pants that fit like kielbasa skin. And that favoured big-woman dress design, gunnysack-with-a-bow, little pleats in front, an outfit that shrieks cocktail party and church, queen-size pantyhose and teensy, tootsy-killer pumps.

Large-size bathing suits are on sale downtown. Some designer doing the bigger ladies a favour has added little skirts to emphasize hips and thighs, a direct steal from the dancing hippos in *Fantasia*.

Where will I find the courage to tuck in my shirt, go sleeveless, wear the bathing suit with the scissored-off skirt in public.

From my mother, who dies in her eighties with a huge red pottery pig on her coffee table? All her life the poor woman hated herself for not growing slimmer, not losing weight. Most of those years she was a reluctant member of a diet club. Every week they weighed themselves. The loser had to take the pig home and keep it on prominent display when friends dropped in. It was ugly and crude and leering, unmissable, probably bought at a street booth somewhere in Mexico. Of course, its presence meant you had to explain why it was there, over and over and over.

"I'm trying to lose weight, you see, and I keep failing."

"I'm fat and ugly like that pig," the words echo underneath. Nobody would want this pig and nobody wants me either" æ which happy thought spikes another urge to drown the feeling of rejection and self-pity and helplessness in food.

When my mother moved, she was given the pig to keep permanently. Oh, she took it as a joke of sorts, but the laugh was missing, and her weight sat on her body like a demon whispering what a failure she was whenever she saw a mirror. She wouldn't buy herself a new dress until she lost some weight. She wouldn't swim, walk, cycle or do anything in public that might have called attention to self and size.

Yet she wasn't what you'd call huge, the kind of contestant they have in mind for one of those bellyflop contests. Through her large bones her mother and her grandmother looked out.

Eighty-three years of what could have been a life, making herself miserable over what was in her genes before she was ever born, passing back and forth in front of that damn pig.

I can still see the paint on its face, black and gilt. And the black despair an guilt on my mother's.

Rose DeShaw is a writer and filmmaker living in Kingston, Ontario.

Appendix C

Communication Case Studies

Your instructor may use the following scenarios as a basis for class discussion or as a foundation for written assignments. You may be asked to apply principles from a specific chapter, or to draw from all of the readings you have done so far, but in each case, you should make explicit use of the theory and concepts you have learned to give the fullest explanation you can of the interaction described in the scenario.

Most of the scenarios are left unresolved, just as our interactions in life often are. You may want to speculate as to what the individuals described might do next, or to evaluate what, if anything, could have been done differently. In all cases, though, your interest is in understanding, as fully as possible, what has taken place. As you prepare your analysis, you should consider the following:

- What are the issues at stake in this situation? Why?
- What misunderstandings have occurred? What has caused them?
- What role, if any, has been played by defensiveness, face risk, footing, self-concept, or interpersonal influence?
- To what extent has context shaped the interaction?
- Is conflict present? If so, what kind of conflict is it? What, if anything, can be done to prevent the situation from deteriorating?
- Does the scenario depict an interpersonal relationship or a single interaction? If a relationship is dramatized, at what stage is it? How does this affect the dynamic of the interaction?
- The rhetorician I.A. Richards once characterized the study of communication as 'the study of misunderstandings and their remedies'. To what extent is this true?

Mike's Revenge

Three days ago, Ken, Mike, Valeria, and Paul received their final grade on the group project they handed in for their professional communication course. The prof, 'Hardline' McAllister, has a reputation as the toughest marker in the college, and the group has received the lowest grade in the class. Mike, who was group leader, was really steamed when they got the grade back, and went immediately to McAllister to complain.

Ken doesn't know exactly what happened in the meeting, but apparently the prof refused to raise the grade. According to Mike, McAllister said the work that was handed in did not appropriately respond to the constraints of the assignment, it was sloppy and ill-conceived, and there were numerous errors in both content and grammar in the written report. Therefore, he says, the grade is more than fair—in fact, under the circumstances it's generous. Secretly, Ken is inclined to agree: it's true that McAllister has a reputation for tough standards, but in this case the grade is probably justified, because the group assembled the report hastily just before the deadline, and all of them knew it wasn't as good as it ought to have been. But Ken hasn't said this to Mike, because Mike's so ticked off, and saying anything would only make him worse. Better to let him bluster for a while until he calms down and can be made to see reason.

Now there's a new problem. Although the rest of the group pretty much agree that the report wasn't very good, Mike just can't seem to let go of the grading issue. Ken isn't entirely clear what took place in that meeting with McAllister, but one thing is sure: Mike is still obsessing about the whole thing, and about McAllister's refusal to negotiate. He's hit on a plan that he brings up every time Ken sees him. Basically, Mike is pushing everyone in the group to log onto the website <www.diss-my-professor.com> and give 'Hardline' a terrible review and rating.

Specifically, Mike has been coaching the group members to say that McAllister doesn't know what he's talking about, that he's unreasonable and unfair; he urges them to declare McAllister incompetent, even to say that he should be fired! This seems out of line to Ken, but when he tries to object, Mike argues that future students have a right to know what McAllister is really like, and that it's the group's responsibility to tell them. Still, the issue seems to have gotten out of hand: Mike is talking to others outside the group about joining in the attack on McAllister, and the thing is, many of the people he's pressuring aren't even in the class. In fact, Ken's pretty sure that some of them have never had a class with McAllister at all.

Ken isn't sure what to do about the whole situation. Valeria has started avoiding Mike entirely, because she can't stand what she refers to as this obsessive crusade of his. Paul has gone ahead and made a posting to the website, not because he especially wanted to, but just to get Mike off his back. He tells Ken that he figures McAllister won't ever see it, and if he does, he won't know who posted it. Besides, who cares what people post to an anonymous website? It's not as if anyone takes it seriously anyway.

But apparently someone does. Ken has learned of a recent case where a student was suspended for using university equipment to post similar illegitimate comments to this website; apparently they can track who's signed in and when, and cross-check that information with which classes they're taking. In fact, there are notices posted in the labs explicitly prohibiting use of university computers for this kind of activity. But Mike is still pressuring him, and Ken needs to figure out what he should do next.

Shelley's Interview

Shelley is about to graduate and has applied for a job in the research division of a local advertising firm. Because this particular job requires record-keeping and report-writing, she has been careful to emphasize on her resumé that her oral and written communication skills are excellent, and she has been invited for an interview partly on the strength of these claims.

As part of the assessment process, Shelley has been asked to provide samples of her written work, and she has chosen to submit the final report from her senior project course. The report received an 'A' and was forwarded for the college's essay prize, so Shelley figures it's a good choice to showcase her writing skills. In fact, the professor who supervised the report is one of her references for this job.

Shelley is pretty confident about that report; she sure spent a lot of time combing through it to eliminate typos, spelling mistakes, and grammar problems. Even so, before submitting the report to the interview committee, Shelley decides to go ahead and incorporate the suggestions for improvement made by her supervisor when he graded the report. His advice was extensive, addressing not only layout and design, but also issues like word choice, sentence structure, and punctuation. Although she is unsure about some of the corrections suggested by her professor, she assumes that he knows better than she does, and she really wants this job, so she makes the changes he advised.

On the day of the interview, everything is going well until one of the interviewers, a senior advertising manager, drops a bombshell. The woman reminds Shelley that the job will require strong writing and editing skills, and asks her to comment on the claim that she is a good writer. Shelley, feeling almost as though she's under attack, confirms again that she is a strong writer, and, as proof, she refers the interviewer to the report she submitted. Then the interviewer hands over Shelley's document, in which numerous errors are red-circled—most of them in places where Shelley incorporated her professor's suggestions.

In a friendly but firm tone, the interviewer asks Shelley to explain why there are so many basic errors in grammar in the report she submitted as a sample of her excellent writing.

Chris Loves Programming

Christian Matthews is a third-year student in electrical engineering at Western Plains University. Last summer, he had a great summer job at Waskasoo College, where he was a computer programmer. He was hired to develop programs intended to assist first-year college students with upgrading their math skills so that they could apply to engineering the following year. While the job didn't pay as well as the jobs his friends had last summer, Chris loves computer programming and was really excited about the idea of contributing to engineering education.

However, the programs he was working on were very detail-oriented, and creating and testing them demanded lots of time. By the end of the summer, Chris had managed to produce only two of the four programs the college had requested. Even so, he had devoted a lot of unpaid time, including weekends, to making sure his programs were bug-free. He reckons that most weeks he worked close to 50 hours instead of the 35 he was paid for. Nobody at the college knew how many extra hours the programming actually took, but at the time that didn't matter. Chris, being Chris, wanted to make sure that his work was bug-free, and in the end his dedication paid off: the programs were really successful, and the students found them easy to use and really helpful.

While he was working at Waskasoo, Chris's direct supervisor was Norman Wells, Head of Technical Certificate Programs. Over the summer, Chris came to think of Norm as both friend and mentor. In fact, when his summer job was over, Norm offered Chris a full-time programming job creating additional programs designed to help students increase their technical skills. Chris had been flattered, but turned down the offer so he could concentrate on finishing his engineering degree. Since then, the college has hired someone else for the position. Nevertheless, Norm has continued to mentor Chris and offer valuable career advice. He has even volunteered to provide Chris with an excellent employment reference.

However, things have begun to get complicated. It turns out that the newly hired college employee isn't as proficient as Chris was. Though he's a competent enough programmer, it takes him longer to produce a finished product and his work isn't as clean. The first time that Norm asked Chris to look at one of the guy's programs Chris didn't mind; he quickly found a couple of small errors and put them right, and Norm was delighted. However, the first time was followed by additional requests, and over the past six months Norm has started to depend on Chris to 'clean up' the other programmer's work. He has often mentioned how impressed he is with what he calls Chris's 'talent' with programming, and seems to think that Chris can find and fix these bugs in a matter of minutes.

During the fall term, Chris helped as much as he could, but by Christmas he found that his own work was suffering because he was spending so much time on Norm's requests. This term, Chris has been getting more and more resentful and frustrated about the college's intrusion on his time. He wants to tell Norm that he can't do any more programming for him. Yet he feels trapped, because he's pretty sure that Norm, who has never done any programming, doesn't have any idea how much time his requests take and would be deeply embarrassed to find out how much he has been imposing on Chris. Chris has been flattered by Norm's belief that he is some kind of programming genius, and has never mentioned how labour-intensive the work is. Now, however, Chris needs to take action. He is heading into finals and will be moving to Calgary to start a new job the day after his final exam. He feels that he simply can't continue this time-consuming work that he is not paid for.

Bob the Nazi

Bob is currently taking a night class in propaganda analysis, which he's enjoying very much. Each week, the group reads a sample of political writing on some controversial topic, and they are expected to assess the course readings using what they are learning about propaganda. The articles always come from some 'respectable' source, and most are written by serious scholars. Many of the topics are hot-button political issues that get everyone going, and the class meetings involve interesting debates and lots of lively give and take.

Take last week, for instance. Among the readings assigned to the class was a historical analysis of Canada's treatment of its Aboriginal populations from the Canadian political journal *Agora Canadensis*. The article compared Canadian government policies to Hitler's 'final solution' and the writer extended this thesis by drawing analogies between residential schools and concentration camps, between the North West Mounted Police and the SS, and between reserve land and the Warsaw ghetto.

While the analogies in the article are dramatic and sure make the guy's point forcefully, Bob believes it's propaganda. Applying the course standard of 'who is saying what, to whom, for what purpose, and who stands to benefit', Bob can't help but wonder about the author's unspoken agenda. In Bob's opinion, Canada's treatment of its Aboriginal peoples is a topic far too important for this kind of grandstanding, and he believes the author undermines serious consideration of an important issue by inflaming and dividing readers. In other words, the article generates lots of heat, but doesn't cast much light. Bob intends to argue in class that the author is using a kind of a fallacy known as '*reductio ad hitlerum*'—the condemnation of something by comparing it to Hitler and the Nazis instead of providing any kind of cogent argument.[1]

When the class meets on Wednesday night to discuss the reading, Bob says pretty much exactly this. Nobody else has thought to come up with this clever interpretation, and Bob has a great time arguing his point with his classmates. The discussion heats up, and one guy in particular gets into it with Bob. When class time is up, the discussion is still going strong, and the prof suggests that the group return to the topic next week with some readings on the whole Hitler-analogy strategy. What a great class! Off and on for the rest of the week, Bob finds himself pondering the discussion and anticipating where the class will go next.

By Monday, however, he's distracted by more pressing concerns—something's not quite right. For instance: he has the impression that people he doesn't know are staring at him, but when he looks directly at them, they quickly turn away. At first he thinks this is his imagination, but the sensation returns when a couple of acquaintances who usually acknowledge him walk right by without seeming to see him. Okay, so this could just be a fluke. Maybe they really *didn't* see him. But there it is again, when he joins the crowd at his usual table in the cafeteria at lunch time. Several people get up, claiming they have to be somewhere else, and conversation among the remaining few is stilted and awkward. Bob has no idea what's happening; is there a pattern, or is he imagining it? There's nothing he can really put his finger on, so he figures he must be having an off day and leaves it at that.

By Tuesday, the whole thing is forgotten. Bob has a really packed day of classes, and he doesn't even get a lunch break until the mid-afternoon. Idling in line at the cafeteria with the rest of the stragglers, he catches bits of the conversation from the two strangers just ahead of him. It's something about some classmate: apparently the guy is a total racist, some kind of Hitler nut and an admitted neo-Nazi. Just imagine the nerve of the guy, turning the last class meeting into a racist diatribe, spewing his poisonous crap right out in public for everyone to hear—and the prof didn't even do anything to stop it! They can only speculate what's going to erupt in the next class meeting.

Bob listens, intrigued. He wonders vaguely if he knows the guy they're talking about, then decides he doesn't. He's sure he'd have noticed someone with views that extreme. He silently sympathizes with the speakers: What a jerk the guy must be. Why didn't the prof call a halt to the whole thing? Did any of the other students say anything? Bob tries to imagine his own reaction if this had happened in a class of his.

When their order comes up, the two in front of Bob collect their trays and turn around to head for the checkout, and he recognizes one of them from the propaganda class. The guy shoots Bob an odd look; until this moment, it has not occurred to Bob that the person they have been discussing is *him*.

Lydia the Tattooed Lady

For as long as she can remember, Lydia has prided herself on being a total original. She wants to stand up and be counted, to challenge other people's perceptions, keep them guessing, go her own way. She doesn't want to be mistaken for anyone else—when she walks into a room, people need to know she's someone to be reckoned with.

Take all the fashion clones, with their predictable, slavish devotion to what the magazines and ads tell them to wear. Their clothes, their hair, their makeup, all their preferences—completely fake and manufactured. Even the guys, these days. You'd think whatever is real in them would disappear with a giant sucking sound, like a giant vacuum pump, leaving only the shell with nothing but its fake corporate surface, completely empty inside. Sucked out. Or sucked in. It's all the same, right?

Even her best friend, the flawless Julie, with her preppie look and her perfect grades and her 'yes-sir-no-sir-three-bags-full-sir' attitude. Sometimes Lydia wonders why they're still friends, except that they've been so since elementary school. And she guesses Julie's all right, in spite of her conventional ways. Still, Lydia likes to tweak her sometimes, just to show her what it really means to be outrageous. And push her to be more adventurous, too.

Unlike Julie, Lydia's no fashion slave. She wouldn't be caught dead in The Gap or LaSenza or any of those other clone-making machines. Nope—her clothes are originals. That is, they're stuff you can't find anywhere else except in places like Value Village or the Sally Ann—things you put together in your own way without caring what anyone else tells you to do. Clothes are a statement, and Lydia is going to make her own statement, not go around like some mindless drip wearing a signboard for Jones New York or Alfred Sung or anybody else. Except herself.

Like the tattoo thing. Lydia remembers when she got her first one. It was only a small one, a bright red and orange flame, right there on her shoulder blade. It sure horrified Julie, not to mention the effect on Julie's straight-laced folks. It hurt like hell, of course, but it was worth it to see the looks on their faces. Her own folks haven't said much—too caught up in their own rat race. But since the first one, she's become more and more daring. The snake around her wrist, the dragon on her calf, the skull and crossbones behind her ear, the bar code on the nape of her neck. Just for fun, the tacky heart with 'Mom' on her bicep and the Tazmanian devil on the back of her left hand. And now, the necklace of thorns around her neck. Pretty much the only place she doesn't have one is on her face—for now, anyway, she's leaving her face alone. It was a small triumph when she managed to talk Julie into getting one, too. Hers is a tiny rosebud, on her ankle. But it's something, a beginning, and a point for Lydia.

But not everything is about the tattoos. Lydia's actually in college, where she's taking drama and history and political science and women's studies. Most of it's pretty dull, and nothing is nearly outrageous enough, except maybe the drama. Still, it's probably better than plugging away at some dead-end job slinging hash in a fast-food dive someplace. At least here Lydia is kind of in charge of her fate, and college will keep her from the brain-numbing drudgery of working for a living. For a while, anyway.

Right now Lydia's amusing herself with a public-speaking class. She's confident, and she figures she's a pretty good speaker, so she expected the class would boost her average. But she can't quite sleepwalk through it as she anticipated doing. In addition to giving speeches, each speaker receives oral feedback on the spot from the prof and the rest of the class, most of whom are the usual clones. It irks Lydia that people who so don't get it are allowed to pass judgement on her like that. For one thing, there's not another original in the bunch. Lydia's the only one. Whatever.

Apparently the teacher isn't that original either. Lydia has just received her result on her second speech, and the grade is about 20 per cent lower than she believes it should have been. Lydia's ticked, and she's pretty sure she knows exactly why she got such a low mark. Does the prof think she can just dish out lower grades on the work because she doesn't like how somebody looks? True, the audience didn't really understand what Lydia was getting at when she talked about corporate containment and individual resistance, but probably her ideas are just too complicated for their little brains, numbed as they are by the cultural vacuum. Anyhow, it's not Lydia's fault that the class is too stunned to see what's out there—this grade just isn't right, and she decides to confront the prof about it. She's used to this kind of prejudice, and she's not going to let it pass unchallenged. It's just one more instance of having to rage against the machine, and Lydia's good at that.

After the very next class, Lydia approaches the prof and says she wants to talk about the grade. The prof agrees that this would probably be a good idea and invites Lydia into her office. Lydia is not one to beat around the bush, so she tells the prof directly that she knows she has been graded down because of her appearance. The woman regards her levelly. She doesn't look mad or anything, but there's a pause before she responds. 'I'm sorry, but I don't understand. You look perfectly normal to me. Is there some reason I should have noticed your appearance?'

Tim's Photo Album

It's been 18 months since Tim's long-term relationship with Rebecca broke up. They had been together for five years, and had been engaged for two; they had moved in together and started planning the wedding, but something just wasn't working out. After months of not getting along, they called the whole thing off and Tim walked out, taking with him only whatever he could carry.

The split was hard on both of them. Tim, who was working on his MBA, chucked school and took off for Mexico, where he lived like a beach bum for the better part of a year. He's back in Canada now, living in another province. He's got himself sorted out, has a halfway decent job, and is even planning to resume his studies. He has some regrets about the way he walked out on Becky, but she's moved on, and he's determined to do the same. He's even started seeing Hecate, a lively, impetuous type who's lots of fun to be with.

Although the relationship with Rebecca is over, Tim has been in touch with her to let her know how he is. Now that he's settled, he's asked her to send on some of the things he left behind—mostly mementos from his childhood. One of the items is a photo album, assembled by his mother as a gift to him. It contains pictures from his childhood, irreplaceable ones in fact, since they have no negatives for any of the shots and no other copies. His brother has a similar album, but with a different set of pictures. Someday Tim wants to get each set copied so that the brothers will both have a complete collection, and having them back in his hands means he'll finally be able to get around to it.

The relationship with Hecate is tumultuous. Impulsive, dramatic, and exciting, Hecate can be lots of fun, but she can also be unpredictable, and sometimes there are arguments. At the beginning, they fought only occasionally, and the blow-ups were always followed by passionate reconciliations.

After six months, however, this roller coaster of emotions has become harder to manage, and more and more of their interactions are fights of one sort or another. Tim has discovered something else about Hecate—she has a violent temper. When angered, she's likely to throw whatever's handy, not caring if it hits him or smashes against the wall. She's already broken a window or two, and once tore up the phone bill when they disagreed over who should pay for an expensive long-distance call. The last time, she even flew at Tim, biting and scratching and punching, and afterwards they didn't speak for days. Tim can't now remember what it was that made him want to walk out on Rebecca.

After that last knock-down drag-out fight with Hecate, things never did get back on track, and Tim decides to end the relationship. Not only is it not fun any more, but it's actually starting to scare him. They meet for coffee and he breaks the news, expecting her to be furious. Hecate takes it surprisingly calmly, saying that she, too, has realized things aren't working out. They actually share a laugh over some of the things they've each said and done, and Hecate says she'll stop by Tim's apartment on her day off the next day, just to pick up a few odds and ends that she has left there. She promises to leave the key on the table for him, and they part as friends.

Tim has to work the next day, so he isn't at home when Hecate comes by to collect her remaining belongings. He returns home in the evening to find the key on the table, as promised, and he is flooded with relief. Beside the key is a large brown grocery bag; Hecate, in a moment of thoughtfulness, must have returned the few things Tim had left at her apartment. When he opens the bag, however, Tim gets the shock of his life. Inside is all that remains of his childhood: his precious photo album, its contents shredded beyond recognition. His irreplaceable photos have been completely destroyed.

Izzy and Sam

For as long as anyone can remember, Isobel has been a protective big sister to her brother Sam. Despite the three years' difference in their ages, they have always been close, and remained so all though their growing-up years in small-town New Brunswick. Izzy looked out for Sam and was always there when he needed advice; Sam, in turn, adored his big sister. Things began to change, however, when Izzy graduated from university five years ago and took a job in Calgary.

Although they talk on the phone at least once a week, the distance has subtly altered their relationship. Sam no longer relies on Izzy for advice the way he used to, and Izzy no longer has an automatic understanding of what's going on in Sam's life. She is married now to Iqbal, whom Sam has met only a few times, once on a visit to Calgary, once when Izzy brought him home to meet their folks, and then again at the wedding.

For his own part, Sam has become an electrical systems technician, graduating after Izzy had already moved to Calgary. He married his childhood sweetheart, Brandi, and six months ago they had their first child, Amy Isobel. Now that they have a child to support, Sam and Brandi have been feeling the pressure financially. Sam makes a decent wage, it's true, but with Brandi on maternity leave, they're feeling the pinch.

Izzy has been telling them for a while about all the opportunities in Calgary for someone with Sam's training, and with her strong urging they have decided to pack up and move out west. Izzy is ecstatic at the idea, and Sam, too, is looking forward to being close to his sister again. He knows that Izzy will be a great support to them as they adjust to life in a new city. In fact, the young couple couldn't afford to make this move if Izzy hadn't generously invited them to stay with her and Iqbal until they can get settled. Sam's never seen their place, but Izzy has assured him there's plenty of room for the three of them and that it will be great to be together again.

And it is—sort of. Except that there was never a baby before, never a pair of spouses to accommodate, never the pressure and crowding. Take the space, for example. It's true that Izzy and Iqbal did have a spare room in their apartment, but what's lots of space for two people turns out to be not so big when there are five. Sam and Brandi have been squeezed into the second bedroom along with the baby. It's the only space in the apartment that Brandi and Sam can feel is rightfully theirs. There is a minuscule third bedroom, but Iqbal needs that for an office, and there's no question of Brandi and Sam taking it over.

Then there's the question of stuff. Not that Brandi and Sam have much: they sold off most of their belongings before coming west. But what they do have is still packed in boxes in the storage room of the apartment complex. And there's the shared kitchen: Brandi and Sam started out buying their own food, but now they just split the groceries with Izzy and Iqbal since there's no room to keep two sets of groceries or make two sets of meals. This is kind of a problem, too: Izzy's tastes have become more international than they used to be, presumably since she's taken up with Iqbal, and they eat a lot of foods that Brandi isn't used to. Sam isn't used to them himself, and sometimes he hankers for some 'comfort' food from home. But apparently their preferences seem just as strange to Iqbal as his do to them, because the few times Brandi has made a meal, Iqbal couldn't eat it.

And the baby. Izzy and Iqbal aren't used to having a baby around, and though they are trying to be nice, you can see it's driving them nuts. Amy's been colicky lately, too, crying half the night, and the soundproofing in the apartment leaves a lot to be desired. Nobody's getting much sleep, and Izzy and Iqbal are less and less subtle about their reactions. Plus, there's the question of the mess and the smelly diapers in the bathroom. Izzy and Iqbal have a bathroom off their own bedroom, but the only bathroom available to Sam and Brandi is the one in the main hallway. This means that not only their own stuff, but all the paraphernalia for a baby is in there, including a diaper pail. Sam and Brandi can't afford to use disposables, and anyway they're trying to go 'green'.

But from Sam's point of view, the worst part is that Izzy can't stop playing the big sister. She seems to think of Sam and Brandi as just kids, and she is inclined to tell them what to do and how to do it, especially when it comes to the baby. Izzy has never had to take care of a baby herself, but she seems to think she's some kind of expert because Iqbal is a medical student. Sam can't remember her being so bossy before—how could he have forgotten? And Brandi feels caught in the middle. She resents what she considers the unwanted intrusion into her child-rearing, but on the other hand, this is Sam's adored older sister and they are living under her roof, so it's hard to say much. All of this comes out in whispered conversations in their cramped little room, late at night when they are hopeful they won't be overheard.

Finally one day it all comes to a head. The baby has been fussing all night, and everyone is tired and irritable. When Iqbal, looking for something in the main bathroom, knocks over the diaper pail, it's suddenly pandemonium. Everyone's shouting, the baby is screaming, and Brandi is in tears. When Sam tells Izzy to lay off, she gives him an earful: they aren't paying any rent, but they expect to have everything done for them. She and Iqbal have made huge sacrifices, do they realize that? This whole arrangement might be saving money for Sam and Brandi, but it's costing Iqbal and Izzy plenty. Iqbal's only a student, so they don't have much money themselves, and this arrangement has cost them their whole lifestyle. They haven't had any friends over for months, they can't come and go freely as they used to do, they can't use their own bathroom without tripping over baby stuff, and they can't even get any sleep any more. Worst of all, not only are Sam and Brandi not even contributing to the rent, but they go around with this crummy attitude like they're the ones being dumped on when really they're the ones who are on the receiving end. Iqbal and Izzy don't mind having her brother and his family with them, really they don't, but they are doing Sam a favour, and a little gratitude would go a long way. Plus, Izzy can't believe how arrogant and pigheaded Sam has become; he never used to be like this before he married Brandi. Now Izzy barely recognizes him. She thought she was getting her brother back, but instead she's saddled with a stranger, and one she isn't even sure she likes very much. Why, they haven't had a single decent conversation since he got here.

Eventually things subside, and everyone is civil again, but there are no apologies. The next day Sam and Brandi go apartment-hunting, and later that week they pack up their stuff. One day while Izzy and Iqbal are at work, they move out. Six months has gone by since the split, and Izzy and Sam have still not spoken.

Anne and Manuel

Anne and Manuel have been living together for more than six years since graduating from university. Though both are impulsive and somewhat volatile personalities, and are regarded even by their friends and families as 'difficult', they nevertheless managed to establish a kind of emotional equilibrium. Family members on both sides think that the relationship has been a blessing, with Manuel providing a calming influence on Anne's legendary temper, and Anne's steadying influence curbing Manuel's tendency to drink too much. Though the two have no immediate plans to marry, they decided two years ago to buy a house together. By all accounts, they've managed to make a success of their relationship.

However, while Manuel's career seems to have plateaued, Anne recently moved from her long-time office job into a better-paid position with another firm, where she has become good friends with Rick, a co-worker. They occasionally have a quick bite or a drink together after work, and a few times have even gone to see a film together, since, according to Anne, Manuel doesn't like to go to the movies any more. Rick is regarded by Anne as a friend to both Manuel and herself, and he appears to regard himself in that light as well. In the past few months, he has begun spending more and more time at the house, where he has been assisting Anne with household renovations: painting, plastering, and wallpapering. They have fallen into the habit of shopping after work to pick up items for the renos, in which Manuel has taken little interest.

Lately, Manuel's other friends have noticed that he has become more withdrawn. He's spending less time with them, and he appears to have reverted to his old habits. For example, twice in the past two months he has run the couple's car off the road; the first time, he damaged the vehicle and broke his leg. More recently, he totalled the car, though he escaped serious injury. It's not clear what actually happened either time, since Manuel won't talk about the accidents at all, and when asked, Anne insists that he simply fell asleep at the wheel. No mention of drinking has been made by either of them.

Last Friday, Manuel put the rental car into the ditch. He walked away from this accident, too, but when Anne found out she packed a bag and went to stay with a cousin. Their families don't know for sure what's going on, since neither Anne nor Manuel is offering any explanation.

Notes

Preface

1. Although the discipline traditionally known as speech, then speech communication, and more recently communication studies is a familiar one in American universities, it has been all but unknown in Canada. With its roots in the ancient discipline of rhetoric, the contemporary department of communication studies offers courses in a variety of areas of specialization, including rhetoric, interpersonal communication, instructional communication, communication theory, philosophy of communication, and organizational communication. Interpersonal communication is offered as a foundational course by most such departments. A brief overview of the discipline is available from the National Communication Association, at: <www.natcom.org>.

2. For my discussion of this phenomenon, see Jennifer MacLennan, '"Canadianizing" an American Textbook', *McGill Journal of Education* (Winter 2000): 31–52.

3. The first departments of speech were formed in 1914, when teachers of public speaking broke away from English and formed their own scholarly organization, Speech Teachers of America (later the Speech Communication Association, and since 1997 the National Communication Association).

4. Ronald B. Adler, Lawrence B. Rosenfeld, and Russell F. Proctor, *Interplay: The Process of Interpersonal Communication*, 8th edn (Fort Worth: Harcourt, 2001), 33.

5. The list is predominantly ethnic: Latino Americans, African Americans, Asian Americans, and Euro-Americans. See ibid., 23.

6. A comprehensive list would be too long to include here, but the following are suggestive: Michael Adams, *Fire and Ice: The United States, Canada, and the Myth of Converging Values* (Toronto: Penguin, 2003); Mel Hurtig, *The Vanishing Country: Is It Too Late to Save Canada?* (Toronto: McClelland & Stewart, 2002); Seymour M. Lipset, *Continental Divide: The Values and Institutions of the United States and Canada* (New York: Routledge, 1990); Michael Adams, 'Moralistic Them, Humanistic Us', *Globe and Mail*, 20 Feb. 1995; Pierre Berton, *Why We Act Like Canadians: A Personal Exploration of Our National Character*, 2nd edn (Toronto: Penguin Canada, 1987); Andrew Malcolm, *The Canadians* (New York:

Times Books, 1985); Richard Gwyn, *The 49th Paradox: Canada in North America* (Toronto: McClelland & Stewart, 1985); Northrop Frye, *Divisions on a Ground: Essays on Canadian Culture* (Toronto: Anansi, 1982); Margaret Atwood, *Survival: A Thematic Guide to Canadian Literature* (Toronto: Anansi, 1972); George Grant, *Lament for a Nation: The Defeat of Canadian Nationalism*, reprint edn (Toronto: Macmillan, 1965).

7. Adler et al., *Interplay*, 39, 41. This assertion would have to be qualified; compared to Eastern cultures like Japan, perhaps Canada is individualistic. But many other studies show a decidedly collectivist pattern when compared with American culture. See, e.g., Adams, *Fire and Ice*; Lipset, *Continental Divide*.

8. For an overview of what rhetoric has to teach us about persuasion, consider the following: Ann Gill, *Rhetoric and Human Understanding* (Prospect Heights, Ill: Waveland Press, 1993); Barry Brummett, *Rhetorical Dimensions of Popular Culture*, Studies in Rhetoric and Communication (Tuscaloosa: University of Alabama Press, 1991); Edward P.J. Corbett, *Classical Rhetoric for the Modern Student* (New York: Oxford University Press, 1971).

9. See, e.g., Richard Weaver, *Language Is Sermonic: Richard M. Weaver on the Nature of Rhetoric*, ed. Richard L. Johannesen, Ralph T. Eubanks, and Rennard Strickland, reprint edn (Baton Rouge: Louisiana State University Press, 2002).

10. Lloyd Bitzer, 'The Rhetorical Situation', *Philosophy and Rhetoric* 1 (1964): 1–15.

11. For a fuller discussion of this phenomenon, see Jennifer MacLennan, 'A Rhetorical Journey into Darkness: Crime-Scene Profiling as Burkean Analysis', *KB Journal* 1 (Spring 2005), at: <www.kbjournal.org/modules.php?name=News&file=article&sid=18>. Also helpful is the sociologist Joseph R. Gusfield's 'Introduction' to *Kenneth Burke: On Symbols and Society*, ed. Joseph R. Gusfield (Chicago: University of Chicago Press, 1989), 1–49.

12. Kenneth Burke, *A Grammar of Motives* (Berkeley: University of California Press, 1969 [1945]); Burke, *A Rhetoric of Motives* (Berkeley: University of California Press, 1969 [1962]).

13. Burke, *A Rhetoric of Motives*, xiii.

Introduction

1. See, in addition to those mentioned in the Preface, Katharine Morrison, *Canadians Are Not Americans: Literary Traditions of the United States and Canada* (Toronto: Second Story Press, 2003); David Thomas, ed., *Canada and the United States: Differences that Count* (Toronto: Broadview Press, 1993); Marjorie Montgomery Bowker, *On Guard for Thee: An Independent Review of the Free Trade Agreement* (Ottawa–Hull: Voyageur, 1988); June Callwood, *Portrait of Canada* (New York: Doubleday, 1981); Joseph Barber, *Good Fences Make Good Neighbours: Why the United States Provokes Canadians* (Toronto: McClelland & Stewart, 1958).

2. Pierre Berton, *Why We Act Like Canadians: A Personal Exploration of Our National Culture*, 2nd edn (Toronto: McClelland & Stewart, 1987), and Berton, *Hollywood's*

Canada: The Americanization of Our National Image (Toronto: McClelland & Stewart, 1975).

3. Margaret Atwood, *Survival: A Thematic Guide to Canadian Literature* (Toronto: Anansi, 1972).

4. Northrop Frye, *Divisions on a Ground: Essays on Canadian Culture* (Toronto: Anansi, 1982), and Frye, *The Bush Garden* (Toronto: Anansi, 1971).

5. George Grant, *Lament for a Nation: The Defeat of Canadian Nationalism* [reprint edition] (Toronto: Macmillan, 1965).

6. George Woodcock, *The Canadians* (Toronto: Fitzhenry & Whiteside, 1979), 292.

7. Robert M. MacGregor, 'I am Canadian: National Identity in Beer Commercials', *Journal of Popular Culture* (Nov. 2003): 276–86; Gregory Millard, Sarah Riegel, and John Wright, 'Here's Where We Get Canadian: English-Canadian Nationalism and Popular Culture', *American Review of Canadian Studies* 32 (2002). At: <www.questia.com/google Scholar.qst;jsessionid=G2QPJ3Rxl4VLvG1QQ1GkpGS6bcJpwN8Zs25brGP1qv6YL kPhsG4V!-124666375!1033568690?docId=5002485379>.

8. Jennifer MacLennan, 'Signposts of Cultural Identity: George Grant's *Lament for a Nation* and Mel Hurtig's *The Vanishing Country*', to appear in *Rhetor*, the on-line Journal of the Canadian Society for the Study of Rhetoric, 2006–7.

9. Jennifer MacLennan, 'Peace, Order, and Good Government: Canadian Values in Pierre Trudeau's 1970 War Measures Proclamation', Canadian Society for the Study of Rhetoric annual conference, Toronto, 25–6 May 2002.

10. Jennifer MacLennan, 'Canadian Documentary Realism and the Dynamics of Identity in Degrassi Junior High', in Michele Byers, ed., *Growing Up Degrassi: Television, Identity, and Youth Cultures* (Toronto: Sumach Press, 2005), 149–66.

Chapter 1

1. L. Barker, R. Edwards, C. Gaines, K. Gladney, and F. Holley, 'An Investigation of Proportional Time Spent in Various Communication Activities by College Students', *Journal of Applied Communication Research* 8 (1980): 101–9.

2. Walter Loban, quoted in Roy Berko, Megan Brooks, and J. Christian Spielvogel, *Pathways to Careers in Communication* (Annandale, Va: Speech Communication Association, 1995), 1.

3. Katherine Barber, ed. *The Canadian Oxford Dictionary* (Toronto: Oxford University Press, 1998), 287.

4. Claude Shannon and Warren Weaver, *The Mathematical Theory of Communication* (Urbana: University of Illinois Press, 1949).

5. Known as the *Precepts*, it was composed in Egypt by Ptah-Hotep. See James McCroskey, *An Introduction to Rhetorical Communication*, 6th edn (Englewood Cliffs, NJ: Prentice-Hall, 1993), 2.

6. The yoking of rhetoric and interpersonal communication is not as odd as it might ini-

tially seem, as is evident, for example, in the following: Marcus L. Ambrester, *Rhetoric of Interpersonal Communication* (Chicago: Waveland Press, 1984); Robert D. Kendall, 'Toulmin, Values, and the Rhetoric of Interpersonal Communication', paper presented at the annual meeting of the Central States Speech Association, Chicago, Apr. 1978; 'Rhetoric and Interpersonal Communication' stream in the Communication and Theater Department at DePauw University, at: <www.depauw.edu/acad/communication/rhetoric.htm>.

7. As the rhetorician and semanticist George Dillon reveals in his study of the 'interpersonal function of language', *Rhetoric as Social Imagination* (Bloomington: Indiana University Press, 1986).

8. Robert Cialdini, *Influence: Science and Practice* (New York: William Morrow, 1984).

9. As she did, for example, in such popular works as Deborah Tannen, *Talking from 9 to 5: Women and Men at Work*, new paperback edn (New York: Quill, 2001), and Tannen, *That's Not What I Meant! How Conversational Style Makes or Breaks Relationships* (New York: Ballantine, 1986)

10. Such as, for example, Communication Studies 240: Rhetoric of Interpersonal Communication, offered by the Department of Communication Studies at Northern Illinois University. See <www.reg.niu.edu/regrec/gened/COMS%20240.htm>.

11. S. Michael Halloran, 'Aristotle's Concept of Ethos, or If Not His, Somebody Else's', *Rhetoric Review* 1 (Sept. 1982): 58–63.

12. Peter Kirby Manning, 'Doubles and Tom Voire', *Sociological Quarterly* 43 (2003): 453–9; Eric M. Eisenberg, 'Building a Mystery: Toward a New Theory of Communication and Identity', *Journal of Communication* 51 (2001): 534–52; W.B. Swann, 'Identity Negotiation: Where Two Roads Meet', *Journal of Personality and Social Psychology* 53 (1987): 1038–51; Mary Jane Kehily, 'Self-narration, Autobiography and Identity Construction', *Gender and Education* 7 (1 Mar. 1995): 23–32; R.S. Zaharna, 'Self-Shock: The Double-binding Challenge of Identity', *International Journal of Intercultural Relations* 13 (1989): 501–26; Peter L. Berger, *Invitation to Sociology: a Humanistic Perspective* (Garden City, NY: Anchor, 1963).

13. Aristotle, *The Rhetoric and Poetics*, trans. W. Rhys Roberts, ed. Fredrich Solmsen (New York: Random House/Modern Library, 1954), 1356a.

14. David G. Myers, 'Close Relationships and Quality of Life', in D. Kahneman, E. Diener, and N. Schwarz, eds, *Well-Being: The Foundations of Hedonic Psychology* (New York: Russell Sage Foundation, 1999); Edward Helmes, Roland D. Chrisjohn, and Richard D. Goffin, 'Confirmatory Factor Analysis of the Life Satisfaction Index', *Social Indicators Research* 45 (1998): 371–90; Keith Oatley, *Best Laid Schemes: The Psychology of Emotions* (Cambridge: Cambridge University Press, 1992); Michael Argyle, J. Crossland, and Maryanne Martin, 'Happiness as a Function of Personality and Social Encounters', in J.P. Forgas and J.M. Innes, eds, *Recent Advances in Social Psychology* (Amsterdam: Elsevier, 1989); Frank M. Andrews and S.B. Withey, *Social Indicators of Well-Being. Americans Perceptions of Life Quality* (New York: Plenum Press, 1976).

15. Petra Bohnke, 'First European Quality of Life Survey: Life Satisfaction, Happiness, and Sense of Belonging', Berlin: European Foundation for the Improvement of Living and Working Conditions, 2003), 4–5, at: <www.eurofound.eu.int/publications/files/EF0591 EN.pdf>; T.M. Beckie and L.A. Hayduk, 'Measuring Quality of Life', *Social Indicators Research* 42 (1997): 21–39

16. For example, Helen Wilkie, 'Communicate Well and Prosper', *Globe and Mail*, 27 Feb. 2004, C1; Peter Morton, 'Communication Key to Success in Engineering Careers', *Polytechnic Online* 127 (28 Mar. 2001), at: <www.poly.rpi.edu/article_view.php3?view= 599&part=1>; A. Terjanian, 'Adequate Communication is Key to Success', PowerPoint Presentation, at: <www.amcham.am/Adequate.ppt>; Paul Aldo, 'Clear Communications: A Key to Success', *Atlanta Journal-Constitution*, at: <jobnews.ajcjobs.com/news/ content/careercenter/features/advice_develop1.html>.

17. Carol D. Ryff and Burton H. Singer, eds, *Emotion, Social Relationships, and Health* (New York: Oxford University Press, 2001); James S. House, Karl R. Landis, and Debra Umberson, 'Social Relationships and Health', *Science* 241 (29 July 1988): 540–5.

18. Employee Health and Wellness, 'Our Relationships Influence Our Physical Health', *Healthworks* (newsletter) (Hamilton, Ont., McMaster University), at: <www.mcmaster. ca/health/employees/monthly%20mentions/relationships.htm>.

19. Northrop Frye, *The Well-Tempered Critic* (Bloomington: Indiana University Press, 1963), 21.

20. Kenneth Burke, *Attitudes toward History*, 2nd edn (Los Altos, Calif.: Hermes, 1959 [1937]), 165–6.

21. Kenneth Burke, *A Rhetoric of Motives* (Berkeley: University of California Press, 1969), 45.

22. Erving Goffman, *Stigma: Notes on the Management of Spoiled Identity* (Englewood Cliffs, NJ: Prentice-Hall, 1963), 51.

23. Ibid., 43.

Chapter 2

1. Roderick P. Hart, *Modern Rhetorical Criticism*, 2nd edn (Boston: Allyn & Bacon, 1997), 36.

2. George Dillon, 'Footing: The Codes of Engagement', in Dillon, *Rhetoric as Social Imagination: Explorations in the Interpersonal Function of Language* (Bloomington: Indiana University Press, 1986).

3. Hilary Bays, 'Framing and Face in Internet Exchanges: A Socio-Cognitive Approach', *Linguistik Online* 1 (1998), at: <www.linguistik-online.de/bays.htm>.

4. See, e.g., Erving Goffman, *The Presentation of Self in Everyday Life* (New York: Anchor Books, 1959).

5. Erving Goffman, 'On Face Work', in Goffman, *Interaction Ritual* (Garden City, NY: Anchor Books, 1967), 5–6.

6. Lloyd Bitzer, 'The Rhetorical Situation', *Philosophy and Rhetoric* 1 (1968): 6.

7. Kenneth Burke, 'Definition of Man', in Burke, *Language as Symbolic Action* (Berkeley: University of California Press, 1966), 3.

8. S.I. Hawayaka, *Language in Thought and Action*, 5th edn (San Diego: Harcourt Brace Jovanovich, 1991).

9. Abraham H. Maslow, 'A Theory of Human Motivation', *Psychological Review* 50 (1943): 370–96.

10. Kenneth Burke, *A Rhetoric of Motives* (Berkeley: University of California Press, 1969), 45.

11. Petra Bohnke, *First European Quality of Life Survey: Life Satisfaction, Happiness, and Sense of Belonging* (Berlin: European Foundation for the Improvement of Living and Working Conditions, 2003), 4-5. At: <www.eurofound.eu.int/publications/files/EF0591EN.pdf>.

12. See <www.mcmaster.ca/health/employees/monthly%20mentions/relationships.htm>.

13. James McCroskey, 'The Nature of Rhetorical Communication', in McCroskey, *An Introduction to Rhetorical Communication*, 6th edn (Englewood Cliffs, NJ: Prentice-Hall, 1993), 17.

14. See, e.g., M.H. Abrams, *The Mirror and the Lamp* (London: Oxford University Press, 1971).

Chapter 3

1. Erik H. Erikson, 'The Problem of Ego Identity', *Journal of the American Psychoanalytic Association* 4 (1956): 56–121. See also Erik Erikson, *Identity and the Life Cycle* (New York: International Universities Press, 1959), 108–9.

2. See Stephen Duck and Julia T. Wood, eds, *Composing Relationships: Communication in Everyday Life* (Belmont, Calif.: Wadsworth, 2006). See also J.S. Atherton, 'Learning and Teaching: Personal Construct Theory' (2005), at: <www.learningandteaching.info/learning/personal.htm>.

3. As is suggested, for example, in the classic work by Beulah Parker, *My Language Is Me: Psychotherapy with a Disturbed Adolescent* (New York: Ballantine Books, 1962). See also Elaine G. Caruth, 'Language in Intimacy and Isolation: Transitional Dilemma, Transformational Resolution', *Psychoanalytic Electronic Publishing* (2006), at: <www.pep web.org/document.php?id=jaa.015.0039a>.

4. Thomas Benson, 'Rhetoric and Autobiography: The Case of Malcolm X', *Quarterly Journal of Speech* 60 (Feb. 1974): 1.

5. Kenneth Burke, *A Rhetoric of Motives* (Berkeley: University of California Press, 1969), 45.

6. Erving Goffman, *Stigma: Notes on the Management of Spoiled Identity* (Englewood Cliffs, NJ: Prentice-Hall, 1963), 56.

7. Ruth C. Wylie, *The Self-Concept* (Loncoln: University of Nebraska Press, 1961).

8. See Susan Harter, 'The Development of Self-representations', in W. Damon and N.

Eisenberg, eds, *Handbook of Child Psychology*, 5th edn (New York: John Wiley & Sons, 1998).

9. M.R. Lepper, L. Ross, and R.R. Lau, 'Persistence of Inaccurate Beliefs about the Self: Perseverance Effects in the Classroom', *Journal of Personality and Social Psychology* 50 (Mar. 1986): 482–91.

10. See, for instance, Carolyn Wood Sherif, 'Needed Concepts in the Study of Gender Identity', *Psychology of Women Quarterly* 6 (1982): 375–95.

11. See Carl Rogers, 'This Is Me', in H. Kirschenbaum and V.L. Henderson, eds, *The Carl Rogers Reader* (Boston: Houghton Mifflin, 1989), 6–28.

12. Carl W. Backman, Paul F. Secord, and Jerry R. Peirce, 'Resistance to Change in the Self-Concept as a Function of Consensus among Significant Others', *Sociometry* 26 (Mar. 1963): 102–11.

13. W. Purkey, 'An Overview of Self-Concept Theory for Counselors', ERIC Clearinghouse on Counseling and Personnel Services, Ann Arbor, Mich. (1988), ERIC/CAPS Digest: ED304630.

14. Robert B. Cialdini and N.J. Goldstein, 'Social Influence: Compliance and Conformity', *Annual Review of Psychology* 55 (2004): 591–621.

15. Abhilasha Mehta, 'Using Self-Concept to Assess Advertising Effectiveness', *Journal of Advertising Research* (Jan. 1999), at: <www.findarticles.com/p/articles/mi_hb3192/is_199901/ai_n7866682>.

16. Sheldon Stryker, 'Identity Salience and Role Performance: The Relevance of Symbolic Interaction Theory for Family Research', *Journal of Marriage and the Family* 30, 4 (Nov. 1968): 558–64.

17. Jan E. Stets and Peter J. Burke, 'Identity Theory and Social Identity Theory', *Social Psychology Quarterly* 63, 3 (Sept. 2000): 224–37.

18. H. Markush, Jeanne Smith, and Richard L. Moreland, 'Role of the Self-concept in the Perception of Others', *Journal of Personality and Social Psychology* 49 (1985): 1494–1512.

19. Erving Goffman, *Interaction Ritual* (New York: Pantheon, 1967), 5.

20. Robert Rosenthal and Lenore Jacobson, *Pygmalion in the Classroom* (New York: Holt, Rinehart and Winston, 1968).

21. E.E. Jones, *Interpersonal Perception* (New York: W.H. Freeman, 1990).

22. William B. Swann, 'The Self and Identity Negotiation', *Interaction Studies* 6, 1 (2005): 69–83.

23. William B. Swann, 'Identity Negotiation: Where Two Roads Meet', *Journal of Personality and Social Psychology* 53, 6 (1987): 1038–51.

24. Joseph Luft and Harry Ingham, *The Johari Window: A Graphic Model for Interpersonal Relations* (Los Angeles: University of California Western Training Lab, 1955). You can find this model described on many websites; see, e.g., Dorothea von Ritter Rohr, 'The Johari Window', at: <www.augsburg.edu/education/edc210/Johari-Ritter-Rohr.pdf>. See also Joseph Luft, *Group Processes: An Introduction to Group Dynamics*, 2nd edn (Palo Alto, Calif.: National Press Books, 1970).

25. Jean-Phillippe Laurenceau, Lisa Feldman Barrett, and Paula R. Pietromonaco, 'Intimacy as an Interpersonal Process: The Importance of Self-disclosure, Partner Disclosure, and Perceived Partner Responses in Interpersonal Exchanges', *Journal of Personality and Social Psychology* 74, 5 (1998): 1238–51.

26. See, e.g., Mark J. Goldstein et al., 'Personal Risk Associated with Self-Disclosure, Interpersonal Feedback, and Group Confrontation in Group Psychotherapy', *Small Group Behavior* 9, 4 (Nov. 1978): 579–87; Richard Nelson-Jones and S.R. Strong, 'Rules, Risk and Self-disclosure', *British Journal of Guidance and Counselling* 4, 2 (July 1976): 202–11.

27. Matthew Kelly, *The Seven Levels of Intimacy: The Art of Loving and the Joy of Being Loved* (New York: Simon & Schuster, 2005).

28. H. Solanoc and M. Dunnam, 'Two's Company: Self-disclosure and Reciprocity in Triads versus Dyads', *Social Psychology Quarterly* 48, 2 (1985): 183–7; Jonathan E. Smith et al., 'Self-Disclosure and Self-Monitoring: The Effect of a Personality Variable on Reciprocal Self-Disclosure', paper presented at the annual meeting of the Southeastern Psychological Association, Atlanta, 25–8 Mar. 1981.

29. Robert L. Armacost, Jamshid C. Hosseini, Sara A. Morris, and Kathleen A. Rehbein, 'An Empirical Comparison of Direct Questioning, Scenario and Randomized Response Methods for Obtaining Sensitive Business', *Decision Science* 22 (1991): 1073–87; Dorothy S. Fidler and Richard E. Kleinknecht, 'Randomized Response versus Direct Questioning: Two Data Collection Methods for Sensitive Information', *Psychological Bulletin* 84 (1977): 1045–9.

Chapter 4

1. Stephen Duck and Robin Gilmour, *Studying Personal Relationships* (New York: Academic Press, 1981), 2.

2. Brian R. Patterson, L.M. Bettini, and Jon F. Nussbaum, 'The Meaning of Friendship across the Lifespan: Two Studies', *Communication Quarterly* 41 (1993): 145.

3. B.A. Winstead, V.J. Derlega, and S. Rose, *Gender and Close Relationships* (Thousand Oaks, Calif.: Sage, 1997), 26.

4. Kenneth Burke, *A Rhetoric of Motives* (Berkeley: University of California Press, 1969), 45.

5. Abraham Maslow, 'A Theory of Human Motivation', *Psychological Review* 50 (1943): 370–96. You can find the entire paper at: <scholar.google.com/scholar?hl=en&lr=&q=cache:pHP5Q5c7Pq0J:sigbus.nove.bg/pool/books/A._H._Maslow_-_A_Theory_of_Human_Motivation.pdf+maslow>.

6. Northrop Frye, 'The Ideas of Northrop Frye', interview with David Cayley [transcript]. (Montreal: CBC Transcripts, 1990), 2. Frye's study of Blake is *Fearful Symmetry* (Princeton, NJ: Princeton University Press, 1947).

7. William Schutz, *The Interpersonal Underworld* (Palo Alto, Calif.: Science & Behavior

Books, 1966), 18–20. For a more detailed account of Schutz's theory than is possible here, see 'FIRO Theory of Needs of William Schutz', in Em Griffin, *A First Look at Communication Theory* (New York: McGraw-Hill, 1991), at: <www.afirstlook.com/archive/firo.cfm?source=archther>.

8. Schutz, *Interpersonal Underworld*, 20.

9. Ibid., 18.

10. Ibid.

11. Kenneth Burke, *Counter Statement*, reprint edn (Berkeley: University of California Press, 1968), 125.

12. Murray Banks, *How To Live With Yourself . . . Or, What to Do Until the Psychiatrist Comes*, sound recording (New York: Murmil Records, 1960).

13. John W. Thibaut and Harold H. Kelley, *The Social Psychology of Groups*, 2nd edn (New Brunswick, NJ: Transaction Books, 1986), 9–30.

14. See, e.g., Sarah Trenholm, *Human Communication Theory*, 2nd edn (Englewood Cliffs, NJ: Prentice-Hall, 1991); Anthony Giddens, *Central Problems in Social Theory* (Berkeley: University of California Press, 1979); Richard M. Emerson, 'Social Exchange Theory', *Annual Review of Sociology* 2 (1976): 335–62.

15. This is part of what Theodore Roszak called 'the cult of information'. See Roszak, *The Cult of Information: The Folklore of Computers and the True Art of Thinking* (New York: Pantheons Book, 1986). Some fascinating excerpts from Roszak's book can be found at: <www.shkaminski.com/Classes/Readings/Roszak.htm>.

16. And it does seem to be a tempting idea, at least to some. Consider the way it's been exploited in television series, through characters such as Mr Spock or Data in *Star Trek*, or the robot Kryten on the British sci-fi spoof *Red Dwarf*.

17. Mark L. Knapp, *Interpersonal Communication and Human Relationships* (Boston: Allyn & Bacon, 1984); Dallas A. Taylor and Irwin Altman, 'Communication in Interpersonal Relationships: Social Penetration Theory', in Mark E. Roloff and Gerald R. Miller, eds, *Interpersonal Processes: New Directions in Communications Research* (Beverly Hills, Calif.: Sage, 1987), 257–77; Stephen Duck, 'How to Lose Friends Without Influencing People', in Roloff and Miller, eds, *Interpersonal Processes*, 278–98; L. Baxter, 'Strategies for Ending Relationships: Two Studies', *Western Journal of Speech Communication* 46 (1982): 223–42.

Chapter 5

1. Verbal communication should not be confused with oral communication, which refers to that which is spoken. When Stan tells Jerry, 'We had a verbal agreement', his statement doesn't make sense. If they had an agreement, it had to have been verbal, since *all* agreements by their very nature are verbal—that is, they are created in language. What Stan probably means is that their agreement was made orally and had not been put into writing.

2. Those who wanted English to be the common language included all of the former Soviet republics, Vietnam, and most of the Arab world. Of the remainder, 40 selected French, and 20 Spanish. See Dennis O'Neil, 'Language and Culture: An Introduction to Human Communication', at: <http://anthro.palomar.edu/language/language_1.htm>.

3. For a discussion of the symbolism inherent in everyday life, see Barry Brummett, *Rhetoric in Popular Culture* (New York: St Martin's Press, 1994); John Fiske, *Understanding Popular Culture* (New York: Routledge, 1991). Also of interest are Margaret Visser, *Much Depends on Dinner* (Toronto: HarperCollins, 1992); Witold Rybczynski, *Waiting for the Weekend* (New York: Viking, 1991); Robert H. Lauer and Jeanette C. Lauer, *Fashion Power: The Meaning of Fashion in American Society* (Englewood Cliffs, NJ: Prentice-Hall, 1981).

4. For instance, see Richard Weaver, *Language Is Sermonic: Richard Weaver on the Nature of Rhetoric*, ed. Richard L. Johannesen, Rennard Strickland, and Ralph T. Eubanks (Baton Rouge: Louisiana State University Press, 1970).

5. Clyde Miller, 'How to Detect Propaganda' (Institute for Propaganda Analysis, 1937), in Jennifer MacLennan and John Moffatt, eds, *Inside Language* (Scarborough, Ont.: Prentice-Hall Canada, 2000).

6. Kenneth Burke, 'Terministic Screens', in Burke, *Language as Symbolic Action: Essays on Life, Literature, and Method* (Berkeley: University of California Press, 1966), 43–62.

7. Described in Barbara Douglas, 'Writers, Readers, Researchers: Beware! Propaganda Ahead!', at: <www.mala.bc.ca/~soules/eng315/textbook/douglas.htm>.

8. For example, S.I. Hayakawa and Alan Hayakawa, *Language in Thought and Action*, 5th edn (New York: Harcourt Brace Jovanovich, 1990). Some others include Richard Mitchell, *Less Than Words Can Say* (Boston: Little, Brown, 1979); Northrop Frye, *The Educated Imagination* (Bloomington: Indiana University Press, 1964); George Orwell, 'Politics and the English Language', *The Orwell Reader* (New York: Harcourt Brace and World, 1956).

9. Edward Sapir, 'The Status of Linguistics as a Science', *Language* 5 (Dec. 1929), in Edward Sapir and David G. Mandelbaum, eds, *Selected Writings of Edward Sapir in Language, Culture, and Personality* (Berkeley: University of California, 1985 [1949]), 69.

10. Benjamin Lee Whorf, *Language, Thought, and Reality* (Cambridge, Mass.: MIT Press, 1956), 212–14.

11. Mitchell, *Less Than Words Can Say*, 23.

12. Walter J. Ong, 'Words as Sound', in Peter Elbow, ed., *Landmark Essays on Voice and Writing* (Davis, Calif.: Hermagoras Press, 1994).

13. Little is known about the effects of 'languagelessness' on adults, because it was long thought that no such phenomenon existed. See Susan Schaller, *A Man without Words* (Berkeley: University of California Press, 1995).

14. Hayakawa and Hayakawa, *Language in Thought and Action*, 5.

15. David R. Heise, 'The Semantic Differential and Attitude Research', in Gene F. Summers, ed., *Attitude Measurement* (Chicago: Rand McNally, 1970), 235–53.

16. See, e.g., Mary Crawford and Danielle Popp, 'Sexual Double Standards: A Review and Methodological Critique of Two Decades of Research', *Journal of Sex Research* 40 (Feb. 2003), at: <www.findarticles.com/p/articles/mi_m2372/is_1_40/ai_101530207>.

17. R.R. Milhausen and E.S. Herold, 'Does the Sexual Double Standard Still Exist? Perceptions of University Women', *Journal of Sex Research* 36 (1999): 361–7.

18. See, e.g., Barry Smith, 'Towards a History of Speech Act Theory', in A. Burkhardt, ed., *Speech Acts, Meanings and Intentions: Critical Approaches to the Philosophy of John R. Searle* (New York: Aldine de Gruyter, 1990), 29–61.

19. Brock Shoveller, 'Your Language Is You', in Jennifer MacLennan and John Moffatt, eds, *Inside Language: A Canadian Language Reader* (Scarborough, Ont.: Prentice-Hall Canada, 2000).

20. Information about this case, which involved Memorial University's proposed degree in Software Engineering, can be found at: <www.engr.mun.ca/~dpeters/sweng/issues. html>.

21. Samuel Hoffenstein, 'Love Songs At Once Tender and Informative (XIII)', *Poems In Praise of Practically Nothing* (New York: AMS Press, reprint edition, 1928). This witty poem can be found at: <writersalmanac.publicradio.org/programs/2001/11/26/ index.html>.

22. Spekkens, who passed away in the fall of 2006, taught linguistics for many years at St Francis Xavier University in Antigonish, Nova Scotia.

23. For more Canadian phrases and expressions, see the collections of word hound Bill Casselman, including *Canadian Sayings* (Toronto: McArthur & Company, 1999) and its two sequels, *Canadian Sayings 2* (Toronto: McArthur & Company, 2002) and *Canadian Sayings 3* (Toronto: McArthur & Company, 2004). You can sample his work at: <www.billcasselman.com>.

24. These have been discussed by numerous scholars and journalists who have revealed many systematic differences between the two cultures—in history (Canadian history is counter-revolutionary, in contrast to the revolutionary spirit of the US); political traditions (Canada's parliamentary democracy contrasts with the American constitutional republic); and sociological context (collectivist, even socialist, in contrast to the culture of individualism that distinguishes the US). Some of these include Jennifer MacLennan, '"Canadianizing" an American Textbook', *McGill Journal of Education* 35 (Winter 2000), 31–52; Seymour M. Lipset, *Continental Divide: The Values and Institutions of the United States and Canada* (New York: Routledge, 1990); Northrop Frye, *Divisions on a Ground: Essays on Canadian Culture* (Toronto: House of Anansi, 1982); Andrew Malcolm, *The Canadians* (New York: Times Books, 1985); Pierre Berton, *Hollywood's Canada: The Americanization of Our National Image* (Toronto: McClelland & Stewart, 1975); Richard Gwyn, *The 49th Paradox: Canada in North America* (Toronto: McClelland & Stewart, 1985). Also helpful are Michael Adams, 'Moralistic Them, Humanistic Us', *Globe and Mail*, 20 Feb. 1995; Richard Gwyn, *Nationalism without Walls: The Unbearable Lightness of Being Canadian* (Toronto: Doubleday Canada, 1995).

25. As is detailed, for instance, in Margaret Atwood, 'Canadian Looks at American Looking at Us' [Review of Andrew Malcolm's *The Canadians*], *Red Deer Advocate*, 4 May 1985, 1B; Atwood, 'Canadian–American Relations: Surviving the Eighties', in Atwood, *Second Words* (Toronto: House of Anansi, 1982), 371–92; Frye, *Divisions on a Ground*.

26. For the centrality of such values to the Canadian psyche, see, e.g., Pierre Berton, *Why We Act Like Canadians: A Personal Exploration of Our National Character* (Toronto: McClelland & Stewart, 1982).

27. Atwood, 'Canadian–American Relations', 373–4.

28. In 2005, the total number of homicides in Canada was 658; the crime rate for homicide stood at approximately 2.06 per 100,000; the US figure for the same year was 5.6 homicides per 100,000. Statistics Canada, 'Crimes by Type of Offense', at: <www40.statcan.ca/l01/cst01/legal12a.htm>; US Department of Justice, 'United States Crime Rates 1960–2005', at: <www.disastercenter.com/crime/uscrime.htm>.

29. See, e.g., Geoffrey Stevens, 'Life in the Land of the Smoking Guns', *Maclean's* 106 (7 June 1993): 60.

30. See Malcolm, *The Canadians*, 78–9; Mr Justice R.P. Kerans, 'Two Nations Under Law', in David Thomas, ed., *Canada and the United States: Differences that Count* (Peterborough, Ont.: Broadview Press, 1993), 215–33, esp. 220–2.

31. Gwyn, *The 49th Paradox*, 58.

32. For another take on Canadian–American difference in cultural assumptions, see Jennifer MacLennan, 'Only in Canada, You Say? The Dynamics of Identity in *Degrassi Junior High*', in Michele Byers, ed., *Growing Up Degrassi* (Toronto: Sumach Press, 2005), 149–66.

33. The most prominent of these is sociolinguist Deborah Tannen, who has written numerous books on the subject of female–male linguistic patterns, including *You Just Don't Understand: Women and Men in Conversation* (New York: Quill, 2001 [rpt]); *Talking from 9 to 5: Women and Men at Work* (New York: Quill, 2001 [rpt]); *'That's Not What I Meant': How Conversational Style Makes or Breaks Relationships* (New York: Ballantine, 1986). Articles drawn from each of these works appeared in the *Washington Post* and are available from her website: 'The Talk of the Sandbox: How Johnny and Suzy's Playground Chatter Prepares Them for Life at the Office', *Washington Post*, 11 Dec. 1994, at: <www.georgetown.edu/faculty/tannend/sandbox.htm>; 'Sex, Lies and Conversation: Why Is It So Hard for Men and Women to Talk to Each Other?', *Washington Post*, 24 June 1990, at: <www.georgetown.edu/faculty/tannend/sexlies.htm>; 'When You Shouldn't Tell It Like It Is', *Washington Post*, 1 Mar. 1987, at: <www.georgetown.edu/faculty/tannend/tellit.htm>.

34. In addition to Tannen, others include: Susan Githens, 'Men and Women in Conversation: An Analysis of Gender Styles in Language', *Threshold* 87 (July 2006): 10–12; Chris Christie, 'Politeness and the Linguistic Construction of Gender in Parliament: An Analysis of Transgressions and Apology Behaviour', *Working Papers on the Web*, at: <extra.shu.ac.uk/wpw/politeness/christie.htm>; Victoria Bergvall, 'Towards a

Comprehensive Theory of Language and Gender', *Language in Society* 28 (1999): 273–93; Penelope Eckert and Sally McConnell-Ginet, 'Think Practically and Look Locally: Language and Gender as Community-Based Practice', in Camille Roman, Suzanne Juhasz, and Christanne Miller eds, *The Women and Language Debate* (New Brunswick, NJ: Rutgers University Press, 1994), 432–60; Victoria Leto DeFrancisco, *The Sounds of Silence: How Men Silence Women in Marital Relations* (New York: Sage, 1991); Robin Tolmach Lakoff, *Language and Women's Place* (New York: Oxford University Press, 1975).

35. Zick Rubin and Steven Shenker, 'Friendship, Proximity, and Self-Disclosure', *Journal of Personality* 46 (1978): 1–22; Dorie Giles Williams, 'Gender Differences in Interpersonal Relationships and Well-Being', *Research in Sociology of Education and Socialization* (1985): 239-67.

36. Ann M. Beutel and Margaret Mooney Marini, 'Gender and Values', *American Sociological Review* 60 (June 1995): 436–48.

37. Carol Gilligan, *In a Different Voice* (Cambridge, Mass.: Harvard University Press, 1982).

38. See William O'Barr and Bowman Atkins, 'Women's Language or Powerless Language?', in Sally McConnell Ginet, ed., *Women and Language in Literature and Society* (Westport, Conn.: Praeger, 1979).

39. See, e.g., Richard D. Ashmore, Frances K. Del Boca, and Arthur J. Wohlers, 'Gender Stereotypes', in Frances K. Del Boca, ed., *The Social Psychology of Female–Male Relations* (New York: Academic Press, 1986); Janet T. Spence and Robert L. Helmreich, *Masculinity and Femininity: Their Psychological Dimensions, Correlates and Antecedents* (Austin: University of Texas Press, 1978). This idea has been challenged by writers who have studied violence by women, including, for instance, Rebecca Godfrey, *Under the Bridge* (New York: Simon & Schuster, 2005); Stacey L. Shipley and Bruce Arrigo, *The Female Homicide Offender: Serial Murder and the Case of Aileen Wuornos* (Englewood Cliffs, NJ: Prentice-Hall, 2003); Carol Anne Davis, *Women Who Kill: Profiles of Female Serial Killers* (London: Allison & Busby, 2001).

40. Some researchers have begun to see aggression in the apparent polite co-operativeness of women's talk and actions. See, e.g., Pat Heim, Susan Murphy, and Susan K. Golant, *In the Company of Women: Indirect Aggression among Women: Why We Hurt Each Other and How to Stop* (New York: Tarcher, 2003[rpt]); Leora Tanenbaum, *Catfight: Rivalries among Women—from Diets to Dating, from the Boardroom to the Delivery Room* (New York: Harper Paperbacks, 2003); Phyllis Chessler, *Woman's Inhumanity to Woman* (New York: Thunder's Mouth Press, 2002).

41. Beutel and Marini, 'Gender and Values', 436–7; K.P. Scott, 'Perceptions of Communication Competence: What's Good for the Goose is Not Good for the Gander', *Women's Studies International Quarterly* 3 (1980): 199–208.

42. See, e.g., Cheris Kramarae, *Women and Men Speaking* (Rowley, Mass.: Newbury House, 1981); Dale Spender, 'Language and Sex Differences', in H. Andresen, ed., *Osnabrucker Beitrage zur Sprachtheorie: Sprache und Geschlecht II* (Oldenburg, Germany: Red, 1979),

38–59; D.M. Siegler and R.S Siegler, 'Stereotypes of Males' and Females' Speech', *Psychological Reports* 39 (1976): 167–70; C. Edelsky, 'Subjective Reactions to Sex-Linked Language', *Journal of Social Psychology* 99 (1976): 97–104.

43. Danielle Popp, 'Gender, Race, and Speech Style Stereotypes', *Sex Roles: A Journal of Research* (Apr. 2003), at: <findarticles.com/p/articles/mi_m2294/is_2003_April/ai_101174062>.

44. Kenneth Burke, 'Definition of Man', in Burke, *Language as Symbolic Action*, 5.

45. Ludwig Wittgenstein, *Tractatus Logico-Philosophicus*, ed. D.F. Pears (New York: Routledge, 1981).

46. Frye, *Divisions on a Ground*, 99.

47. Hayakawa and Hayakawa, *Language in Thought and Action*, xiii.

48. Charles Barber, 'What Is Language?', in Barber, *The Story of Speech and Language* (New York: T.Y. Crowell, 1964), 9.

Chapter 6

1. Albert Mehrabian, 'Communication without Words', in C. David Mortensen, ed., *Basic Readings in Communication Theory* (New York: Harper & Row, 1973), 91.

2. Most famously, Julius Fast, *Body Language* (New York: Pocket Books, 1970), or, more recently, Jo Ellan Dimitrius and Mark Mazzarella, *Reading People: How to Understand People and Predict Their Behavior, Anytime, Anyplace* (New York: Ballantine, 1999).

3. Geert Hofstede, *Culture's Consequences: International Differences in Work-Related Values* (Beverly Hills, Calif.: Sage, 1980).

4. See Ingrid Randoja, 'Julia Sweeny', *Now Toronto*, 18–24 Mar. 1999, at: <www.nowtoronto.com/issues/18/29/Ent/cover.html>.

5. M. Dittman, 'Standing Tall Pays Off, Study Finds', *APA Monitor* 35 (July–Aug. 2004): 14, at: <www.apa.org/monitor/julaug04/standing.html>.

6. Terry Poulton, *No Fat Chicks* (Toronto: Key Porter Books, 1996).

7. Peter T. Katzmarzyk, 'The Canadian Obesity Epidemic, 1985–1998', *Canadian Medical Association Journal* 166 (16 Apr. 2002), at: <www.cmaj.ca/cgi/content/full/166/8/1039>.

8. L. Lampert. 'Fat like Me', *Ladies' Home Journal* (May 1993): 154, 215; C.S. Crandall, 'Prejudice against Fat People: Ideology and Self-interest', *Journal of Personality and Social Psychology* 66 (May 1994): 882–94.

9. 'Nri Sikh Teen's Hair Cut Off in Beating: Police, Community Leader Appeal for Calm after Hate Crime', *Vancouver Sun*, 1 June 2005; 'Calls for Charges against Richmond Sikh Boy for Fake Assault Claims That Five White Men Cut His Hair', CBC News, 6 June 2005, at: <www.nriinternet.com/NRI_Discrimination/Canada/2005/2_Sikh_teen_hair%20cut%20f%20.htm>.

10. See, e.g., Rosaleen Croghan, Christine Griffin, Janine Hunter, and Ann Phoenix, 'Style Failure: Consumption, Identity and Social Exclusion', *Journal of Youth Studies* 9 (Sept. 2006): 463–78; Laurel Horton and Paul Jordan-Smith, 'Deciphering Folk Costume: Dress Codes among Contra Dancers', *Journal of American Folklore* 117 (2004): 415–40;

Barry Brummett, 'The Building Blocks of Culture: Artifacts', in Brummett, *Rhetoric in Popular Culture* (New York: St Martin's Press, 1994), 11–17.

11. Ian Hanomansing and Peter Mansbridge, 'Sikh Mounties Permitted to Wear Turbans', CBC News Report, 15 Mar. 1990, at: <archives.cbc.ca/IDC-1-73-614-3302-10/on_this_day/politics_economy/sikh_mounties_turban>.

12. Edward Hall, *The Hidden Dimension* (New York: Anchor Books, 1966); Hall, *The Silent Language* (New York: Anchor Books, 1973). For a summative discussion of Hall's theories, see Nina Brown, 'Edward T. Hall: Proxemic Theory, 1966', Centre for Spatially Integrated Social Science, at: <www.csiss.org/classics/content/13>.

13. Non-verbal influences such as tone, style, diction, sentence structure, grammar, spelling, punctuation, handwriting, and document design affect how our written messages are received and interpreted by others.

14. Rosini Lippi-Green, *English with an Accent: Language, Ideology, and Discrimination in the United States* (New York: Routledge, 1997); Levent M. Arslan and John H.L. Hansen, *Language Accent Classification in American English*, Technical Report RSPL-96-7 (Durham, NC: Robust Speech Processing Laboratory, Duke University, 1996).

15. For instance, see Neera Kuckreja Sohoni, 'Fortune Cookies and Ethnocentrism: When Making Fun of Accents Isn't Funny', *PaloAlto Online*, 26 Apr. 1995, at: <www.paloaltoonline.com/weekly/morgue/spectrum/1995_Apr_26.BOARD26.html>.

16. Michelle LeBaron, 'Cross-Cultural Communication', in Guy Burgess and Heidi Burgess, eds, *Beyond Intractability* (Boulder, Colo.: Conflict Research Consortium, University of Colorado, 16 Nov. 2006), at: <www.beyondintractability.org/essay/cross-cultural_communicastion>.

17. H. Bakwin, 'Emotional Deprivation in Infants', *Journal of Pediatrics* 35 (1949): 512–21.

18. For instance, Marc Mogil, *I Know What You're Really Thinking: Reading Body Language Like a Trial Lawyer* (n.p.: Authorhouse, 2003); Dimitrius and Mazzarella, *Reading People*; Gerard Nierenberg and Henry H. Calero, *How to Read a Person Like a Book* (New York: Barnes & Noble, 1990).

Chapter 7

1. Neil Postman and Charles Weingartner, *Teaching as a Subversive Activity* (New York: Dell, 1969), 3–4.

Chapter 8

1. For two different points of view on this issue, see 'Good Riddance to the Gun Registry' (editorial), *National Post*, 20 June 2006, at: <www.canada.com/nationalpost/news/editorialsletters/story.html?id=8536ee16-eece-40b7-9a02-618108485f83>; and 'Reasonable Control: Gun Registration in Canada' (editorial), *Canadian Medical Association Journal* 168 (18 Feb. 2003), at: <www.cmaj.ca/cgi/content/full/168/4/389>.

2. Canadians have traditionally valued the interests of the collective over individual freedom, as the Canadian philosopher George Grant explains in his famous *Lament for a Nation* (Toronto: Macmillan, 1965). For other explorations of Canadian values, particularly as they diverge from American ones, see Michael Adams, *Fire and Ice: The United States, Canada, and the Myth of Converging Values* (Toronto: Penguin, 2003); Seymour M. Lipset, *Continental Divide: The Values and Institutions of the United States and Canada* (New York: Routledge, 1990); Richard Gwyn, *The 49th Paradox: Canada in North America* (Toronto: McClelland & Stewart, 1985); Pierre Berton, *Why We Act Like Canadians* (Toronto: McClelland & Stewart, 1982).

3. The psychological and interpersonal principle of commitment is discussed more extensively in Chapter 10.

4. Kenneth Burke, 'The Rhetorical Situation', in Lee thayer, ed., *Communication: Ethical and Moral Issues* (London: Gordon and Breach Science Publishers, 1973), 266–71.

5. Such as, e.g., Michael Schrage, 'Technology, Silver Bullets and Big Lies: Musings on the Information Age' (interview with Educom Review Staff), *Educom Review* 33 (Jan.–Feb. 1998), at: <www.educause.edu/pub/er/review/reviewArticles/33132.html>; John Fiske, *Understanding Popular Culture* (London: Methuen, 1989), 24.

Chapter 9

1. Katherine Barber, ed., *The Canadian Oxford Dictionary* (Toronto: Oxford University Press, 1998), 1085.

2. Kenneth Burke, *A Rhetoric of Motives* (Berkeley: University of California Press, 1969), 172.

3. See, e.g., M.C. Miller, 'Hollywood: The Ad', *Atlantic Monthly* 265, 4 (Apr. 1990): 41–54.

4. Jen Van Evra, 'Headlines vs the Bottom Line', *Adbusters* 22 (Summer 1998): 13–14.

5. A helpful discussion of how form can function as persuasion can be found in Rebekah Bennetch, 'The Gospel According to Glamour: A Rhetorical Analysis of *Revolve*: The Complete New Testament', MA thesis (University of Saskatchewan, 2006).

6. Jennifer MacLennan, 'Canadian Documentary Realism and the Dynamics of Identity in *Degrassi Junior High*', in Michele Byers, ed., *Growing Up Degrassi: Television, Identity, and Youth Cultures* (Toronto: Sumach Press, 2005), 149–66.

7. Jennifer MacLennan, '"Canadianizing" an American Textbook', *McGill Journal of Education* 35 (Winter 2000): 31–52.

8. Most famously, Chaim H. Perelman and L. Olbrechts-Tyteca, *The New Rhetoric: A Treatise on Argumentation*, trans. John Wilkinson and Purcell Weaver (South Bend, Ind.: University of Notre Dame Press, 1971). See also Norman Fairclough, 'Discourse, Common Sense, and Ideology', in Fairclough, *Language and Power* (New York: Longman, 1989), 77–108.

9. Aristotle, *The Rhetoric and Poetics*, trans. W. Rhys Roberts, ed. Fredrich Solmsen. (New York: Random House/Modern Library, 1954), 1357a.

10. Ibid., 1355a.

11. Vance Packard, *The Hidden Persuaders* (New York: Pocket Books, 1961).

12. Robert Cialdini, *Influence: Science and Practice* (New York: William Morrow, 1984).

13. Jennifer MacLennan, 'Answer the Big Question', in MacLennan, *Effective Communication for the Technical Professions* (Scarborough, Ont.: Prentice-Hall Canada, 2003), 351.

14. See, e.g., Cialdini, *Influence: Science and Practice*.

15. M.B. Sperling and S. Borgaro, 'Attachment Anxiety and Reciprocity as Moderators of Interpersonal Attraction', *Psychological Reports* 76 (Feb. 1995): 323–35.

16. Social proof, also known as 'bandwagon', is frequently used for propaganda purposes. In addition to Cialdini's work on the subject, see Clyde Miller, *How to Detect Propaganda* (New York: Institute for Propaganda Analysis, Records, Manuscripts and Archives Division, New York Public Library. Astor, Lenox, and Tilden Foundations, 1937).

17. Assar Lindbeck, 'Incentives and Social Norms in Household Behavior', *American Economic Review* 87: Papers and Proceedings of the Hundred and Fourth Annual Meeting of the American Economic Association (May 1997): 370–7; Dan M. Kahan, 'Social Influence, Social Meaning, and Deterrence', *Virginia Law Review* 83 (Mar. 1997): 349–95.

18. Richard Weaver, *Language Is Sermonic: Richard Weaver on the Nature of Rhetoric*, ed. Richard L. Johannesen, Rennard Strickland, and Ralph T. Eubanks (Baton Rouge: Louisiana State University Press, 1970).

19. Kenneth Burke, *A Rhetoric of Motives* (Berkeley: University of California Press, 1969), 172. Burke, of course, defines persuasion quite broadly to refer to any attempt at identification.

Chapter 10

1. For example, G.B. Graen and M. Uhl-Bien, 'Relationship Based Approach to Leadership', *Leadership Quarterly* 6 (1995): 219–49; W.H. Drath and C.J. Paulus, *Making Common Sense: Leadership as Meaning-Making in a Community of Practice* (Greensboro, NC: Centre for Creative Leadership, 1994); J. Belasco, *Teaching the Elephant to Dance: The Manager's Guide to Empowering Change* (New York: Plume, 1990); W.W. Burke, 'Leadership as Empowering Others', in Srivastra and Associates, *Executive Power* (San Francisco: Jossey-Bass, 1986); Robert K. Greenleaf, *The Servant as Leader* (Newton Center, Mass.: Robert K. Greenleaf Centre, 1970).

2. For example, Peter Guy Northouse, *Leadership: Theory and Practice* (Thousand Oaks, Calif.: Sage, 2004); Pamela Tierney, Steve M. Farmer, and George B. Graen, 'An Examination of Leadership and Employee Creativity: The Relevance of Traits and Relationships', *Personnel Psychology* 52 (1999): 591–620; S.R. Levine and M.A. Crom, *The Leader in You: How to Win Friends, Influence People, and Succeed in a Changing World* (New York: Simon & Schuster, 1993).

3. For example, Northouse, *Leadership: Theory and Practice*; D. Tjosvold and M. Tjosvold, *Psychology for Leaders: Using Motivation, Conflict, and Power to Manage More Effectively* (New York: Wiley, 1995); J.P. Kotter, 'What Leaders Really Do', in W.E. Rosenbach and

R.L. Taylor, eds, *Contemporary Issues in Leadership* (Boulder, Colo.: Westview Press, 1993); C.C. Manz and H.P. Sims, *Superleadership: Leading Others to Lead Themselves* (New York: Prentice-Hall, 1989).

4. Such as Philip Heymann and Ronald Heifetz, 'The Intellectual Architecture of "Leadership"', in Ellen Pruyne, Roundtable Rapporteur, *Conversations on Leadership 2000–2001*, Harvard University Leadership Roundtable (Cambridge, Mass.: Harvard University Center for Public Leadership, 2001), at: <www.ksg.harvard.edu/leadership/the_intellectual_architecture_of_leadership.html>; R.J. House and T.R. Mitchell, 'Path-Goal Theory of Leadership', *Journal of Contemporary Business* (1974): 81–97; Fred E. Fiedler, 'The Effects of Leadership Training and Experience: A Contingency Model Interpretation', *Administrative Science Quarterly* 17 (1972): 455.

5. For instance, Boyd Clarke and Ron Crossland, *The Leader's Voice* (New York: Select Books, 2002); James M. Kouzes and Barry Z. Posner, *The Leadership Challenge* (New York: John Wiley, 2002); B. Nanus, *Visionary Leadership* (San Francisco: Jossey-Bass, 1992); John Gardner, *On Leadership* (New York: Free Press, 1990).

6. Richard Bolden, 'What is Leadership?', *Leadership South West Research Report* 1 (Exeter, UK: Exeter Centre for Leadership Studies, 2004), at: <www.leadership-studies.com/documents/what_is_leadership.pdf>; Belasco, *Teaching the Elephant to Dance*; J.P. Kotter, *A Force for Change: How Leadership Differs from Management* (New York: Free Press, 1990); Donald A. Schon and Chris Argyris, *Theory in Practice: Increasing Professional Effectiveness* (San Francisco: Jossey-Bass, 1974).

7. James M. Kouzes and Barry Z. Posner, *Credibility* (San Francisco: Jossey-Bass, 1993); J.A. Conger, *The Charismatic Leader* (New York: Jossey-Bass, 1988); K. Blanchard and N. Pearle, *The Power of Ethical Management* (New York: Fawcett Crest, 1988); D.E. McClelland, *Power: The Inner Experience* (New York: Irvington, 1975).

8. Arthur Shriberg, Carol Lloyd, David L. Shriberg, and Mary Lynn Williamson, eds, *Practicing Leadership: Principles and Applications* (New York: John Wiley and Sons, 1997), 6.

9. Jonathan Shay, 'Aristotle's Rhetoric as a Handbook of Leadership', at: <www.d-n-i.net/fcs/aristotle.htm>.

10. Clarke and Crossland, *The Leader's Voice*, 5.

11. Kurt T. Dirks and Daniel Skarlicki, 'Trust in Leaders: Existing Research and Emerging Issues', in R. Kramer and K. Cook, eds, *Trust within Organizations* (New York: Russell Sage Foundation, 2004), 2, at: <www.olin.wustl.edu/faculty/dirks/trust%20in%20leader%20chapter.pdf>.

12. Shay, 'Aristotle's Rhetoric'.

13. James M. Kouzes and Barry Z. Posner, 'The Ten Most Important Lessons We've Learned about Learning to Lead', in Shriberg et al., eds, *Practicing Leadership*, 179.

14. Stephen R. Covey, 'Three Roles of the Leader', in Shriberg et al., eds, *Practicing Leadership*, 186.

15. Aristotle, *The Rhetoric and Poetics*, trans. W. Rhys Roberts, ed. Fredrich Solmsen. (New York: Random House/Modern Library, 1954), 1356a.

16. S. Michael Halloran, 'Aristotle's Concept of Ethos, or If Not His, Somebody Else's', *Rhetoric Review* 1 (Sept. 1982): 58–63.

17. Shay, 'Aristotle's Rhetoric'.

18. B.M. Bass, *Bass and Stogdill's Handbook of Leadership: Theory, Research, and Managerial Applications*, 3rd edn (New York: Free Press, 1990); Marvin E. Shaw, *Group Dynamics: The Psychology of Small Group Behaviour*, 3rd edn (New York: McGraw-Hill, 1981).

19. Gardner, *On Leadership*.

20. For example, the Ohio State studies that observed two dimensions of leadership behaviour: 'consideration' and 'initiating structure', at: <changingminds.org/disciplines/leadership/actions/ohio_state.htm>; also the University of Michigan studies that described 'employee-centred' versus 'job-centred' behaviour, at: <changingminds.org/disciplines/leadership/actions/michigan.htm>. Also of interest are House and Mitchell, 'Path-Goal Theory of Leadership'; Fiedler, 'The Effects of Leadership Training and Experience'.

21. Ralph K. White and Ronald Lippit, 'Leader Behaviour and Member Reaction in Three "Social Climates"', in White and Lippit, *Group Dynamics*, 3rd edn (New York: Harper & Row, 1968), 318–35; Ralph K. White and Ronald Lippit, *Autocracy and Democracy* (New York: Harper & Row, 1961).

22. George L. Dillon, *Rhetoric as Social Imagination: Explorations of the Interpersonal Function of Language* (Bloomington: Indiana University Press, 1986).

23. Ibid., 45.

24. In addition to Tannen's *Talking from 9 to 5: Women and Men at Work* (New York: Quill, 2001), see Sally Helgesen, *The Female Advantage: Women's Ways of Leadership* (New York: Currency Doubleday, 1990); Carol Gilligan, *In a Different Voice* (Cambridge, Mass.: Harvard University Press, 1982).

25. Shay, 'Aristotle's Rhetoric'.

26. Clarke and Crossland, *The Leader's Voice*, 6.

27. Mercer is, of course, the actor, writer, and satirist who hosts *The Rick Mercer Report* for CBC. You can read his blog—and several examples of his storytelling skills—at <rickmercer.blogspot.com/>.

28. McLean is the host of CBC Radio's *Vinyl Café* and a prolific storyteller. You can find his works at <stuartmclean.zunior.com/>.

29. The popular historian and television personality was one of Canada's greatest storytellers, having written more than 40 volumes of Canadiana. See 'Pierre Berton', *The Canadian Encyclopedia Plus 1997* (CD) (Toronto: McClelland & Stewart, 1996); Jeff Craig, 'The Last Patriot? Surely Not, but Pierre Berton's New Work Predicts a Troubled Future for Canada', *Edmonton Sun*, 28 Sept. 1996.

30. 'Canadian Storyteller Dips into Indian Myth', *Deccan Herald*, 24 July 2005, at: <www.deccanherald.com/deccanherald/jul242005/finearts1439322005722.asp>.

31. Kurt Dirks, 'Trust in Leadership and Team Performance: Evidence from NCAA Basketball', *Journal of Applied Psychology* 85 (2000): 1004–12.

32. Shay, 'Aristotle's Rhetoric'.

Chapter 11

1. S. Michael Halloran, 'Aristotle's Concept of Ethos, or If Not His, Somebody Else's', *Rhetoric Review* 1 (Sept. 1982): 58–63; William M Sattler, 'Conceptions of Ethos in AncientRhetoric', *Speech Monographs* 14 (1941): 55–65.

2. See, e.g., Nan Johnson, 'Ethos and the Aims of Rhetoric', in Robert J. Connors, Lisa Ede, and Andrea Lunsford, eds, *Essays in Classical Rhetoric and Modern Discourse* (Carbondale: Southern Illinois University Press, 1984); Halloran, 'Aristotle's Concept of Ethos'; Arthur B. Miller, 'Aristotle on Habit and Character: Implications for the *Rhetoric*', *Speech Monographs* 41 (Nov. 1974): 309–16.

3. William Kilpatrick, *Why Johnny Can't Tell Right from Wrong: Moral Illiteracy and the Case for Character Education* (New York: Simon & Schuster, 1992).

4. See, e.g., Margaret Sommerville, 'Ethical Dilemmas in Medicine', McGill Faculty of Medicine Mini-Med Study Corner, at: <www.medicine.mcgill.ca/minimed/archive/Sommerville2002.htm>.

5. Aristotle, *The Rhetoric*, trans. W. Rhys Roberts, ed. Friedrich Solmsen (New York: Random House/Modern Library, 1954), 1356a. You can find the entire text of *The Rhetoric* at: <www2.iastate.edu/~honeyl/Rhetoric/index.html>.

6. Quintilian, *The Institutes of Oratory*, Book 2, Chapter 15, at: <www2.iastate.edu/~honeyl/quintilian/1/index.html>.

7. George Campbell, *The Philosophy of Rhetoric*, ed. Lloyd Bitzer (Carbondale: Southern Illinois University Press, 1963), 43.

8. A small selection of these includes James M. Tallmon, 'Casuistry', in Thomas O. Sloane, ed., *The Encyclopedia of Rhetoric* (New York: Oxford University Press, 2001), 83–8; Paul M. Dombrowski, 'Survey of Ethics in Communication and Rhetoric', in Dombrowski, *Ethics in Technical Communication* (Needham Heights, Mass.: Allyn & Bacon, 2000), 12–37; Marshall Gregory, 'Ethical Criticism: What It Is and Why It Matters', *Style* 32 (Summer 1998); Richard M. Weaver, *The Ethics of Rhetoric*, reprint edn (New York: LEA, 1995); Wayne C. Booth, *The Company We Keep: An Ethics of Fiction*, reprint edn (Berkeley: University of California Press, 1989), 194–221; Lee Thayer, ed., *Communication: Ethical and Moral Issues* (London: Gordon and Breach Science Publishers, 1973).

9. B.J. Diggs, "Persuasion and Ethics', *Quarterly Journal of Speech* 50 (1964): 360, 363.

10. Such behaviour actually signals a disregard of others' well-being, a failure of socialization, and even possible psychopathology. See Paul Babiak and Robert Hare, *Snakes in Suits* (Toronto: HarperCollins, 2006); Sgt. Matt Logan, 'The Psychopathic Offender: How Identifying the Traits Can Solve Cases', *Royal Canadian Mounted Police Gazette* 66 (2004), at: <www.gazette.rcmp.gc.ca/article-en.html?&article_id=39>. See also the classic work, Harvey Cleckley, *The Mask of Sanity*, 5th edn (Augusta, Ga: Emily Cleckley, 1988), at: <www.cassiopaea.org/cass/sanity_1.PDF>.

11. For a more extensive and highly readable discussion of the root and nature of ethics, see Peter Singer, *Practical Ethics*, 2nd edn (Cambridge: Cambridge University Press, 1993).

12. Erving Goffman, *Interaction Ritual: Essays on Face-to-Face Behavior* (Garden City, NY: Anchor Books, 1967); Goffman, *The Presentation of Self in Everyday Life* (New York: Anchor Books, 1959).

13. Such as that offered by John C. Maxwell in *The 21 Irrefutable Laws of Leadership* (Nashville: Maxwell Motivation, 1998), Review and summary by Dee Pink, Project Management Institute, Iowa Chapter, at: <www.pmi-centraliowa.org/BookReview_Laws ofLeadershipnotes.doc>.

14. Many of these can be found at the Center for the Study of Ethics in the Professions, at: <ethics.iit.edu/codes/>.

15. Including, e.g., those posted on-line by Queen's University: <www.queensu.ca/secretariat/sen ate/policies/codecond.html>; University of Toronto: <www.utoronto.ca/govcncl/pap/poli cies/studentc.html>; Athabasca University: <www.athabascau.ca/calendar/page11.html>; McMaster University: <www.mcmaster.ca/univsec/policy/StudentCode.pdf>.

16. Martin Buber, *I–Thou* (New York: Touchstone, 1993 [1923]).

17. Illinois Institute of Technology, 'Codes of Ethics On-line', at: <ethics.iit.edu/codes/>.

18. Andrew Olson, 'Authoring a Code of Ethics: Observations on Process and Organization', Illinois Institute of Technology, Center for the Study of Ethics in the Professions, at: <ethics.iit.edu/codes/Writing_A_Code.html>.

19. Cristina Sewerin, 'What is a Licensed Professional?', *Engineering Dimensions* (Sept.–Oct. 2004), at: <www.peo.on.ca/publications/DIMENSIONS/septoct2004/Webwatch.pdf>.

20. Ibid.

21. Canadian Council of Professional Engineers Code of Ethics, at: <ethics.iit.edu/codes/ coe/can.council.pro.engineers.a.html>.

22. American Association of University Teachers Code of Professional Ethics, at: <ethics.iit.edu/codes/coe/amer.assoc.univ.prof.pro.ethics.1987.html>. Curiously, the Canadian Association of University Teachers shows no similar code on its website.

23. PMAC Code of Ethics, The Purchasing Management Association of Canada, at: <pmac. ca/about/ethics.asp>.

24. American Library Association, 'History of the Code of Ethics 1939 Code of Ethics for Librarians', at: <www.ala.org/Template.cfm?Section=coehistory&Template=/ContentMa nagement/ContentDisplay.cfm&ContentID=8875>.

25. 'Four Core Boy Scout Values', *DELTA: An Ethics in Action Program for Boy Scouts*, at: <pinetreeweb.com/delta-1.htm>.

26. The code can be found at the Centre for the Study of Ethics in the Professions: <ethics.iit.edu/codes/coe/ca.curling.coe.html>.

27. For some interesting discussions of policies of dehumanization, see Haig A. Bosmajian, 'Defining the "American Indian": A Case Study in the Language of Suppression', *Speech Teacher* 22 (Mar. 1973): 89–99; Bosmajian, 'The Language of Sexism', *ETC: A Review of General Semantics* 29 (Sept. 1972): 305–13; Bosmajian, 'The Language of White Racism', *College English* 31 (Dec. 1969): 263–72.

28. This was underlined by the famous Nuremberg war crimes trials of 1945–9. See Doug

Linder, 'The Nuremberg Trials' (2000), at: <www.law.umkc.edu/faculty/projects/ftrials/nuremberg/nurembergACCOUNT.html>.

29. Goffman, *Interaction Ritual*, 5.

30. Corporations and bureaucracies get a lot of heat on this score. See, e.g., Joel Bakan, *The Corporation: The Pathological Pursuit of Profit and Power* (New York: Simon & Schuster, 2004), 60–84; Noam Chomsky, *Profit over People* (New York: Seven Stories Press, 1999).

31. Criminal Code of Canada, Article 219(1): 'Every one is criminally negligent who (a) in doing anything, or (b) in omitting to do anything that it is his duty to do, shows wanton or reckless disregard for the lives or safety of other persons.' At: <laws.justice.gc.ca/en/c-46/267361.html>.

32. You can find this justification at the secretmessage website by clicking on 'learn more' in the blue box headed 'Care To Say'.

33. Claude Lanzmann, *Shoah: An Oral History of the Holocaust* (Paris: Editions Fayard and Claude Lanzmann, 1985).

Appendix A

1. Jennifer MacLennan, 'Teaching Interpersonal Communication: The Personal Icon Assignment', *Speech Communication Teacher* 12 (Summer 1998): 13.

2. Forced disclosure was the case in the Department of Speech Communication at the University of Washington when I was a Ph.D. student; I was told that it was standard practice in many such departments in the US. I found it invasive and potentially dangerous, since the instructors—usually graduate students with little classroom experience—were not trained to handle therapeutic disclosure.

3. For a typical confidentiality agreement, see the one described in the course outline for Texas State University's Comm 2315: Introduction to Interpersonal Communication, at: <www.finearts.txstate.edu/commstudies/Faculty&Staff/Mostyn/Comm2315 Mostyn.pdf#search=%22interpersonal%20communication%20course%20confidentiality%20agreement%22>.

Appendix B

1. Emily Dickinson (1830–86) and Robert Frost (1874–1963) are well-known American poets.

2. See, e.g., Michael Huemer, 'Student Evaluations: A Critical Review', at: <home.sprynet.com/~owl1/sef.htm>; Susan Lang, 'Study Examines Use of Student Ratings of Teachers', *Cornell Chronicle*, 23 Oct. 1997, at: <www.news.cornell.edu/chronicle/97/10.23.97/teacherratings.html>; Annie Tao, 'Course Evaluations Flawed, Unreliable', *UCLA Daily Bruin*, 25 Oct. 2005, at: <www.dailybruin.ucla.edu/news/articles.asp?ID=34638>.

Appendix C

1. The term was first coined by University of Chicago ethicist Leo Strauss.

Index